THE TORRINGTON DIARIES

VOLUME TWO

Follies
Committed
in
1791,
by
Edwd. Bohun.

TITLE-PAGE FROM THE JOURNAL OF THE
TOUR IN LINCOLNSHIRE, 1791

THE TORRINGTON DIARIES

CONTAINING THE TOURS THROUGH
ENGLAND AND WALES
OF THE

HON. JOHN BYNG

(LATER FIFTH VISCOUNT TORRINGTON)

BETWEEN THE YEARS 1781 AND 1794

EDITED BY

C. BRUYN ANDREWS

VOLUME TWO

BARNES & NOBLE, Inc.
New York
METHUEN & CO. Ltd
London

First published, 1935

This edition reprinted, 1970
by Barnes & Noble, Inc.
and Methuen & Co. Ltd.

Barnes & Noble ISBN 389 04048 7

Methuen ISBN 416 15680 0

Printed in the United States of America

CONTENTS

ILLUSTRATIONS

vii

ILLUSTRATIONS

VOLUME ONE: ADDENDA AND ERRATA

Owing to an unfortunate oversight a reproduction of Ozias Humphry's portrait of the Hon. John Byng was printed in Vol. I without acknowledgment being made to the owner of the copyright photograph. The editor and the publishers wish to express their indebtedness to Dr. G. C. Williamson for his permission to include this portrait from his important book on Ozias Humphry, R.A., and to apologize for the omission of the acknowledgment in the first edition.

p. xxx, l. 6, *for* 'Mrs. Byng' *read* 'Mr. Byng'.

p. xxxiv. The date of Lord Torrington's death is variously given as 1st January (*G.E.C. Peerage*) and 8th January (*Burke's Peerage* and *Gentleman's Magazine*, Feb. 1813).

p. 18. *From Needwood Forest.* The beauties of the Forest of Dean reminded Byng of Mundy's poem on the beauties of Needwood.

p. 26, l. 10, *for* 'height' *read* 'weight'.

p. 36, l. 4. The family of Cotterell were associated with the post of Master of the Ceremonies at Court.

p. 45, l. 18, *for* 'birds gardens' *read* 'Bird's Gardens'.

p. 56, l. 33, *for* 'alteration' *read* 'altercation'.

p. 61, note 5, *for* 'Godwin' *read* 'Goodwin'.

p. 64, notes 32 and 33, *for* 'Bellasye' *read* 'Belasye'.

p. 105, l. 6. Byng was probably informed (wrongly) that Eastbury belonged to the Dorset family of Erle. The house was not pulled down finally till 1795.

p. 110, note 17, *for* 'Cornwall' *read* 'Cornwallis'.

p. 111, note 23. Omit.

note 26, *read* 'Richard Grenville, Earl Temple'.

p. 199, note 5, *for* 'William Wilkins' *read* 'John Wilkins'.

p. 199, note 38. The references to Captain Plume and Mr. Worthy are to Farquhar's *The Recruiting Sergeant*.

p. 200, note 23, *for* 5th *read* 2nd.

p. 202, l. 44, *for* 'papers' *read* 'pipes'.

p. 202, note 57, *read* 'Dr. L— is probably Arthur Loveday, who had just been made a D.C.L. of Oxford. Dr. T— was almost certainly Thomas Townson, D.D. (1715-92), an intimate friend of the Lovedays' (see *D.N.B.*).

p. 214, l. 27, *for* 'partridge' *read* 'Partridge' (*i.e.* the character in *Tom Jones*).

p. 292, note. The reference to James Bindley is to the book-collector (1737-1818). See *D.N.B.*

p. 370, l. 25
p. 381, note 21
$\Big\{$ The recovery of a missing volume of the Tours reveals that W. W. was not William Windham, but W. Wynn, who was the diarist's companion on the Tour in the Midlands, 1789.

A TOUR IN THE MIDLANDS
1789

At the time when this edition of Lord Torrington's Diaries was prepared for press the first volume of the manuscript of the Tour which follows was missing, but happily it has now been discovered. It has not been practicable, however, to incorporate it in the present edition, but it can be obtained separately through any bookseller or directly from the publisher, Patrick Smith, care of Messrs. Simpson, Printers, Marlow, Bucks. In this manuscript the tour is entitled :—

A MOST LABORIEUSE JOURNEYE INTO DISTANT COUNTEYES
PERFORMYD BY JOHN BYNGE JUNE 1789

and in this first mss. volume the travellers make their way from London Northwards, before the opening of these later portions of the Tour, when they have arrived at Newark.

Day	Weather	To What Place	Inns	County	Miles
Wednesday June 10	—	To Worksop Manor, Welbeck, &c. An evening ride.	—	Notts.	
Thursday June 11	—	To Roche Abbey, Sandbeck, Tickhill, & to Rotherham.	Red Lion. T. Crown. V.B.	Yorks.	
Friday June 12	—	To Sheffield. To Dronfield. To Chesterfield.	Tontine Inn. Golden Castle. G.	Yorks. Derbyshire.	
Saturday June 13	—	By Hardwick to Bolsover & back.	Swan. T.	Derbyshire.	
Sunday June 14	—	To Chatsworth. To Cromford	Eden Greyhound.		
Monday June 15	—	By Haddon to Bakewell & back.	White Horse. G.		
Tuesday June 16	—	To Ashburn.	Blackamores Head. G.		
Wednesday June 17	—	To Okeover, Ilam, Dovedale, &c.	—	Derbyshire.	
Thursday June 18	—	To Ector Mines, Warsall and back.	Greyhound Ale house	Staffordshire.	
Friday June 19	—	By Snailson &c, to Derby.	George B.	Derbyshire.	
Saturday June 20	—	By Morley &c to Shardlow. To Ashby-de-la-Zouch.	Rose & Crown. T. Queens Head. G.	Derbyshire. Leicestershire.	

A

Day	Weather	To What Place	Inns	County	Miles
Sunday June 21	—	An Evening Ride.	—	—	
Monday June 22	—	By Caulk &c to Castle Dunnington & back.	Turks Head. G.	—	
Tuesday June 23	—	To Loughborough & to Leicester.	Bulls Head. Three Cranes. G.	Leicestershire.	
Wednesday June 24	—	An evening Ride to Scrapthorp & back.	—	—	
Thursday June 25	—	About the town.	—	—	
Friday June 26	—	To Bosworth. To Atherstone.	Bulls Head Ale-House. Swan. G.	Leicestershire.	
Saturday June 27	—	To Merevale. To Coleshill.	Swan. T.	Warwickshire.	
Sunday June 28	—	To Maxtoke. To Meriden.	Bulls Head B.	—	
Monday June 29	A Windy squally day.	To the Butts; and An Evening Ride.	Butts Head. B.	Warwickshire.	8
Tuesday June 30	A Fine Day.	To Coventry. To Rugby	Kings Head. B. Bear. B.	—	19
Wednesday July 1.	Rainy morn afterwards tolerable.	To Daventry. To Towcester.	Saracens Head T. Saracens Head B.	Northamptonshire	26
Thursday July 2.	A Fine Warm Day.	To Fenny Stratford; to Wooburn	Swan. T. George. G.	Bucks. Beds.	20
Friday July 3.	Hot Weather.	About the Park and to Dunstable.	Bull B.	Beds.	17
Saturday July 4.	Heavy, Rainy.	To Barnet. To Duke Street.	L. Red Lion. T. B. B.	Middlesex.	34
			9	5	124

G = good ; T = tolerable ; B = bad.

As I did musing lie,
   With sundrie thoughts opprest,
Seeking to salve my carefull minde,
   Of pain to be redrest:
And pond'ring how my Youth
   Full ydely I had spent,
In scilence only wrapped up,
   My minde it did torment.
From darknesse into light
   I thought it best to call
By setting forth some little booke,
   Which profite might us all.
And that I did intende
   Is brought now to effect,
At Yode houres I did it penne
   As time would me direct.
      A Schole of Wise Conceytes. 1569

A Tour in the Midlands
1789

Newark Soon after my return, P.[1] and W[ynn][2] came back from an ineffectual fishing scheme; and seem'd to regret with reason, their not having shared my pleasant day.—Our supper was good; and to each other we related our several adventures.—

The Sessions House is a fine building; and has cost a Tuesday, June 9 fine sum: The Assembly Room therein is 90 feet by 30: behind it are shambles and shops; and at one corner, a very old kind of chapel, call'd St Johns of Jerusalem.

My boots which were made by P. of Wale's bootmaker in a light genteel taste, were sent to a cobblers, to be welted, look very ungenteely, and to feel very comfortable.—Our charge at Newark was cheap, and the cooking good; our first supper, consisting of roasted chickens, spitch-cock'd eels, cold ham, with tarts and custards, was but three shillings; the people were very civil: but a town inn is always a dismal, noisy, thing. My further enquiries about my lost cloak-bag were in vain; so I left directions where to send it, if found.—On every side of the town are the remains of the fortifications thrown up in the Civil Wars.

At parting from Newark, I gave another look and many farewell thoughts on the castle, so long steady in the cause of Royalty, to which was owing its demolition.

Passing over Kellham Bridge, we ascended Delby-Dale Hill, whence is a very fine view over the vale of the Trent, with frequent catches of the river; and at a great

5

distance Lincoln Cathedral. W. W.'s mare went so lamely as to threaten falling; and appears to be founder'd; He acted unwisely in letting the horse that P. has bought slip through his fingers.—Our road was very chearful, passing thro' several villages and a pleasant country; at Wellow (where Sr F. M[olyneux]³ has a house, and a kennel full of pointers,) we quitted the high road, and in a mile **Rufford** enter'd the avenue leading to Rufford Abbey; and thro' tall shady woods to that house; to the old part of which, built upon the monastick foundation, has been added a lofty ugly addition.

There are few trees of much size; and the water is ugly, running ditch-like in front of the house; in short it is a place, gloomy and ill-imagin'd; water without management, gloom without grandeur, and shade without timber. We were shewn the House which is an useful building; The newer rooms are lofty, and well tapestry'd, with a long gallery, containing some good Saville portraits.

The old rooms, now disused, are very melancholy; the old brick'd hall, as well as the chapel appear so likewise; but this may rise from the want of inhabitants. The kitchen, on the contrary, seem'd gay and comfortable, being well warm'd by a noble fire, before which two well laden spits were turning, seeming to proclaim a celebration of sheep-sheering, amidst the servants, and their friends.

Quitting these grounds, we came upon Sherwood Forest, where mistaking the steeple in sight for Ollerton, we rode considerably out of our way, to Edwinstone, a pretty village, where stands a pleasant seat of Capt. Mills, looking to the two only remaining woods of the forest, Birkland and Billah; and these will soon be eradicated, as all the trees are marked for felling.—At the end of Billah is a gay, new-built house of Dr Alridge; an happy cribbing from the forest.

Ollerton The Hop Pole Inn at Ollerton is pleasantly situated

6

upon a trout stream, and fronting the forest woods; a house of good stop, and station.

Here we fared comfortably; and of the port wine, seemingly better than usual, we drank two bottles; and the host was of a communicative turn; nor did we think our stay, of two hours, tedious, except the time thrown away at looking at the new church, as ugly, and ill-contriv'd, as ever was built.—

FLOWER.

HOP POLE INN.

OLLERTON.

						s.	d.
Dinner -	-	-	-	-	-	3	0
Supper -	-	-	-	-	-		
Tea and Coffee	-	-	-	-			
Wine -	-	-	-	-	-	5	0
Negus -	-	-	-	-	-		
Punch -	-	-	-	-	-		
Rum -	-	-	-	-	-		
Brandy -	-	-	-	-	-		
Cyder -		-	-	-	-		
Porter	-	-	-	-	-	0	6
Ale -	-	-	-	-	-		
Servants Eating & Ale	-	-	-			
Horses Hay & Corn	-	-	-			
Fire -	-	-	-	-	-		
						8	6

At a short distance from Ollerton, (keeping thro' Billah Wood, where the trees are wonderfully thinn'd) we came into Thoresby Park, and soon to the house; passing by this spot, where in a print, the late Duke's[4] father is described taking his favourite diversion. _{Thoresby Park.}

The made water above the house, is of a bad fashion, and intention; and about, and near the house it runs in ditches, and canals, except where forming a paltry, (play house) cascade in front of the south aspect.

7

The house seems like one in St James's Square, fitted up with French furniture; all for shew, as if the Dss,[5] and Mrs Cornellis[6] had clubb'd tastes. All which gaudy furniture, and useless china will find its deserved price within these few days:—and to view which, were assembled all the gaiety, farmers, &c of the neighbourhood, gaping about at the mock marble, the gilding, the shells, and the crookery ware;* and, no doubt but much petty larceny must be committed, of lace and other easy moveables. The foolish expence and vanity of this dutchess is visible in every room!

*THORESBY. NOTTINGHAMSHIRE.

by

M. V. Christie.

_____

On the premises on Wednesday June 10th and eleven following days (Sunday excepted)

All the rich and elegant household furniture, pier glasses of distinguished magnitude, suits of tapestry in fine preservation, capital pictures, collection of fine Dresden, old Japan, and enamelled porcelane; extensive collection of curious and valuable fire arms, plate, linen, wines, mathematical instruments; a collection of thorough-bred pointers and spaniels, and a great variety of curious and valuable effects, late the property of

HER GRACE THE DUTCHESS OF KINGSTON,

deceased.

at her Grace's Seat, at Thoresby Park in the County of NOTTINGHAM.

To be viewed on Saturday, Monday and Tuesday, preceding the sale, which will begin each day at eleven o'clock. Catalogues (at half a crown each, which will be presented to purchaser) may be had on the premises; at the White Lion, Nottingham; Kingston Arms, Newark; Red Lion, Worksop; Tontine Inn, Sheffield; Angel, Chesterfield; Swan, Manfield; and at Mr Christie's Pall Mall.

The following articles will be sold as undermentioned, viz:

The Linen on Thursday—the 2d day's sale.
Fire Arms on Tuesday—the 6 day's sale.
Fine Dresden Porcelaine on Thursday—the 8 day's sale.
Collection of Pictures & Tapestry on Friday—the 9 day's sale.
Wine on Saturday—the 10 day's sale.

8

After much time loiter'd away in pushing thro' every doorway, we remounted, and rode to the park end; and then turn'd about to take our survey of this, certainly grand seigneurie: but it is neither a pretty place, or of taste, or comfort. The woods of the forest as the adornment of the approach, so are they likewise the beauty of the backing view.—Close adjoining this domain, we enter'd the later commenc'd improvement of Clumber Park[7] (the Clumber Duke of Newcastles) which is in wonderful, and hourly improvement.

This is the soil and situation for planting; to work on upon a light soil with proper husbandry, and every lasting planting and sowing of timber, must not only afford infinite pleasure, but also an advancing adequate profit; but then great schemes can only be undertaken by great purses; and here luckily was one of amplitude to maintain every hope.

After much admiration at the beauty and growth of the plantations, and surprise at the quantity of the pheasants, we came to the new bridge, whence, down the water (which is of a long and noble sweep) the house is best seen to advantage.—What can be so useful, so noble, or so gratifying, as this, forming, from sterility, a charmingly cultivated, wooded domain?

My wishes wou'd extend to fix, within, and around such a place, my honest dependents, and firmest friends; by placing the former in various lodges; (pension'd, and rent-less;) where they might pass the easy evening of their days, in feeding, and rearing poultry, &c. As for my friends, them I wou'd endeavour to tempt about me, by building charming houses around the boundaries of my grounds, with every advantage of view and land; at a pepper corn rent.

As for poverty, rags, and misery they should not exist in my village; for the cottages should not be only comfort-able and low-rented, but attached to each should be, at least, 2 acres of ground, which on first possession the

9

hirers should find well cropped with potatoes, and planted with fruit trees;—teach them how to proceed, redeem the poor from misery, make a large public enclosure at the end of the village, for their cows, &c; and then poverty would soon quit your neighbourhood: As for the very aged, and helpless, I should revert to that good, old, (now neglected,) Custom of Alms Houses; by a charge ever-lasting, upon the estate, therein I should place 12 of the most pitiable and deserving aged poor, with each their several slips of garden ground; where such as were able might employ themselves: before their doors, a shady walk of trees fronting the south, with some benches, would tempt forth the, not unhappy, lodgers, to bask in a sum-mer's sun, or to endeavour at a winter's walk.—

Is not this a reasonable, a cheap, an heartfelt satisfac-tion? And why, in God's name, is this country to be swallowed up by poor rates? And the oppress'd, miserable inhabitants to be hunted about from village, and village; and at last to be starved to death in a work house!!!

Everything here is in good keeping; but I must be sur-prised that rabbets, such dangerous and distructive crea-tures, should be suf. er'd to abound; and that a gentleman, who pays so much per head, for their destruction, shou'd not soon perceive that he is only encouraging their breed, and making the fortunes of his cunning park-keepers! The house, built about 20 years, of stone front, is placed (somewhat to my taste) low, and looking up to its sur-rounding beauties; whereas most modern houses are placed upon the pinacle of a mountain, overlooking their own beauties, and seeking those, which the caprice or axe of their neighbours may in an instant destroy.—No house can be fitted up with more grandeur, or comfort; (I think it the best house I ever enter'd;) with many and magnificent apartments: the library, and gt dining room are of the most spacious dimensions, and furnish'd with all the proprieties of such rooms of enjoyment; in the latter are 4 most capital pictures of fish, fowl, greens, and game.

The bed rooms are proportionate: but the chapel is in the modern, frippery, Adametic, stile, and glazed with the modern stain'd glass, flurrying the sight, and of no awful gloom.

The kitchen is noble; and the adjoining pantries, with the larders for raw, and cold meats, are in the very first capacity. From lack of time, or curiosity, we did not walk round the kitchen, and pleasure gardens as we ought to have done; (but I fancy we were idle, or hoped for yet grander things.)

The grounds continue northward from the house, and are verged by some old wood; when we enter'd a skirt of the foresty heath, the woods of Worksop Manor being about a mile in front. Some rain now falling, hurried us on without taking the notice, we otherwise shou'd, of the rich prospect from the hill above Worksop town; where we Worksop soon enter'd the Red Lion, a paltry looking inn; taking possession of a poor parlour, and ordinary supper. As the rain now fell fast, we were confined to our stable inspection; and awaiting the arrival of some (miserable) stew'd mutton chops and pickled salmon. Nothing occur'd to us of comfortable conversation, or to make much harmony.—

My repose was of the worst kind, upon a sweltering *Wednesday* feather-bed, with a straw-kind of mattrass. P. and I, com- *June 10* monly sleep in double-bedded rooms, but never talk; for he goes to bed early, and rises late; I am in no hurry for bed, and eager to rise in the morning.

Before breakfast I walk'd about the castle hill, behind this inn; where, from the keep, are beautiful views over a rich country, and to Worksop Manor Woods.

When return'd, I was obliged, lacking my own materials, to use a barber's puff and powder. We now assembled to breakfast, and afterwards walk'd over the bridge at the town's end, where the canal passes, bringing up coal at 8 shillings the ton; happy purchase!

At the end of two fields, we came to Radford Abbey,

11

Old
Worksop

(now call'd Old Worksop;) and enter'd, after much admiration of the outside, this old church.

The pulpit is of a respectable age; and the font yet more. The pillars are large; and the body of the church is lofty, and well-lighted by three tires of windows: painted glass is gone; and but a remainder of an old tomb, with three old stone figures newly placed against the wall, are left. Beneath the gallery are several maiden garlands,[8] several of which were lately, most insolently cut down by some mad puritan:—I had forgot to mention, that at Thurgarton were many of those white silk Chaplets, that were borne before the corpse at the interments of batchelors, and maidens; a custom of much honor, as descriptive of their innocence. But country customs, whether sacred, honourable, or of exertion, are now all laid aside!

P— remark'd that, from the prevalence, and neighbourhood of the Norfolk Dukes, the Catholick faith had taken root here; if so, said I, why will he not beautify Radford Abbey, and enclose the beautiful remains of the chapel near the church? (where many stone coffins have been dug up). This chapel, and the gateway, will be better explain'd by the two beautiful prints from Sandby's drawings, than by any description of mine. In front of the gateway, whereon is much curious carving, and antient sculpture, is an handsome remainder of a cross, with steps entire; on which we sat for some time, ruminating on this scenery of former grandeur. In this gateway is a large room with this great window, to which we ascended, and found a school at business. The master whereof, who was very civil, I remarked to P—, must be a conceal'd priest, placed there purposely to make converts, with the artful, sheepish look, they commonly carry.

Worksop
Manor

We did not begin our horse expedition till eleven o'clock; then enter'd the lodge gate, adjoining to this town, which leads to Worksop Manor,[9] long famed as the seat of the Dukes of Norfolk.

But the noble old mansion was, with most of the antiquities, pictures, &c, burnt in the year — and the present pile, only a fourth part of the intention was then begun.[10]

This was the old house and was reckon'd, I believe, to be of great curiosity and grandeur.

W. W. immediately remark'd its likeness to a front of Somerset Place. Want of residence will render a place dull; but no residence could render this place otherwise, for it is so ill-imagin'd. The offices are spacious. In the north front of the house are 75 windows. The stair case is very lofty, and dark; and all the lodging rooms lead from one to the other.—On the ground floor are several very long rooms, and various others, out of descriptions; except the drawing room, which is of a noble size, and hung with Gobelin tapestry of the same pattern as the French ambassadors lately sold, and thereon are likewise depicted red crabs, and crimson lobsters crawling ready boil'd out of the sea! The tapestry is much faded, owing as the housekeeper thought, to the sun, but I shou'd rather think that, when it was put up, the walls were not sufficiently dried. The adjoining dining room is likewise a very fine room, and in it are two valuable and pleasing landscapes.—Of the chapel expecting much I was much disappointed, as not being of the adornment of a popish chapel, except a heavy gilt altar and a crucifix. The Duke, tho' he may have for many reasons renounced the errors of the Church of Rome, still maintains the priesthood at his several seats. Supposing much superiority at Welbeck, we did not enter the kitchen garden. The ground in the southern, unfinish'd front, is much neglected, and there are several miserably shaped stagnate ponds; but the uphill woods are bold and royal.

We took this course to Welbeck Park; whose separation Welbeck from that of Worksop Manor is not more than 100 yards. Mistaking the right drive, we much improved our ride by going thro' some young plantations; but had soon a sight of the house, which, with the whole ill-keeping about it, but little answer'd my ideas, and hopes.

13

In this place I was much disappointed, for I had heard of it much vaunting account; and so had kept it with expectation for a bonne-bouche. In these Duckeries there is an everlasting tide, one flows, another ebbs; and

'Sure Life itself can little more supply,
Than just to look about us and to die.'

Pope.

I cannot refrain my paltry wonder at the possessors of these charming domains, sacrificing health, and fortune, at the shrine of politics!

It was formerly the boast of this country that their nobles, sometimes retired in London, were only to be found in true magnificence in the country; there were they in glory, real patriots, and protectors; their mansions famed for hospitality; and their cellars overflowing with ale: but times are sadly changed; for one does see many noblemen, either dependent on ministry, or so linked to an ever-losing opposition, or so reduced in fortune, by gaming, or elections (the worst folly of all); that a country residence, at first tiresome, becomes at last impossible; down falls the house, down comes the timber; whilst the fine air of Marybone parish is enjoyed to the highest perfection on two closets and a cupboard! The poet well advised,

'Couldst thou resign the park, and play, content,
For the fair banks of Severn, or of Trent,
There might'st thou find some elegant retreat,
Some devious Senators deserted seat;
And stretch thy prospects o'er a smiling land,
For less than rent the dungeons of the Strand.'

This house is mean, ugly and ill-built; and the water, not in front, but at one corner, runs weedily thro' a flat: the offices appear to be very useful; but the old, grand, stable of the Marquis of Newcastle[11] is not quite quitted.— We put up our horses; and then enquired for Mr S[peechly] the gardener, to whom I had hoped for a preceeding letter of introduction, and thence to receive civilities, and many

14

grapes, and strawberries: but he was gone to Harrogate, and the grapes and strawberries were not near ripe.

Of the garden I expected wonders, and saw none: we enter'd a pinery, but it was the pinery of a private gentleman; nor is there any pleasure ground, or roses, or flowers, or orange trees for my lady Dutchess!

Tho' I shou'd suppose that Mr S.[12] understands his avocation,* yet I must own that I disagree with him, as to his practice of plucking most of the leaves from his fruit trees; which may make the fruit toast, and ripen quickly; but how is the flavour to be preserv'd, or those dews which cherish, and enlarge the fruit, this way, to be retain'd? Of such treatment of cherry trees, I have no doubt of the disadvantage.

* Welbeck. May 1. 1789

PROPOSALS

FOR PUBLISHING BY SUBSCRIPTION

A

TREATISE

ON THE

CULTURE

OF THE

VINE, &c.

By W. Speechly.

Gardener to the Duke of Portland at Welbeck,
in Nottinghamshire

and dedicated, by permission, to His Grace.

———————

This work, which is in great forwardness, will be printed on a fine paper, and comprized in one handsome volume 4-to. embellished with fine copper plates, engraved by Bafire.

The price to subscribers is 1£ 5s. to be paid on the delivery of the book.

Gentlemen desirous of encouraging this work, are requested to send their names, with the number of copies subscribed for, to W. Speechly, at Welbeck, near Mansfield, Nottinghamshire.

Subscribers names are also received by the following booksellers;— J. Debrett and J. Stockdale, Piccadily; E. Jeffrey, Pall Mall, London, and J. Drewry, Derby.

15

The inside of the house is of no account; without pomp, without pictures, (some very few,) and not of the luxurious establishment I expected; and I also expected an ancient pile, but nothing remains of antiquity, but the chapel, which is in mean attire. What has been done by the present Duke, are three respectable, modern rooms, the great hall is fitted up in the most contemptible attempt at antiquity, being stuck over with a white trimming, just like the sugar ornaments of a second-course cake.—But, if in the house little is for admiration, there is on one side a grove of oaks, near the water, which is scarcely to be equalled, such noble chieftains of the wood, of the tallest stature, and of the greatest girth; under the command of their old, (and now in his latest decay) monarch of the grove, *The Green Dale Oak*; whose majesty is propp'd by various crutches; and yet partly exists after some violent paralytic strokes, that have destroy'd his noblest limbs.

> 'And when the sun began to fling
> His flaring beams, the Goddess bring
> To arched walks of twilight groves,
> Or shadows brown of sylvan loves,
> Of pine or monumental oak,
> Where the rude axe with heaved stroke
> Was never heard the nymphs to daunt,
> Or fright them from their hallow'd haunt.'
>
> *Milton.*

From Welbeck Park, we took a detouring ride, returning by the north front of Worksop Manor, which for a mansion of that sort, shou'd not have been placed so near the road; but in the centre of its noble park.

Our dinner was very bad, and our inn is very bad, but it is a good station, and so on a tour must be abided. P— and W— preferring a walk, I took a creeping ride, in the evening, by Gatesford wooded common, to Mr Hewet's seat at Shireoaks[13] (where the counties of Derby, York and Nottingham meet) which is a good old place, shaded and green; tho' he has lately fell'd a fine avenue. For here, as elsewhere, they levell all the timber, and as if to prevent

Shireoaks

16

BOTHAM,

RED LION,

WORKSOP.

	£.	s.	d.
Dinners			
Suppers			
Tea			
Coffee			
Claret			
Madeira			
Port			
Sherry			
Lisbon			
Negus			
Punch			
Brandy			
Rum			
Hollands			
Cyder and Perry			
Porter			
Ale and Beer			
Servants			
Cards			
Rush Lights			
Chamber Fire			
Hay and Corn			
Chaise			
Saddle Horse			

(Gates, Printer.)

future supply, root up and narrow the hedges; so that if any man after a death of 100 years, cou'd look over the enclosed and wooded country he remember'd, it would appear to him a naked wild. I return'd at 8 o'clock, by the old tall house of the D. of Norfolk's steward, Worksop Lodge; and we then sat writing, till it was nearing to order supper; after which, having ginned ourselves without being strangled,[14] we retired to our truckles.

Worksop

Thursday June 11

In my ride of yesterday evening I gain'd such intelligence as determin'd us not to go southward, as we at first intended, but to make a little northern detour, and so quit our thought of going to Mansfield. Nothing can have been nastier than our inn at Worksop: with ill cookery, stinking feather-beds, and a conceited fool of a landlady:—but I endured, in my old quiet way, knowing there were much worse to be found. My morning account is allways of the same narration; Up early—feed the horses, strole about the town, then breakfast. Think how much time lost, and how many miles forward I cou'd have been; for it is the early setting forth that makes journeying easy: my comrades to this answer, 'Why you think but of doing this, or of going there? And when there so early?' My replies are, 'Because distances are uncertain;—because things should be seen leisurely; because at every stop, there is the town, church &c, to see; something in the neighbourhood to hear of, and time to us allotted for an evening lounge, as fishing, &c; and because by being early, you have the command of our intentions, are never benighted, or balk'd of your pleasure.' At 10 o'clock we had paid our bills at Worksop; when the baggage being ordered forward, we took the Doncaster road, for some time, till we came to the village of Carlton, over which, and to the church, and to an house of Mr Ramsden's, is a very pleasing view.— These we rode down to; the church is neat, the village well-built, and Mr. Ramsden's is a chearful-looking place: in the church yard I took down the two following inscrip-

Carlton-in-Lindrick

tions; in the first of which the lines are most happily divided!

> 'Go home, dear friends, and shed no
> Tears I must lie here till Christ
> Appears and at His coming I hope
> To have a joyfull rising from
> The grave.'

> 'Hard Fate, why shou'd you thus bereave of life
> The best of mothers and the dearest wife
> Must the weak aged parent yet survive
> To mourn for one so beautiful alive
> And why shou'd Death obtain his cruel ends
> And snatch her from her kindred and her friends?'

After this village we soon enter'd the wooded grounds of Mr Knight,[15] and passed by his ancient house, opposite to which are new and spacious offices.—From his grounds we came to a high land commanding a very rich prospect, with the village of Firbeck in the bottom; and soon to Sandbeck Park Gates;[16] leaving these on our right, we descended to the village of stone, where is something of romantic scenery of craggs over the stream. Here, the path near the mill leads into Roche-Abbey grounds; but of Roche Abbey this being ignorant, we continued thro' the wood, till we enter'd into a further quarter near the wider water, where were several gentlemen fishing (of the Lumley family, I believe) who directed us the way, after our expressions of admiration at the water, woods, and keeping of the place, just like a garden.—

At a small distance, embower'd in most delightful scenery, stand the ruins of Roche Abbey; and surely nothing was ever more happily placed for comfort, and contemplation; on one side the rocky cliffs, where it derived its name, and stone for building, and on the other, the most pastoral and translucent stream, over shaded by woods: for fishing there cannot be a better situation; or for love or for contemplation. Our observation here was most hasty; for we sat down for a long time at several points. Tho'

19

undemolished it is not properly guarded; and the plantations are too studied and gardenish; and, certainly, there
shou'd not have been a modern lodge built close to this
picturesque old gateway of entrance.

A house, and inhabitants are necessary; but then it
shou'd have been in concealment; or hallow'd out of the
rocky bank, and to suffer the abbey to be made a lodgment
for carts, rollers, &c, &c, is most intolerable!!!

In a mile hence we came to Sandbeck Park Gate, which
opens opposite to the abbey garden, the chief beauty of
this seat, rebuilt by the late Ld Scarborough.

After having lately seen so many houses (and a modern
house cannot be worth the trouble) and being drag'd
about by a foolish housekeeper, I was not sorry at being
refused admittance here; for there was a family here, part
of which I suppose we saw fishing in the Abbey waters. It
may be a good house, but around it are no particular
features.—What a folly it is for people to over-build themselves; knowing, as they must do, that the mortgage so in-
curr'd must prevent their heirs, inhabiting their grand
buildings; being only mausoleums of vanity, when the
next possessors never behold, without arraigning their
predecessors ill-taste, and folly.

Tickhill By a lane whence is a fine view to the left, we came into
the turnpike road that soon brought us to Tickhill, a mean
market town; and glad we were to put up, and quickly to
partake of cold lamb, eggs and bacon, (and some bad
collops at the young man's desire) when we ate as for a
wager. Unluckily we are too early for beans and peas. Our
dinner finish'd, and some Burton-ale drank (but not by me)
we walk'd to where stood the castle,[17] wherein formerly
resided, in feudal and princely pomp the Plantagenets
themselves.

The old gateway is venerably perfect; and close-adjoin-
ing is an iron barr'd door, which was the wicket, with this
inscription, 'Peace and Grace be in this Place'. Within the
castle-walls, still very thick, and in places very lofty, is

20

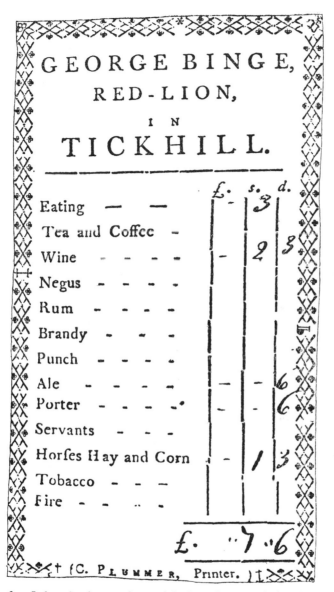

GEORGE BINGE,
RED-LION,
IN
TICKHILL.

	£.	s.	d.
Eating — —		3	
Tea and Coffee -			
Wine — — —	-	2	8
Negus - - - -			
Rum — - -			
Brandy - - -			
Punch - - - -			
Ale - - - -	-	-	6
Porter - - - -	-	-	6
Servants - - -			
Horses Hay and Corn	-	1	3
Tobacco - - -			
Fire - - - -			
	£.	7	6

C. PLUMMER, Printer.

At first I thought that my host might have been a relation, but in his name they pronounce the G, soft as in hinge, &c.

21

built a good seat of Mr Berridges; who was not at home, nor did we see any one to molest, or guide us: so we climb'd, with some toil, to the summit of a steep keep; tho' there was an easy twining path, that we found to descend by: the ditch is yet fill'd with water, and now, shaded by lofty trees. At our descent we enter'd the church a tolerably good one, (by the wall lays a perfect stone coffin) wherein are some old tombs, the writing about which I took not the pains to decypher; but was more pleased at the clerk's telling me that they were those who were stewards to one Mr Lancaster, who formerly lived in the castle. W. W. rang the church bells, and brought the boys into the belfry.

In going home I observ'd a custom, to me new, (and seemingly savage, like fleeing alive) viz, the barking of the oaks some time before they are fell'd; and numbers in this naked, condemned, condition stood within our view.— Maltby woods are large; and Maltby village is in a pretty vale where there is a good house of Mr Basires. Bramley is a neat well built village; and Bramley Grange[18] a fellow told me had been a good house, and was as good and habitable now as any house in the county.—The eggs and bacon had made me so dry that I stopp'd here to take a pint of milk. Finer children than in this country I never saw; and such white curling polls cost me many a halfpenny, thinking of my Frek. and wishing he was here to walk with, and talk to me: the happiness and growth of these children depend upon their having the nourishment of warmth.

By a country of much beauty, hill, dale and wood, we
Rother-
ham enter'd the town of Rotherham, and went to what is call'd the best inn, the Crown, but a more dreary, blacker, tumble-down, old casemented ruin cou'd not be. In a front room, upstairs, uneven as a plough'd field, we drank tea, and then with melancholy faces survey'd our shatter'd beds, windows broken, paper hanging down, blankets, and curtains torn; and everything number'd for sale, if purchasers can be found: for the master of the inn has got a

patent (a very odd one)[19] for making marbles for children, which he can do of all descriptions, so well, and expeditiously, that he will soon supply all the school boys of the world.

I proposed a walk; when we pass'd thro' the church yard, by the church of great size, and with a very lofty steeple, to the stone bridge, over the River Don; below which is a fine broad fall of water.

On the opposite side over the river, is a new-built, flourishing town, arising from the cannon founderies, and great iron works, established by Mr Walker;[20] who not only maintains the neighbourhood, but has so, honourably, enriched himself, that he and several of his sons live in magnificent villas, built on several eminences about the town; where, I said that they ought to invent signals for invitations, and announcements of all kinds.

In Mr Walker's work-yard, we survey'd an arch of an iron bridge, just cast; and with much pleasure the surrounding population, who are render'd warm, and happy, by the coal pits, which are every where by the road side; and down which we peep'd, and flung stones: how the little children escape falling into them is miraculous! All the people employ'd in the founderies are allowed coals; the other poor may have a cart-load for 5 shillings! From the hill, at our walks end, we cou'd discover Sheffield spires, at the end of the vale; in front the sun setting; behind us the town of Nottingham; and in the valley beneath, the furnaces vomiting forth their amazing fires, which make this country in an eternal smoke.—We made our walk as long as possible, from the dread of our dreary inn; where we supp'd on some thick chops, and unscraped asparagus.

I pass'd a very uncomfortable night, from the badness *Friday* of my bed; and from being waked several times to be *June 12* told of the arrival of P.'s and W.'s baggage; for which they had Express'd great Alarms.—I wonder where mine is gone to!

23

P— having spoken a great desire to pass much time in Sheffield; but I disliking all thoughts of a great black manufacturing town, rose early to push forward my own way, and await them at night.—After a peep thro' the windows into Rotherham church, (which contains nothing curious within, or without, but that all the grave stones lie horizontally, except one which was the old font,) I walk'd my horse gently to the iron forges; (by the way, viewing

the sun dispell the mist from the mountain tops;) where dismounting I saw the flowing of the lava, the dross whereof makes materials for road mending.—A bye lane brought me to the river, which the water being low, I Sheffield cou'd now cross. The country hence to Sheffield, is full of collieries, and trade. The Tontine Inn at Sheffield makes a magnificent appearance.[20a]

My first direction was to the hair-dressers room, where he dress'd my hair, and where I shaved myself; receiving many compliments (for the first time) on my adroitness: 'Never did he see a gentleman shave so well!'

This is a great flaring inn, of noise, and uproar. After

breakfast, I paraded the town, and try'd two booksellers shops for old books, where I receiv'd the usual, provoking answer, 'That they had lately sold a large Parcel'. I next survey'd the new market house; went to Mr Tudor's[21] manufactory, and there inspected all the business. The play house[22] adjacent, being open, I entered it, and seated myself in the front boxes; it is a neat, well-built theatre, and they say will hold, at the advanced prices of next week, 100£.; for then Mrs Siddons[23] will act here, beginning on Wednesday next, the 17th, with the character of Isabella in the Fatal Marriage. The waiter told me, 'That she wanted to put up at the Angel Inn, but they wou'd not take her in; and so she had hired lodgings'.

At my return to the inn I found that my comrades were arrived; saw W— at his toilette, and met P— in my way out of town.—

Passing Healy turnpike, I came into Derbyshire, (whence is a fine view of the country, and of Sheffield town,) and enter'd into conversation with a farming kind of man going my way, who was very communicative, and acquainted with the country around, which is full of good houses: with him I quitted the high road, and descended to a small village call'd Woodseats, and very properly Wood- from being surrounded by woods; and below it, a very seats noble one belonging to Lord Fitzwilliam. To the right is a view of the bold hills, where the Peak Country begins. Here my guide left me: and I soon came to Beauchief Beauchief Abbey, where formerly the religious seated themselves in a most happy situation for beauty, and retirement.

The clerk's daughter shewed me the church; of which only the gutted bellfry, the chancel walls, and a small portion of the body exist; and these in great decay:—as to the modern divine service therein, that she said was almost left off, for the parson was so *neglective*, that few folks came.—There are around the church, much burying ground, and many heaps of foundation; and in the old church many grave stones; as there are also under some

25

tall ash trees, which the girl call'd *Craw* trees; this at first
I did not understand, till I saw the rook's nests.—There
cannot be a finer view, than from the abbey. (Let the
monks chuse spots for my residence) over a glorious wood,
belonging to Ld Fitzwilliam; and it is back'd by lofty
wood-sides.

On the hill, above it, is a comfortable old seat of Mr
Pegg's,[24] (an ancient family in this county), and close to the
lane, some superb sycamores: I wish to know why this
noble, shady tree that flourishes well in a rocky soil, and
can endure the sea breeze, finds so few encouragers,
and is so selldom seen in our modern plantations? Which
are now pitifully reduced into larches, and Lombardy
poplars! Hence I blunder'd my road a little, but at last
deigned to ask a direction; and then by a horse road passing
Dronfield thro' Stubley, soon came to Dronfield; a market town of
pleasant situation, and with a large church.

This town I rode thro'; when feeling the day hot,
and myself hungry, I turn'd back to a small alehouse
(the Golden Lion) where I procur'd some slices of
fried gammon of bacon, and eggs; and being refresh'd,
sought the key of the church, which is best of the outside, tho' within there are grand pictures, of Moses and
Aaron, of Death and of Time; the chancel is in a ruinous
state.

The clerk's wife said 'There would be a *Rory Tory* in
a few days, and the Sheffield men to sing it'.—For since
the fame of the abbey musick, the country has gone wild
in its imitations: which indeed may be of use, as drawing
people to see the inside of churches.—The church yard
appear'd to be barren of poetry: I only carried off these two
lines,

'The loss of friends is much, the loss of life is more,
The loss of Christ is such as no man can restore.'

I stay'd long at my inn, for I was lazy, and had much
writing to bring up—my charges here were

					d.
Dinner	-	-	-	-	6
Hay and Corn	-	-	-	-	5
Brandy	-	-	-	-	5
Servants	-	-	-	-	0

	S1	4

The evening ride was at extreme leisure; the weather and country beautiful.—Three miles brought me to the village of Whittington, and to the Revolution House;[25] Whittington where, in the best parlour, I seated myself in the same chair that one of these noblemen might have occupied.—

The house is too bad for a tea shop, else I had ponder'd here for some time.—Our thoughts must arise from any classical ground we tread upon;—in the theatre, upon Shakespeare; in the House of Commons upon our country; —and so shou'd the mind ever employ itself in pleasure, and improvement:

Who then being at Whittington must not revolve on the consequencies of this meeting?—Most of my opinions live, and dye, in my own bosom: but every one knows that in the haste of alteration and reformation, more is done than is consistent with reason, or with justice!

On the 5th of November 1788, the hundred anniversary of this revolution was celebrated here—the Revd Mr Pegge preached in the morning, to a noble and numerous congregation; who afterwards marched in succession to view the inn, and the room, but they being in-adequate to receive the company, a new room was annexed in which was saved a cold collation.—The procession then moved towards Chesterfield, consisting of several thousands of people with the Duke of Devonshire, the Earl of Stamford, the Cavendish and Osborne families, with most of the neighbouring gentry, (preceeded by the militia music, at their head); who fill'd the inns at Chesterfield at dinner, and afterwards attended at the evening ball; having given beer &c to the populace.—

27

On the neighbouring common, whence the grandees were driven by the rain, are numberless coal-pits, and the Chesterfield Race Course.[26]

An intention is mention'd of erecting on this spot, a column in honor of the revolution; but unless these projects are instantly put into execution, they commonly end in vapour.

Chesterfield

Chesterfield steeple stands most curiously awry; the market place is spacious; where at the Castle Inn* I put up. Most of my evening, (for I was here at six o'clock) was pass'd in writing, (for I receiv'd the first letter from town); and in guarding a good parlour that I had engag'd. This house after our last bad stops, seem'd quite a palace. At eight o'clock my comrades arriv'd, having dined at Sheffield, where they had view'd the manufactories.—Together we walk'd about the town till dark; supp'd at ten o'clock, very well; retired to bed at eleven.—

Saturday
June 13

I will now indulge in a little hasty vanity, and satisfaction, in thinking how pleasant my tours will be to readers, an hundred years hence; if they, or the ink of them shall abide. Tour-writing is yet a novelty; our ancestors never thought of such a thing. Till the beginning of this century I never heard but of few (the best Mr Anthony A. Wood,[27] about Oxfordshire), and those were very short, and unde-

* Castle Inn,
Chesterfield.
March 12.   1789.

With all possible deference and thankfulness, Bluett, late of the Carte Inn, in Swines Green, begs to inform his numerous and very respectable friends, as well as the public in general, that he is now removed to the Castle Inn and Post House, on the lower side of the market place; which he has fitted up with great neatness; and where he hopes, by assiduity and Unremitting attention, to merit a continuance of the many invaluable favours he has already received.

N.B. Neat post chaises with able horses, and careful drivers.

The mail, Leeds, Halifax, and Birmingham coaches, set out from the above inn.

28

scriptive; neither were any engravings made (but the very few by Hollar,), of antiquities, castles, seats, &c).

Oh that a critical tourist had minutely described, before the Civil Wars, the state of the castles, and of the religious remains, and of the mode of living of the nobility, and gentry; 'er the former were dismantled, the monuments of religion demolish'd; and that the entrance of folly, by high roads, and a general society had introduced one universal set of manners, of luxury, and of expence.—Of all the tours I read I like my own the best, (Well said, master!) because all others are so cramm'd with learned investigation, and new fangled drawings; perpersly to forward a sale, whilst all pleasure minutiae are left out, as unworthy of the public eye.—This vanity is the overuling planet, and governor of all our actions. Be we brave, or cowardly, wise or foolish, active, or torpid, still vanity reigns triumphant in all our works, and supports us under every disappointment: nothing can be greatly done by another, to confound this passion in ourselves; which has the bound of a tennis ball, and the unceasing toil of a spider! For vanity hints, that had we been in the same places, at the same times, we should have atchiev'd the wonders of heroes. It makes us to bray as well of folly, as of learning; of gluttony, as well as abstinence; of age, being happier than youth; and of diminutiveness being preferable to stature: every false taste it adorns into a virtue; and every impotence into an honesty: our meaness it makes prudence; our apathy, resolution; and our cunning, wit.—So that, in fact, vanity becomes the healing balsam of life; and therefore let no man deny having a full share.

We were upon our horses by half past nine o'clock, and rode thro' Normanton, a village, where May Pole was, as others of this county, richly adorn'd by garlands, composed of silk, gauze, and mock flowers; and around which (a woman told me) they danced in the Morris-way; but not in honor of the goddess Maia on the 1st of her month, but, rather in memory of the Restoration, upon the 29th of May.

29

An intricate road led to a heath, where, before us, on a lofty hill crown'd with wood, and looking like a great, old, Hardwick castle of romance, stood seated, Hardwick Hall—the 1st object of our ride.—The right approach is thro' grass grounds with white gates; but after passing thro' several, we were much vex'd, at finding one fast lock'd, to return back, and to seek another way by a blind lane.—

On entering Hardwick Park,[28] we admired the liberality of nature to this place, in the boldness of the ground, the growth of the timber; and a running water, now only forming great pools, but which might be made most superb. When we had climb'd the hill, we had to observe the older house, in lofty ruins, only one end of which is inhabit'd: but for the newer—it astonish'd me! Such lofty magnificence! and built with stone, upon a hill! One of the proudest piles I ever beheld. And I was highly pleased to find myself mistaken in having supposed it a deserted ruin; as much repair has been done within some last years, and many masons here now at work in the inside.—The housekeeper was fetched from the old house, and found us seated in the great hall, in admiration of its grandeur, tapestry, old oaken tables, elks horns &c, &c.— My mind bethought itself of old Bess of Hardwick, the first and richest female subject of Queen Elizabeth, who married 4 husbands, men of rank and respect. She was with her husband, the Earl of Shrewsbury, the guardian of Mary Queen of Scots, in this house. (I think that this print much resembles the original picture, here, from whence it is taken).

The dining room on the ground floor, is now repairing, so that the pictures are removed: in it, as in most of the other rooms of this pompous house, are the Cavendish arms, in stucco, over the mantel peices; with the motto

'The conclvsion of all thinges
is to feare God, and keepe
His commandemantes'.

E. S. 1597.

These two rooms, with a dismal decay'd chapel, were all we saw upon the ground floor, except the kitchen, and servants halls; for nobility, and grandeur, formerly dwelt aloft:

On the second floor are a profusion of fine apartments, with painted oak doors, and lofty mantel pieces; all hung with tapestry, except those of Marys; whose work of gold figures upon black silks, and velvets, for hangings, still cover the walls.

In her bed room, are the old bed and great chair; and over the door her arms carv'd in wood and around it 'Marie Stewart par le grace de Dieu Rayne d'Ecosse, douariere de France;' crest, a lion; motto, In my defens.

She pass'd 13 years of her captivity, either here or at Chatsworth, or at Wingfield Manor in this neighbourhood.

Upon the second story, I was struck with wonder at the grand drawing room, which is near 70 feet long, and 50 feet wide; the lower part is hung with tapestry, and the upper part, of about 10 feet in height, is of emboss'd stucco, in colour, of huntings, forests &c.

This is a room of the most surprising grandeur, and in perfectly good order, for the floor is matted; which as all the others of the house are form'd of a composition;[29] and all the stairs are of stone; oddities these in an old house! In this room is a curiously inlaid oak table, of arms, &c, with this inscription, which I cannot clearly make out.

THE REDOLENT SME
OF AEGLENTYNE
WE STAGGES. EXAVET
TO THE DEVÆYNE.

Above it are the Cavendish stags, to which it alludes.— The wainscotting is painted with heads, the chimney piece is of marble, superbly pillar'd; and there is a very ancient cabinet, that I wish'd to have explored.—This room fill'd me with lofty ideas of the grandeur and living of the lady builder, who was the richest subject in Europe: the adjacent old house, wherein she was born, she call'd her cradle. The great gallery being repairing the portraits belonging to it are now placed about the great drawing room. These portraits of great antiquity and from the very commencement of painting, I had not time to examine; they had been, and are much neglected, and many in great decay; tho' yet restorable. These are some I remark'd.

Queen Elizabeth.	Henry VIth.	Countess of Shrewsbury.
Lady Jane Grey.	Henry IVth.	Charles Ist.
Lord Darnley.	James Ist.	Henry VIIth.
Henry VIIIth.	Stephen Gardiner.	Sr Wm Cavendish.
James V. of Scotland.	Queen Mary.	Sr Thos Wyat.
Richard III.	Arabella Stuart.	Hobbs aged 89.
Cardinal Pole.	Countess of Salisbury.	Countess of Exeter.

With many others; besides, one, inscribed, *Maria D G Scotiae püssima Regina Franciae Doueria* 1578. *Anno regni* 36 *anglica captiva* 10. and tho' these are many, and curious, yet are they quite insufficient for such a gallery. 200 feet in length, with—I believe—about 9 recess'd windows, and two lofty chimney pieces.

Tho' I was pleased at the Dukes making any reparations, yet I stared at the execution, for all the new doors, skirting boards, &c, are made of deal, and only befitting a farm house. I said to my friends that the first expence about this house, were I to command, wou'd be an allotment of 3000£ for carpets, and grates: most necessary *Gratifica*tions; and of more use than a journey to Spa!!

After a very long and critical examination of the apartments, we mounted to the leads whence is a beautiful view of the country and park, and down to the water, which might be render'd visible from the lower floors: upon these leads are six very good rooms, and they are environ'd by balustrades, and a quantity of S's.

We now quitted this magnificent seat, which is placed in a noble park, with fine timber, water at will, and abundant of

32

every thing to render it a place of admiration. It is the fore-most old manor I ever saw: and yet I have now seen many.

The older mansion, has been gutted for the advantage of Chatsworth building, and displays a sad skeleton of ruin; upon the walls are some chimney pieces, and stucco bas relief: pull it all down, and good.— —At the further end of it, where the housekeeper, and a family reside, there are some magnificent rooms, and one of the largest, and loftiest apartments I ever saw, call'd The Giant's Room, from two figures over the chimney, 10 feet high and yet not out of proportion to their situation. In the next room, tumbling to pieces, are these verses on another chimney piece alluding to the Cavendish Stag.

'A fountinge Stagge the water brooke desireth,
Even so my soule the lyvinge Lorde requireth.'

So much for Hardwick. I never did, and probably never shall see such another house of antiquity. At our quitting the park P— expressed a wish to see the neighbouring church of Hucknall, hoping to find therein many Caven-dish monuments, (for P— is a great genealogist, and fond of heraldry, and family blazonings); so we turn'd into some meadows, and were soon lost, and obliged to turn back. W. W. was now detached forward to our dining stop; for we all began to grow hungry, peevish and tired. I must not forget to mention that in the older Hardwick house are the remains of a library, which was removed to Chatsworth. For a library I allways enquire, and in the chamber here, I found myself amidst a large parcel of pamphlets, letters, and accounts: amongst them there appear'd to be some valuable classics; and W. W. said that he saw some letters directed to the old Countess,[30] which he said *ought to be saved*,—and which wou'd bear an hearty rummage. Of this old and miserable church of Hault-Hucknall we did with difficulty get the key; therein Ault is a good monument of a Countess of Devonshire, with Hucknall a later description 1627; also a later inscription to the

c   33   T.D. II

memory of Thos Hobbes of Malmesbury, age 91. There is also these verses to the memory of a park keeper;

'Long had he chas'd
The red and fallow deer
But Death's cold dart
At last has fix'd him here.'   1703.

Brasses on grave stones are now either lost, or so disregarded that those who will save them are to be commended; under this principle I wrenched up a brazen figure, (about 15 inches long;) which is now fix'd in the cloisters at Chicksands.

Hence we rode to Glapwell,[31] a small village on a hill on the Chesterfield road, where there is a house of Mr Hallows; and in two more miles came to Bolsover, a mean town, of most elevated situation; after having endured much heat, and a long detour.

W— had provided for us, all that was to be had at The Swan Ale House, viz, stew'd mutton chops, sallad and tarts; and to them we sat down, with the eagerness of savages.

We ate, we drank, without form, without compliments; not till, full, and somewhat rested, cou'd we speak to each other. Our nags were lodged in a bad hovel; but the hot weather prevents any mischief, and they were as hungry, and thirsty, as ourselves. Our meal (at another time wretched,) being finish'd, we enter'd the walls of Bolsover Castle:[32] the Windsor Castle of Derbyshire. My first wish was to see the riding house where the Marquis of Newcastle trained his managed horses; (for I have ever had a wish, and some little ability, in putting horses upon their haunches; having look'd up to the methods of Sr Sydney Meadows,[33] and endeavour'd to do likewise.) This was very narrow, and must have been very inconvenient. Adjoining was the long gallery, and many fine apartments, built by this nobleman, but now unroof'd; the chimney pieces, stone window shafts, and strong walls remaining, it might easily be render'd habitable.

34

This old strong turretted building, standing on the edge of the hill, and commanding a most extensive prospect, the D. of Portland keeps a good repair; within, there is a curious old hall, and a dining room like a chapter house, with a centre pillar, and an arched roof; with walls of wonderful thickness.

Above stairs there is a drawing room and a number of bed chambers; with walls so thick and kept so well that by additional furniture it might in a few hours be render'd habitable: but it surprises me that the Duke does not gratitiously offer it for a residence; which shou'd allways be done with these old houses. A school wou'd warm it well.

We climb'd up to, and walk'd upon the leads, a miniature of Hardwick. From the outer court is a remarkably strong single eccho.—

At our return to the inn, the weather continuing hot, we stay'd tea; when W: and P: going forward, I remained, as usual, the paying of the bill: then led my horse down the long and steep hill, often looking back at the bold castle; the steep of which is most rugged, and, probably, has been wooded.

					s.	d.
Dinner	-	-	-	-	-	2	0
Liquor	-	-	-	-	-	2	4
Tea	-	-	-	-	-	2	0
Horses hay & corn		-	-	-	1	3
					7	7

The road and soil of the vale are so deep and bad, that I should think there was no stirring in winter. My pace being very slow, I overtook not the advancing party; at Duckmanton were some young fellows playing at quoits, a game much in vogue hereabouts; of the weight of the quoits, and length of the cast, I ask'd particulars of a remarkably fine young fellow, whom I eyed with the looks of a recruiting officer; and he answer'd, that the former weigh'd 10 llb, and that the cast was 25 yards.

35

Chester-
field

At my return to Chesterfield I found Thos. Bush just arrived from London, with letters, and a trunk of new accomodations for me; but as I have gone on so far with 3 shirts, and 3 pr. of stockings, (and enough too,) I shall send this back to town tomorrow, with the sheets also, that came in it; for already there is a weight of baggage enough to load a horse. It now became necessary to account for this strange appearance of Thos Bush; (to be sure, I did wish for him all the way, but then we must each of us have had a servant, and have travell'd at a great expence, with a train like a comet;); and this was the cause; viz, that W. W. chusing to return to town sooner than we did, desired T. B. might be sent for to lead Mr L—'s[34] horse back, whilst W. W. might hasten to London in a post chaise.

If ever I shou'd tour again, (and that I shall scarcely do, without much forethought,) an equal share of baggage shall be allotted to each man; the weight being equalised: then take the sort of luggage you list. Light baggage and quick movements for my army.—We had a good supper, and were well attended; for this proved a good inn.

P— who has long resided abroad, and is now upon the verge of Matrimony, has been inquisitive during our tour at every place, about the price of lodgings, meat, butter, fuel, &c, &c; and discovered, to his great surprise, that in even this not distant country from the capital, everything except the wages of servants, were much cheaper than in France.

> 'Now the worlds comforter with wearie gate,
> His dayes hot taske hath ended in the west;
> The owle (nights herauld) shrieks, tis verie late,
> The sheepe are gone to fold, the birdes to nest;
> The cole-blacke cloudes that shadow heavens light
> Do summon us to parte, and bid good-night.'
>
> W. S.

Sunday
June 14

At ten o'clock we took our road of departure, and our leave of the good inn at Chesterfield. Passing thro' Brampton village, we soon came upon a bleak, healthy

country, (wherein are grouse); in our descent, towards the
vale, is the Robin Hood Alehouse, and under the sign
these verses.

> 'You gentlemen, and archers good
> Pray call and drink with Robin Hood;
> If Robin Hood be not at home
> Pray call and drink with little John.'

At Baslow village we turn'd up the vale to the left, and
soon enter'd Chatsworth Park,[35] thro' which we rode; and
then skirting by the house, came to Edinsor Inn in the
village of that name; there leaving our horses, and ordering
dinner, we walk'd back to Chatsworth; where the porter
was *so obliging* as to find the gardener, and the housekeeper
for us; who are allways *ready* to attend to strangers. Under
the guidance of the first, we had the long temporary cascade in front of the house let loose for us: this, when dry, is
a disagreeable sight, and not much better, when cover'd
with the dirty water they lower from the hill.

Chats-
worth

Next some fountains were made to squirt aloft for us;
and a leaden tree (worthy only of a tea garden in London)
to sport about us. Nor cou'd I refrain from remarking
what I suppose all others do, at the ground remaining un-
sloped to the vale and river; which the gardener said might
be completely done for 2000£. As for the river, of clear
water, meand'ring thro' the meadows, it is now but a pitiful twine, which, under an owner of spirit wou'd be made
equal, if not superior to the Blenheim Water: but here is
no taste, no comforts display'd. All is asleep! More money
may be lavish'd in follies, or lost at cards, in one year than
wou'd render this park a wonder of beauty.

Seeing this little of garden, cost us much money; because we were shewn about by a wou'd-be gentleman, and
felt ourselves to be really so. The housekeeper next took
us in tow, and shew'd us all the foolish glare, uncomfortable rooms, and frippery French furniture of this vile
house. If nothing has been done abroad to beautify, if
nothing has been done within for true luxury, yet the

37

Dutchess has made a fine display of French tables, gilt chairs, uneasy sofas, and all what is call'd charming furniture.—To complete the French-hood, the oaken floors of the great apartments are all wax'd, so that ice is rougher, and every step upon them is dangerous.

Of pictures, there are some portraits, and much indecency in the other paintings and the tapestry: a great Hampton Court stair case, and a Sr John Vanbrugh chapel make up the total. Hardwick House a house of grandeur as a house of comfort is worth a dozen Chatsworth.

We now return'd to our inn, where we eat grayling, out of season; and P— slumber'd after dinner.

Edensor

Edensor is a small and pretty village, the poor where of, the gardener told us, had a right, after having parted with their commons, to turn a certain number of cows into Chatsworth Park, for some months, at 25s. per head.

EDENSOR INN.[35a]						s.	d.
Dinner	-	-	-	-	-	4	6
Porter	-	-	-	-	-	0	6
Brandy	-	-	-	-	-	0	3
Wine	-	-	-	-	-	2	6
Tea	-	-	-	-	-	2	0
Horses Hay & Corn		-	-	-	-	1	6
						11	3

The weather was so warm, (for the wind has been long at east,) that we made a long stay here; then crossing the park, left Rowesly village to the right, where is a rural stone bridge over the River Derwent.—

Darley

A lovely road with the river on our right, brought us to Darley village, where at ye church gates stood the clerk, who usher'd me, and P, into the church; wherein are two old monuments,[36] of Whitehall, and of old John of Darley; in the church yard is a most reverend and aged yew tree, probably one of the largest existing, being 33 feet in girth, and containing 1800 feet of solid wood. Darley Priory stood at a small distance, and the remains there of were pull'd down about 16 years ago, as is usually done, with little gain, and much trouble: the clerk said (licking his lips) that in the oven he had seen 8 sheep hide for shelter. By a variety of most beautiful country, we arrived at Mat- Matlock lock village.

To oblige my friends I came through this part of the country; for at Chatsworth, and Matlock I have been before; and I do abominate seeing modern houses, and modern furniture, or entering within the vortex of public places: I seek not company, and noise; I turn not my head to look at a woman; for I leave London that I might see Nature in her wild, and most becoming attire: at pictures I could glut my eyes at my neighbours Mr A[ngerstein]'s;[37] and satisfy them by staring at the beauties in Bond Street.

I come abroad to view old castles, old manors and old religious houses, before they be quite gone; and that I may compare the ancient structures, and my ideas of their taste, and manners, with the fashions of the present day:— I enjoy a grove of venerable old oaks; feel transported at the sight of a wild water-fall; and taste the animation of a fox-hunter at the unkennelling of a fox, when I discover a castle, or a ruin.

So that the flirtations of Matlock I leave to younger men; and the charms of Chatsworth-Gardens to its master; who, perhaps,

'Tired with the joys, parterres and fountains yield
Finds out at last he better likes a field'.

Darley village continues to the village of Matlock, where is a bridge, and waterfalls of much beauty; thence the ride by the river, with the rocks, and the high-torr to the left, is sweetly romantic; and the river is as clear as crystal. Matlock Wells, which we rode by, did not appear to be full of company; and by new buildings, and an increase of lodging-houses, the quiet and society of the place is lost, and it begins to become noisy, and divided into parties.—

39

Below Matlock a new creation of Sr Rd Arkwright's[38] is
Cromford started up, which has crouded the village of Cromford
with cottages, supported by his three magnificent cotton
mills. There is so much water, so much rock, so much
population, and so much wood, that it looks like a Chinese
town. At our inn (the Black Dog) T. Bush having gone forward, had prepared, (as he knows well to do) our beds, and
our stables.—We took a meand'ring walk around these
little mills, bridges, and cascades; and went to where Sr
R: A[rkwright] is building for himself a grand house
(Wensley Castle) in the same castellated stile as one sees at
Clapham; and *really* he has made a *happy* choice of
ground, for by sticking it up on an unsafe bank, he contrives to overlook, not see, the beauties of the river, and
the surrounding scenery. It is the house of an overseer
surveying the works, not of a gentleman wishing for retirement and quiet. But light come, light go, Sr R[d] has honourably made his great fortune; and so let him still live in a
great cotton mill! But his greatful country must adore his
inventions, which have already so prosper'd our commerce;
and may lead to yet wonderful improvements.

An Act of Parliament[39] is soon expected to pass to
render the river navigable to Cromford, from which much
benefit must accrue to these works, and much destruction
to the beauty of the river,—for when was any river made
navigable that its beauties were not demolished?

An event, at our return from this walk, somewhat em-
barass'd us; an old lady, a young man, and two young
women desired to join our company, and to sup with us:—
This desire I stubbornly opposed, and went out, as em-
bassador, to say that we were met upon urgent business,
and cou'd not be disturb'd.

Indeed I believe that this strange request sprang from
their ignorance, and being unused to travelling! We did
not sit up late; for W. W. eager (as he thinks) for fishing,
had order'd a man to attend him at 5 o'clock in the morning; (at which I smiled) and P. was eager to go to Mat-

lock: not so I, being neither eager for bed; for fishing in an easterly wind; or for joining the company at Matlock-Bath; my desires were to see the country.

Having breakfasted at 9 o'clock (Mr W., the angler, *Monday* not being risen!!) I, and poney took our way.—Just below *June 15* the great house at Matlock, are new stables &c built, much to the disfigurement of the place, and to spoil the view. In the overhanging woods was much melody; and a nightingale accompanied me all the way to Matlock village.

'Everything did banish mone,
Save the nightingale alone,
She (poor bird) as all forlorne,
Leand her breast up-till a thorne,
And there sung the dolefulst dittie,
That to heare it was great pittie;
Fie, fie, fie, now would she cry
Teru, Teru, by and by:
That to hear her so complaine,
Scarce I could from teares refraine;
For her griefes so lovely showne,
Made me thinke upon mine owne.
An' (thought I) thou mournst in vaine,
None takes pitty on thy paine;
All thy fellow birdes doe sing
Carelesse of thy sorrowing.—
    Whilst as fickle Fortune smil'd,
Thou and I were both beguil'd.
Every one that flatters thee,
Is no friend in misery:
Words are easie, like the wind,
Faithfull friends are hard to finde;
Every man will be thy friend,
Whilst thou hast wherewith to spend,
But if store of crownes be scant,
No man will supply thy want!
He that is thy friende indeede,
He will helpe thee in thy nede:
If thou sorrow, he will weepe;
If thou awake, he cannot sleepe;
Thus of every greefe in heart
He, with thee, doth beare a part.

41

These are certain signes to know
Faithful friend from flatt'ring foe.'
Willm. Shakspeare.

Since we came from Wandesford we have never eaten peas: strawberries are not ripe; and this is not the county for flowers! And, owing either to plenty of coals or employment, we have never been teiz'd by beggars!!

As I pass'd by Matlock Bath, I purchased a sixpenny spar watch, for my Frek; and had some foolish thoughts of laying out money, for presents, in the spar ware;[40] but a sensible *wherefore* stopt me, especially when I found them as dear as in London.

Some of my riding and touring pleasure is lost from the want of an intelligent, and gayly-roving spaniel; who wou'd divert me by day, and guard me by night. Poor Jock did this, and never offended; when you chuse it, he wou'd stay in the stable, with your horse; eat any thing offer'd to him, and never required more than table scraps: for at inns, they will fancy you fine, and charge in proportion, if you call for meat for your dog.

To-day, I turn'd to the left, over Rowesley Bridge; and soon came under the wall of Haddon Hall park,[41] now quite dismantled, and the timber fell'd. I cross'd over a bridge to the house, of awful, and melancholy look, as if deploring its forlorn state; the river, below, finds tears. The farmer, who inhabits the farm near the Gate, (part of the old out houses,) most civilly put up my nag; and then attended me.

This poor abandon'd place is totally deserted; (tho' surrounded by an estate of 8000£ pr ann:) and uninhabited, because then not subject to the window tax!

As a place it might be made of greater beauty, by the power of water and a romantick county, than cou'd ever be the nasty stare-about Castle of Belvoir. The walls and roof are all sound and good; so only furniture and fuel are necessary, to make it habitable: nor, were I Duke of Rutland, shou'd I visit it for more than 2 summer months; but

Haddon Hall

42

I cou'd not suffer its decay, and that the gallery and kitchen shou'd not be warm'd. The river is so brilliant, and so rapid, that it wou'd form a lake of the utmost magnificence; and, as abundant of trout, of much diversion.—One nights losses at play of the late duke had made this a charming place.

Planting & paling	-	-	-	4000
Repairs & additions	-	-	-	4000
Furniture	-	-	-	4000
The water	-	-	-	3000
Roads & turning	-	-	-	1000
				16000

Nor do these wasteful, idle nobility know what they possess: for in the old hall is a full length picture that I and Monsr Secard[42] (picture dealer in Pall Mall) wou'd put into good order; and there is another in the gallery of rare account.—The stewards room, next to the hall, is the oldest room I ever saw; the old wainscot whereof, almost black, is curiously carved with heads, armorials, &c, and E.P.'s (Black Prince) with the arms of England: in the windows is much stain'd glass. Above—there is a room of the same size, with ancient tapestry, and many others; in one of which is a grand bas relief of Orpheus attracting the brutes by his lyre. The gallery is very noble, tho' not of the grandeur, or length, of that of Hardwick, being but 110 feet long; yet it is full state of antiquity, finely wainscotted, finely window'd, with much stain'd glass; and to my great surprise, a modern table spread with eating preparations,—as cold ham, &c, &c.

To these presently came in the steward, and several ladies, (from Bakewell) for a fishing party; and very civilly offer'd me of their entertainment.—The chapel, at one corner of the inner paved court, is very dirty and neglected; but the east window was highly to be admired for the very curious, and antique painting, till one of my brethren (antiquaries) (a sad dog!) lately cut out 5 of the saints faces. The date in the chapel is 1427. At the door of the chapel is placed a Roman altar, beneath the print of which, I have written as many letters as are easily legible.

The old kitchen is woefully damp. 'Aye', said the farmer, 'twou'd kill a fly in five minutes in summer! Unlike to former times, Sr, when Sr George Vernon (call'd King of the Peak) treated Prince Arthur (Hen. VII son) here and when he kept open his house for the 12 days of Xmas, as he allways did, and was allways done (even at the beginning of this century) by the Rutlands.'

In a room, below, hung with tatter'd tapestry, call'd the wardrobe, are many remains of rusty armour. 'Sr,' quoth the farmer, (my intelligent guide) ' many gentlemen will stay hours in this house, and prefer the observation here to the being in Chatsworth'. 'That's just my case'. 'And some, Sr, will desire to take away pieces of armour'. 'That I shou'd like to do, too'. 'Why then, Sr, as you seem fond of these things, there is a sword hilt, with part of the blade, said to be worn by the Vernons in the wars of France'; and so I instantly carried him off.

I wou'd not disturb the fishers, to whom the farmer went; after advising me to go to Bakewell, a market town two miles distant, to view the monuments of the Vernons and Manners's; for this estate came to the Manners's by their marriage with a daughter of Sr G. Vernon.

I found Bakewell to be a much better place than I expected, and the inn, the White Horse, a very good one. The landlady instantly brought before me a quarter of cold lamb, a cold duck, sallad, tarts, and jellies; and I was eager to enjoy them: nothing so pleasant after fatigue, (at a certain age, too) as eating and drinking.—Being satisfied, I sought the clerk, and found him in his day school, amidst his scholars; who appear'd to be quite happy at a little respite, for he seem'd to be a great tyrant. He said to me 'I am master of this parish'. 'How so, my friend?' 'Why, Sr, I govern the boys; they govern their mothers;

BAKEWELL BRIDGE

[see pp. 44 and 191

BENTLEY CHURCH
from sketches by the Diarist [see pp. 48 and 166

the mothers govern their fathers; and so, Sr, in fact I rule the parish'.

The church stands loftily, and closes well the vale from Haddon. Upon a large tomb in the church yard, is this most pompously foolish inscription.

'Know posterity, that on the 8th of April in the year of grace, 1757, the rambling remains of John Dale, were in the 86th year of his pilgrimage, laid upon his two wives.

> This thing in life might raise some jealousy,
> Here all three lie together lovingly:
> But from embraces here no pleasure flows,
> Alike are here all human joys and woes.
> Here Sarah's chiding John no longer hears,
> And Old John's rambling Sarah no more fears,
> A periods come to all their toilsome lives,
> The good man's quiet, still are both his wives.'

In the centre of the chancel is a very ancient tomb, well engraved, and lately cover'd by a new, ill-fancied, Derbyshire marble slab, with the old written Latin inscription to the memory of a Vernon; which, to the schoolmaster's surprise, I read fluently. 'That has been a great puzzle to most people; and you Sr. read it off at once! That I never saw done before!!' He next led me to admire the Vernon and Manners monuments, which are very lofty, very magnificent, being made of the Derbyshire marbles; and are well preserved, being guarded by folding deal doors.— With this *learnede Clercke*, I pass'd much time; and then went to the house of Mr Watson.[43]

I trailed my way back, much at my ease, and again in contemplation of the old turrets of Haddon.

> '. . . The lon'ly tower
> I also shun'd; whose mournful chamber hold
> So night struck fancy dreams the yelling ghost.'

till I came opposite to Matlock-Bath; where W. W. hail'd me from a window; and I was obliged to go up into the great room, where some parties were at tea. This house was not of the pleasure of those lately past; for what had I to do in this society, but to stare and be stared at. I was glad to get away, and to find myself, as it were at home, at Cromford, which affords, however, but a bad noisy inn. My latter day here was pass'd (as may my latter day of life be) most peaceably; for I found a sequester'd walk thro' a wood, overhanging a trout stream, and many small cascades: returning I sup't alone; nor did the gay flirters of Matlock return till eleven o'clock, having supp'd there.

Cromford

BAKEWELL, DERBYSHIRE.

WHITE WATSON,

(Nephew and Succeſſor to Mr. HENRY WATSON, late of *Bakewell.*)

BEGS leave to acquaint the Nobility, Gentry and others, that he executes Monuments, Chimney Pieces, Tables, Vaſes and other Ornaments, in all the variety of Engliſh and Foreign Marbles, agreeable to the modern Taſte and upon the moſt reaſonable Terms.

W. WATSON, having attentively collected the Minerals and Foſſils of *Derbyſhire*, is now in poſſeſſion of a valuable Aſſortment ready for the inſpection of the Curious, and undertakes to execute orders for the like Productions, properly arranged and deſcribed.

Tuesday June 16

A collector and seller of all this sort of work, and curiosity; but which is to be seen to more perfection in many shops in London. If Mr W. hoped for a Buyer in me, he was mistaken.

Being determined to oblige W. W. in his wishes; or fancies about fishing, I did not make the stay here I had intended; and in riding to view Wingfield Manor House, and the many druidical monuments, &c, in the neighbourhood of Winstre.

My intentions overnight were to have risen at six o'clock this morning; but I went to bed, feverish, and flutter'd; so having taken many James's Pills, I passed a sudorific, uncomfortable night, and did not rise till 8 o'clock.

P. and I, having breakfasted, left W. W. to settle the .account; and climbing the steep hill, cast back many a look

W. MATTHEWS,

WHITE-HORSE, BAKEWELL.

Neat Post Chaisee, with able Horses.

	L.	s.	d
Eating,		1	1
Tea and Coffee, —			
Wine,		1	1½
Rum and Brandy,		0	3
Punch,			
Ale, and Porter,			
Cyder,			
Tobacco,			
Servants Eating & Liquor			
Rush-Lights,			
Chamber Fires,			
Hay and Corn,		0	5
Post Chaise,			
L	0	2	9½

The White Horse Inn is a very tolerable one, and my charge, you will perceive to be exceedingly cheap: think what a service I had.

47

over the beauties of Cromford Vale, and at Sr R. Arkwright's house, which thence appear'd to an advantage, it
does not deserve.

The country above the hill is very stoney, and dotted by
lead mines. The road to the right, (neither the best or most
frequented I believe) carried us to Middleton, a long
straggling village, amongst stone walls, in a bleak country;
and thence we continued over a rocky wild, to Brassing-
ton; to Bradborn; and so to Tissington, where is a good
old house of Sr Willm Fitzherbert's[44] whose family have
long resided here.

Tissing-
ton

The church of Tissington is surrounded by fine old
trees; as I search in every church yard for what is best to
be found, so is this the best inscription I cou'd here find;
spelt and letter'd as I have mark'd.

ANNE ENDESOR. 1766.

Beneath this stone, a virtuous dame here lies
Fair, modest, artless, innocent and wise,
The meekest *patron* of her sex designd.
The softest manners, and the gentlest mind;
Good without show, obliging without art,
Her speech the faithful dictates of the heart.

(I do not recollect whence these lines (of pleasant import) are borrow'd.)

Having pass'd the grounds of Sr Wm Fitzherbert; we
came into the turnpike road from Buxton, and in three
more miles, thro' Bentley village, and by much up hill and
down, arrived at Ashbourne. T. B. who has the care of *the*
Baggage, is to come as he can; for neither horse or carriage
are to be hired at Cromford. We had suffer'd much heat in
the last hour; and were tolerably fatigued, and hungry.—
Booksellers shops a vain pursuit! No letters awaiting us
here!! I walk'd up the principal street, and made fruitless
enquiries after Dr Johnson's memory; (whether any letters, inscriptions by, or memorials of him, were to be
found in this town;) for here was his frequent summer
residence at Dr Taylor's.[45]—The church[46] is large, and
crowded by pews, with a shabby chancel, and a miserable

Ashbourne

organ, that W. employ'd himself upon. Our dinner was serv'd at two o'clock, We were all very muzzy and sleepy.

If travellers (Cocknies) expect, when in the country, to revel in fruit, to eat trout, and to purchase venison, they will be sadly mistaken; for fruit is not to be bought, trout are not to be caught; and venison (good) is not even to be had in gentlemen's houses, as they delay, relative to the season, too long e'er they kill deer, and for age, and flavour, never wait long enough, by three years!—

For fruit, for wine, for fish, for venison, for turtle, London is the only mart in the world.—So that tourings and country visitings only serve to whet desire for London quiet and London luxuries. A London gentleman steps into a coffee house, orders venison, and turtle, in the instant; and (if known) a delicious bottle of port, or claret: upon a clean cloth, without form, he dines at the moment of his appetite and walks away at the moment, he is satisfied; neither importun'd by civilities, or harrass'd by freedoms; he labours not under obligation, he has not submitted to ridicule, or offended from a want of high breeding.—To these thoughts I am urged, from seeing our inn yard crowded by chaises full of company, going to a grand dinner in this town; there to be overwhelm'd by dress, compliments, hams and fowls, ducks, custards, and trifles; losing their time, their peace; and not improving their politeness.

Yet with these ideas, I am no hermit; for I love society that I know, and approve of me; but when I do go, (as I sometimes must,) upon a genteel visiting party, I feel myself a bewilder'd, unhappy wretch, struggling for words to utter, and for schemes to escape; at last, home I come, so happy, clap on my bed gown, my slippers, take off my gaiters, ease my neckcloth; and am most comfortable: next day, comes another card of invitation, and I am not rich enough to hazard a refusal, and dare to be happy, and free; which, however, had I no children, I do declare I wou'd.

In the evening, W. W. having engaged the (father) barber, opposite, (who is an expert fisher) to attend him we walk'd together over *Bentley Bridge*, to the banks of the Dove.

PISCATOR. 'Why, this, Sr, is call'd Bentley Brook, and is full of very good trout, and grayling: but so encumber'd with wood in many places, as is troublesome to an angler.'

'From that sweet book—*The Compleat Angler*'.

Now I never was, or ever shall be a fly fisher: for such eternal whiskings require a quicker sight than I possess. The fishing that I like, is either sitting peaceably over a pearch hole, with strong tackle, and a float; or else troaling for pike, in a quiet sedgey stream. Here all the people are fishers (alias poachers,) and every spare hour are at work. —W. W. knows as little of fly fishing as myself, and wants my perseverance; P, and I, look'd at his, and the barbers no success, till we were tired; then cross'd over meadows to Mappleton, by the way getting a draught of milk. This is a sweet village upon the banks of the River Dove; fronting Mr Okeovers house, [47] on the opposite side, in Staffordshire; who has with most bourgeois taste, whiten'd the ends of the cottages and the church, that they look like ornaments in a desert. Near the whiten'd bridge were many *pauvre miserable picheurs*, some of whom had caught (especially the barbers son) several small salmon, about six inches long; which they speak of as a dainty, and must be very good to pot. In a summer house of a bowling green, the neighbouring squires were assembled in noisy mirth, (hard to determine whether merry or quarrelling): I remark'd to P—, that the truest derivation of *Bowling-Green* was from the number of *Bowls* of punch and negus drunk thereon.

We took a new, and very pleasant walk home, and again by Bentley-Stream, where we talk'd much to an angler about fly-fishing; these fellows, I am confident, know but little of the science in comparison of a gentleman angler; just so it is in regard to the huntsman; and a gentleman who will attend to and hunt his own hounds; the former may ride, and halloo, and murder, but is totally ignorant of the refinement and the true pleasure.

I once tour'd a small distance with a lady, who used to be so *witty* with the waiters, that they never attended to our wants;—just so, with my two companions, talking so much to the maid waiters, that I grow sulky, and say 'We shall now get nothing, from this chatter; let me bring the wine, and necessaries; and talk to her afterwards'. To which they answer 'You are an old fellow'; 'Aye, so I am', I reply, 'and know how much better it is to be well waited upon, than to make servants impertinent by familiarity'.

W., returned fishless, as we were going to supper; but he *thought* that *one* trout did rise at his fly! He, W, leaves us tomorrow, returning to Sheffield in Yorkshire to see Mrs S[48] act there!! I make few comments: but must think that touring cannot be taken alone; and for company to draw together becomes almost impossible.

My Master Walton[49] says 'That Ashbourn has allways in it the best mault, and the worst ale in England:' Come 'Take away, and bring us some pipers, and a bottle of ale, and go to your own suppers'.

The middle of the day is now very hot; but by a trav- *Wednesday* eller, or a tourist must be borne, unless they will be very *June 17* early in the morning, and so make a double day.—I suppose that in former times either the laws terrified, gentlemen controul'd or inferiors were humble; and that when our forefathers hunted, and fished, there was plenty of game: for the more laws, the more evasion; and their multiplicity has render'd them ridiculous.

When Isaak Walton was an angler, he walk'd out near London, and caught his fish; and when Cotton angled these streams, there was no interruption of vagabonds; now, go where you will, every one is a sporter, alias poacher; every market place is overrun by grey hounds and pointers; and all people say that the game is not preserv'd! If an estate, on which I shou'd reside, were left to me, I shou'd, at first, endeavour to preserve the game, and fish; but if I found that impossible, that they were deem'd ferae naturae, and that every person was abroad after them; why then (sooner than permit such inroads, see my fences broken, my grass trodden down, and myself trampled upon,) I wou'd make a general distribution; poison every fish; destroy every nest; and unfairly demolish every hare: no creature shou'd find game upon my estate; for their breed shou'd be annihilated. Now, by most gentlemen they are partially preserv'd, at the expence of some poor starving objects, for the advantage of the insolent maroder. But any game or fish brought to my door, I shou'd purchase; and avow my intention of so doing.

W. W. adhering to his design of quitting us, (for the novelty of Mrs S's acting!) was alert this morning, and soon after 9 o'clock in a post chaise; at going he gave orders to T. B. about his journey to town on Mr L. L.'s horse, where he ordered him to drive on Saturday: but no sooner was he gone than I call'd T. B. to prepare his horse to ride with us; 'for there is no need of our going to town, as I have previously written to Mr L. for the loan of his mare'.

So now we are greatly attended! P— owing to the shew of fine weather left his great coat at home; as for old careful he never parts from his gt coat, and his nt cap. Wou'd I had my sheets too; then I had not kick'd off those of last night, and slept on nasty blankets. Till this day, the 17th of June, we have had, at least since Coultersworth, a suc- Mapleton cession of fine weather.—We rode by Mappleton church, and over the whiten'd bridge, to Mr Okeovers red house; ordering our groom forward (in a *genteel* way) to enquire if we might enter.—

We were permitted to go in, (at P.'s desire I come) and saw two habitable rooms; in the second, the dining room, are some good pictures; but our object was to see the fine

52

Raphael, for which Mr. O— has been offer'd great sums, (according to the maid's report £7000)—we admired; and I do believe it to be an undoubted picture; and a very pleasant one it is.—P— and I did not agree about the keeping of such a picture; 'What', said I, 'shall a private gentleman have his dining room eternally enter'd to see a picture, which he might sell to such advantage; which must be kept, allowing for interest of money, at such an excessive cost; which Time or Fashion may under value; which is out of place, and out of pleasure, in a country seat'!—P—, per contra, felt for Mr. O.'s pride; and talk'd of likings.—But I continued; 'A private gentleman, with only an easy estate, does an injustice to himself, and family, by harbouring such a picture; and is as mischievous as if he indulged in proper pleasures at a great waste: when he dies, or distress shou'd come, and the picture must be sold, Christie's hammer will knock it down for £500;—or in 20 years, another person will boast the original, and this be proved a copy.' This picture was found in the garret, cover'd with filth; nor does the hanging of it over the fire place, subject to heat, and smoke, shew the knowledge of the possessor!—As for Mr O.'s place, tho' in a lovely vale, it is kept in wretched taste; with white rails, clip't hedges, and shroven[50] trees; either his notions, or mine, are best; both of us cannot be right: and I deride his taste.—

Hence we came (how tired I am, and any reader must be of 'Hence we came', and 'then I rode', but what can I say?) Hence, then, we came to the hilly country where stands Blore church, (we are now in Staffordshire,) a dismal place; but as it might be productive of curiosity, we wou'd have enter'd cou'd the key have been found at the clerks; so cou'd only peep thro' the windows, and get a look at one old monument.

Descending the hill, we came to a lock'd gate of Mr Port's of Ilam,[51] when sending forward our groom, the gardener with a key soon appear'd.—Here nature has

Ilam

53

done wonders; an amphitheatre of wood, a rapid stream, with the curiously formed hill, call'd Thorp Cloud, to close the valley, altogether form an assemblage of the most picturesque and beautiful scenery: but the banks of the water are not sloped, nor is it properly staunched to produce cascades, or fullness.—We meander'd about this place with the civil gardener, who agreed with me as to the indolence of his master; who, surely, shou'd not with a great family, enter in expence; but yet 2 labourers with spades and mattocks might do wonders of walks here! Thro' the rock, near the house flows so rapid, and so cold a stream as wou'd kill trout to a certain distance; and being distinctly heard; and if let loose at the hill top, (as I think it might be) wou'd form a wonderful cascade over the rocks, thro' the wood.—The gardener made us observe a small grotto with a table, wherein he said that Congreve often sat, and where he wrote his play of *The Distrest Mother*. 'Hold you there, Master Gardener; probably Congreve was here, but he did not write the Distrest Mother; was it not The Mourning Bride?' (It was the Old Batchelor) but the gardener perservering, I gave it up!—

I saw, in passing by the house, Mr Port's young family, but did not much notice them, from the preference I gave to *Old Port*!—At our departure from Ilam, on the gardener desiring our names, P—, in strange fancy, added to my name that I was a nephew of the late Adml Byng! which, tho' no family shame, was a misfortune, and the causes whereof not to be explain'd to a gardener.—

Dovedale   We now meant for Dove-Dale; but were somewhat puzzled in our road, till we found a poor man working at a gravell-pit, who offer'd to attend us, and a boy to assist in taking round our horses; our companion proved to be a civil, quiet old man, and an accustom'd guide.—On quitting our horses I smiled at P—, for leaving his gt coat at home; and put on mine as the sky began to lower.— The passage of this vale is truly romantic; on either side, banks and woods, varying at every turn; with the charming

River Dove rippling to our left;—but e'r long, the
threat'ning storm urged us briskly forward to the cavern,
call'd Reynard's Hole; to which the ascent is very steep
(unlike this description) and very laborious.—The rain
now fell violently, and the thunder rowl'd tremendously.
—At our arrival to the cave, we found it occupied by two
native burghers, who fled at our approach; viz, two formid-
able goats, refuging from the thunder, at which they are
much alarm'd;—this scene was truly in the manner of
Robinson Crusoe. They, however, maintain'd a neighbouring station, whilst we remain'd here, for a long half hour,
during the tempest; which added double solemnity to the
scenery, and made the rocks rebound most formidably.—
Sr Wm Fitzherbert, to whom the land on this side belongs,
had built a stable near the cave; had found the ascent easy;
and had made a cellar at the end of the cave, and had put
up benches, &c: civil intention, but foolish performance!
Had he blown up by gunpowder an inside for a house in
the rock, and therein fix'd a family, or two, who cou'd have
preserv'd the place, and accomodated the tourist, he had
done well; otherwise he must know that the speedy hands
of time, and mischief, wou'd demolish every thing.

The ascent to Reynard's Cave is now very steep, all-
most unsurmountable by women; above the larger cave is
one of a smaller size, call'd The Cooking Cave. Upon the
decrease of the rain we push'd forward, tho' but a little
way, till we sheltered in another cave; and here we remain'd a tedious hour, having, except the thunder, only to
listen to the accounts of our guide, about the place, the
fishings, the birds, the game, and of the opposite hill of
wood cut down by Mr. Port: after these generals, he
related the history of his family, in a very artless way, and
in language and pronunciation often unintelligible; he well
remember'd (being 71 years of age) the coming of the
rebels into those parts in the year 1745, and that they
press'd several people to carry their baggage, but none
took in with 'en. From our second retreat, we sought a

third call'd The Dove-Holes, large and beautiful caverns; below which, on the river's brink, we saw George Hastings, an expert angler, catch a good trout.

Tho' it yet rain'd fast, we quitted the vale, and by a twining path betwixt hills came to a farm house, Hasingdon Grange,[52] where our horses were station'd;—and here, after our forgetfulness of bringing liquor or food with us, we trusted to the hospitality of Mr Gould, the rich farmer: —but this old sullen hunks suffer'd us to remain at his stable door, (whilst we were dying of hunger and fatigue) without a single offer, tho' our worthy guide spake every broad hint to him! Such an old rascally curmudgeon, so unlike the run of farmers, who in most counties wou'd instantly have relieved us, hurried us away at the first clearing up of the weather; and then we posted off T. B. to Ashburn, (it being past 4 o'clock) to get us dinner. In our return we stop'd at a poor alehouse, The Dog and Partridge,[53] in Spend Lane, and ate and drank furiously of some soft bad oaten cakes, cheese, and ale.—In our inn at Ashburn, there being much company, we were put into a large upper room, where we dined on beef steaks and plum pudding, and were not sparing of the liquor.—A letter was now deliver'd to me, open'd which had been sent to a Mr Byng in this neighbourhood; a distant relative I believe him to be, and long thought dead;—

In the evening one of his two daughters (both married to two brothers of the name of Banks) dress'd in a shabby genteel, waited upon me, with explanations and apologies about the letter, seem'd highly pleas'd with my acknowledgment of relationship; and said that their father lived at a village some miles distant, where he hired a small farm, which added to his half pay as Lieut. of the Navy, serv'd to support him: when I ask'd of her the profession of her husband &c, she answer'd 'That he was a farrier (alias blacksmith) and much addicted to liquer.'

After our dinner, at about seven o'clock, we view'd the church yard—wherein is this epitaph most *happily* divided:

Ashbourn

56

All people
that do pass me by
As you are so once was I
But as I am so must
You be.
Therefore prepare
To follow me.

In the church is, now, Boothby Chapel, formerly belonging to the ancient family of the Cockaynes, of whom there are many old monuments; and the following description to the memory of a Cokayne, who served in the wars in France under Henry VIIIth.

'Here lyeth Sr Thomas Cockaine.
made Knight at Turney and Turwyne.
Who builded here fayre houses twayne
With many profettes that remayne
And there fayre parkes impaled he
For his successors home to be
And did his house and name restore
Whilst others had decayed before
And was a Knight so worshipfull
So vertuous wyse and pitifull
His dedes deserve that his good name
Lyve here in everlasting fame.

In another part of the church are some fine recumbent figures of the Bradbornes of Bradborne; one male figure is very gigantic.

At the other end of the town is the seat; and grounds of Sr Brook Boothby,[54] (descended to them from the Cockaines) with all the disadvantages of the town noise, and neighbourhood, with paths thro' the grounds: the water has been removed from its natural channell, into an upper cut in the meadows; where were great boats punting about.

We now return'd to our writing; and to a cold supper; and were in bed before eleven o'clock.—

I cou'd have wish'd to have gone forward to-day; but *Thursday* P— hearing of the copper mines at Ecton,[55] urged me to go *June 18* thither, fearful that I was too hasty in my scheme of return; which is fallacious reasoning, there being allways enough to lead off, and to employ the time. We breakfasted at 8 o'clock, and at 9 o'clock the road of our return of yesterday, till we were directed at a turnpike gate, to turn to ye left, which we did by a most stoney road, till we cross'd the River Dove; and amidst mountains of height and beauty, came to the village of Austenfield. Here we enquired our road, and turning to the right over mossy commons with much fatigue to ourselves, and horses, arrived

Ecton at 12 o'clock at the Ecton Mines, the most valuable property of the Duke of Devonshire.—Our horses were led forward by T. B. to the village of Warsell, where dinner was to be provided for us.—One of the managers of the mine conducted us up the shaft to the water engine, which drains the mine; and a dirty and tedious walk it was; the manager, a miner, P— and myself, with each a lighted candle in our hands. In this infernal region one cart of ore passed by us. At the water engine we were stunn'd by the noise, and astonish'd at the body of water; one river flowing above, and one below us. Next, we were carried to the smeltings of the copper, and lead, saw several siftings, and the many children employ'd in the laborious pounding of the stone, by which hand work they *may* gain 6d. per day. The women wash the ore. In the several branches are employ'd many hundred labourers.—At the end of our survey, which lasted about an hour and a half, we had to

Warslow endure a most desperate rain to the village of Warsall, which is call'd $\frac{1}{4}$ of a mile distant, but where, at our best speed, we did not arrive in $\frac{1}{4}$ of an hour, till my gt coat was almost wet thro', and P— (without gt coat!) soak'd to the skin.—The Greyhound and Hare, was as miserable an alehouse as cou'd be seen, with only one dreary parlour, where T. B. had very properly prepared a great fire, and had ordered bacon and cabbage to be boil'd; which as soon as out coats were put to the fire, we attacked with much vigour, as also the brandy and ale. P— had luckily his one great coat to put on.—Our employ, and our apartment strongly reminded me of the Boor Schaft[56] in Germany, after a severe march; but then I had my servants about me, and my canteens well stored.—After we had dispatch'd much bacon and many eggs (the rain falling with surprising violence,) P— composed himself to sleep, (which I never yet did out of bed; tho' in a course of years it may be necessary) and I had luckily my tour writing to employ me; and I will not get fat.—Such an heavy rain is rarely to be seen!—

T. B[ush] was of the greatest use to us, for he waited at table, dry'd our cloaths, and had to attend to the horses at a distant stable.—At 5 o'clock the weather began to clear up; and our reckoning was call'd for, which amounted for 3 dinners, 3 horses hay, and double fed with corn, brandy, 2 quarts of ale, tea, and fire, to the no very extravagant charge of 6s. 3d. and thus I will suppose the division.

					s.	d.
Horses	-	-	-	-	1	6
Dinner	-	-	-	-	1	6
Tea	-	-	-	-	1	6
Brandy	-	-	-	-	1	2
Beer	-	-	-	-	0	7
					6	3

Our road to this place had been so steep, and stoney, as much to fatigue ourselves, and our horses; so we enquired for (if possible) another road of return, and they said, that at a short distance we might get into a turnpike road, but that it was about.—By all means, said I, let us rather go twenty miles of good way, than, again, such another 12 miles that we founder'd thro', this morning.

Till we reach'd the turnpike, the road was bad; then to the village of Hartington, (by the way my poney went lame from a stone in his foot, which we with difficulty extracted): the vale of Hartingdon is rocky, and romantic, leading for two miles to the great road to Buxton, 9 miles from Ashburn; this way may be 3 or 4 miles about, but then it was excellent, and we spun away, and I was eager, from seeing more rain in the wind, which made me (in spite of P.'s counter opinion) hoist all my canvass, from Sr Wm Fitzherbert's gates; and well I did, for I nick'd the time to a minute, when the rain thoroughly return'd.—

The sight of Ashburn is now hateful; and so wou'd be the prettiest town, in touring, after passing three days in it.—

This is the first day that the peas have appear'd here; so from travelling north, and returning south, we shall lose both peas, and strawberries, for in our way out, they were not ripe, and at our return they will be past.—At our supper of to-night I was not agreeably surprised by two pacquets from Mrs B[yng] which requiring much deciphering, and much answering, fully employ'd me till bed time.

Friday
June 19 A lovely morning after the rain. Passed a bad night from a pack of barking dogs!—I left P— to settle the bill, for I meant to go a round about way, that I might visit the old cousin of mine, to whom my letter was missent.—He

Snelston resides at a small village call'd Snailston; in going to which, I stop'd on a hill to admire a most beautiful prospect over the River Dove, to Mathfield church, and towards Mr Okovers Park, Thorp Cloud, &c.

Near the church of Snailston, at a neat farm house I found this aged cousin, (who rents 26 acres of land, and keeps 6 cows;) in a clean dress, in his kitchen;—he shook me by the hand, and was glad to see, once more, one of his name, and kindred; but seem'd very old, and nearly worn out. His face, hair, and air, much resembled those of old Mr Kemble,[57] but he is much taller. The man who held my horse (a deputy of Mr Banks, one of his sons-in-law) wou'd shew me some of my road, and led me to the top of the pastures, where he pointed out my course. [The stay of yesterday was against my wish, for I abominate the sight of mines, and miners, as unproductive of pleasure; and the

60

wretches who work in, and about them, seem devoted to darkness, dirt, and misery: the happiest hours of a tourist are those of passing thro' the country, when his eyes, and lungs are gratified by fresh scenery, and fresh air.—Besides this, I never wou'd (if possible to be avoided) abide in a market town, in noise and dirt, a witness of forlorn idleness, or offensive drunkenness].

I easily found my way, which was good but splashy, and leading thro' a pleasant country to the villages of Evely, Rodesley and Shirley, and entering the turnpike road near Brentsford; where I stop'd at a small alehouse for a draught of milk, and some bread and cheese, and whilst in the kitchen had the history of my hostess, 'That her husband was a waggoner, that she had a cow, and seven hens,' and she had likewise, one of the finest children in a cradle I ever saw.

From Brentsford is a very fine view to the Staffordshire hills. I hence, pass'd thro' Longley and Markworth,[58] below which in a vale is Mr Mundy's seat at Markeaton, a flaring red house without shade; there is a verging plantation, but that neither cools the house, or the walkers from it.— Derby looks well in approach, especially the steeple of All Derby Saints Church; and the entering street is handsome.

P. was arrived an hour before me. The George Inn stands awkwardly; and is one of those dark, narrow, noisy town inns that I abominate.

The town is crouded by the county militia, assembled for their *annual exercises*. At the booksellers shop I cou'd find neither old books, nor intelligence about the county; most of those I enquire from, whether stayers at home, or professors of travelling, are puzzled at the 2d. question. The loss of my map, intentions, &c, in my portmanteau, has been a great distress to me; tho' it has been luckily recover'd, and is now in Duke St.—A bad dinner, and bad wine.—

In the evening we took the town survey. The great church of heavy Grecian architecture, attach'd to the fine

61

old Gothic steeple, contains the burying place of the Cavendish family, and the monument of Bess of Hardwick (before mention'd) with a long Latin inscription, descriptive of her titles, her husband's children, and buildings. The clerk, a pedantic puppy, keeps a spar-shop of useless ornaments.

The silk mills[59] quite bewildered me; such rattlings and twistings! Such heat, and stinks! that I was glad to get out: we shou'd be full as happy, if silk worms had never been.

This town is over run by the drunken militia: having given my opinions before, I now apply'd to P. to remark the truth of them; being brought from home to be let loose upon their country men in fights, and insults, of which we saw various instances;—as well as their (*steady*) Rollcalling!!—

Being in all the distress that idleness and a great town occasion, we had only to saunter about the streets, where I made much enquiry about the Pretenders abode here in 1745; and enter'd the house, and saw the parlour where in these hasty, misguided adventurers quarell'd so fiercely, before their return. To me it appears strange that in a bad season he shou'd suffer his whole army to march on foot; and did not press the country for horses—for their forward march—or quick retreat—: but probably the want of breeches, and ignorance of riding, might prevent it.

They still speak of the rudeness of this army, and of their plunder of the town.*

*'Gazette Extraordinary. Dec. 12th. 1745.

Derby. Dec. 8th. The Rebels behaved tolerable well in their march southwards, but have plunder'd the country in their retreat.—Many of the best houses here have suffered. Two of them were taken with their arms, between Ashburn and Derby, by a farmer and two boys, and were sent to the camp at Meriden Common. In this town they demanded billets for 10,000 men; but those who computed their numbers as exactly as possible, assure us, that they did not exceed 6,300, horse and foot. The horses are extremely jaded and in a bad condition. In the numbers above were many old men, and boys of 15 and 16 years of age, all without shoes and stockings.'

All the officers of the militia are gone to dine with Mr M[undy] of Markeaton. There is a coffee house, a gloomy hole, upon the market place, where in we went to read the papers; and of the burning of the opera house,[60] which must have been the work of intention! Our supper was slight, and short.

P— often tells me that we are too forward, and I am allways hurrying along. Surely, said I, 'it is right to employ nimbly our time; and it is only extending our plan, if too soon of our intention;—and besides—bad weather'. *Saturday June 20*

This morning began with a heavy rain; this continuing for a day, or two, wou'd impede us exceedingly:—however at eleven o'clock it clear'd up, and enabled us to crawl abroad.

How *pleasant* for the sick, or studious, must be the clattering of fifes, and drums, in narrow streets! The musick of the militia parade was not of an offensive nature, being scarcely audible. Tho' in this tour I was appointed pilot, for a general conduct, yet I have never commanded the time, or interfered with the delays, by which several days have been lost. Disinclinable to see what might be

June 19.   GEORGE from DERBY.

Salmon	-	-	-	-	-	2 6
Loyne Lamb	-	-	-	-	2 0
Peas	-	-	-	-	-	1 0
Bread and Beer	-	-	-	-	1 0
Wine	-	-	-	-	-	2 3
Tea	-	-	-	-	-	1 6
Suppers	-	-	-	-	-	2 0
Brandy	-	-	-	-	-	1 0
Wine	-	-	-	-	-	1 2
Malt Liq.	-	-	-	-	-	0 6
Breakfast	-	-	-	-	-	1 6

16 5

Horses - - - - 4 9

£1 1 2

63

seen to more advantage in Bedford St Covent Garden, I accompanied P— to the porcelain manufactory,[61] where, being denied seeing the process (from good reasons, I suppose) we had only to admire the beauty, and good painting of their works; and I learnt from one of the proprietors some hints about our progress. At our return from the china shew, and having paid our bill, we left Derby by the old bridge;[62] (soon to be rebuilt;) and passing over a hill, whence is a pleasant view adown the vale of Bradsol, soon

Morley came to the village of Morley; seated upon a hill, and commanding fine prospects: nothing can be better placed than the church and the ministers house.

At the entrance to his grounds stands an old cross, which has been properly restored.

To the left, is the old gateway, which led (I believe) to some noble manor house:[63] how barbarous to pull down old ruins, as is commonly done; to fill up cart-ruts! Here Mr Wilmot, the minister,[64] has with that conserving taste, that I so much commend, not only left unmolested the cross, and this gateway; but also this piece of old wall, whereon is a stone clump that may mean to represent a heart and flames; and probably was an ornament of the old mansion.—A boy now brought the key of the church from the distant clerk's house; and we were attended by a civil, hearty neighbour, (who had been a great hunter, and brag'd of the *gamm* hereabout,) and by a hind of Mr Wilmot's, whose house seems a good one.—In the church are many old tombs of the Stathams,[65] who built it, and of the succeeding family, the Sacheverells; but I search'd in vain for a monument of the famous doctor, (whom I have since learnt was buried in St Andrews Church, Holborn.) who must have been buried here.—There was some stain'd glass in the windows, and some broken pieces laying upon a monument, where I *cou'd not reach*; the fraction of this window was made by the entrance of a *sacrilegious fellow* to steal the church plate.

Whilst I was employed, for five minutes, in making my

RUINS AT MORLEY
from sketches by the Diarist

[*see p.* 64

drawings on a paper upon the poneys back, P— and our guide walk'd to a little distance to a mount, (whence is a noble view to Belvoir, Nottingham Castles, Ld Middletons, &c.) by the side of which are the remains of a surprizing ash tree:—

This mount and broken trunk I included in my works, making, as I think, the prospect viewers like two dancing dogs.

(I must here intreat a candid criticism upon my drawings; and inform the perusers that I never learn'd to draw; and that this tour contains my (almost) first attempts: on a future day I shall hope to improve my pencil; gain an idea of shade; and be able to give some kind of grace to my trees.)

‾eaving Morley, after a pleasant and long survey, we were directed, by bridle gates, over grass closes, to Stanley; and thence to the object of my pursuit, standing in a sweet valley (as they all did) what shou'd remain of Dale Abbey.[66] Of all that is described in the print, as existing Dale only 60 years ago, (belonging to noblemen, to whom we Abbey join an idea of taste) nothing now remains but the lofty arch, which P. did not walk down to, but I took post as near as I dared from a vicious bull, and executed a drawing with more success (I think) than usual.[67] Indeed this bull was its only guard: and I must again express my wonted surprise that a nobleman (of taste I have heard Ld Stamford to be) who owns, and sometimes visits it, shou'd not enclose, and plant about it; and then it wou'd appear to great advantage.

About Dale are many coal pits.—A private road, which we sometimes mistook a little, brought us to the summit of Hopewell Hill; upon whose brow I seated for some time, and P— survey'd with his glass, the extensive prospect before us, with the course of the River Derwent for many miles.—We soon cross'd the Nottingham road, and keeping a straight course, on a light soil came to Ogbrook,— and shortly to Willne Parva; to which church we had been Wilne directed, as an object of curiosity, by the master of the Parva china factory. We had now been on horseback too long, without a bait; and unluckily the clerk lived at a village we had passed; so T. B. being sent back thither, gave us a delay of $\frac{1}{2}$ an hour, when I hunted the church yard for inscriptions, which are selldom legible upon the grey slate stone of this country.

This was the only one I took down—

> 'Now I have ended all my toilsome years
> And now re-linguish'd from all worldly cares
> And here I lie in this cold urn of clay
> To meet the Bridegroom on the final day'.

A circle of lime trees around the church yard have been lately fell'd.

At last the clerk came; for hungry as I was, it appear'd to be a long time. Within the church (our object) is a remarkably old font; and the well kept, well screen'd-off burying place of the Willoughbys, whose monuments are very respectable.

But the stain'd-glass windows thereof, tho' somewhat damaged, are now properly guarded by shutters, and are, for their number, as fine as can be, as fine, I think, as any part of those at Fairford: there are 3 of them, 1st our Saviour in the manger, (rather damaged;) the 2nd, (the finest) His Crucifixion, is most gloriously pencill'd, and colour'd, as well the fore and back grounds, as the soldiery in armour, with the temple, and the distant hills;—the third (much broken) is the Sepulchre.—We thought ourselves much obliged to the china man for having directed us to this good observation.—

At the bottom of the adjacent meadows is a cotton mill, and a ford over the River Derwent, as deep as to make me lift higher my legs; which brought us upon the navigation of the Trent to the Mersey, around which at Shardlow, are built so many merchants houses, wharfs, &c, sprinkled with gardens, looking upon the Trent, and to Castle Dunnington Hill, as to form as happy a scenery of business and pleasures as can be survey'd.

Here, to our comfort, we put up at 4 o'clock, at The
Rose & Crown, just placed to my wishes, exactly different
from The George at Derby; tho' the hostler being drunk,
and the women of the house sulky were great drawbacks.
But we had a good room, and our horses sweet hay; our
dinner of lambs chops was greedily eaten, and I now (finding no bad effects) drink of their sweet ale. Being easy as to
our time we stay'd two hours.—Near this inn is an old
seat, occupied by Mr Parkins, in a very bad state of
improvement.—

As my intention (after many enquiries at Derby abt inns
&c,) was only to proceed few miles further, and without a
doubt of finding a tolerable inn, and having a charming
evening, we walk'd slowly thro' the villages of Aston, and
Weston, to Swarkston upon the Trent; where is that wonderfully long bridge, reckon'd a mile long. T. B. was
detach'd forward for preparation, but came back with a
woful face, to say that the house we expected to sleep in,
was a most wretched ale house.

Whilst they advanced to the opposite side—for a better
quarter, I rode down on survey of the ruins of an old hall,
which has been a grand place, and where the great lodge
at the end of an avenue is still perfect in shell. I had then to
wonder at the bridge, which is certainly the longest I ever
saw.

At Swanton, the village on the opposite shore, I found
P— at a small inn, who instantly said that we must proceed
further, for 'this house wou'd not do, that T. B. must be
sent forward, and that he had order'd tea'.

This was a blow upon me, who love roosting, like a
turkey, at sunset! But P— was pleas'd with the idea of a
night ride; said 'how pleasant it was, and a novelty, and
that I was allways for stopping too early.' To this my answer was, 'Aye, certainly, I do', and ever shall,—to prepare
beds, supper, &c, and to be early in the morning;—and
not ride a country in the dark, that we came to view, in bad
roads, at some peril, and much melancholy;—and with an

encroachment upon the next day, when it becomes impossible to get away in any time:—Arrived, too, your horses are neglected, your sheets can't be aired, and you disturb, and distress the inn! Besides, this look'd to me like a tolerable house, wherein we shou'd have done very well.

T. B. being gone, we followed, and were away at 9 o'clock! The road soon became stoney, and unpleasant; I kept silence, and blunder'd slowly forward; P— went faster, and in two miles I was alone and in the dark. I came to the village of Tickenhall, a long straggling place, and had much inclination to have put up at a public house; but I push'd forward, and in process of time, arrived at a common of a thousand tracks, and cover'd by coal pits; after crossing this common I came to a cottage, and enquired my road, which, after a crawl of two miles, down a tedious lane, where I had only the glow worm to amuse me,

Ashby-de-la-Zouch

brought me at eleven o'clock, to Ashby-de-la-Zouch, a market town in Leicestershire;—having lost so much country;—tired of myself and horse;—and arrived at an hour when other tourists go to bed. P— was surprised to have lost me!! and had not order'd supper! I did not talk much; I was not in a frisky humour:—but bustled about for some cold meat, and some liquor, which were finished by ½ past twelve o'clock.—

Sunday June 21

My watch was not wound up; so I waked at, I thought, seven o'clock, but found it to be nine; the consequence of our unpleasant night ride!

I took T. B. to task—'I thought that you, T. B., knew me better than to encourage such a night ride!' 'Sr, it was Mr P— that did not like the house; the stables were good, and I saw nothing against our stay'.—The quantity of grass in this country exceeds any former produce; there are horses and cattle feeding in grass of 2 loads pr acre; and most idly and wastefully destroyed, as why not tether them, or cut it green for them? Whatever God sends of His bounty, selldom advantages people of middling fortunes,

from the tricks, and rogueries of great farmers and sales-
men; for now they say that no one will send cattle to London; so that I may pay more for my meat, because it is a
most fruitful season!!

In Ashby are no soldiers; nor have we seen but half
dozen, (at Eaton) since our coming out! After a late
breakfast, we walk'd to see the ruins of Ashby Castle.
The first appearance, on the north side, coming from the
town is a chain of irregular buildings erected in different
ages, which, altogether form a pompous pile of ruins.
Many of the stone shafts are perfect; and if the whole
were clear'd from adjoining buildings, and, (as I so often
repeat) fenced around, with a lodge of entrance, the ivy to
spread around, trees to spring up, and the ruin only to
proceed of itself, its fall wou'd be mark'd with decent
pride. The view to the south and towards the old gardens
(still traceable) and the park exhibits a much bolder display of grandeur; and is well described in one of my
prints—

Adjoining to the castle, on the eastern side, is a long
timber'd building, said (by a man near us) to have been
built for the reception of the suite of K. James Ist when he
visited here: part of this building is used as a concert room,
and at another end is a Methodist chapel, under the
guidance of the Dowager Lady Huntingdon,[68] the lady
patroness of this persuasion; and to which (service time
now beginning,) there went 5 to the one that went to
church; and no wonder, as here may be fervour, and devotion.—To church we had thoughts of going, until we
heard that the preach was not to be heard; and I heard
that there was an organ:—which has driven out the old
melody, and singing, all together.—After a walk about
the town, we return'd (service being finish'd) to see
the church, wherein is the vault, and a most gorgeous
tomb 1561, the richest we have yet seen, with a canopy
over it, and curtains around, of Henry Hastings, Erle of
Huntingdon.

There is also a modern marble mausoleum of the last earl, with a pompous inscription relative to his travells; saying that he not *only* visited France and Italy, but *even* Spain; as may be said of me, that I not *only* visit Nottinghamshire and Derbyshire, but *even* Leicestershire!

There is over it, a bust of the present dowager embracing his urn.

During this present travell, I have seen many grand chapels in several of the great houses we have enter'd, which have all been lumb'ring, marble monuments; and not to my idea of taste. Were I to build a chapel in my house (we suppose the great fortune) for no house of size can be otherwise complete, I wou'd send for drawings of several cathedral quires, and of several college chapels of Oxford and Cambridge; frcm them, I shou'd select one, and then build mine of a size equal to my house, or establishment, with Gothic pillars, roof, and windows, *richly dight*; I cou'd first have a small exact model made; perhaps one of Kings College Chapel of Cambridge.

P— and I do not agree about the following matter:—

He chooses, when at meals, to have the waiter (commonly a woman) attend behind his chair, and hand to him every thing he wants; now my way wou'd be, to get every thing necessary; beer, wine, water, &c, &c, upon the table, before dinner; then dinner being serv'd, I say to the waiter, 'You need not stay, I will ring when we want you': and now let us talk our talk, and eat our meat at our leisure.

Instead of a nasty, dirty wench, watching you all the time, picking her nails, blowing her nose upon her apron, and then wiping the knives and glasses with it; or spitting and blowing upon the plates. Surely, with a great fortune, there is nothing so comfortable for a small company as dumb waiters; as for myself, I am uneasy when a fellow stands behind me, watching me, running away with my plate, and winking at his fellows.

At my inn, particularly, when people come in tired,

they are as greedy of food, as of venting their mind to each other of their past travells, and future intentions; and this they cannot do before attendants.

I remember to have stop'd at this inn to change horses, 13 years ago, when travelling with the Messrs B[ertie]s, on an unadvised expedition in November; and my advising, after eating some excellent cold beef, a stay here for the night; which had done us much better than a very bad inn at Burton-upon-Trent, where we nearly perish'd with wind, and cold. Last night, a spaniel came into our room at supper, whom nobody knew; we fondled, fed him, tied him up, and meant that he shou'd attach himself to us: but to-day, being let loose, he went into a neighbouring shop in the town, where he lived, and was owned.

Soon after dinner we determined upon a ride; and after consulting our landlord, intended for Bretby Park, a deserted seat of Ld Chesterfield (who may feel more pleasure in living in a hired house near Windsor, than in restoring and inhabiting any of his fine old seats) who has almost levell'd the noble old hall, and fell'd the timber; but still they said it was worthy our curiosity. E'r we had gone 2 miles, the clouds thicken'd and the rain commenc'd, and for some time we shelter'd under a tree; but forseeing more, we push'd forward, and at lucky time got into a barn at Butts Houses, on the Buxton road; and were kindly receiv'd by the old farmer. For an hour, did I never see such a deluge of rain, with thunder and lightning: to vary the scene, we sometimes enter'd the house, and convers'd with the family—civil decent people, till a glimmering of sky appear'd; when the storm pass'd dreadfully down the vale. Seeing more bad weather in advance, we thought it best to retreat, and give up my thoughts of Bretby; so trotted back in haste, the 3 miles, to our tea at Ashby, where they thought we must have been drown'd. Coals are cheap in this county; the best at 7d. the 100 weight. It was lucky that we return'd when we did, for the rain soon return'd, and continued with much gloom, and violence, during the evening. What can exceed the dullness of a country town on a Sunday evening, in a heavy rain? This made us anxious to call for early supper; and early beds.

Monday June 22

The comforts of having T. B. with me are that I know my horse is taken care of, without my watching every fresh hostler; that my bed is made well; and my sheets are put before a fire. To have a comfortable, high-headed smooth hard bed, must be impossible in inns, till the bolsters and pillows be better stuff'd, and the mattrasses are more abundant.—The slowness of answer in this country is very irritable; when I stop to ask the plainest question, as the name of our road to, any village, they being with 'Why as to that' 'Let me consider' 'You seem to be out of your way' 'And so I was saying'. Here I ride off; for life were not long enough to hear them out.—After a night of heavy rain we were abroad at 9 o'clock.—Passed 2 miles on the Loughborough road thro' a country of wood, and verdure; then turn'd upon some roads, torn up by coal waggons, to

Staunton Harold

Staunton-Harold, a flaring, lately-built, ill seated house of the Earl of Ferrers.[69]

Here is a profusion of brick work, with grounds in disorder, unfinish'd, unlevelled; the church close to the house, we did not enter, as the clerk lived at a distance; nor did we think it worth our trouble to go into the house, promising nothing curious, old, or new. There is a kind of a park, and many woods around it; with some bad water meant, I suppose, to have been improved.—a very short distance brought us into the grounds of Sr H. Harpur at Calk;[70] (for these two parks have formerly almost join'd;) and soon espied, to our right, the church well shaded by trees: P— thought it had been a pigeon house, till he saw the enclosure, and the grave stones; and most time it is, however unsanctimonious, that the small steeple is a dovecot, whence cooings instead of bells must invite to prayer. —I walk'd around it and endeavour'd at a sketch; within, I cou'd discover the pulpit, and altar to be hung with black cloth, and escutcheons, for the death of the late Sr H. H.

The house, which stands at a small distance, seems to be a very bad one, built in an ill chosen spot: it is now under repair; and many men are employ'd in blowing up a long extent of hill, in front, which is done, at perhaps no expence, as they burn the lime-stone of which it consists.

The quantity of coal pits about Stanton-Harold is amazing; and the land itself is as black as if the coal lay above ground.

Leaving the park, we cross'd a country, now enclosing, for 2 miles, with a smart rain at our backs, to Mellbourn village, which is large and well looking. The church[71] had so antiquated an appearance, that I must needs enter; but there was nought to observe but the size of the columns, supporting Saxon arches; and one very old, recumbent, stone figure. At the west end of the church is so reverend looking a house that I desired the woman to shew us about it, which she did into the several bed rooms, cheese chambers,[72] &c; and told us that it was once the bishops house, and did now belong to some chapter: it has a beautiful view over a large piece of standing water, with a fringe of wood.

At the east end of the church is Lord M[elbourne]'s house,[73] a decent mansion, with such an old fashion'd garden of yew hedges, fountains, and alleys, as now becomes a curiosity, and to be admired for that shade so much wanted in modern shrubberies: there is also an interspersion of wall'd garden, where we ate, for the 1st time of cherries; and there was allso a blow of roses (one noble moss rose tree) for the decoration of our bosoms. The gardener's wife attended us, and soon discover'd the bent of her mind; for upon my observing that a fountain was stopt, she remark'd that it was by the will of God, who ruled all things; and upon P.'s attention she went on in a strange cant about St Austin's being converted in a garden by the Spirit of God, and that God govern'd all things &c, &c:

Melbourne (margin note)

73

'Aye', says P— 'and giveth the increase', upon which she instantly pluck'd cherries, and roses for him: talk'd of their preacher, Lady H[untingdon] and proved her mind to be under the management of some Methodist; who may likewise have an eye to the daughters conversion, who is a pretty wench.—She made us observe a statue of Perseus, and another of Andromeda, which she call'd St George, and the Queen of Egypt; and also a little naked leaden boy, who squirts up a stream of water in a most ridiculous manner. In two miles we came into a turnpike road (Castle Dunnington park to our left)[74] when finding ourselves hungry, that it was a proper house for dinner, and that the rain was coming on, we trotted to Castle Dunnington village; there putting up at a good looking public house, The Turks Head.—This is a large well-built village, with many creditable Houses, in a dry soil, and lofty situation.

Castle
Donning-
ton

At coming in, the hostler recognised my pony for an old friend, saying 'that he knew Mr H—, whose sister lived in this village; and that when Mr H— was last here, the poney stood in these stables.'

As a snug inn this came near to my wishes, for the landlord was so attentive, the hostler so busy, and the house so neat. During the time that mutton chops were sending for, we found a boil'd leg of mutton, not quite cold, upon which we seiz'd, and despers'd our appetites e'r our landlord return'd from the butchers. During our meal the rain commenc'd;—at a lucky time for us.—After dinner, combing my hair, and turning my neck cloth (like a good soldier in the morning) I went to pay my respects to the Miss H—'s and behaved, with propriety, I hope.—This finish'd, I walk'd to the hill top, where are but few remains of the castle wall; forming one side of a cottage; wherein P— was housed. Here is a very fine view of the Trent vale, of Nottingham Castle &c. But the rain that has fallen has made Trent too wide in his course, which encroaches upon the hay meadows. At an interval—I took out my pencil and book; (and upon my afterwards, shewing this to Mr N—

74

he instantly said 'Part of the old wall of Dunnington Castle'.)

As soon as cou'd be, I ran back to the inn, and sent to P—, his great coat; we then drank tea; and had the rain continued, we had done very well (I dare say) in the sleeping way.

T. B. knows my ways so well, and that I am sometimes too quiet, and inclinable to stay, that he came in, with 'Come, Sr be going, or you will lose the day!' 'Well then, I will'. Our bill was very cheap; and our reception very good.—If there were many such landlords, and inns, I cou'd travell alone.

HEARSON. TURK'S HEAD.

C. DUNNINGTON.

June 29.

2 Dinners	-	-	-	-	-	1	6
Ale & Porter	-	-	-	-	-	0	6
Brandy	-	-	-	-	-	1	0
Wine	-	-	-	-	-	1	2
Lighting & paper	-	-	-	-	-	0	1
2 Teas	-	-	-	-	-	1	4
Horses Hay & Corn	-	-	-	-	-	2	0
						7	7
Ostler	-	-	-	-	-	0	8
						8	3

In a mile and a half (our road over-looking the now-tremendous Trent) we enter'd Dunnington Park, the seat of the Earls of Huntingdon; when I much expected much old grandeur of house;—but when I saw it, I took it for a gardeners, or some lodge.—However having sent before, we enter'd it.

Here I must remark with surprise, our not having met any family of any house we have stop'd at, except Sandbeck; marking the desertion of the country, or the extraordinary short time of quitting London:—old people

75

shake their heads, and say 'Aye, I remember rare doings, formerly, at the hall; merry doings at Xmas: but, lackaday my Lord now only comes in September, for a fortnight's shooting!'

Dunnington House is of a capacity for a gentleman of 2000£ a year, squatted in a hole, of most ugly building; and what was added by the present earl—is of the worst taste, a low dining room, with a tea room above it, like a mean addition to a villa near London.—But where are all the old pictures of the Hastinges's; and of the Erles of Huntingdone?—There is one picture of a Duke of Suffolk, and 2 of an Earl and Countess of Huntingdon; those are all, I believe. There is a vile daubing of the Duke of Clarence: a full length of Lord Rawdon, with some modern warriors, as The Emperor, &c, are stuck upon the stair case.—The bedchambers are very tolerable; and the house is no bad house, but not worth the getting off a horse to see.—Around it, the park grounds rise pleasantly; but the old oaks are wither'd into most decrepid stumps; and there is not an addition of young trees.—We return'd home by a good turnpike road, thro' the village of Breedon, which stands under a lofty lime stone hill, on the summit of which is the church, to be seen from all quarters. After our return, it began to set in for wet, and we set in for writing;—My brain was ransack'd for rhyme —in a letter to Mrs S[oames] as followeth—

TO MRS SOAME.

Madame.   June 22. 1789.

I

For you, my Muse attempts to flow,
Altho' her stream runs very low,
        As wand'ring thus I roam;
Yet, for an offering of the heart,
She, e'n, her follies dares impart
        To generous Mrs Soame.

76

2

My Muse, like Po, of things the least,
Creeps gently on, like Sancho's beast
    By Rozinantes side,
Your nephew wholly took the lead,
Excell'd me both in pen and steed,
    In this our second ride;

3

But smitten by dramatic fire,
He chose from dullness to retire,
    And Sheffield's road to take;
What conquests he must there have made,
Or how the Siddons has repaid
    Such journey for her sake,

4

I'm still to learn, but be it known
On such strange parting skies did frown,
    With plaintive drops they wept,
The lightnings spake, and growled the thunder,
Agreed to urge their mutual wonder,
    To see me thus *so* left!

5

At a bad inn I lonely sit,
Not as expectant when in pit,
    Within old Drury's dome;
No Siddons here each heart alarms
No poetry, nor music's charms,
    No sight of Mrs Soame:

6

No abbe with sardonic grin
Tight-buckled curl, and cock'd-up chin
    Conceitedly offends;
Instead of Crouch's[75] warbling note,
From fenny ditch, with husky throat,
    The frog his croaking sends.

7

But, tho' alas, I cannot find
Much entertainment for the mind,
   My body well I treat;
The currant tarts are very good,
Those you'll allow delicious food,
    With cream, thats thick, and sweet.

8

Whilst you emerg'd from senseless noise
Of fashions fools, of fashions joys,
    To Tunbridge-Wells retire;
On Ephraim's mount the opening rose
Around her subject garden throws
    Sweets that can never tire.

9

How plays the music of the year?
Too much God save the King, I fear!
    Your hired horse safely carries?
Pray, is your jockey most gallant?
Do you take cherries, en passant,
    From pursy Mrs Harris?

10

Your neice, I hear is quite the thing,
The first named toast is 'Dear Miss Wynne',
    That Speechly's most attractive;
That Mrs Wynn has an intent
To dance with any Man of Kent
    If *young*, *like* me, and *active*:

11

That neice has so much sense, I know,
'Tis finely pencill'd on her brow
    And blazon'd in her voice;
She n'er will play the coquettes part
Prudence will nicely steer her heart
    To make a proper choice.

12

For different minds, a different taste;
Tunbridge, to me appears a waste,
  Where thoughts can never rally;
Where idle girls, and ill bred boys,
Raffle eternally for toys:
  A country Cranbourn Alley![76]

13

Sometimes, at Sprange's door you sit,
With Cumberland,[77] that various wit,
  Of elegant array;
Who chides all thoughts of going home,
Intreats 'that with him you wou'd come'
  And hands you to the play.

14

Whilst thus each chearful hour beguiles,
Or walking on the hot pan-tiles,
  Or cheap'ning of a bonnet,
Some poet may (*of force like me*)
In hopes of praise, or hopes of fee,
  Present you with a sonnet.

        E. B.

In a letter received from Mr L— (who accompanied
us to Wandersford-Bridge) he relates the circumstances of
his having been robb'd upon Hounslow Heath—with his
dangers from the foot-pads. I never was robb'd:—but I do
not attribute this so much to luck, as to my observance of
early hours.—I neither see the use, or taste the pleasure of
travelling in the dark!—Modern, young gentlemen, after
dawdling away their day in London, think it polite to
travell in the dark, and knock up inns; there they stop all
the following noon, and then enjoy a subsequent night of
clatter; wheels breaking, horses falling;—then demanding
applause or pity (which I shall never bestow) for the mischief they have sought; and for being encouragers of
roguery!

I will not hazard my weak opinions against the great voice, that now brawls aloud in favour of Sunday schools, and on the uses of reading and writing: nor can I presume to say that ignorance and innocence are inseperable companions: the subject has been, no doubt, ably investigated; and the verdict commonly given for the wise-seeming side of the question; as not supposing that immorality cou'd be taught by books, or that forgery was, ever, the consequence of learning to write. I care not to be the champion even of innocence and truth, against the passions of the day, and the fine affected sentiments of ignorant morality. If I now introduce any transcript abt Lillee[78] (the astrologer) who was born in this neighbourhood, it is not as being for, or against, the foregoing argument; but, merely, from having read his foolish life, with pleasure, (*all Diaries are pleasant*) which spake of this county; and so it pops in, as an interlude of relief, amidst my dry narration.

'I was born May 1st 1602 in the county of Leicester, in an obscure town, in the north west borders thereof call'd Diseworth, seven miles south of the town of Derby, one mile from Castle-Dunnington, a town of great rudeness, wherein it is not remembered that any of the farmers thereof did ever educate any of their sons to learning, only my grandfather sent his younger son to Cambridge.—

Upon Monday, April 3rd 1620, I departed from Diseworth and came to Leicester; but I must acquaint you, that before I came away I visited my friends, amongst whom I had give me about ten shillings, which was a great comfort unto me.

On Tuesday, April 4th, I took leave of my father then in Leicester Goal for debt, and came along with Bradshaw the carrier, the same person with whom many of the Duke of Buckingham's kindred had come up with. Hark how the waggons crank with their rich lading! It was a very stormy week, cold and uncomfortable: I footed it all along. We could not reach London until Palm Sunday, the 9th of April, about half an hour after three in the afternoon, at which time we enter'd Smithfield. When I had gratified the carrier, and his servants, I had 7s. 6d. left and no more: one suit of cloaths upon my back, two shirts, 3 bands, &c, &c.'

Tuesday
June 23
All last night the rain continued unmercifully; and must now do mischief; especially in the low country. My mode of travelling shou'd be this; but it might not suit a

party.—I call for the bill in the night before my departure; rise early; eat a slice of bread and butter, and drink some milk, that I took upstairs with me; then ride 10 miles to breakfast; there shirt and shave; by which means I get a forward day, and my horse baits while I dress; whereas by waiting, (at the bed-inn) for a barber, and a breakfast, the finest hours in a fine weather are lost; and the delay may lead to a *dark evening ride*!

QUEEN'S HEAD. ASHBY.

1789.

							s.	d.
June 20	2 Suppers	-	-	-			2	0
21	Breakfasts	-	-	-	-	-	1	6
	Dinner	-	-	-	-	-	4	0
	Supper	-	-	-	-	-	2	0
22	Breakft	-	-	-	-	-	1	6
	Supper	-	-	-	-	-	2	0
23	Breakfast	-	-	-	-	-	1	6
	Wine -	-	-	-	-	-	5	10
	Brandy	-	-	-	-	-	3	0
	Ale & Porter	-	-	-	-	1	3
	Paper	-	-	-	-	-	0	6
						£1	5	1
	2 Teas	-	-	-	-	-	1	4
						£1	6	5
	Booidoo Horooo		1 3	9d.				
	Servts.	-	-	1 1	6d.	1	5	3
						£2	11	8

At last, after this our long abode, we took our leaves of Ashby; betwixt 9 and 10 o'clock: I walking forward, whilst P— stayed to pay the bill; and was not overtaken in a mile. We soon came to the village of Coleorton (from the numerous coal pits) which stands high, and with pleasant views.

Here we housed (as *some people might say*) under a tree, to avoid a smart shower: and then continued our slow route, till another storm pent us up under another tree near to the ruins of Grace-Dieu Nunnery: a scenery of wretchedness, and the shelter of cattle; in the last state of dilapidation. At one end is a mean house.

P— soon rode off; but I walked around the place, and did, as well as I cou'd with my pencil; some practice, will, I hope, improve me.

Charn-
wood
Forest

I overtook P— when enter'd upon Charnwood Forest which is steepy ground, bare of wood on this quarter, and with many rocky cliffs.

To our left stands the village of Belton, famous for a castle and horse fair.[79]

We soon pass'd by a park of Sir Wm Gordon's; then, fearing a storm, we took ourselves to a small farm, where in crossing the yard in haste, Po was as nearly swallow'd up; which occasion'd a laugh, sadly sustain'd by me. We were lucky in our shelter, which saved us a marvellous soaking. Here ends the forest on this side.—In two miles

Lough-
borough

of good road, we came to Loughborough; and were civilly treated, and soon employ'd on a comfortable dinner.

After dinner I walk'd to a booksellers, (more intelligence and of better books than I have seen in my tour; but, nothing, however to tempt so dainty a collector as I am. We then stroll'd about the town, and the church yard; where I got the two best, (these following) inscriptions—

WILLM WILLSON. DRAPER

Tis not the Brother we lament alone,
The father, friend and guardian likewise moan,
Yet happier Wilson in Heaven's blest abode
Pities our efforts, and implores his God.

(This is placing Mr Willson in a grand situation, truly; being certainly gone to heaven, where he feels so much commiseration, and possesses so much interest!)

TWO WIVES OF JOTh. HOWARD.

T'was Heaven's high will to take them hence,
Then let our hearts no more repine,

> Removed from scenes of time, and sense,
> They rest, we trust, in bliss divine.

(How easy and resign'd does Mr Howard appear to have been under such *severe losses*: especially as they were removed from 'scenes of time and sense'!!)

This is a very cheap charge for a good dinner, at a large, much-frequented inn, owing to the gloom of the evening, and dirt of the road, our ride was melancholy and tedious; expecting as one might at this season, brilliant suns, and dry boots.

BULLS HEAD. LOUGHBRO'.

Dinner -	-	-	-	-	-	3	0
Wine	-	-	-	-	-	2	3
Porter -	-	-	-	-	-	0	3
						5	6
Horses -	-	-	-	-	-	2	0
					0	7	6

Quarndon-Woods appear'd handsome to our right; the River Soar flow'd to our left.—At Mount Sorrell, which is a long, ill-paved town, overhung by a rocky cliff, I dismounted, and walk'd up to the hill top, where stands a Maypole, whence is a wide view over the country.—In the market place as in all others formerly, was a cross.—Now this, tho' destroy'd as a cross, has been repair'd by new topping, and wou'd be much admired, were it not hidden by the roof of the market house, which cuts it off in the middle. _{Mount Sorrel}

The old popular tradition of the names of the places on this road, is that the devil mounted his horse at *Mountsorrell*; took a surprising jump to *Wanlipp*; killed him at *Burstall*; and buried him at Belgrave!!

After this, we soon saw the spires of Leicester; and enter'd that town, and the Three Cranes Inn, at $\frac{1}{2}$ past six o'clock. _{Leicester}

Tea finish'd, I walk'd about the town, tho' it was a

wetting, dark evening; try'd at a booksellers; and then read at the coffee house the latest London papers.

A plan which I have of the town, 1610, becomes a curiosity: at present from manufactories, it is exceedingly increased in houses, and inhabitants.

Wednesday, June 24

We supp'd last night, at half past nine; and having nothing but writing to do, were early in bed.—P— having a great taste for newspaper reading, I recommended a breakfast this morning at the coffee house, which we found very bad, very unlike what we shou'd have had at home, for the master of our inn is very civil, the cook (from our last night's specimen) very good, and the port wine very likeable. On entering this town, we passed by the great new-built house of the famous Dr Arnold,[80] who therein treats his patients as Dr Willis does; and has now a namesake chaplain to the King, and many men of fortune under his care: in a neighbouring house the patients of a lower order are confined.—The parade of the light dragoons, upon the market place, was a treat to me; for it was very clean, very orderly, very attentive; and the commanding officer, (a very rare circumstance!) was clear, and intelligent.—

We next enquired our way to the abbey remains; and crawl'd thro' this long town, whose streets are wide, but, generally of low houses: the market place, however, is gay, and spacious. The abbey ruins, or rather those of a house that did belong to the Devonshire family, are at some distance, on the other side of the River Soar; environ'd by old walls, gardens, and orchards, most gloomy and forlorn. We prowled about these ruins, I took out my pencil, at several times, sketching the ruins as well as I cou'd; as also the old wall, and gateway, leading into a side lane; and this archway, standing in the garden grounds.

At coming back, P— and I took different routes; he, to order dinner, and I to find out a gentleman I wish'd to visit. In my way I walk'd around St Margaret's church yard, and carried off this couplet, from the tombstone of Wm Heaford,

> By swimming I my pleasure oft have sought,
> By sinking I to sudden death was brought.

There is allso a grand cumbrous monument, with a pompous inscription to the memory of a Scotch Lord (Rollo I believe) who died there.

The first strawberries of this year we have eaten to-day (24th, June); and we had also a regale of newspaper reading at the shabby coffee house.

Our dinner at two o'clock, was well serv'd, duck and pease, and cold beef; our landlord a Swiss[81] of good manners, advised us to go in the evening to Mrs —— house at Scrapthorp, not far from this town 'dere to see her mount, and her schrubberie, whiche alle de gentlemen like to inspect'.

Since our leaving Ashby, there has been a continuance of gloomy rainy weather, that has wither'd all touring descriptions: this evening Mr Sol returned to us again, and made us smile in turn, and to resolve upon a ride; else we might sleep in our chairs! The players come here next Monday: we cou'd have wish'd, in our course, to have seen some; and especially in such weather.——In 4 short miles, east of this town, we came to Scrapthorp Hall, now hired as an hunting seat by Mr Harvey, where are the gardens we were advised to visit; and so we did, and went to a mount with a summer house at the top, where is a good inland view; here a very old large seat of Mr Ashley's[82] at Quenby, presented such a venerable appearance, that I wish'd I had gone in the morning to see it. The walks here are very shady; and in, and about the gardens, are abundance of hares.

Our ride here, and back and our walk, employ'd 3 hours of the evening: the latter part of which, was pass'd at tea, strolling on the market place, or sitting at a booksellers shop, where I met Mr O[liver] our distributer, upon

85

whom I had call'd in the morning: here likewise came in an old drunken knave, of a wild wit run to waste, who preferring idleness and misery, to business and comfort, seem'd to subsist by patriotic charity; he made to me a violent declamation upon Whigs politics; such a one as is often spoken in St Stephen's chapel!

AN ODE ON THE CENTENARY OF THE REVOLUTION ADDRESSED TO SIR GEORGE ROBINSON, BART, and COLONEL POCHIN, PRESIDENTS OF THE REVOLUTION CLUB AT LEICESTER.—

> Old Time has with unerring hand,
> A hundred rounds revolv'd his wheel;
> Since Albion's highly-favour'd land
> Did freedom's genial influence feel:
> And as the time-describing God,
> The azure-vaulted system rod,
> With trumpet of aethereal make;
> He made the constellations shake,
> And this proclaim'd to every passing sphere;
> The next to Venus from the sun,
> Behold a radiant planet run;
> Within this orb an isle is found,
> Envy'd by all the nations round,
> For liberty has rear'd her temple there.

> Let passive bigots ask how freedom reigns?
> Or where the place that gave her birth?
> 'Twas heav'n! The blessings which she deigns,
> Belong to all the sons of earth.
> What tho' the *Tyrant* and the *Priest*,
> By fraud enslav's the hapless east,
> When on his banks where Tygris flows
> Nimrod, the first of despots rose,
> Still liberty inherent is in all;
> Of Albion 'twas try happy fate,
> This glorious truth to prove tho' late;
> When by collected fire and might,
> Thy sons asserted nat'ral right,
> With blood cementing what shall never fall.

> Let tyrants ceaseless war provoke,
> And deluge half the world in blood;

86

Let vassals smart beneath the smoke,
   Yet tamely think it *Public Good*.
Britannia can a sovereign boast,
   Belov'd, obey'd, but not from dread,
Who, when the God of War, his host
Calls out for freedom's legions led.
And O historians! as you're fine, be bold
     Impress the aera with a type of gold;
      When reason scorning threats of pow'r,
        Took courage with all-guiding hand,
     And in a dark tremendous hour,
     From vilest slavery sav'd the land,
Re-throned full liberty by gen'ral choice
And guarantee'd her with a people's voice.

CHORUS.

Then let this choral throng,
To heaven's high arches raise the song,
And whilst we pity nations round
Fast in the chains of Slav'ry bound;
     Let ev'ry Briton 'neath the sun,
      What his great sires for him have done,
     And shew his progeny that all their blood
     Is nobly spilt, if spilt for publick good.

This, from him, entertain'd for once; and I paid a shilling for it; which, they said wou'd keep him drunk, and from home, till spent! These verses were written by him for the Revolution Club,[83] of which he is secretary; and worthy the pen of a poet laureat.

It shou'd seem to me, from my (trivial) observations, *Thursday* that noblemen, and gentlemen have almost abandon'd the *June 25,* country; that yeomanry is annull'd, and that dowagers *mer Day* have gone away:—So, amongst the first great people, now residing there, may be reckon'd the inn keepers, the tax gatherers, and the stewards of great estates who with the lawyers rule the country. Justices—the few there are—are afraid of the felons; constables are not to be found; the poor must plunder because not provided for; ladies dare not live in the country; taxes are evaded; enclosures of

common field land, and commons, are general; corporations are venal; trade and manufactories are over strained;
banks and bankruptcies in and over every town; laws,
from being multiplied beyond comprehension, cannot be
enforced; London markets and London prices govern the
whole kingdom; and as that encreasing Wen, the metropolis, must be fed the body will gradually decay: all the
canals, all the roads must be forced to supply it; and when
they have brought all they can, and it shou'd by oversize,
or particular seasons, want more—why then there will
come a distress, a famine; and an insurrection; which the
praetorian guards, or the whole army cannot quell; or
even the Parliament pacify; the latter; because they
have connived at the (now general) alarm, from having been constantly employ'd in struggles for power;
and regardless of the peace and interior happiness of their
country!!)

This now was a cold morning, and so rainy as wou'd
have detain'd a hunter at home in November: unlike to
every idea of a midsummer day! Roses, garlands, hay-
making, the dame on the green, the lovers whisper, the
assistant twilight, and the nightingales song:—Being
weather bound, we impatiently awaited the arrival of the
mail, for the reading of the news papers; by this speedy
conveyance, the evening papers came 100 miles, by 10
o'clock in the following morning! (How much better was
it when Mr Lillee was 5 days crawling up with the
waggon?)

When I was here, on a short touring intent, 16 years
ago, our company, being scant of cash, were obliged to a
Mr Bursby; an old and rich merchant, for a supply: so
now, being taper of the said necessary commodity, I was
obliged to recruit from Mr Oliver (distributor of stamps,)
who has been very attentive to us; and this morning shew'd
us every corner of this good inn, with the cellaring, which
is incomparably stock'd with the best wines; for this inn is
frequented in winter by fashionable sportsmen, who

require delicacies, and cookery: the master, (he died soon after) a Swiss, who has lived in the gay world, knows how to treat, and talk to, a gentleman.

During much of this morning, Mr O— was our companion, and walk'd with us as far as St Martins Church; adjoining to which is an hospital for poor people, founded by Sr Wll. Willsden;[84] their chapel is very antient, and the windows have been much adorn'd by stain'd glass; which is, now I find, in general, thought to be a dirty nuisance!— I believe that I have remark'd 500 times that people upon the spot never know of, or enquire after, anything near them; now to-day, just before dinner, I ask'd of Mr O— 'if the bed in which Richard 3d slept in at an inn here in his march to Bosworth, was not in this town?' After his expressions of denials and ignorance, he return'd to say, that it was at a house within two doors of him; but that till that instant he had never heard of it!

To see it we went; and a great curiosity it is; of most massive oaken pillars, back, and tester, and has been, in parts, gilt.—Mr Drake, the owner, an auctioneer, lately purchased it at a sale at the inn, the Blue Boar, where it had remain'd. It is curiously carved and well worth the seeing. —Tradition says that an innkeeper of the name of Cartwright, in the reign of James Ist. finding the bed posts, which were hollow'd, to be filled with gold coin, purchased a house, &c, in the town; and was afterwards robbed, and kill'd by his 2 servants, who were executed at Leicester, for the murder. Mr. O— has promised to get a drawing of the bed for me.

Mr. O— now beginning to smoke me for a bit of an antiquary, brought me for copying, this original and unpublish'd letter: it is written in a good stile, and in a firm, and pathetic manner.[85]

This underwritten copy was taken from a curious letter (in the possession of Mr Oliver of Leicester) written by King Charles 1st, soon after his defeat at Naseby: the hand, seal, &c, are so well known as to have no doubt of its authenticity. The stile is manly, and pathetic; and of a better manner than in most of his letters.

Cardiff.

31st July 1645.

ORMOND.

It hath pleased God by many successive misfortunes to reduce my affairs of late, from a very prosperous condition to so low an eb as to be a perfect tryall of all mens integrities to me; and you being a person whom I consider as most entyrly and generously resolved to stand and fall with your King, I doe principally rely upon you, for your utermost assistance in my present hazards. I have commanded Digby to acquaint you at large with all particulars of my condition; what I have to hope, trust too, or fearer; wherein you will fynde that if my expectation of relife out of Ireland be not in some good measure and speedily answered, I am likely to be reduced to great extremities. I hope some of those expresses I sent you since my misfortune at the Battaile of Nazeby are come to you, am therefor confident that you ar in a good forwardness for the sending over to me a considerable supply of men, artillery and ammunition: All that I have to add is, that the necessity of your speedy performing them is made much more pressing by new disasters; so that I absolutely command you (what hazard so ever that Kingdome may run by it) personnaly to bring me all the forces of what sort soever you can draw from thence, and leave the Government there (during my absence) in the fittest hands that you shall judge to discharge it.—For I may not want you heere to command those forces which will be brought from thence, and such as from hence shall be joynd to them. But you must not understand this as a permission for you to grant to the Irish (in case they will not otherwaise have a peace) anything more in matter of religion than what I have allowed you already; except only in some convenient parishes, where the much greater number ar Papists, I give you power to permit them to have some places which they may use as Chapels for their devotion, if there be no other impediments for obtaining a peace; but I will rather chuse to suffer all extremities, than ever to abandon my religion, and particularly ether to English, or Irish rebels; to which effect I have commanded Digby to wryte to their agents that were employed hither, giving you power to cause deliver or suppresse the latter as you shall judge best for my service. To conclude, if the Irish shall so unworthily take advantage of my weake condition as to press me to that which I cannot grant with a safe conscience, and without it to reject a peace; I command you, if you can, to procure a further cessation; if not, to make what division you can amongst them; and rather leave it to the chance of war between them, and those forces which you have not power to draw to my assistance, than to give my consent to any such allowance of popery as must evidently bring distruction to that profession wch by the Grace of God I shall ever maintain through all extremities. I know, Ormond, that I impose a very hard task upon you;

90

but if God prosper me, you will be a happy and glorious subject, if other-
wise, you will perishe nobly, and generously, with, and for Him who is
Your constant reale faithful Friend
CHARLES R.

To the Marquiss of Ormond
His Maties.   31st July 1645.

Rec. 18th Aug.
by R.ob' Smith.

At two o'clock our good dinner came on; that, and our
bottle of port finish'd (for we did not exceed, tho' the
cellar afforded much temptation,) we hoped to get away;
but the weather continued so bad, that nothing but
obligation cou'd have forced us away: and we are on a
party of pleasure, you know! That Leicester has been a town
of great antiquity may be seen in the following prints.

Much black slate, cut thick, is used here for hearths,
chimney pieces, &c, looking very black and shining; but
the coarser sort, used for tombstones, is very bad for us
travellers, as the letters thereon are soon unintelligible. In
the evening tho' it rain'd hard, I essay'd 20 short walks
upon the market place; and to the coffee house and to the
booksellers: and right glad we were, when there was an
excuse for supper.

Our treatment at, and the wine and the cookery of this
inn have been very good; but, after all, a good country inn
makes but a bad London tavern, as a good street of a
country town wou'd make but a paltry figure in London.

It may not be amiss, here to remark the fashions of old *Friday*
time, even with regard to the manners of inns; and, as I am *June 26*
frequently rubbing into old books, to ascertain former customs, and the methods of our fore-fathers, I will transcribe
from a B.L. book in my possession, (date 1585) this account
of an hoste, and his family, &c, &c; forming a striking
contrast to the insolence, and blasphemy of modern inns.

'In my last return from Edenborough in Scotland, coming homeward
through Yorkshire, I traveled somewhat out of the common high London

91

way, of purpose to see the countrie—And one day among others, towards
even, I chanced to come to a little thorough fare town, call'd Rippon, where,
at the very ent'ring into the town I met a poore old woman, of whom I
asked if there were any good lodging in the town: she answered me that
there was lodging at the Signe of The Great Omega—And thither I went

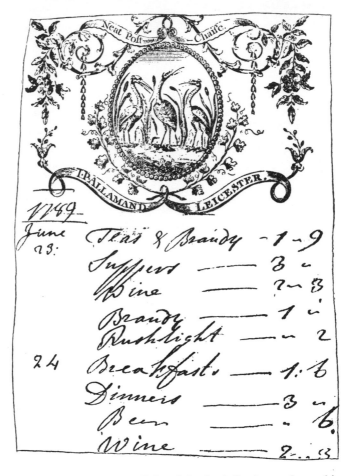

and ent'ring into the house, I found in the hall, the goodman, his two
sonnes, his chamberlain and his hostler singing the CIIII Psamle of David
very distinctly and orderly; the goodwife with her two daughters sat spinning at their wheeles a little distance from them.

So I bad them God speed. The hoste very curteously arose, and bad me welcome: so did the wife also, and asked me whether I meant to tary all night. I answered yea.—Then he asked me if I would see my chamber. No, gentle hoste, (quoth I,) I will not hinder so much your good exercise, for I am sure I cannot be lodged amisse in this house. Not so, sir (quoth he) but ye shall have the best that we have, and welcome. I gave him hasty thanks.

Neat Post Chaise.

I. P. ALLAMAND.
LEICESTER.

1789.							£	s	d
June 23.	Teas and Brandy	-	-	-	-		0	1	9
	Suppers	-	-	-	-		0	3	0
	Wine	-	-	-	-	-	0	2	3
	Brandy -	-	-	-	-	-	0	1	0
	Rushlight	-	-	-	-	-	0	0	2
24.	Breakfast	-	-	-	-	-	0	1	6
	Dinner	-	-	-	-	-	0	3	6
	Beer	-	-	-	-	-	0	0	6
	Wine	-	-	-	-	-	0	2	3
	Teas	-	-	-	-	-	0	1	6
	Suppers	-	-	-	-	-	0	2	0
	Brandy -	-	-	-	-	-	0	1	0
	Wine	-	-	-	-	-	0	1	2
	Rushlight	-	-	-	-	-	0	0	2
25.	Breakfast	-	-	-	-	-	0	1	6
	Dinner -	-	-	-	-	-	0	3	0
	Beer	-	-	-	-	-	0	0	6
	Wine	-	-	-	-	-	0	2	3
	Coffee	-	-	-	-	-	0	1	6
	Supper	-	-	-	-	-	0	2	0
	Porter	-	-	-	-	-	0	0	3
	Wine	-	-	-	-	-	0	1	2
	Brandy	-	-	-	-	-	0	1	0
	Rushlight	-	-	-	-	-	0	0	2
26.	Breakfast	-	-	-	-	-	0	0	9
	Horses Hay & Corn		-	-	-	-	0	14	3
							£2	9	7
	Servt. -	-	-	-	-	-	0	14	0
							£3	3	7

Then he enwuir'd of mee, of whence I was, where I had been, and whether I was bound. I tolde him I was a southern man borne and dwelling, and that I had been at Edenborough in Scotland; and was thus farre in my way homeward. In good time, sir, (quoth he) and yee are hartely welcome into this part of Yorkshire. I thank ye, gentle hoste, (quoth I) &c. &c.

Tho' in my *hostes* house at Leicester we never heard him, or his hostler singing psalms; or ever saw the *good* wife Allamand spinning; yet had we good reason to be contented with his civility, his wine, and his bill; two *gemmem* living 3 days in a grand inn—with their 3 horses in the stable, for 3 guineas, cannot be supposed to make the fortune of the inn keeper.

The sun shone as he ought to do this morning, at 5 o'clock, but that was too early an hour for my rising; but at seven, T. B. aroused me; and after our long sojourn at Leicester, I was eager to get away. In a few minutes I was dress'd, and in a few minutes having eaten some bread, and butter, I was ready to go; and T. B. led my horse forward: he loves an early march, and said 'Why, Sr, you are not so soon abroad as you used to be'. Tho' I had made enquiry here for curiosity or antiquity I was left to find (as I did this morning) the old gateway of approach, call'd the Newark, which formerly led to the castle; now used by the soldiery for their magazine.

Within this area is the new ill-built hospital lately erected upon the scite of the very old one. Beyond these buildings stands the church of St Marys; and the sessions house, built where the old castle was. In the neighbouring street, High Cross, is The Blue Boar where Richard 3rd rested in his way to Bosworth; (it was then The White Boar). This inn, lately relett, and vamped up, has now lost all remains of antiquity; together with the bed, (lately mention'd,) which was suffer'd to be sold for the weight of its wood; else preserv'd here, in an ancient chamber, and announced properly, it had brought great advantage to the house.—

T. B. returning from the towns end, I took the field

alone, (at eight o'clock, having lingered some time in my walking inspection). The morning fresh, and gay; and to my pleasure, and surprise the road continued very fine for 6 miles; when turning to the right, I blundered and plunged thro' a most deep and dangerous way to Desford; thence by a nasty track and a wet common to Newbold; (hard work for poor little poney).—From Newbold, some long stoney lanes brought me to Bosworth-Park, looking more like a common, and with as bad roads; and so into Bosworth town, if any thing so mean can be call'd one, Bosworth for it is a wretched place, and wou'd be unheard of but for Shakespeare; and he brought me here; and glad I was that it was not to be a night stop.—At the Bull's Head Alehouse I breakfasted, shirted and shaved; but before I had finish'd, in came P—: and T. B. who had found a much better road than the one I had plung'd thro'.

An early dinner was order'd; tho' I had first break-fasted; and we immediately met a boy with the fowl, that owed his death to our arrival. At the end of this place is the ugly seat of the Dixies, where there is a good view over the country, and of many steeples. (Mr D, the brother of the present possessor, resides here, and it is lucky for the place that anyone wou'd reside on so ugly a spot!) The late Sir Wm D— having an address to present, from the county, to the late King; to whom was hinted a question; —they thus communicated (K) 'I hearde that was a great fight at Bosworth?' (D) 'Aye, Sir, but it is very extra-ordinary that you shou'd have heard of my battle with the barber'. In the church have been the common demolition of antiquities, arms, brasses, and windows; as also the ex-tinction of psalmody by their late rector[86] (Dr Taylor of Asburn), who cou'd not *endure their filthy* manner of sing-ing, so this was abolish'd; and none other establish'd in its place! There is one modern monument of the Dixies,[87] and several of their achievements, with their motto—*Quod Dixi Dixi.*

Of intelligence relative to our topography, and history, I was much entertain'd, yesterday, and to day; when P— enquiring of a travell'd gentleman (at Leicester) his abode —was answer'd by him that it was at Bosworth, near the famed field of battle; and, here, being solicitous to find— could not for some time learn any tidings of him; till at last we were told that he resided at Husband-Bosworth, a village in a distant part of this country. Ye travell'd gentlemen, wou'd it not be as well to know something of your own country, before ye declaim of your foreign travells; and your knowledge of the topography of Italy??

A fowl kill'd in honor of our arrival, with a large quantity of thick beef steaks, flank'd by a stack of asparagus, each one foot in height, satisfied me; (who had not eaten for two hours).

My pursuit here being urged by our immortal bard, and now treading almost on his classic ground, we order'd a guide to shew us the road to, and give some tradition of, the Bosworth field.

BULL'S HEAD. BOSWORTH.

					s.	d.
Dinners	-	-	-	-	-	3	0
Malt Liquor	-	-	-	-	0	8
Wine -	-	-	-	-	-	1	2
Brandy	-	-	-	-	-	1	3
Horses	-	-	-	-	-	1	3
					7	4

My imagination, heated by Shakspere felt most glowing, when arrived upon the ground; and in my mind's eye, I grasped all the heroes of the field.

'Here pitch our tents, e'n here in Bosworth Field'.

It appears to me, that Richards army was encamp'd upon the hill with the village of Sutton in his rear and the wood covering his left flank; and that Richmond was on the opposite smaller hill, well chosen for his body of troops, with the wood to his right, and the marsh in his front.

'My Lord, the foe have passed the marsh already'.

So that the battle was maintain'd on the small heath betwixt the two armies.—We gave the ground every due observation; and saw King Richards well, where were steps but it is now rush grown, and running waste.

There are the remains of two deserted cottages near the palace of action—discharging our guide (who knew nothing) we soon came to a good road, and in a mile to Thenton village; near which is a field call'd Kings Field, where Richard is supposed to have harangued his soldiers. Near Stoke, likewise, are places call'd Crown Hill, and Halloo Meadows: whereon Henry was crown'd after the action, and where his army shouted applause.—

In the village of Shankton stands a venerable old hall, which I was tempted to enter; and found it to consist of, as usual, a large old hall, a grand apartment above stairs, with a massive oak stair case; P— awaited my return at the church yard rails.

Hence we journey'd in a pleasant evening, without any occurrence, till our crossing of the little River Anker, (which divides the counties of Leicester, and Warwick,) now so swelled by the late rains, as to make my passage unsafe, even by the help of a bridge; for my boots were well soaked.—T. B. was sent forward to the Swan Inn at Atherstone, a neat clean house, in this pleasantly-placed Atherstone town.—The old parlour was of my sort, with clean wainscotting; and our little, odd landlord, made us smile by the particularity of his manners; and he wou'd drag us about, to shew us the bowling green, and to hear all his stories, about his living at Cambridge, and elsewhere; and when I began to speak to him about supper, he said 'Let me alone, don't speak, I will give you a pretty little supper'. We next took a tour about the town, and to the navigation canal, and afterwards by the pleasantest walk possible to the village of Manceter, the parish church, (for I had before observ'd with surprise, that there was no burying ground about the church of Atherstone).—The evening was very fine, and our promenade remarkably gay; nothing can be more chearfully placed than the church yard of Manceter. (The River Anker now swell'd into a beauty, the village and steepled church of Witherly with the surrounding vicinage so simple, so rural, and everything so corresponding; except one finely dressed out lady, walking in Mr Millward's garden; where the roses shrunk from the smell of the musk! Under what thought can any female trick herself out in a guise, so useless, so unfit for the country; and so manifest of folly, and absurd fashion? A neat, short, gown with a chip hat[88], tied with a rose-coloured ribband, strong shoes, and easy stays (if stays be necessary at all?) form a truly ornamental dress for any lady in the country; and I shou'd fancy would make a stronger impression in the eyes and hearts of men, than all the toilsome troubles of the toilette.

Passing our way back, we met many ladies walking abroad; when return'd to our inn, there was (really) an elegant cold supper serv'd to us, by day light. P— is allways in haste for bed. I cannot write alone; so we retire too early.

Saturday June 27

Cold sheets I felt, and cold feet also, last night; so I was obliged to rub them upon the wool: my bustlings awakening P— we discours'd, and T. B. hearing a noise came to enquire the occasion.

Most luckily our landlord had a Dugdales Warwickshire, of some use to us; but maps—or old books are not to be bought.

As Merevale Abbey was near, I resolv'd to rise early, and visit it, and return to breakfast; so I was down stairs by seven o'clock, and into the kitchen, where the maid was happily busied in washing my upper and under waiscoats, which may be imagined to want some ablution; these being dry'd, I went forth on my inspection, with a large piece of

bread and butter at my mouth,—passing near the grounds
of Merevale Hall, I came to the old church of Merevale, Merevale
beyond two large and beautiful pools, with many orchards,
and old walls, proclaiming the proximity of the abbey,
whose ruins are extensive; to which I was led (whilst Po:
was shut into a stable) by the clerks son, an active, anti-
quity-hunting boy, who pointed out this, and made me to
observe that: here is a large farm house; about it the farm
yard, and in the garden, much is remaining: as part of the
refectory, or chapel, five gateways, and many walls and
doorways of the old mansion. The church is very antient,
with two fine recumbent figures of the Deoncur family;
and it can boast a beautiful window of stain'd glass, as all
the ruins have been.—In the farm yard is a stone coffin;
which make useful troughs for cattle! The boy said that
the squire, disliking the parson, never came to this church.

Now for my business of an early visit. My friend T.
P[almer] is now a guest at Merevale Hall; so I would not
pass him, and Mr H. his landlord, and had intended to
leave a letter of enquiry and compliments; but now being
at the gate, I rode up to the house; and went up to Mr
P[almer]'s bed room, e'er he had risen. He, pleased to see
me, urged my stay, and to send for P—; 'That we must
breakfast, and dine here, at least. (Mr R. whom I knew,
was in the next bed room;) so easily prevail'd upon, as I
allways am, I sent, for B[ush] to come immediately, and
after receiving the civilities of Mr H. we took the walk of
his wood, I in admiration of the prospects, and in wonder
of the oaks, each tree fit for a main mast, and such as I
never saw before, but at Welbeck, (and if there uncertain).
But what wou'd grieve me as tenant,—tho' it is a wonder
that any man, but a pauper, wou'd be a tenant, would be to
see the surrounding timber, felling every year, so that the
axe will soon come to the parlour door. Some oaks of 40£
price, of these magnificos, (the only product of the world
not to be obtain'd—at the time of wish—by all the wealth
of the East) sometimes 50, sometimes 100, are annually

fell'd; so that the hills lately cover'd by these stately curiosities, are now become a wild: surely some trees, dotted about, might have been left! At the brow of the now remaining grove, are erected butts, the pursuit of this house, and the present fashion of this county: an elegant, manly, sociable exercise.

P— now arriving, and Mr Bush with my clean shirt, &c, (be it known that I had fitted myself out at Mr P.'s toilette) a grand breakfast followed and much civility: after which, and many bows of mine to Mrs H., we attended the archers to their butts, (Mr R. taking another course). Here Mr H. has built a root summer house, for a retreat for the archers; which is much in character; and I cou'd wish that it had been portray'd by a better pencil.

This proved a good shelter to us, during some hasty showers; a little boy attendant on the archers, gave signals of their success, with much neatness; that for hitting the goal, was a low bow.

At our return, I had to undergo another toilette, preparatory to dinner, which if required, wou'd make me abhor country visitings; for I will not submit to such a loss of time, and the accomplishment of so much folly. (It *sometimes* happen that a husband is an easy good humour'd landlord or rather wou'd be so; and that his wife is an uneasy peevish—: that for a certain time he can maintain his country life; but at last, harrass'd out, and for the advantage of his daughters education—that's the phrase, I believe,—he gives up health and comforts for a box at the opera, and a villa at Richmond!) The situation of this house is very charming, commanding a rich and extensive view; Atherstone town in the bottom, with Bosworth Park at the distance.

(Thus far my tour book went on, but a subsequent loss of one from my pocket—carried away the description of some time, which shall be noticed; and which I am now obliged to repair from a bad memory: (Jan. 1790): so that

any little incidents are forgotten, as well as several epitaphs, &c, which I have taken down.)

The pools below the house, and which adjoin to the abbey,
are now hired by Mr H. who thence procures excellent
fish: the tench, particularly, are so large, that Mr H. said
he took out, at one draught, 8 tench that weigh'd 40lb!!

Being resolute for departure, (tho' we receiv'd from Mr
H. every pressure to stay,) and the evening coming on, our
horses at last were sent for from Atherstone: we are upon a
touring, not a visiting scheme. In Merevale Hall, we were
treated with much civility, and much good cheer; but in
how few houses cou'd I abide long? and, in general, when
compared to a inn, what are they? At the inn, surrounded
by civil attendants, you command your own hours, order
your dishes, at your own hours; pulls off your boots, and
your gaiters, when you list; have grooms and waiters at an
instant of order, to wait upon you, and your horses:—At
the private house forced civility and forced manners keep
one ever in awe; the groom watchers, and the chamber-
maid threatens. In short freedom and independency are
wanting, nor can be hoisted the national cockade of liberty.

Mr H. has collected in Italy, several marbles, and mutilated statues; such as I dare say possess much merit; but,
lack-a-day, I never was in Italy, or ever saw Mr Jenkins;[89]
and therefore must want a true taste for these curiosities of
sculpture, of which we are *supposed* to have none in this
country. *Of this subject more hereafter.* At 6 o'clock in the
evening, we took our leave of M— Hall, and its company;
with an hope of a speedy remeeting. Below, and on one side
of the hill of Merevale, lay a forest of fallen timber; such
magnificent sticks are rarely to be seen in a dock yard!

A road of retirement, goodness, and beauty trail'd us
along, passing thro' some small villages, and near the
church of Whitacre; then cross'd the river where we
descry'd before us, the high steeple of Coleshill, and Coleshill
enter'd the Swan Inn at 9 o'clock. This town lying on the

Chester road, is placed upon a pleasant hill. After a crawl up and down the street, we return'd to our dull and shabby inn; so were likewise ourselves, and our supper.

We now seem to be upon our near return; and indeed, my leave of absence almost expired. Wou'd any one know, or wish to recollect my conversation relative to information, that frequently occur in a country travell. I shall relate such as almost daily pass'd between me, a country man or an inn keeper.

B. and countryman.—(B) what is that place?—(C) I am a straunger.—(B) Where does that road lead to?—(C) I am hard a hearing.—(B) Is your old priory, or any part of your old castle remaining?—(C) I never heard of such places; I'm sure there's none such here, or ever was!!

B. and innkeeper. (B) Do you know this county well? —(I) Aye, perfectly well.—(B) Anything worth seeing hereabouts?—(I) Nothing that ever I heard of.—(B) Do you know such a place?—(I) Know nothing of it.—(B) Which is the road to ——?—(I) I never was that way.— (B) Do many people go to see ——?—(I) Not that ever I was told.—(B) Have you any shews in town?—(I) I can't say.—(B) Whose house is that by the road side?—(I) I don't think I ever enquired.—(B) When will your fair be? —(I) I can't recollect exactly.—

I was up early, from a bad bed, and to the appearance of a cold low'ring morning: knowing that the park and seat of the Digby[90] family was adjoining the town, I took my walk that way; here is an old park in wretched plight, and some mutilated avenues; but all the timber is gone; at present nothing can be more forlorn, tho' there is a running stream, capable of every magnificence. The mansion house is very large, of the old striped sort, and was the seat of hospitality in the time of old Ld Digby, who lived in the beginning of this century the friend of the famous, and ever to be revered Dr Hough,[91] Bishop of Worcester. Being alone, and the rain falling fast I hurry'd back to breakfast; after which we sat confined by the gloomy weather; only sallying forth before service time to view the church.

This church contains many old monuments of the Digby family; and this font, on which the crucifixion is well carved.

What a pity that amongst the engravings that antiquaries do seek for, there shou'd be such an omission of sounding boards, pulpits; and of fonts, with their covers; many of which, having survived depredation, become great curiosities of carving, painting and sculpture; and, in general, much more worthy preservation and observation, than most of the *marbles* imported from Italy.

When we return'd to our inn, the rain continuing we debated if it wou'd not be better to make an early dinner, and trust to a long fine evening: this determined, we wrote letters, and read newspapers, till the arrival of the very good, house, dinner. This finish'd and the weather clearing up, we continued our ride, back to Blythe Hall,[92] now modernised, wherein formerly Sr Wm Dugdale resided; and then turn'd thro' fields to Maxtoke[93] Castle, Maxstoke to which we bore an introductory letter from Merevale Castle Hall.

Supper -	-	-	-	-	-	2	0
Wine -	-	-	-	-	-	2	4
Brandy -	-	-	-	-	-	1	0
Tea -	-	-	-	-	-	1	8
Rushlight	-	-	-	-	-	0	2
Horses. Hay & Corn		-	-	-	-	5	6
						12	8
Dinner -	-	-	-	-	-	2	0
Brandy -	-	-	-	-	-	1	0
Wine -	-	-	-	-	-	1	2
						16	10

Nothing cou'd be more picturesque of antiquity, than our reception at this ancient castle; for near the gate stood the old gentleman, the owner, Mr D[ilke] who, upon receiving our letter, order'd the gates of his castle to open. These gates are cased with iron, and are beneath a beautiful gateway; highly resembling that of Borstal House, Bucks.*

Luckily for us we were under the guardianship of the old governor else we might have been devour'd by the lean greyhounds, and other starv'd dogs, that bay'd about us, longing for our blood. The upper part of this gateway is, prudently, converted into a pigeon house.

The appearance of this castle, so correspondent of romantic history, and legendary tale, highly engross'd my thoughts and attentions.—

A clear, surrounding, moat, an inhabited fortress of 60 yards square, turreted, and preserv'd with battlements; all this serv'd much to my inspiration!

When the old gentleman, Mr D— (a family of long residence here,) led us in, we were receiv'd by the young knights of the castle; who were truly attentive, and finding my eagerness of curiosity, indulg'd it amply by shewing me the cellars, hall, kitchen, turrets, &c, &c.—

An old hall ill kept up, and without furniture; a large dining room uninhabited; and many other rooms, in great dirt, and disorder, compose the building.—Of antique preservation there is nothing; not a piece of armour, a pannell picture, or a pane of stain'd glass! (How it might be deck'd up).

The young gentlemen are healthy and lively; the old gentleman has had his day;—in the castle was an active preparation (very becoming of the spot) for the approaching archery meeting at Meriden. Maxtoke Castle is certainly in the highest preservation of any place in England,

---

* The following antient custom I omitted to insert.—'They have an antient custom at Coleshill in the county of Warwick, that if the young men of the town can catch a hare, and bring it to the parson of the parish, before ten of the clock on Easter Monday, the parson is bound to give them a calves head, and a hundred eggs, for their breakfast; and a groat in money.'

as a fortified house; such as I will suppose were common, in old times of defence or depredation: around it has been a park of much extent, now under farming; and what little wood, or small number of deer are left are brought to good account.

After every civility, at Maxtoke Castle, we cou'd wish for, and an invitation to partake of the good honest dinner we saw preparing, we departed with a groom to guide us the intricate road of our intention, which led thro' fields, and grass, to the small village of Maxtoke, where might remain some ruins of Maxtoke Priory.

The front of the old gateway of approach is yet in a good state, and leads to the farm house, built upon the old ruins, in the building of which a large stone arch is very discernable.

The farmer came out upon us, in very civil guise, offering us his company and information: beyond the house, at a small distance stands this noble steeple which has lately suffer'd by a dilapidation at one corner; most extraordinary that it has so long weather'd winds and time! Around it are many walls, and such heaps of rubbish as to make me think I cou'd plainly trace the dimensions of the church. Below it were the fish ponds, clearly mark'd out, tho' now dried up. In short, there is much to observe; and for admiration, the lofty steeple and gateway; enough to draw an antiquary many a tedious mile, and well to repay him. Beyond the circuits, within a moated ground, is an old farm house, which our farmer said was the abbots retiring house; and it might be upon that spot.—

On the other side of the enclosure is the present church yard; and the little, mean church, which charmingly setts off in comparison what remains of the Gothic pile.

> Who sees these dismal heaps but would demand
> What barbarous invader sackt the land;
> But when he hears no Goth, no Turk did bring
> This desolation, but a Christian king;
> When nothing but the name of zeal appears,

'Twixt our best actions, and the worst of theirs,
What does he think our sacrilege would spare
When such th' effects of our devotion are.

Denham.

(Surely this poem is not very fine!)

Nothing cou'd be civiller, or fuller of his offers, than the farmer, except our attendant servant, who insisted on seeing us forward in our road, which tho' bad, and tedious, was rather beguiled by the history of this hunter and the hounds of the country: nor did he quit us, till we enter'd Packington Park, Ld Aylesfords;[94] when we *thank'd* him for his civility.

P. Park is a dead flat; and the new church building on the spot, is a wretched erection; the whole park is dotted by low stone pillars, which are the roving butts that Lord A: shoots his arrows at; a sport of which he is furiously fond, and a most capital performance—perhaps the best gentleman archer in the kingdom. We left the house to our right; which is large, new, and apparently a very good one.—There is a flow of water which is form'd into a grand lake above, and a twining stream near it; this, and the ground, are, may be, as well managed as possible; but nothing that can be done will ever make it a place of such charms as arise from hills of wood, and a velocity of water. Quitting the park by a bad, and seemingly unfinished approach, we came upon what was Meriden Heath.

In the village of Meriden is the inn of much notoriety, and what I have heard so much spoken of, The Bulls Head;[95] here we took up our quarters; and after receiving our letters, were surprised to hear that the gentleman bringer was in the house, viz, Mr L— (our quondam fellow-traveller at the beginning of this tour) who was in his way into Cheshire, and hoped to meet us here.—His mare, on which T. B. mounted, was claim'd by Mr L.'s (elegant) groom, as if it had been stolen; and I much fear'd, wou'd not continue with us, till Mr L— assured me, that he did not want her, and beg'd she might continue

Marginal notes: Packington Park / Meriden

in our service, to London.—I had now to view this far-famed inn: which is deficient of every comfort, has old casements, folding doors, and only fit to receive waggoners!

Around it is a strange profusion of little ponds, and foolishly fanciful buildings, with chimes playing for the diversion, and for the peace of the company, in winter, there is a dog kennel behind the inn.

In the evening there was a happy bustle from the arrival of the M[arquess] of B[uckinghamshire][96] the Ld Lt of Ireland, in his way to his seat at Stowe in Buckinghamshire; his son Ld T[emple][97] with some (Irish) attendants, sported for some time, in the garden. Several fat, stupid, female servants attended us at tea; and at our bad, ill serv'd supper. Mr L— spake of the pleasures of London and Oxford; and we retail'd to him, part of our touring occurrences.

I rounded my tour this way, that I might be present at *Monday,* the archery meeting; and, of a certainty, meet Mr T. *June 29* P[almer], and probably my friend Mr W. P[almer].[98] Being up early I first walk'd about the garden, and then, (by a circuitous course, having had to hunt forth the clerks,) to the church of Meriden, which stands, upon a hill, in a pleasant country, half a mile from the inn. The morning was black, and drooping; and after the clerk had shewn me the inside of the church, wherein I noticed little but two old recumbent figures, (and some memorials of the landlords of the Bulls-Head Inn, particularly of the old man, who had laid out so much money about it) and that I had taken down some epitaphs (lost in my book), I was obliged to shelter, for some time, in the church porch, or under a famous large yew tree in the churchyard. Then hurry'd back to breakfast in our inn, where soon a company began to assemble, and the company from Mereval, all equipp'd in a green uniform, round hats and black feathers, with their apparatus of bows and arrows; giving me a chearful tho' unpleasant feel, as not joining in their sports. Nothing seem'd wanting to enliven, but a fine day; but the weather was very blust'rous and strong.

In my way to the butts, I stopp'd for 5 minutes during a shower; at a cottage; where to rivet my old opinions there pass'd betwixt the woman, and me the following conversation.

(B) Has Meriden Common been long enclosed? (W) Ah, lackaday, Sr, that was a sad job; and ruin'd all us poor volk: and those who then gave into it, now repent it. (B) Why so? (W) Because, we had our garden, our bees, our share of a flock of sheep, the feeding of our geese; and could cut turf for our fuel.—Now all that is gone!—Our cottage, as good a one as this, we gave but 50 shillings a year for; and for this we are obliged to pay £9 10s.; and without any ground: and coals are risen upon us from 7d to 9d the hundred. My cottage with many others is pull'd down; and the poor are sadly put to it to get a house to put their heads in. !!! Heigh ho!

> HEAR THIS, YE PITIERS OF MONEY-BEGUMS.—
> HEAR THIS, YE FREERS OF BLACK SLAVES.—
> HEAR THIS, YE REPRESENTATIVES OF THE PEOPLE.—

When I had finish'd the reading of this too-true description, to a lady; she remark'd—'Ah it is but too true, for I have just quitted the country where the misery of the cottagers is not to be described; but we,' said she, 'work'd for them, gave them assistance, and did all we cou'd to help them'. 'That was,' answered I, 'highly commendable;—but charities will not remove the evil; the poor must have land allotted them for their support; else under their present oppression, they can have no hope but from vice, and theft. Then every apple above ground, and every esculent from beneath, would afford food and rayment; comfort would encourage honesty, and industry lead to virtue; whilst on the other hand, misery destroys shame, and hunger will break down stone walls.'

The place of archery has been lately enclosed, turf'd, and planted, by Lord A[ylesford] in the stile of an extended bowling-green; and there is a rustic building erected by the club, for their meetings, dinners, &c—which are furnish'd by the inn.[99]

At the top of the hill, at the village end stands a repair'd cross.*—

The company, of about thirty gentlemen of the county, divided into two squads, shot, for some hours, at their separate butts; whilst myself, L., P., and a few others, were spectators.—Tho' the rain and wind made it unpleasant, and at times drove us all for shelter into the house, yet the sport continued till 3 o'clock (the house of H. gaining much honour), when a long table was well spread with cold victuals &c, &c. We, the spectators, receiv'd from Lord A.[100] the cheiftain (bugle) of the season, every civility of invitation; so play'd away upon the hams, and fowls, as well as the best of the archers cou'd do.—

A round of adapted toasts follow'd our collation, when I was thinking of Shakespeare's Arden &—'Sit down—& eat'—&c &c.

Our dinner ended; and the archers returning to their butts, I mounted my horse, (before order'd,) that I might take the round of Packington Park, and the country; for not being a party in the archery sports, I tired of the meaness of being only a spectator.—This evening I had P[n] Park to myself; so wander'd all about it; passed by the old house, and to end of the Park, of which my former opinions remain'd; and I wonder'd why rabbets cou'd be encouraged to the destruction of plantations, and soil.—

*In my detour I have seen the remains of many crosses, which but for puritanism had continued entire; but, in this age of better taste, and of fewer rages about religion, many of them are guarded, (as at Grantham and Newark) and many have been drawn by young artists, who begin to feel that antiquaries abound.

This, of Meriden, tho' uncross'd, and ill-repair'd, has been luckily sketched by Mr Carter, who means well; but wants guidance and encouragement.

What trees of age are left, are low, or pollarded.—The water in sluggish stream twines thro' the meadows, and beneath the small church of Packington-Parva; to which I walk'd, and could discover that there was painted glass in the windows; the view thence is very pastoral, and pleasing.

Here I came into the Coventry road; and, at a foot's pace, passing Stone-Bridge, returned in two hours to the Archery House; where, (the sports now concluded,) the company were assembled at tea, Lady A: presiding.—We now all parted, as many of the woodmen had many miles of return; but I, near at home, still enlarged my ride, and was overtaken by Mr Gd,[101] whom I accompany'd 2 or 3 miles in his way to his seat at Guys-Cliff.

Night coming on, I rejoin'd my company at supper; when we were obliged to eat furiously of hot ducks; not so hard upon us as the taking leave of our pleasant companion Mr L. who pursues his journey into Cheshire tomorrow.— —

Tuesday, June 30   This inn at Meriden is a most blackguard stop, where we never saw master, or mistress, or any attendants, but some fat, greasy maids; or any eatable, or drinkable fit for others than carriers.

For Mr L——, to whom we are so much obliged for his mare, we long awaited breakfast; then having settled our bill, *kindly* borrow'd 5 guineas of him, and receiv'd his orders about the mare, we parted, taking our course south-

Allesley   ward: some pleasant miles brought us Allesley, where I dismounted to survey the churchyard, which stands well. —The clergyman, from his garden, spoke to me, in praise of the view. To one remaining Gothic isle of the church has been added a Venetian brother; proving which looks best; the venerable Goth, or the tasteless Italian. Over the church door, is written an exhortation to the people to come in: that wou'd do much!—In the churchyard, (whence the prospect over Mr Neales grounds is very pleasing,) I transcribed 3 epitaphs,—lost in my tour

book.—At Coventry Towns End, I dismounted; near to Coventry
one of those, so disdainfully spoken of, *Romish* chapels.
The streets are narrow, and meanly built. Close to our inn,
The King's Head, is the figure of Peeping Tom, project-
ing from the front of an house, dated 1700; and, after the
fashion of that day, he is equipp'd in a large laced hat, and
a full wig!—Being eager after strawberries, I immediately
went in search of them, and did buy some quantity; (but
where out of London are they to be found good?) and sur-
survey'd the spot, whence the wise corporation of Coventry
removed the ornament of their town, their old beautiful
cross: upon which they ought to have expended 500£ in
reparations.—If blockheads will pull down these monuments of antiquity, that wou'd attract the attention of
strangers, why do not noblemen of the neighbourhood
carefully remove them to their parks, and gardens, and
there restore them to their primitive glory.—St Marys
Hill (formerly call'd St Katherines Gild) where the corporation feasts are held, was fill'd by burgesses swearing to
their freedoms; a most necessary, and pleasant thing to
these gentry on the approach of a new election, which is
commonly well contested.—On the centre of the gateway
roof is a curious old bas relief.

The stairs, the hall, the roof, windows, &c, are as old
as any antiquary wou'd wish, with many ancient pictures,
and the armoury that might have been used in former pro-
cessions. There is an old chair is very grand and of much
curious carving.

Having now found the clerk (an intelligent, jolly fellow,)
we enter'd St Michaels Church, a grand and lofty building, much out of repair, with an huge organ, and a good
eastern window; but for antiquity look not into great town
churches: for aldermen are ashamed of seeing painted
windows, and old tombs: some however have survived!

The clerk discovering that he, and I, were brother antiquaries, offer'd to conduct us about the town; and my surprise was great when I found all the old gates were pull'd

down.—The two last remaining, the Sponne, and the Grey Friars Gate,[102] (with the steeple of G. Friars) I here insert.—He likewise led us to the oldest foundation, the White Friars, now let out into small tenements; however there were an archway of entrance, much arched ceiling, and some part of the cloisters left.—We then cross'd into the park, a large extent of ground belonging to the P. of Wales, and now granted to the Earl of H^d,[103] who makes a pretty advantage of it, and has lately fell'd a row of trees, which must have been an ornament; and comfort to the town. The spire of the Grey Friers Church, hollow to the top, is left standing in a garden.—In the Grey Friers Street is a most venerable hospital; formerly founded for lepers; now a retreat for aged poor.—We then went back to the clerks house, to see some carvings he had preserv'd from the church; and I told him that I wish'd that all clerks wou'd preserve more, as brasses, glass, &c; and then we antiquaries (a bold word) might come in for a bit of plunder.

Our wretched Black Town Inn, gave us a very bad dinner, and bad wine: (a wonder not to have a tolerable inn here!) and we are glad to depart from Coventry.—At a miles distance we cross'd Gosford Green, whereon was the grand combat to have been fought betwixt Henry D. of Hereford and Mowbray, D^e of Norfolk.

BOLINGBROKE. Pale trembling coward, there I throw my gage,
              Disclaiming here the kindred of a king,
              And lay aside my high bloods royalty,
              Which fear, not reverence, makes thee to except, &c.
MOWBRAY. I take it up; and by that sword I swear,
              Which gently lay'd my knighthood on my shoulder,
              I'll answer thee in any fair degree,
              Or chivalrous design of knightly trial, &c.

                                      W. S.

Binley New Church, built in the Venetian ball room taste, we pass'd by: the fall of old churches seems to be at hand; nor do I conceive how, without a *special care*, (suitable to my superstitious notions) so many—neglected, as they are—have lasted so long.—A pleasant group, near this place, of a gentleman with 4 or 5 children, girls and boys, nicely mounted on clever ponies, much engaged my attention.—Mean is the entrance into Coombe-Abby[104] Park; a place, of which I had heard much, and where my friend Capability Brown was allow'd to act;[105] so modern taste, join'd to antiquity, I hoped wou'd produce great things: but B— here sadly deceiv'd me; for he has ruined old avenues, and not planted in their place, half enough; the water is stagnate, and there is no inequality of ground. The old part of the abbey is venerable; the newer, tasteless and ugly.—In front, at a short distance, is a poor attempt at castle building, for the front of a dog kennell.—(Of this kind of architecture I conceive myself a good judge, from being in the practise, for a 4th part of a century.) Our horses being stabled, we enter'd the old cloisters, now glazed up; and so hornified are their walls, as to give *horrible presage;* their being horns of all sorts of wild cattle, and one amazingly large stuff'd wild cat, kill'd here, of which they say there are many about; I never saw a live one.

The old hall, now the great dining room, is a lofty and magnificent apartment.—The great drawing room at the top of the large stair case is in the same superb stile; a kind of room they will not, now, build!! It is preserved in old state, with old sashes; and is a room I shou'd dote upon: the long gallery adjoining is cover'd by noble portraits of the Cravens, of Gustavus Adolphus, and those warriors distinguish'd in the Palatinate War.

The gallery is narrow and low; and all the pictures have been shamefully clean'd. To enumerate all the grand portraits here were impossible; those of Prince Rupert, and Prince Maurice, please me most; as well as one of Charles Ist, when young, by Mytens; and several of the Queen of Bohemia, the heroine of this house, whose love made Craven a warrior.—She has a pleasant sensible look, with the gloomy family cast. This was the Lord Craven not only so famous in his youth for his love and courage, but who was afterwards noted for keeping horses, ready saddled, in London, to attend fires; which drew from Rochester this answer to K. Charles 2d's enquiry 'if Craven was at the Great Fire?' 'Yes, please your Majesty,' answered R., 'and has already had two horses burnt under him'.——

In the newer part of the house, particularly in the drawing-room, are many charming pictures; some by Morillio, I shou'd think. We survey'd every part of the house, with pleasure, and delay; and were only surprised at the want of a chapel.

General Monk's picture frequently occurs; as well as several of that beautiful concubine, the Duchess of Cleveland.

I must own that I expected more at this place, (as I had before at Welbech); but my sanguiness *here* arose entirely from fancy. When I am walking in gardens, and about gentlemens farms, I often wonder that more invention is not studied about hedges; which might be composed of a variety of double blossom'd thorns, hollies and various plants of fragrance and resistance; tho', in general, (if not almost altogether,) the eagerness of our cultivation, and a desire of hasty gain, has annihilated all beauty of wood; and landscape; nor can there, now, be any where seen a forestry display of ground, or of rough and lofty trees overhanging pools, and rivers: (as is to be view'd in Prints and pictures): for timber has now no place to flourish, and revel in; even that of woods is so frequently cut, and kept under, as to produce only small crook'd stuff, and faggot wood; by haste and folly, the profit of wood is as much destroy'd, as wou'd our pleasure be by drinking port-wine when a year in the bottle.——

We enquired our road here, which was reported bad and intricate; and so indeed we found it: at quitting the park, we kept a long cut thro' a wood, and then a continuance of muddy, stoney lanes, much untrodden (not highly agree-

able to a man upon a small grey poney) to the village of
Bretford; where, in the meadows, was the first display of
hay-making we have seen.

> Now swarms the village o'er the jovial mead:
> The rustic youth, brown with meridian toil,
> Healthful and strong; full as the summers rose
> Blown by prevailing suns, the ruddy maid
> Half naked, swelling on the sight, and all
> Her kindled graces burning o'er her cheek.
> Even stooping age is here; and infant hands
> Trail the long rake, or, with the fragrant load
> O'ercharged, amid the kind oppression roll.
>
> *Thomson 'Seasons'.*

Here we cross'd the River Avon, (now in its early
course,) and by a tedious road thro' an unpleasant country,
in 5 more miles, passing near the village of Church-Law-
ford, at last came to Rugby: where a most tremendous Rugby
sign of The Bear and Ragged Staff invited us into a very
ale house; tho' the best of the town.

> 'They all with admiration stare
> And think him a prodigious bear.'
>
> *Gay.*

No sooner was I enter'd, than I miss'd my tour book
from my pocket, (a loss of a disagreeable nature and what
memory cou'd not repair) so T. Bush saddled his mare,
and was to retrace these bad roads; hunting a needle in a
bottle of hay, but still there was a hope of recovery.—This
was a small trial of philosophy: which is allways required
in the usage of inn pens and ink.

Rugby Church is no *grete thinge*; (as Leland wou'd say)
and over the porch are some lines of threat to those who do
not frequent divine service: but not half so much to the
purpose as this well-chosen couplet,—

> Those who do not willingly come to church
> Are always afraid to be brought there.

The town entirely depends upon the (new flourishing)
school; for who shou'd sacrifice their sons to Eton, and

115

Westminster: tho' here indeed is a want of lock-up, and walls, as the boys board at lodging-houses, as at Eaton; but then vices are not so near at hand.——We walk'd about the town, and the school walks, whilst light lasted; and then foresaw a low'ring night, after a day of hope that the rain were done.—— ——

> —Now the soft hour
> Of walking comes: for him who lonely loves
> To seek the distant hills, and there converse
> With nature.

At supper we were put into the upper long room; which I allways dislike, as being too far from attendance, and the kitchen; and where you may ring in vain. I was very melancholy at supper, for the loss of my book; T. B.'s ride; the bad weather; and the altogether:—For one of my great pleasures of touring wou'd be lost, cou'd I not chew the cud of my travells for the 6 following months, till they are written, completed, and bound.

My sheets were so damp, and the blankets so dirty and stinking, and the room so smelling of putridity, that I slept very little; tho' I took off the sheets, and employed all the brandy, near a pint, in purifying the room, and sprinkling the quilt, and blankets.—

T. B. return'd without success, at $\frac{1}{2}$ past eleven o'clock; having ridden 24 miles of bad roads. [So here ends my memory relation.]

Wednes-day, July 1

All the latter part of June has been November weather; and the roads are as bad as in midwinter:—this has made us inactive, and prevented our venturing into the cross roads of Northamptonshire; but we must rest contented, that we have done, and seen so much. In the night much rain fell; as I knew who frequently rose, and look'd out of the window: and glad was I to rise, tho' with an head-ach, and gloomy as the day.—Opposite our inn is erected a very grand new pillory, upon which I did not know that

116

gentlemen were ever placed in the country; and I forgot to ask the question here, and why such expence?

This our Rugby charge—*for one night—two meals and*

Joseph Richardson — Black-Bear. RUGBY.	£	s	d
Eating	–	2	
Tea	–	1	4
Coffee			
Wine	–	2	–
Negus			
Punch	–	2	–
Cyder			
Ale & Porter			
Tobacco			
Serv.ts Eating & Ale			
Horses Hay & Corn	–	4	3
£	0	11	1

3 *horses*, will prove touring to be no very extravagant pleasure; and silence the ignorant assertions I often hear, that all travelling is wonderfully expensive.

117

In 4 miles from Rugby, we came into the high road at Dun-Church; and soon to Braunston, there crossing the Banbury Navigation: and here I must express my (ignorant) surprise, (as I believe I often do) that land owners shou'd not bore their estates for coal: shou'd I say this country has a coal aspect, there is lime-stone all around for burning; the answer will be 'There is none': my reply 'Have you tried?'—People waste money in every idle pursuit, and won't try for coal in these inland perishing counties; where, certainly it abounds, and will be found hereafter.—The hill above Branston has every appearance of earth that I have observ'd about colleries.— —

Daventry

It now began to rain; so we push'd briskly forward to Daventry, and housed at The Saracens Head—pronounc'd The Serjeants Head; say Saracen and you wou'd not be understood.—It was market day; and there were many lean cows, leathern breeches, with much gingerbread.—I enquirèd at our inn, if there were any remains of the old priory; and was answer'd (as usual) that there never was any here:—and in 5 minutes I saw these remains adjoining the new church, which is low steepled and Venetian-window'd. What exists of the old priory serves as an habitation of the poor.—

In the church yard is this inscription,

WILLIAM PEASCOE AND WIFE.

The aged couple who lie here
Were man and wife near threescore year   An excellent
They lived in love and dyed in peace   triplet!
We hope their souls are gone to rest
To dwell with Christ amongst the just.

There is the best booksellers shop here, that I have seen since Loughbro'; tho nothing curious to be got; and the old bookseller was very crusty, and unpleasant.

Dinner ended, we hasten'd to go and I must needs ride up an hill to an encampment; where is nothing of notice or view. This threw me back; so that I did not overtake

P— till we came to Weedon-in-the-Street. At a short distance to the right of the road is ye Church of Stow churches; but, by mistake going first to the village, which lays wide, we made an unnecessary detour of two miles.—
In the church yard is the following inscription upon

ELIZABETH SMITH, aged 21.

Lost in the flower of my age,
   I seized was by death;   Metre much to
My life was but some hours   be admired.
   All flesh must come to earth.

Within the church is this (*happy*) inscription to the memory of the beauty, and virginity, of

Mrs Elizth Acam, aged 15 years, 1701.—

For it is appointed for all once to dy
Death tane mee away in my virginity,
No arte, no skill for me would serve,
No cordiall helps could mee preserve;
At last weak nature did decay,
My beauties flower past away,
Friends do lament my unripe fall,
Earlie or late death takes us all.

There are also three monuments; one of an old crusader, cross-legg'd, shielded, &c; one of Dr Turner, of much pomposity, and expence; and not ill executed; but the third, exceeding all my hopes, and all my former observations, is the almost-recumbent figure of the Lady Elizabeth 4th daughter and coheire of John Latimer &c, &c,— with a long account of her marriages, children &c; her 6th daughter, Dorothy, by her Ist husband Sr John Danvers, was married to Sr Peter Osborne.
—— —— —— Such a sculptory of white marble, so fancied, so executed, I never saw; (for I have never been in Italy; and those who have, let them look in here.) She is in dress, in figure, in looks, most exactly resembling Mrs Siddons in her reposing scene of Queen Catherine in Henry VIIIth.—So light, so well executed is the work-

manship—that touch her, and she wou'd rise. One hand lies upon her breast, one by her side, her eyes half open, and just ready to repeat her vision.—Had I presumption, I wou'd declare that nothing in Westr Abbey came up to this; or, indeed, any thing I have seen (tho' I have view'd many works of Roubillac)! Such a sight in a hopeless day revived me.—

Towcester Our ride hence was dull, and dreary; and the roads nothing but stones and mud.—As we enter'd Towchester, (where T. B. had prepared us) it began again to rain: (I only wonder how we lately kept on; and done so much!)

In all my walks and of all the clerks, who have shewn me churches, (and I have seen some few) I have allways asked, from hope and curiosity, 'Have you any person of remarkable old age in your town?' The answer being, for ever, no, has terrify'd me: but to-night, reading this in the county paper, had rather comforted me.—

'April 27th, 1789, Mr James French, of Fritwell, 90 years of age, walked from thence through Aynho to Banbury before breakfast, being about nine miles. He appears remarkably healthy for his age, has a fine bloom on his countenance, enjoys a good appetite, and seems likely to live many years. He informed the editor of this misellany, that he was for a good part of his life a servant in the Mr Child's family, (where we hear he was much respected and esteemed) by whom his faithful service is rewarded with an annuity of 20£ during life. Not long since he walked to London in three days, and there, amidst the multitude observed, that he could not find an old man. He eats but two meals a day, and never drinks any strong liquors, nor very often ale, but generally mixed beer.

I met to-day, several broad-wheel'd waggons with the Phoenix Insurance fixed upon them;[106] which is a novel safeguard, many having taken fire.

The road had been so wet, and slippery, as to prevent observation: gay suns make the country appear happy, and chearful; otherwise all nature desponds.—Thats the prettiest place that is seen under the gayest sun, at the luckiest hour.—The evening was only good for tour writing; and brought up my running arrear: as well as mv recollection of the contents of the lost pocket book.

In touring, never expect, or call for what is not likely to be met with, good; then you will be easy and happy; otherwise, you seek your own distress and peevishness.—For instance, I allways oppose those who call for, and expect to find, oil in alehouses,[107] and small beer in great inns; because it is not for the interest of an inn to assuage your thirst with small beer, or to inform soldiers that such a thing is to be had.

When alone, I allways make my noon stops at snug village public houses; but that won't do for people, who cannot wait upon themselves, tie up and feed their own horses; but sit ringing the bell, calling for oil, Kayan pepper, wash-hand glasses and tooth-picks!!—The second rate houses upon the North Road are capital inns to the best on the Chester; and on the North Road, horses are well lodg'd, and attended to.—Unluckily for our intention, the M^{ss} of Buckingham is return'd to Stowe, else we had thoughts of surveying it.—

Before breakfast I paraded the churchyard, which is low, large and ugly; and without any good metre.

In the church were a couple making those vows, which, probably, will soon be broken, or forgotten.—Close to the church, are some old porches and walls, which proclaim the scite of 'A college, valued at the Dissolution at £19 6s 8d pr annum'.

And here let me remark that all the valuations of the religious houses made before the Dissolution are supposed to be much under the true income; as both the monks, and the new proprietors, from motives of cunning, (except in some few instances) wanted to conceal the extent of their property: and from the hour of the fall of the smaller foundations, the larger houses lavish'd away, or conceal'd their effects.

After breakfast, I proposed a walk to Easton-Neston, the seat of Ld Pomfret, built on the hill above the town; a great, staring, unpleasant dwelling, of neither comfort or content; surrounded by great offices, adorn'd by statues, and commanding an offensive view. Such a place I shou'd be tempted to . . . Sr G. P. Turner,[108] who has pull'd down, and sold the materials of his several houses.

The church stands close to the house. In the church-yard there is one grave cover'd by a large iron cradle; and on one tombstone an inscription certainly written by the *late* Lord,

BENJAMIN ROLFE. 1777.

As honest a little fellow
as ever was born.

Tho 10000£ were to be expended on such a place, and everything done that cou'd be done, it wou'd still continue a wretched place: and there is no living in a dirty stoney country; better to dwell on a wild sandy heath, where walking and riding may be allways had without dirt, and danger.—

After settling our bill, we pursued our quiet course, by the forest side to Pottersbury, to old Stratford, and to Stoney-Stratford, adjoining, a town with two churches, and of better account than Towcester: here we enter'd Buckinghamshire. Another hour of the Ist fine day we have seen for some time, brought us in good appetite, at near two o'clock, to a good, little inn, The Swan in Fenny-Stratford: where a motherly old landlady instantly brought in some fine cold lamb, cold ham, and tarts; what more to be wish'd for? Nor have they fire enough in small inns for fresh cookery; but just enough to boil a tea kettle: but let those who seek for tedious luxuries, think not of touring.

Fenny
Stratford

SWAN INN.   F— STRATFORD.

							s.	d.
July 2.	2 Diners	-	-	-	-	-	2	0
	Banday	-	-	-	-	-	1	0
	Wine	-	-	-	-	-	1	2
	Bear	-	-	-	-	-	0	5
	3 hore's hay and corn	-	-	-	1	7		
						£0	6	2

Nothing so gratifying to my taste and temper, as the immediate dinner after exercise, and without form: when thus seated, how my mind revolves with contempt, on fashionable dinners, serv'd up at ridiculous hours; where ease gives place to fine breeding, where you eat not what you like or drink what you list; nor have you time for digestion, or communication, from the impatient civility of the inviters, and the worry of their servants.—I, in general, dislike dining out most excessively; as I have no time for eating, or drinking, from the civilities of observation, and restraint; and with—'You eat nothing', 'You are the least eater I ever saw'!—I bow—and grumble inwardly—'How shou'd I, when the dishes won't stay upon the table.' To dine abroad you must give up much of morning intention; and break away from some certain pleasure, to come home at 4 o'clock to dress:—then you are hungry —and wish for your meal; but no, you must stay another hour of fatiguing impatience, e'r you reach the house of appointment, and seat yourself in a formal circle till the dinner is announced: then you are obliged to hand some old ugly woman down stairs; and soon to find yourself placed near the windy door.—Dinner ended, much form continues whilst the ladies stay; and then ignorant of each other, and finding the wines thick, and bad, (having been long brought up, and decanted by the servants) the gentlemen are silent, stupid and wishing for retreat.—

When this shall be read, I shall be deem'd a sulky blackguard (however inwardly the reader may agree with me.)

In this tour, to my wonder, we have met no tourists, seen no shews, interfered with no clubs, nor have heard of any players.—After dinner we survey'd first the churchyard of the opposite chapel where were these three inscriptions—

'Within my silent grave I ly, all temporall affliction i defy
To rise a gain i know i must, and hope to be amongst the just
Seeing all earthly things are transitory, bend your whole mind to ensure
    eternal glory'.

'Farewell vain world, and worldly pleasure, death will not tarry no
   mans leasure,
Farewell my wife, and children small, for I must go now Christ
   doth call.'

'O savage Death what have you done, I am shure I had much
   Rather you had took my daughter or my son so youd but spared
   My father. But now my loving husband dear have from my bosom
   Torn and left on earth with me in tears six infant babes to
   Mourn but now my loving baby dear since twas the Lords
   decree let us for heav'ns you prepare our father dear to see'.

In this last, the words are written to the end of the cross bar; and so,
luckily the rhyme is entirely lost.

The chapel of red brick, built by subscription about 60
years ago, is of no bad model or intention, and being well
adorn'd, and with a painted roof of the subscribers arms, I
cou'd see pleas'd P— from his fancy of other chapels. The
eastern window is of good old stain'd glass, brought from a
neighbouring old destroy'd mansion.

After a long stay here, for we had time enough, having
not more than 4 miles for our evening ride, we re-em-
bark'd; and now we are upon comfortable sandy roads,
where one can indulge sight, and thought, without fear of
falling.—On the left on a high hill, stands the solitary
church of Bow-Brickhill (repair'd, as I think, by Dr Willis,
Little   so often quoted in this tour); we pass'd thro' Little Brick-
Brickhill   hill, and then left the high road: I had here my church-
yard round, but was now satisfied of inscriptions, tho'
there were some not bad; this being short, I took it down.

'Dear friends weep not for me, but rather than be glad,
   The sooner I was gone, the lesser sin I had.'

Passing by some pleasant woods (for a good soil gives
Woburn   pleasure) we soon came to Wooburn (Bedfordshire) and to
the George, an inn of manners and method, unlike the
alehouses of Daventry or Towcester.—Here we drank tea,
read and answer'd letters, (for this was a station where I
cou'd have wish'd to have met Mrs B[yng] and then
walk'd into the park, a scenery of grandeur, and of toler-

able keeping; for where is the comfort of any place that is not in keeping and cleanliness? Almost all we have seen except Clumber, have been abandon'd, half-finish'd places. —We pursued a clean, and pleasant walk that carried us to the new kennell, there to see his Graces fox hounds, which are established in a pompous stile.—The huntsman has a charming house.—

Upon this subject, knowing something, I may speak; and suppose a very unnecessary expence when I see 70 couple of hounds, fed upon flesh and oatmeal, and laying upon straw all the summer:—talking of whey, low feeding, garden-stuff, &c, was I found, Hebrew to the huntsman; as were all my (foolish) questions about a garden of roots, and if they had cows, and if they boil'd with milk, for weak hounds in winter.

When I keep fox hounds (don't laugh,) they shall not out run the fox in the first mile; and all their attendants (in the field) shall be two, quiet, civil young men, who wou'd pretend to nothing but obeying my commands.—

This huntsman, for his place, was a civil man; for I shou'd suppose his situation, as to salary, respect and estimation, infinitely better than a Commissionership of Stamps, or any such *paltry* place under Government.

The P. of Wales was here 2 days ago; and *then* felt he wou'd be a fox hunter.—After our long visit here we walk'd towards the house, thro' the woods; where I was shock'd and surprised to see that the axe had been most busy. What is the D. of B[edford] doing to imitate Sr G. P. T[urner]? Or is it to pay for the new roofing of the abbey? Nor wou'd I disgrace any park with a dog-kennell, and the eternal yelping of hounds: loving my woods and rides to be quiet, and only cheer'd by the rook, and the ring dove;—but the clamour of hounds, unless when in the field, is an everlasting torture.—We took our seat, on a bench on the hill, above the front of the house. It is a grand place, with finely surrounding woods; but the water is ill-managed and of bad effect: there are more deer upon such a space than I ever saw (electioneering) who came around us in a most quiet manner; and who might surely be tamed like sheep, and led as easily to slaughter, without being shot at, badly wounded, and half of their flesh spoil'd.—The sporting of the fawns was inexpressibly gay, and elegant; and of such sweet simplicity, that I long'd to have Frek to turn out amongst them, and join their frolicks. We were so pleased with our evening, (one of the first that we have walk'd in,) that we stay'd out till 9 o'clock; for the park, close to the town, was alive with walkers, mushroom pickers, and the quality of the place.

As a country retreat, or as a station for some days, none are so good as those on the edge of a great park, and place. For therein is to be had everlasting walking and riding, whether during the heat beneath the groves, or when the moon is up in pleasing glades; shou'd you be well with the owner, he may permit you to Angle in his ponds, and have a run in the park for a couple of horses; and shou'd you be well with the parkkeeper, gamekeeper, and gardener (as it is easy to be) your table may not be ill accomodated. But wherever a tourist halts, let it be, if possible, by a park side.—Our supper, preceded by strawberries, was very good; and we had every reason to be contented with the inn.

Friday
July 3

We have now nearly finish'd our circle. To settle another, (if another can be) different arrangements shall be adopted: baggage of equal weight,—unless a gentleman chuses to take his own chaise, or his own servant, at his own charge; hours must be stated thus, where shall we dine, tomorrow, if possible? And where is our bed stop? Then the active may set off early, and make a good, and active pursuit; without watching and delaying for the inactive; who may settle the bills.

There must be an equality of baggage to equalise comforts; so weigh away,—my sheets against others bedgowns and breeches.—Last night I lay in blankets; this

126

night, probably, I shall again; and, tomorrow I hope to enjoy my own sheets.

Wooburn House is only to be seen on a Monday; so that visit must be deferr'd: but we mean to ride the park this morning.—Tho' of the park I did not exactly know the rides, yet I had a tolerable guess; and I hate a guide to worry, watch and confound.

In the intention of my great progress I have luckily steer'd as well; as I did to-day in this small ride.—

Finding the gate of the evergreen drive open, we pursued that drive quite to the end; and there call'd for a key to let us out: we were now in wide park, and safe as to road. The having an evergreen, dry, side of the park, for a winter ride, and a contrast to the damp green shades of the opposite part, is truly delectable: and here, I shou'd go on with extension of paling and plantation over the high sandy country, and farm it with every new invention, of corns, grasses, and trees; and then what thousands of partridges and tame fowls might I rear thereon: on the side of some of these dry hills, shou'd be erected my dog-kennell, fronting the eastern sun; not shut up, as it now is, amidst damp groves, a nuisance to the house by the noise; and where, in the servants hall, are allways the kennell attendants to be found, instead of living everlastingly upon the spot, for the safeguard of the hounds.—We met a pack of younger hounds coming in from their exercise at eleven o'clock: is that an hour in an hot summers day for hounds to be abroad??! The upper hills of the park command good prospects, and are beautifully cloth'd with wood; so as to form a grand amphitheatre around the house: but the trees being, in some places, rather *too* thick, the Duke has been *advised* (I suppose) to thin them, which proposal suiting *his Graces taste*, he has laid furiously about him; and will most amply repay himself for the roofing and repairs of his house: as a steward when order'd to cut down 50£ worth of timber for repairs, allways cuts down 100£ that they may be *nobly* done!—This upper part of the park

127

wants much draining; and none of the old root holes of the trees are fill'd up.—Passing the back of the kennells we made the distant detour, and so down to the bridge, whose pyramids I shou'd instantly levell; then crossing by the kitchen garden we made our exit at the town gate where we enter'd.

Hay making now being the general employ, this market was thinly attended; if Father Time were ever wellcome it wou'd now be with his scythe. We saw the D. and Mrs D.[109] angling, at an hour, 2 o'clock, when sport was not to be had; but perhaps this is the only time *they* can command, for breakfast, is but just finish'd, and they dine too late to have any evening.—If I cou'd I wou'd come to this good inn for a stay of some days, as there are several (little distant) places worth seeing, and the park is an eternal pleasure for riding and walking; besides I might hope to be allow'd to angle, and to *look* about the kitchen garden.— As for the Duke and his late visitor,[110] they are fallen into *pleasant* hands, who understand their cards.—

We have lately been very unlucky in the weather; no gaiety of season but allways a lower; evermore great coating, and skulking under trees or into barns: now we are returning, summer is setting out upon his progress.— But perhaps we had been from want of alacrity, more deaden'd and knock'd up by heat; than by the cold and latter damps. After all, I remember (in this tour) but one morning, and one whole day of confinement: my pleasantest and fullest days of touring were those to Southwell, and Bakewell; and they both ended WELL.—In the park, today, my poney was so frisky at the sight of the hounds as to alarm me; and does return in such courage and fatness, as shews he wou'd bear exercise double to what I gave him.— Wooburn steeple has walk'd down from the church, and stands by the side of it.—

We were well treated at The George, but were charg'd as we have been unaccustom'd to, in the grand tavern stile.—

From Wansford Bridge to this place, our charge has been at so much a head; but now we smell London, and all its extravagance. Leaving Wooburn, we rode, after dinner, as gently as cou'd be; for Poney is so fat and lazy, that he dislikes to, and will not hurry himself. Hockliffe—our half-way, looks cooly in a hot summer day, but must be wofully dirty in winter.—Before seven o'clock, we arrived at Dunstable at the Bull, the wrong inn; as I am pretty certain that the Sugar-Loaf had done us infinitely better.— After tea, we walk'd to view the remains of the priory church, which now serves the town.—

In the church-yard is this epitaph

'Weep not for me my parents dear, I am not dead, but sleepeth here;
'Tis a fate prepared for all, we must obey when God doth call;
Now I lie in the lonesome grave, companions none but worms I have,
Untill I hear a voice to say, Arise young man, and come away.'

Close to the west front of the church, are these remaining walls, and gateways that led to the priory.—

This being the sweetest evening we have seen, and it being our last, we employ'd fully in walking thro' the corn fields, in enjoying the finest moon, and avoiding the worst inn; where we were press'd to eat of ducks for supper, which we needed not T. B.'s hint to refuse, as we found them dead, or dying in every corner of the garden.

The last Bill

BULL INN. DUNSTABLE.

Tea	-	-	-	-	-	1	8
Suppers	-	-	-	-	-	2	0
Wine	-	-	-	-	-	2	6
Brandy	-	-	-	-	-	1	0
Breakfast	-	-	-	-	-	1	8
						8	10

The closing day. —

For myself I can boldly assert that I have put forth, thro' this tour, the best exertions of my temper, and the highest powers of my philosophy: powers of limb, or powers of conversation have never been required; cards we have never touch'd; walking we have never try'd; talking we have never attempted: about religion I have made some enquiry, (having been in so many churches) and find it to be lodged in the hands of the Methodists; as the greater clergy do not attend their duty, and the lesser neglect it; that where the old psalm singing is abolish'd, none is establish'd in its place; as the organ is inconvenient, and not understood; at most places the curates never attend regularly, or to any effect, or comfort, so no wonder that the people are gone over to Methodism.

Our day was a gloomy mixture of many showers, and some thunder.—Passing thro' Margate and Redborn we soon came to St Albans—where P.— never having seen the old abbey church dismounted for a survey, whilst I slowly walk'd forward; nor did he overtake me for some miles, when he seem'd gratified with his inspection of this magnificent old pile.—

St. Albans

We dined at the lower Red Lion at Barnet, where they talk of the amazing price of straw; and that in London, it is dearer than hay: what's the reason? Shall I tell you? It is because London is so overgrown; and so crowded by horses, that the consumption of straw is, within these few years, doubled; consequently, the adjacent counties, that are much under grass, cannot supply the metropolis, as formerly; straw then must be fetch'd from afar. This devilish increase of London will in time, cause a famine, because it cannot be supply'd:

However I must abide therein;—and so I return to Duke St, and to my business in

SOMERSET PLACE

Amen
Never emprinted
before
in London.

EDITOR'S NOTES

(1) This P., unidentified, has obviously from the context nothing to do with either of the Palmers who appear later in this tour (p. 99, and see note 98).

(2) This is certainly W. Wynn, nephew of Mrs. Soames, and perhaps son of Mrs. Wynn and brother of the toast, Miss Wynn, who is mentioned in the long poem on p. 76.

(3) Sir Francis Molyneux.

(4) Evelyn Pierrepoint, 2nd Duke of Kingston (1711-73), with whom the dukedom came to an end. The reference to 'father' should probably be 'grandfather', *i.e.* Evelyn, 1st duke, d. 1726.

(5) The only daughter of Colonel Thomas Chudleigh, born in 1724, maid of honour to Augusta, Princess of Wales, secretly married Augustus Harvey, a lieutenant of H.M.S. Cornwall, separated from him in 1747, and did not meet him again. In 1749 she contracted a liaison with Evelyn, 2nd Duke of Kingston, a man of mature years, plotted to cancel her first marriage, and was at length pronounced by the Ecclesiastical Court to be 'a spinster', and then married the Duke of Kingston in 1768. Five years later the Duke died and left her everything, disinheriting his eldest nephew. In 1775 she was arrested on a charge of bigamy (in spite of the decision by the Ecclesiastical Court) and convicted, but pleading excuse on account of her rank, was discharged on payment of the fees of the court. She died in 1788 at the age of 63.

(6) A famous eighteenth-century night club, mentioned in Hickey's *Memoirs*, Casanova's *Memoirs* and many other contemporary writings. See *D.N.B.* under Cornelys, Theresa (1723-97).

(7) The original Dukes of Newcastle were associated with Welbeck. There were frequent creations on account of failure of male heirs, and it was after the third creation, when default of male heirs again seemed likely, that the Duke persuaded the King to grant special remainder to the male heir of his sister, the Countess of Lincoln, through whom the dukedom became for the future associated with Clumber.

The Duke at the time of Byng's tour was the second, Henry Fiennes Clinton (1720-94), who succeeded to the dukedom in 1768.

Clumber was built by the second Duke of the third creation in 1769-70, and Wright was the architect. It had a large central block with four wings. This was the house seen by Byng. A fire destroyed the centre in 1879, and it was rebuilt by Barry. A library was added by the 9th Duke and a state drawing-room by the 5th.

(Clumber Park is now the chief attraction of the well-known 'Dukeries'.)

131

(8) An old custom of carrying garlands at the burials of unmarried females on their way to the grave and then hanging the garland up in the church as a memento of the departed one. The custom continued in Derbyshire long after it ceased in other parts, and in the Peak District almost within the memory of the older inhabitants of to-day. They were made of real flowers once, but gradually paper, ribands, etc., supplanted the flowers as they lasted longer. Often a glove or handkerchief of the deceased was added, inscribed with the name, age and date of death of the maiden. There are one or two instances still remaining of garlands suspended from the beams of the roof—at Ashford-in-the-Water, for example. Those from Matlock Church have been removed to the local museum.

(9) The first Worksop Manor was built by the Earl of Shrewsbury and his wife, the famous Bess of Hardwick, on the site of Worksop Priory, the nave and beautiful thirteenth-century Lady Chapel of which still remain as the parish church of Worksop. It was a private residence of Bess, and Mary Queen of Scots was confined here under Shrewsbury's charge until the Babington Conspiracy led to her removal. The estate passed by marriage to the Dukes of Norfolk about 1740. Bess of Hardwick's house was burnt to the ground in 1761, with a loss in paintings and statuary alone of £100,000. The Duke of Norfolk decided to build in its place the finest and largest mansion in England, and commissioned Paine as architect, the foundation stone being laid in 1763. Part of one side of the quadrang e was finished, but even that was 300 ft. long, and had 500 rooms, four storeys and a portico of six Corinthian pillars supporting a large pediment. From a print of the building it does appear rather like Somerset House, and this was the house seen by Byng. In 1840 it was sold by a later Duke of Norfolk to the Duke of Newcastle, who razed it to the ground rather than meet the expense of its upkeep.

(10) This was begun in 1776, the east and west wings being used in 1785. (See Newnham and Webster's *Somerset House*.)

(11) The Marquis of Newcastle is mentioned in connection with Welbeck in this note referring to Charles I's visit in 1645. He was *then* the owner, but in Byng's time the abbey had become the property of the Dukes of Portland by the marriage of Margaret, the daughter of the Duke of Newcastle of the second creation with Lord Harley, who became 2nd Earl of Oxford. Their only child was a daughter, so the earldom of Oxford lapsed; but this daughter married the 2nd Duke of Portland, who, on Lady Oxford's death, inherited Welbeck. It has belonged to the Dukes of Portland ever since, and it is to the Portlands that Byng refers. Lady Oxford before she died built the great Gothic hall and extended the south front. The hall is the one referred to so scathingly by Byng. Byng's description of the house and grounds is much at variance with the somewhat eulogistic account of them given by Horace Walpole in 1756, and Mrs. Delaney in the same year.

(12) William Speechley's *Treatise on the culture of the Vine* was regarded as a very important work when it was first published in 1790. In 1779 he published a *Treatise on the culture of the pineapple,* and the great horticultural writer, J. C. Loudon, referring to the two works, said that they opened quite a new era in that department of horticulture and laid the foundation for the improvements which have followed, in rapid succession, to the present time (1828). Before the appearance of these treatises there was little on record that afforded any material information to the cultivators of the vine and the pineapple.

(13) Shireoaks Hall belonged to the Hewitt family from the sixteenth century to the beginning of the nineteenth.

(14) 'Those infernal monsters (children's nurses) throw a spoonful of gin down a child's throat which instantly strangles the babe. When searchers come to inspect the body and inquire what distemper caused the death, it is answered "convulsions".' Burrington, *An Answer to Dr. William Brackenridge's Letter,* 1757, quoted by Dr. George in *London Life in the Eighteenth Century.*

(15) Mr. Galley Knight of Firbeck.

(16) This house was built in 1750. It has a well-wooded deer park, and in a ravine at the west end of the park are the ruins of the Cistercian foundation—Roche Abbey.

(17) There is an excellent account of this castle in Hauter's *Deanery of Doncaster.*

(18) At the time of Byng's tour Bramley Grange was the residence of the Spencers. The house is still standing, but is in use as a farmhouse. Hanging in the house are still the family portraits of the Spencers who were connected with the old Sheffield family of that name, who were living at Attercliffe Hall early in the seventeenth century.

(19) Patent No. 1635 of 1788, granted to J. G. Hohmann of Rotherham.

(20) These iron works were started by Lord Fitzwilliam towards the middle of the eighteenth century, and Mr. Walker at one time acted as manager. Samuel Walker came from Grenoside in the West Riding of Yorkshire, and his son Joshua built a fine Adam house, now the Rotherham Museum, in 1783; another son built Ferham House, and a third Eastwood House. The main branches of the family left the district many years ago, but the present-day firm of J. & J. Walker are said to be family connections of the original Walkers.

(20a) The Tontine Inn was built in 1785 and demolished in 1850. Sheffield Market Hall now stands on its site. James Watson was landlord from 1785 to 1793, when he was succeeded by a man named Carnelly.

(21) Mr. Tudor's manufactory at Sheffield was built about 1770, and carried on as a silversmith's business under the title of 'Tudor and Leader'. Mr. Tudor resided in a fine Adam house across the street. This was demol-

ished by the Sheffield Corporation about the year 1900, and the site is now occupied by the new Sheffield Library.

(22) The building erected in 1763 and described in 1764 as 'large and commodious, capable of containing eight hundred spectators, handsomely decorated, and having some very good scenery' was taken down and rebuilt on a larger plan in 1773. This is still the Theatre Royal notwithstanding the drastic changes both internal and external. The profile of Shakespeare and some dramatic symbols executed for the original builders by a poor wandering tramp named Renilowe are housed in the city museum.

(23) On special occasions the great actors of the time were brought down from London. Mrs. Siddons was one of the first persons of repute to break through the prejudice which regarded summer 'strolling' or starring in the provincial theatres as a degradation. She was here in June 1789, and again in 1799, and the names of her famous brothers are closely associated with the theatre.

(24) The Peggs or Pegges are a well-known Derbyshire family dating back to the beginning of the sixteenth century at least; there are several branches all taking important parts in the history of the county of Derby. *The Beauchief branch* was established at Beauchief in 1648 by the marriage of the daughter and sole heir of William Strelley, Esq., of Beauchief Abbey, with Edward Pegge, who was the son of Edward Pegge of Ashbourne. The member of the family residing at Beauchief when Byng was there was Peter, a great grandson of the original Edward Pegge of Beauchief Abbey. He was Sheriff of Co. Derby in 1788 and died in 1836. One of the best known members of the Pegge family was Rev. Samuel, LL.D., who was rector of Whittington and died there at the age of 91 in 1796. He was a well-known antiquary and combined in his person two branches of the family, as his father was an Osmarton Pegge and his mother was a granddaughter of Edward Pegge of Beauchief.

(25) The Revolution of 1688 is said to have owed its origin to the meeting of a few 'friends of liberty and the Protestant religion', held in the early part of that year on Whittington-Moor, at which the Earl of Devonshire (afterwards Duke), the Earl of Danby (afterwards Duke of Leeds), Lord Delamere, and John Darcy (son and heir of the Earl of Holderness) are known to have attended. It is said that in consequence of a shower of rain, they adjourned to a public house on the moor, called the Cock and Pynot, or Magpie, which acquired from this circumstance the name of the Revolution House; and the small room where these distinguished guests retired, that of the Plotting Parlour. The armchair in which the Earl of Devonshire sat still forms part of the furniture of this room, and this would be the chair in which Byng sat in 1794. The centenary celebration of the event took place at Whittington and Chesterfield in Nov. 1788; at Whittington divine service was held in the church, at which the rector of the parish, Rev. Samuel Pegge, though 84 years of age, preached an excellent sermon.

(26) The races were held on Whittington Common, about a mile from the town; they were patronised by the Duke of Devonshire and some of the leading gentry in the neighbourhood and were generally held about the end of September.

(27) Anthony Wood of Merton College, Oxford, was born in 1632 and died in 1695. He made collections for a History of Oxfordshire and pub‑‑lished a book on the University and a Dictionary of Oxford writers. He was expelled from the University for a libel on the Earl of Clarendon contained in his *Athenae Oxonienses*.

(28) A seat of the Duke of Devonshire. 'Bess of Hardwick' was born in the old mansion. She built the present hall in 1590-7. She married Sir Wm. Cavendish for her second husband, and their grandchild became Earl of Devonshire, ancestor of the present Duke of Devonshire, and inherited Hardwick Hall. The older hall (of which Byng speaks as possessing the remains of a library) was left standing when the Countess built the new hall, to accommodate the large number of retainers that were required for so large an establishment.

(29) It is not unusual to find composition floors in English houses of the sixteenth century.

(30) Christina, daughter of Edward Bruce, Baron Kinloss, who married William Cavendish, M.P. for Derby 1621-6, in which latter year he became 2nd Earl of Devonshire, succeeding his father. He died in 1628, but the Countess lived until 1675, and was a great supporter of the Royalist cause. The good monument of a Countess of Devonshire, with a later description 1627, that Byng mentions at Hault Hucknall Church, is to the memory of Anne, daughter of Henry Highley and wife of William, 1st Earl of Devonshire. She died in 1628.

(31) Glapwell is part of the parish of Bolsover. There do not appear to be any references to a Mr. Hallows of Glapwell Hall, but about 1790 a Mr. Chaworth Hallowes was Rector of Pleasley, which is less than two miles from Glapwell Hall.

(32) The present building and the one which Byng saw was the keep (in imitation of a Norman one) built by Sir Charles Cavendish in or about 1615, to replace the ruined Norman castle (built originally by William Peverel), and a stately range of domestic buildings continued by the Earl, afterwards Duke, of Newcastle on the death of his father, Sir Charles Cavendish, in 1617. On several occasions the Earl entertained Charles I and his Queen here; and in the Civil War it was captured by the Commonwealth troops and the buildings unroofed and otherwise damaged. This damage the Earl, now promoted to a dukedom, repaired; but the buildings were again allowed to go to decay in the eighteenth century, when the Duke removed the contents of the house to Welbeck. To-day the keep continues in good repair and is inhabited; and the riding house is still standing, but the stately rooms are now mere shells. The house was evidently going to decay when

135

Byng saw it, but was still capable of speedy repair and restoration to habitability.

(33) Was appointed Knight Marshall on January 16th, 1758, six weeks after the death of his father, Sir Philip Meadows, age 95, who had been Knight Marshall since 1700. The office of Knight Marshall continued until comparatively recent times. There is the following entertaining account of Sir Sidney Meadows in his obituary notice in *The Gentleman's Magazine* for 1792. (Vol. 62, Part 2, pp. 1060 and 1061):

'At his seat near Andover, Hants, aged 93, Sir Sidney Meadows, brother to Mr. M. of Richmond Park, and uncle to General M. and to Evelyn and Pierpoint M. Esqrs. He was Knight Marshall to the Marshalsea Court in Southwark, given him by the late Duke of Chandos, as Lord Steward of the household. The nominal value of this place is only 26£ per annum; and the Court consists of the Lord Steward and Knight Marshall as judges, a steward and deputy steward, a prothonotary and deputy, four counsel, six attorneys, and six Marshallmen, at 20£ per annum each. The prison is for privates and other offenders at sea, and debtors; and in all civil actions tried in this court, both the plaintiff and dependent must belong to His Majesty's household. Its jurisdiction involves 4 counties, extending 12 miles round the palace of Westminster, the city of London only excepted. Sir S. was so extravagantly fond of horsemanship, that he has been known to hire eleven horses in a day at his manege, and in the last yr of his life four: Nor was his exercise in walking less. He died extremely rich, in personal property as well as in land. It was said of him that he had not been on the East side of Bond Street more than twice a yr for the last 30 years, and that was in his way to receive dividends at the Bank. He was buried on the 22nd at Andover, for it was his will to be interred in the parish where he died; but the family burial place is at Kensington, and to that village he walked or rode from his house in Picaddily almost every morning of his latter years.'

(34) There is insufficient evidence in the diary to permit the identification of L——. His robbery on Hounslow Heath (see p. 79) is not to be distinguished from those of other unlucky travellers, in the news-sheets for June.

(35) The house was an old hall or manor-house up to about 1550; then Sir William Cavendish began to build another on a much larger scale, which, on his death in 1557, was continued and completed by his widow, Bess of Hardwick. This house remained until 1687, when the 4th Earl (and 1st Duke) of Devonshire began to replace it by a great palace with Palmer as the architect. He built first the south front, then the east side, which was not finished until 1700, in which year the old west front was demolished and rebuilt, and the north front in 1704, the whole house not being completed until 1706. The 6th Duke of Devonshire added another great wing in 1820, which took twenty years to complete. Byng saw the house before this wing, which spoilt Palmer's original design, was added. The 'Dutchess' to whom Byng refers was Georgiana, eldest daughter of the 1st Earl Spencer and wife of the 5th Duke of Devonshire, whom she married in 1774, and who

lived until 1806. She was renowned for giving a kiss to a voter in exchange for his vote for Fox, for whom she was canvassing in the Westminster election 1784.

(35a) Arthur Young (*Eastern Tour*, I, 213 f.n.) says: 'It will not be improper to warn the traveller against depending on the Inn at Edensor. . . . He will find there nothing but dirt and impertinence.'

(36) The oldest monument in the church is that assigned to Sir John de Darley, 'Old John of Darley'. There is no inscription on the slab, but its style agrees accurately with most of the era in which John de Darley flourished; and Cox, the authority on Derbyshire churches, agrees with this decision. John de Darley was the most eminent man of his time, and his family flourished in Darley in the thirteenth century. 'Old John' was custodian of the Peak Castle and lord of the whole manor. The knight is represented clad in a surcoat over the suit of mail, with his legs crossed below the knee, a sword before him on the left thigh, and holding a heart in his hands, which are raised to his breast. The sword is broken and the figure somewhat mutilated, but it shows the head uncovered, and he has long curled hair and a short beard. The feet rest on a cushion.

The other old monument referred to by Byng as 'Whitehall' is an incised alabaster slab to the memory of Thomas Columbell and his wife Agnes. This family built the manor of Nether Hall, or Whitehall, which was a second manor in the parish of Darley, from 1370. Previously this manor also belonged to a branch of the De Darleys, but came into the possession of the Columbells when Thomas married Agnes, the sister and heir of Sir Ralph Darley. The Columbells held this manor for eleven generations, until 1687. In 1790 Sir Richard Arkwright, the cotton spinner, bought it and pulled down the house and used the materials to build a new house lower down the hill.

The aged yew tree referred to by Byng was still in existence in 1877 when Cox wrote the history of the Derbyshire Churches. He thinks with other authorities, that it dates from the twelfth century. He measured it in 1877 and found its circumference at the widest part to be a few inches over 32 feet. The tree is still flourishing, or was in 1928.

(37) John Julius Angerstein, of Pall Mall, whose collection was bought for the National Gallery. There is a good deal of information about his collection in W. T. Whitley's *Art in England, 1821-37*, published by the Cambridge University Press.

(38) Willersley Castle was begun by Sir Richard Arkwright shortly before his death in 1792, but he did not live to occupy it. It was burnt down before it was ever used and had to be rebuilt.

(39) This Act of Parliament refers to the Cromford Canal, which was built by the Arkwright in 1793 and ran for a distance parallel to the River Derwent. It was a great success up to 1850 (when the Matlock Railway was opened) and used to carry not only lime, coal and all sorts of merchandise,

but also passengers to the baths at Matlock. It did not interfere with the river or destroy its beauty as Byng feared it might do.

(40) This was made of stone found in the natural caverns which abound in this district, or quarried from the rocks even in the town itself, which is much disfigured by these quarries. The chief mineral of which they are made is *fluor-spar* and its beautiful variety Blue John, which when polished make objects of great beauty.

(41) Now thoroughly renovated and inhabited by the Duke of Rutland, whose family have possessed it since the marriage of Dorothy Vernon, daughter of Sir George Vernon (1508-67) with John Manners. Before that it belonged to the Vernons and had been inhabited by them for four hundred years. The hall was fully furnished and used continuously until 1702, in which year the Duke of Rutland abandoned Haddon for Belvoir, though it was not dismantled till 1730. He and his successors continued to keep the fabric in good repair, and the above dates agree with Byng's statement that open house was kept for the 12 days of January and 'was allways done (even at the beginning of this century) by the Rutlands.'

(42) The death of Mr. Lewis Secard, 'a considerable picture dealer in Pall Mall', who died in March 1793, is recorded in the *Gentleman's Magazine* of that year, Vol. I, p. 378.

(43) In a Directory of Derbyshire for 1829 there is at Bakewell 'White Watson, F.L.S., professor of mineralogy and sculptor, Bath House', probably the same.

(44) The first baronet, created 1784, was born in 1748, son of William Fitzherbert and Mary Poyntz Meynell of Bradley, and died in 1791. The Fitzherberts are a very old family who trace their pedigree back to Thomas Fitzherbert, *c.* 1268, and they came into possession of Tissington Hall, a fine Elizabethan mansion, by the marriage of Nicholas with Margaret Frauncis about 1450.

(45) Dr. Taylor was born at Ashbourne, or baptised there, on March 18, 1710. Son of an Ashbourne attorney, he went to Mr. John Hunter's school at Lichfield, where he became acquainted with and remained the lifelong friend of Dr. Samuel Johnson. He went to Christ Church, Oxford, March 1728-9, and became an M.A. in 1742 and an LL.D. in 1752. He was intended for a lawyer, but decided to take orders and was admitted sometime between 1736 and 1740. He was never Vicar of Ashbourne, but preached occasionally in the church, and Dr. Johnson composed many of his sermons. He resided chiefly at Ashbourne, occupying himself with breeding cattle, horses, pigs and sheep, and with other agricultural pursuits. He was J.P. for Leicestershire and later for Derbyshire, and held a prominent place in the public and social life of the place and was called 'the King of Ashbourne'. Dr. Johnson visited him on many occasions, often staying with him for several months. The most notable visit was the one in 1777 with Boswell, who records the incidents of the visit very fully in his *Life of*

Johnson. Johnson also came to stay with Taylor in the last few months of his life in the hope that it would improve his failing health. Dr. Taylor read the burial service over Dr. Johnson at Westminster Abbey on 20th Dec. 1784. He himself died at Ashbourne on the 29th February 1788, and is buried in the parish church.

(46) The present edifice was consecrated in 1241—the original tablet recording the fact still exists—and is a beautiful Early English building with late additions, especially the graceful decorated spire 212 feet in height. In 1789, when Byng visited it, the walls were whitewashed, many of the beautiful lancet windows bricked up, 'to keep the church warm', and there was a lath and plaster screen enclosing the organ. The spire is termed 'the Pride of the Peak', and George Elliot described the church as 'the finest mere parish church in the kingdom.' Byng evidently saw the building under the worst conditions. There is an account in the Church Reports dated 10th May, 1710, of the erection of the 'great organ' on which Wynn played. It was made by Henry Valentine of Leicester and completed by the following September, when a series of elaborate services and concerts were held to celebrate the opening.

(47) The seat of the Okeovers is on the opposite bank of the River Dove at Okeover, in Staffordshire. The River Dove is the boundary between Derbyshire and Staffordshire for a large part of its course. To the Okeovers also belongs the village of Mapleton on the Derbyshire side of the river. The Okeover family have been Lords of Okeover for upwards of 800 years, being one of the few old families which have held the same manor and lands without intermission since Saxon times. The Raphael picture mentioned a little later is still in the Okeover drawing-room at Okeover Hall—a Queen Anne house, red brick with stone facings and portico. Cf. description in Young's *Tour Through the East of England*, I, p. 189.

(48) Mrs Siddons. Cp. note 23.

(49) Isaac Walton's *Compleat Angler*, Part II, chapter ii.

(50) The word 'shroven,' used also in the Tours of 1781, 1790 and 1792, may have been employed in error as the past participle of the verb 'shrive', which J. Wright in his *English Dialect Dictionary* records as having been used in Kent in the sense of 'to prune trees', 'to clear the small branches from the trunk of a tree.'

(51) The hall, at which Mr. Port lived, is in a beautiful valley on the banks of the Manifold River about a mile before it pours its waters into the Dove. The Port family held Ilam from Tudor times until the beginning of the nineteenth century. The old house which Byng saw was pulled down in 1840 and rebuilt by Mr. Jesse Watts Russell. In a grotto in the grounds (which is still shown), Congreve, the dramatist (1670-1729), is said to have written some scenes of his comedy *The Old Batchelor* in 1693, at which time the Ports lived at Ilam. The west side of Dovedale, which is in Staffordshire, belonged to the Ports of Ilam in those days; the eastern side is in

Derbyshire and was owned by Sir William Fitzherbert. The Fitzherberts still own that side of Dovedale; and recently acquired the Staffordshire side by purchase, so that the whole of Dovedale is now in the possession of the present representative of the Fitzherberts of Tissington. Arthur Young (*Tour through the East of England*, I, p. 190) says: 'the gardens are the most romantic in England.'

(52) Hasingdon is an error—it has never been called anything but Hanson. Hanson Grange is a fine old Derbyshire homestead on the hill-top at the side of Dove Dale, and its antiquity is shown by the fact that it was in possession of the abbey of Buxton as early as the beginning of the thirteenth century.

The Goulds, an old-established Derbyshire family of yeomen, came into possession of Hanson Grange by a union with the Beresfords at the beginning of the eighteenth century, and Nat Gould, the author, was a member of this family.

(53) This inn is still in existence between Ashbourne and Dovedale. It is an old-fashioned stone house with thick walls and small windows, and is now conducted as a hotel and patronised by visitors to Dovedale.

(54) In Byng's time Sir Brook Boothby owned Ashbourne Hall, which was situated at the east end of the town, with the main entrance to its grounds opening out at the end of the main street. The hall did not 'descend to them from the Cockaines'; it was bought by Sir William Boothby, Bart., from Sir Aston Cockayne in 1671. He had got into pecuniary difficulties and had to sell, though the hall and manor of Ashbourne had been in the possession of the Cockayne family since the reign of Edward I.

Sir Brooke Boothby was the 6th baronet. He succeeded his father, Sir Brooke, 5th baronet, in April 1789 (the year of Byng's tour), and was the father of the famous Penelope whose monument in Ashbourne Church by Banks is one of the masterpieces of sculpture.

The hall has no pretentions to architecture, beauty or even interest. The old hall is noted as the resting place of the Young Pretender and his officers on their way through Ashbourne both on the disastrous march to Derby and on the retreat a few days later. The names of the party were chalked on the doors of the rooms; one of the doors was preserved in the new building, that of Prince Charlie's room, and is still shown, though the park and grounds have been cut up and built over and the hall converted into flats, the Boothbys having left the neighbourhood early in the nineteenth century.

(55) In Staffordshire. These mines are reached by crossing the River Dove below the village of Alstonfield—Austenfield in the Diary—and the horses were sent on to Warslow—called Warsall by the diarist.

The mines at Ecton, which run horizontally into Ecton Hill, one of the hills that bound the Manifold valley, were worked chiefly in the eighteenth century, and at that time produced a fair amount of copper and lead. They belonged to the Duke of Devonshire, and with the proceeds of the mines he built the Crescent at Buxton (completed in 1789), which town he was at that time making great efforts to establish as a spa in opposition to Bath and Cheltenham.

Byng refers to the 'body of water' in the mine. The mines were in limestone, in which there are often underground streams; such underground streams are very common in this neighbourhood. The River Manifold close by disappears beneath the ground, and in dry weather runs for some miles altogether underground.

(56) The word 'boor' is probably a phonetic rendering of the first syllable of the German word *Bursche* or *Burschen*, referring to the colleges and student life of Germany. The societies of students were called *Burschenschafts*—a word invented in imitation of *Landsmannschafts*, the name given to the guilds of workers or traders. The word *Bursche* referred at first to the groups of students who lived together in a burse or college, and it was such a burse which was called to Byng's mind by his apartments and surroundings in the village inn at Warslow.

(57) No doubt Roger Kemble—actor and theatrical manager—1712-1802, Mrs Siddons' father.

(58) The manors of Markeaton and Mackworth have always been held together, and came into the possession of the Mundy family about the year 1516, when Lord Audley sold them to John Mundy, citizen of London and Lord Mayor in 1522. The manors had been held by the Mundys, and the family have resided at Markeaton Hall until recently, though the old hall of wood and plaster was pulled down in 1755 and the present mansion built in its place. To-day the two manors are separated, Markeaton being owned by the Corporation of Derby.

(59) The manufacture of silk was in the exclusive possession of the Italians until a native of Derby, John Lombe, went to Italy and managed to procure by bribery and otherwise, drawings and models of the machines necessary for the undertaking. He returned to England in 1717 and decided on Derby as the most suitable place for a mill, and acquired from the Corporation an island in the River Derwent and there established his mill. The industry rapidly increased during the early part of the nineteenth century, but after 1861 declined owing to the competition with France. The manufacture of silk in Derby came to an end in the early part of the present century, and the old mill was pulled down by the Corporation.

(60) There is a good and dramatic account of the burning of the Opera House on June 18th in the *Annual Register*, 1789 (p. 211).

(61) The industry was established in Derby in 1750 by William Duesbury and remained in his family for two generations. The eldest of the Duesburys bought the Chelsea factory and plant at Bow, closing these two works and manufacturing only in Derby. The industry was enlarged in 1876 to try and capture the overseas market. It continues to-day under the title of the Royal Crown Derby Porcelain Company Limited.

in 1877 by Mr. Phillips of the Worcester Royal Porcelain Works, and still continues under the title of the Derby Royal Crown China Company.

(62) St. Mary's Bridge, on which was a chapel, 'St. Mary Chappell,' which has recently been restored (1931). The bridge was rebuilt (as Byng said it was going to be) in 1788, because the old one was very lofty and narrow.

(63) The manor-house, the family mansion of the Stathums and Sacheverells, did stand quite close to the church at its north-west angle, and there was a private entrance from this house into the church.

(64) The Minister or Rector of Morley in 1789 was Robert Wilmot, appointed 1777 and died in 1804. As Byng said, the church and vicarage have a fine situation; and the church has many old and interesting features. The cross is still there, and originally stood on the village green. It is of fourteenth-century date.

(65) (Or Stathums) who owned Morley for four generations; and many monuments to their memory are found in the church. In the sixteenth century the estates came into possession of the Sacheverells by the marriage of Joan, sole heiress of Henry Stathum, with John Sacheverell, whose descendants have held them until the present day. A union with the Sitwells gave rise to the Sacheverell Sitwells, whose descendants hold an important place in literature, etc., at the present time.

(66) Was dissolved and the church destroyed in 1539. The materials were brought by Francis Pole of Radbourn, who removed the carved work to the church of Radbourn, while the stained glass and the windows in which it was placed were taken to the church at Morley and there erected.

(67) Byng's water-colours in the Diary vary considerably both in spirit and workmanship. The best have a remarkably modern appreciation of design. (See article in *The Studio*, 1934.)

(68) The Countess of Huntingdon, wife of the 9th Earl, was converted to Methodism about 1735. She knew the Wesleys and employed White-field and others as chaplains to the chapels she built and established, first at Brighton and then in London, Bath, Tunbridge and many other places. Her branch of Methodism was called 'Lady Huntingdon's Connection.'

(69) The earliest member of this family was Henry de Ferrers, who came over with the Conqueror. He held 220 lordships, including 114 in Derbyshire. His son became Earl of Derby and Earl Ferrers. There have been many branches of the family, and many connections with illustrious English families, and many seats associated with them. The present earldom is not continuous from the Earls Ferrers of Norman times. The Earl Ferrers of Byng's day was a Shirley and was descended from the Ferrers of Chartley, County Stafford. Their chief seat at the present day is at Staunton Harold, as it was in 1796.

(70) Calke Abbey is adjacent to the estate of Earl Ferrers at Staunton

Harold. Henry Harpur, the 1st baronet, was created baronet in 1626 and came of an ancient Warwickshire family. The Harpurs moved into Derbyshire in the reign of Elizabeth. The 9th baronet (great grandson of Sir Henry) married one of the co-heiresses of Lord Crewe, and the 7th baronet assumed the name of Crewe in 1808, and his descendants have been styled Harpur-Crewe ever since that date and still live at Calke Abbey. The present house was built at the beginning of the eighteenth century, and would be the house seen by Byng. It stands on the site of the old Austinian Priory (founded in the twelfth century), and part of the old building was probably incorporated with it, as some of the walls of the house are over 6 ft. thick. The present church is not the one described by Byng, as it was rebuilt in 1826.

(71) There is good early Norman work of the eleventh century (not Saxon, as Byng says).

(72) All the old farm-houses and many of the manor-houses had rooms for the storage of cheese, which was made largely in Derbyshire up to the end of the nineteenth century. This particular building at the west end of the church of Melbourne is an old tithe-barn of the Bishops of Carlisle, and would certainly have cheese rooms.

(73) Melbourne Hall was built about 1700, but is of no special interest, though the gardens are famous for their topiary work and are in the original Dutch style introduced by William of Orange. The hall descended by the marriage in 1740 of Thomas Coke's daughter to a Mr. Matthew Lamb. He was created a baronet, and his son, Sir Peniston, was raised to the peerage in 1780 with the title of Baron Melbourne. His grandson became Viscount Melbourne, Queen Victoria's first Prime Minister.

(74) Donnington Hall, in Donnington Park, near the village of Castle Donnington, became the principal residence of the Earls of Huntingdon when Ashby Castle was demolished in the seventeenth century. It is described in 1789 as a 'patch work of different periods, blazoned out with disgusting yellow colour.' It was pulled down in 1793 by Lord Rawdon, who succeeded to the property on the death of his uncle the 10th Earl of Huntingdon, and was rebuilt by him in a pseudo-Gothic style. The park was converted into a motor-cycle racing track in 1932, the mansion being used in connection with it.

(75) There is a full account of Anna Maria Crouch, the 'vocalist' (1763-1805), in the *Dictionary of National Biography*.

(76) Cranbourne Alley, now Cranbourne Street, Leicester Square, was in the eighteenth century famous for cheap bonnets and millinery, and the phrase 'Cranbourne Alley' came to be used in the same pejorative sense as 'Brummagem'.

(77) George Cumberland, the author of many plays, well known at the time; he was born in 1732 and died in 1811. Byng recounts having seen a

performance of his *West Indian* at Cheltenham in 1781. The life of Cumberland is fully described in the *Dictionary of National Biography*.

(78) The well-known astrologer and prophet (1602-81), who was satirised by Butler in his *Hudibras*. Lillie's autobiography was published posthumously in 1715.

(79) Belton is included in William Burton's *Description of Leicestershire*, 1622, and it is stated (p. 42) that 'this town hath two fairs, one upon the Friday after Trinity Sunday; another upon the 15th of August.'

(80) Thomas Arnold, M.D., 1742-1816, the physician and writer on insanity, was born at, and practised at Leicester. He was deservedly popular and was the owner and conductor of a large lunatic asylum. 'In a word, he was an enlightened ornament of his native town.' (*Gentleman's Magazine*.) Francis Willis, M.D., the physician (1718-1807), was called in on George III's first attack of madness on December 5th, 1788. Although a specialist on mental diseases his views were always considered rather unconventional.

(81) John Peter Allamand (†1790), freeman of Leicester, 1778. (See Hartopp's *Freemen of Leicester*, II, p. 11.)

(82) Arthur Young (*Tour through the East of England*, 1781, I, pp. 80-81) speaks of Schuckburgh Ashby (not Ashley) of Quenby Hall very highly. 'It is an old house, built in the reign of *Elizabeth*, but what is very extraordinary, in an admirable situation, being on a very high eminence, finely wooded that commands all the country. . . . Around the house is a great terrass which commands a great variety of prospect. . . . These works are very noble: they ornament a country, promote industry,—promote that useful circulation which should ever attend the residence of a man of fortune.'

(83) This club was founded in Leicester for the cultivation of principles of political progress and parliamentary reform, and was called the Revolution Club in recognition of the principles secured to the English people by William III. Mrs. T. Fielding Johnson's *Glimpses of Ancient Leicester* (1891) and many other books on Leicester give accounts of it.

(84) This no doubt refers to Sir William Wyggeston's Hospital, of which there are full accounts in Thompson's *History of Leicester*, Vol. I, 217-21, and in Mrs. Fielding Johnson's *Glimpses of Ancient Leicester*, p. 132.

(85) After his defeat at Naseby. The original is now in the British Museum, having passed through various sale rooms in 1855, 1869, 1876 and 1917.

(86) Rector of Ashbourne. Dr. Taylor was *not* Rector of Ashbourne. He was a parson and held many curacies, but resided in Ashbourne in a house now called The Mansion which was left to him by his father, an Ashbourne attorney; and he had a large estate and spent his time breeding cattle, horses, bull-dogs, etc. He occasionally preached at the church of Ashbourne, and Dr. Johnson wrote the sermons for him; but he had no official connection with the church. (See note 45.)

(87) Bosworth Hall is a good example of the English Renaissance, and was built about the year 1700. It was the seat of the Dixie family for about 300 years until forty years ago. Sir Wolstan Dixie purchased the hall in the time of Queen Elizabeth, and it was a descendant, another Wolstan Dixie, who by his overbearing pomposity and dictatorial manner as a trustee, caused Dr. Johnson in 1732 to give up the ushership of the Grammar School of Market Bosworth after holding the appointment only a few months.

(88) A hat made of thin strips of wood, probably willow.

(89) Thomas Jenkins, painter, banker and dealer of antiques in Rome. Died 1798.

(90) *The Beauties of England (Warwickshire)*, by John Britton, F.S.A. (1814), has a good account of Coleshill and the Digby family.

(91) John Hough (1651-1743), Bishop of Worcester (see *D.N.B.*).

(92) *The Beauties of England (Warwickshire)*, by John Britton, F.S.A. (1814), gives details of Blythe Hall and Dugdale.

(93) Maxstoke Castle, the seat of the Dilke family, is fully dealt with in the *Views and Seats of the Noblemen and Gentlemen of England, Wales and Scotland*, by J. P. Neale, 1821, Vol. IV.

(94) Heneage (Finch), 4th Earl of Aylesford (1751-1812). His principal amusement is said to have been 'pistol-shooting.' The estate of Packington came into the family with Mary Fisher, wife of the 2nd Earl, and is the principal Aylesford residence.

(95) For another traveller's opinion of the Bull's Head, see Cobbett's *Rural Rides* (Cole's edition), p. 853.

(96) George (Granville), 1st Marquis (cr. 1784), Lord Lieut. of Ireland for four days in 1783, and again from 1787 to 1789 (September 30). He returned to England the same October.

(97) Richard (Temple-Nugent-Brides-Chandos-Grenville), the eldest son of the 1st Marquess of Buckingham (1776-1839), was known (1784-1813) as Earl Temple. Married the only daughter and heiress of the 3rd Duke of Chandos and was created (1822) 1st Duke of Buckingham and Chandos.

(98) Are probably Thomas and William Palmer. (Cf. *Torrington Diaries*, Vol. I, Tour into North Wales, 1784.)

(99) In Neale's *Views of the Seats of Noblemen and Gentlemen*, 1821, Vol. IV, it is stated 'At a short distance from Packington is the Forest Hall, a small but pleasing building erected for the accommodation of a society of archers called "The Woodmen of Arden" who hold periodical meetings and exercise the bow for honorary prizes.'

(100) Lord Aylesford, whose residence was Packington Park.

(101) Mr Greathead of Guy's Cliff, mentioned also in Tours of 1781 and 1785.

(102) 'These two last remaining gates' evidently refers to the two that are still standing and have recently been restored (1933).

(103) Probably Francis, Earl (1793, Marquess) of Hertford (see *Dictionary of National Biography*).

(104) The seat of the Craven family.

(105) The famous Lancelot Brown is mentioned several times in these Diaries. He was the great reviver of the 'natural' type of landscape gardening, which eventually, however, became in itself a mannerism.

(106) It is possible that the reference is to advertisement signs, corresponding to the present-day poster, supplied to agents to affix outside their premises for advertising purposes, and that an enterprising local agent was sending them round the countryside following a sensational fire or series of fires, possibly on farms. Or, more likely, the wagons themselves were insured and bore metal badges similar to those the insurance companies used to put on all houses insured by them.

(107) Probably to replace the rushlight with what Byng calls 'its expiring stink.'

(108) Sir George Page Turner, Bart., of Battlesden House, Bedfordshire, near Woburn Abbey, who inherited the baronetcy in 1766 and died in 1805, adding the name Page in 1775.

(109) The Duke of Bedford would probably be residing at Woburn Abbey in 1789, as it was the principal ducal residence. The Duke at this date was Francis, 5th Duke of Bedford, who succeeded to the dukedom at six years of age. He was born on the 23rd of July, 1765, and died on the 2nd of March, 1802, unmarried, at the age of 36. He was succeeded by his brother John, who married Georgina Elizabeth Byng, second daughter of George, 4th Viscount Torrington.

(110) The Prince of Wales.

A TOUR IN THE MIDLANDS: 1790

Day	To What Place	Inns	Miles
Monday June 7	From 7 o'clock this morning till 2 o'clock in the next morning in the stage coach.	Bell.	100
Tuesday June 8	By a roundabout to Castle Dunnington	Turks Head. G.	20
Wednesday June 9	By — To Derby.	Bell. T.	16
Thursday June 10	To Ashburn. To Buxton.	Blackamoors Hd. Hall's Hotel. T.	33
Friday June 11	To Tidswell & back.	New George. T.	15
Saturday June 12	To Macclesfield. To Knutsford.	Angel. T. George. G.	23
Sunday June 13	To Altrincham. To Stockport.	Unicorn. T. White Lion. T.	16
Monday June 14	By — To Dishley.	Rams Head. G.	10
Tuesday June 15	Morning ride; and to Buxton.	Hotel. T.	16
Wednesday June 16	—	—	—
Thursday June 17	By — To Bakewell.	White Horse. B.	15
Friday June 18	By Winstre, &c, To Cromford.	Black dog. T.	15
Saturday June 19	To Wingfield Manor; and back.	—	12
Sunday June 20	To Buxton. To Dishley.	White Hart. B. Rams Hd. G.	30
Monday June 21	To Altrincham & by D.M. To Manchester.	Unicorn. T. Bridgewater Arms. B.	25
Tuesday June 22	Manchester.	—	—
Wednesday June 23	Towards London.	—	—
Monday June 28.	In the stage coach to Wansford-Bridge	Haycock. G.	84
Tuesday June 29	Riding in the morning.	—	6
Wednesday June 30	A morning ride. In the evening to Stamford & back.	—	16
Thursday July 1	In the evening to Thorney.	Dukes Head. B.	15
Friday July 2	To Crowland. To Spalding. To Boston.	Marquis Granby. B. W. Hart. T. Peacock. T.	34

Day	To What Place	Inns	Miles
Saturday July 3	To Holbeach.	Chequers. G.	16
Sunday July 4	To Wisbich.	White Hart. B.	34
	To Chatteris.	George. G.	
Monday July 5	To Ely.	Lamb. B.	28
	To Cambridge.	B. Bull.	
Tuesday July 6	To Arrington;	Talbot. T.	27
	To Huntingdon.	George. G.	
Wednesday July 7	To Alconbury Hill.	Wheat Sheaf.	20
	To Wansford Bridge.	Haycock. G.	
Thursday July 8	To Elton and to Fotheringay	—	12
Friday July 9	To Easton &c; and back.	—	13
Saturday July 10	Morning & evening rides.	—	10
Sunday July 11	To Apthorp, Kings Cliff, and back. Evening ride.	—	16
Monday July 12	To Elton & Chesterton.	—	10
Tuesday July 13	A morning ride.	—	5
Wednesday July 14	A short ride.	—	6
Thursday July 15	A do.	—	6
Friday July 16	Around Burleigh Park & back.	—	14
Saturday July 17	Fishing.	—	—
Sunday July 18	To Apthorp & back.	—	10
Monday July 19	To Alconbury Hill;	Wheatsheaf. T.	41
	To Eaton;	Cock. T.	
	To Biggleswade.	Sun. G.	
Tuesday July 20	In the stage coach, (45 miles) to London.	—	—

A Tour in the Midlands

1790

I AM just old enough to remember turnpike roads few, and those bad; and when travelling was slow, difficult, and, in carriages, somewhat dangerous : but I am of the very few, (perhaps alone,) who regret the times (I mean not living in them) when England afforded to the pleasure of the observant traveller, a variety of manners, dress and dialect.—In former tours I have (*gravely* and *wisely*) remark'd upon the influx of vice pour'd in upon every corner of the country by the quick and easy communication of travell.—In the days of bad roads, the country cou'd not be strip'd of its timber, or despoil'd of its honesty, cheapness, ancient customs, and civility: every gentleman, then, was bow'd to with reverence, and 'A good morning to you, master, Good evening, Good journey to you Sir', were allways presented; with every old-fashion'd wish, and compliment of the season: now, every abuse, and trickery of London are ready to be play'd off upon you.

A priggish, impudent waiter from Covent Garden, has succeeded the drawer, with his bushy wig, and blue apron; and pert jockeys, and conceited chambermaids, have driven out the steady hostler, and the careful chamberlain. —I have been told, that a century ago, people made their wills, e're they began a long journey.—When the Prince of Orange was press'd by the Earl of Danby to land in the north, in 1688, his advice was overuled by the statement of the very bad roads near London; even till lately, there were hollow ways from Grays-Inn Lane to Kentish Town, and a long, deep water to be waded thro' from Mother Red-Caps in the road to Highgate. All the Hertfordshire roads were deep ravines. The following extracts from a touring account will exhibit the strange touring of travelling in thirty-five years.

Nottingham,
White-Lion,
Sunday, July 20, 1755.

Dear Brother and Sister,

After a very delightful journey of two days, our friend Mr B. and myself arrived here in good health: and as I promised to give you a particular account of every thing I thought worth notice in our travels, without further ceremony, I begin as follows.

We set out *Friday* the 18th, at five in the morning, from *St John's* Street, most miserably equipt with an old tatter'd two-wheel'd post-chaise, and a couple of founder'd horses; the harness was mended three times before we finished our stage at *Barnet*; but when we found both cattle and tackle belonged to a collar-maker there, we were not surprised, concluding the horses were only purchased for their hides, which he took care to weat sufficiently before they were converted into leather. We set forward from thence somewhat better accouter'd for *St Alban's*, where we breakfasted;

From *Northampton* we set out at five the next morning for *Market-Harborough*, where we breakfasted, but found nothing worth notice. From thence to *Leicester* we went in a two-wheel'd chaise, with a comical boy for a driver, who had all the airs and motions of a horse-courser, which he practised in so affected a manner as gave us great diversion; a monkey on horseback could not have cut a more droll figure.

We passed by a fine seat of Lord *Byron's* at *Newstead*, and got to *Mansfield* to dinner.

Here we met with a difficulty how to get any further; one chaise only was to be had in the town, and that an open four-wheel'd one with a coach-box; but no driver was to be found, except the hostler of the inn, a raw ignorant fellow, not a descendent of the family of *Jehu*, and who knew not a step of the road; however we made a virtue of necessity; and being informed he was sober, and would be careful, we accepted him, and also took a guide to conduct us by *Balborough* to *Chesterfield*.

A two-wheel'd post-chaise, with rotten harness and founder'd horses, was hired of a collar-maker! From Market-Harboro' to Leicester they went in another two wheeled chaise, driven by a boy unused to driving! How

'Upon a sufficient horse, with a small portmanteau behind me, like this old-fashioned traveller, so well engraved by Hollar'

[*see p.* 151

could people submit to such inconveniences as these; or
how people brave the races, and dangers of modern travelling, is to me wonderful: when horses of safe, and quiet
conduct are easily to be procured! To me, who feel every
wish to move at my own pace, at my own hours; and, if
upon a sufficient horse, with a small portmanteau behind
me, like this old-fashion'd traveller, so well engraved by
Hollar.[1]

Nor could Mansfield afford more than one open four
wheel'd chaise; for which a driver was with difficulty
found. The road from Mansfield to Chesterfield, now so
broad, beaten and frequented by mail-coaches, then required a guide! Happy days; when the traveller had food
for observation in plenty, as well as animal food on the
easiest terms; as we read in the following bill of fare, and
charge, at Burton upon Trent.

'Burton consists of one long, regular street, at the top of which is a cross
street, forming a T; at the end of the cross street is the bridge, supported
upon 37 arches, and at least a quarter of a mile in length, tho' it has not a
very stately appearance, the arches being equally too low, and too narrow.
At this town we fared cheaper than at any other place in our journey: we
ordered two fowls for supper, and had beside, a dish of tarts, and cheese and
butter; for the whole of which, including bread and small beer, we were
charged but eight-pence a head, and a groat for our servant. Here we
lodged, and next morning discharged our *Mansfield* vehicle.'

As for the expenses on the road, they are finely varied
from those of the present day; provisions then kill'd, must
be dress'd at home, and cou'd not be pack'd off in the instant to London, to supply that enormous stomach.

Most inns, now, are kept by, and for a change of post
horses, as fine gentlemen never step out of their chaises in
the longest journies; and all others travell in the mail, or
post coaches: so that the tourist who wants only a supper,
and a bed, is consider'd as a troublesome unprofitable in-
truder; nor is it necessary to tempt him by good liquors,
and civility. However I who love the passage thro' fresh air,
and a new country, will continue to stop at inns, and there
to revert to former times, when the jolly host with his civil

helpmate, having loaded the crackling hearth, awaited with impatience the arrival of the stage coach from London.—

So much for the ideas of past travell. Now let me indulge my notions on the arrangement of any future party I may engage in; and none can I ever listen to, unless these rules will be observed, as a basis of peace, and pleasure; and for the prevention of misunderstanding, or laying a foundation of dislike:—Here they follow

1. If one servant; a mutual payment: and the baggage of each to be weigh'd; and to be of equal weight.—
2. If horses are fed equally, then to be paid out of the stock.
3. As no two people can agree about hours, the hours and intended places of dining, and sleeping, shou'd be named; then come, if you can, or will.
4. Meals apart, to be paid separately.—
5. A settlement of stock-purse once a week.—
6. One halting day (at least) in a week:—more, if necessary, or agreed to.
7. If each person takes a servant, then they may carry what luggage they like; and feed their horses as they like.
8. Choice of beds, if a difference, decided by a toss up.
9. Whoever stays latest at the inn, in the morning, settles the reckoning.
10. No luxuries, unless paid separately, to be called for; but by mutual agreement.

Monday June 7

Buxton strikes me as a good excuse for hurrying from London, to relieve a set of nerves nearly worn out; or like an old huntsman flying from a pack of hounds just ready to devour him: 'And since it's hard to combat, learns to fly.'

I leave town, every year, with more pleasure, from being incapable, (call it so,) of tasting the *delights* of fashionable hours, and from ignorance of the fashionable tongue; hoping that, even yet, there must exist in the country, by the want of baneful intercourse, somewhat more purity, and civility; where you may escape eternal insult, and viewing the ill-treatment of every animal who cannot resist:—Be-

152

sides, the uproar of a small London house, with stairs like
Jacob's Ladder, makes my blood to boil; in every sense of
the word.—I believe that nurses are selldom either honest,
or sober; but I leave Mrs B. on the mending hand, and
find myself, without quiet, or country air, to be on the un-
mending hand.—T. B[ush] is gone forward, 3 days in advance, upon a black Galloway; leading my grey poney:

At 7 o'clock in the morning I was push'd into the
Manchester coach with three women: one fat creature like
a cook; one large, and younger in a linnen great coat; the
third, older, in a blue great coat; and then learnt that we
were to take up two more females at Islington: tho' the
coach cou'd but just hold four.—When we had receiv'd
and stow'd our complement; much frippery discourse
arose about London, its delights, and fine places, as Bagnigge Wells,[2] &c. Glorious weather: I skulk'd at a corner,
and endured. The blue gt. coat, going to Manchester, was
escorted by a young man, who rode on the coach box, and
drove; the large great-coat, the cook, and the two young
Islingtons were going to Derby; these two last had never
been far from home.—Change horses at Kitts-Inn;[3] at Redburn; and at Dunstable; where dinner was prepared for Dunstable
us at 12 o'clock.

Here arose a schis'm; for the young delights of Islington, with the blue-coat, and the young man, disdaining
dinner, wou'd walk forward; leaving the two large ladies,
with an outside woman, to feast on a coarse, boiled leg of
mutton, and a large neck of veal roasted; which I did allso,
and order'd, at *mine own charge*, a pint of red *wine* to entertain the ladies.—My company now remark'd, with much
asperity, on the strange behaviour of the others; and Miss
H., the bouncing gt. coat, in her anger, declared them to
be *significant* and *illiterate* creatures.—After my dinner of
two ounces, I walk'd on, and had almost joined the
advanced party, when the coach overtook us; being re-
pack'd, there began a sparring match; for Miss H., on
seeing the poor, stop, man, at Dunstable Hill, declared,

'That when she came to town, the *then-genteel* passengers collected for him 2 shillings; but then *they* were not a *stingy, mean* party'! This roused the spirit of an Islington miss, who sharply answer'd, 'That some *folks* might *flash away* without being able to afford it'.—Here, luckily, the contest drop'd; and we sulk'd along in much heat, and inconvenience: as for myself, being bodkin'd and surrounded by high, and wide flat caps, I cou'd neither stir, or breath, or see out of the windows; but was as much conceal'd by my guards, as could be the Grand-Signor by his Janizaries Turbans.—

Pass Woburn; drag thro' the sands; change horses near Newport: and, after a tedious crawl, reach Northampton at 8 o'clock.—Northamptonshire is a dreary, stoney, county, devoid of features; and if there are seats in it which appear to some advantage, from a contrast, they can only suit a fox-hunter.—Here were quarter'd the Nthn. Regiment, whose drums rattled the Retreat with unusual clamour: surely these noises must be a sad, and dangerous nuisance. —Whilst a change of coaches was preparing, the older ladies revell'd in tea, and the Islingtons sipp'd coffee, who were reproved by me for being all new dress'd; 'Your old worst cloaths, (I told them,) were fittest for travelling'. Resuming the coach, the tea (which caused *strong* perspirations) sat the ladies tongues a-wagging, and developed their characters; for now the younger four (the cook and I taking no part) began an elaborate discourse about fashions, feathers, robes, bodies, French backs, &c. &c. and then Miss H— proclaim'd herself a mantuamaker, told them for whom, and at what prices she work'd; (meaning to serve the Miss Islingtons;) and brag'd of her getting silver'd muslins; and that she had equipp'd, last year, the Sheriff's lady going to *a consort* at Leicester:—The old-blue also spake so scientifically, that I should think they were of the same business, and that they had been up to town to see, and study fashions; and to view (as they said) 'The *Qualaty* going into the birth-day,[4] and who walk'd in

St. James's Park of a Sunday evening, and who were dress'd so *fancically*.'

Never was heard a greater flow of English language more barbarously treated!—Night soon overshading us, the fat cook took from her pocket a pint bottle of Nantz, which I, and the old blue, likewise, held to our mouths; whilst the refined party, complaining of head-achs, wou'd only be cheer'd by salts. It was eleven o'clock when we reach'd Harboro'; there chang'd horses; and at ½ past one we enter'd Leicester:—My legs cramp'd double, and my hips sore. Leicester

To please ladies, of the above description, in conversation, I cannot, for they require a second hand, servants hall ribaldry, or an affected refinement. Miss H— spake of ladies being lighted, who had been with child; and she brag'd of the Derby market, as abundant of meat, and *what not*, and likewise of garden stuff; at which the Islingtons were much surprised; she also said that the quantity of pots sold was astonishing; to which I remark'd 'That was a very necessary article.'—A cold supper was prepared at the Bell Alehouse; but my intentions being, if possible, for quiet, comfort, and a good supper at the 3 Cranes, to that inn I went; but in vain did I bawl, and thunder at the gate, as no one wou'd, or cou'd hear me: so in despair I return'd to my *agreeable* friends, and to the coach supper; and then, by the softest language, prevail'd upon the landlady to give me a bed; which was a miserable press, at a corner of a large, smoking club room, wherein I toss'd about till the morning, with the impatience of a school-boy for the 1st day of his holidays.

An early morning without doubt. No abiding in such an alehouse.—Paid a shilling for supper; a shilling for brandy; and a shilling for my bed, which was sheeted, contrary, to my orders; but they were put to their best purpose, height'ning my boltster. *Tuesday June 8*

At seven o'clock, taking my parcell under my arm, I

went to the 3 Cranes; and there found (much to my satisfaction) my horses in excellent plight. After ablutions, shaving, &c, I sought Mr O[liver] Distributer of Stamps,[5] desiring his company at breakfast; when he speedily came, and then, full of civility, not only furnish'd me with the means of procedure, but wou'd be my guide.

We left Leicester at eleven o'clock: the 3 Cranes Inn has suffer'd much by the death of the landlord, I. P. Allamand, whose widow is going to quit the house; there has been an inventory taken of the stock amounting to 6000£.

A true Leicestershire road, of stones and sloughs, brought us to the village of Anstey; and soon after to the confines of Bradgate-Park.—In most of my tours I have been held back; but now I am alone, and resolv'd to move, and keep my own hours.—Bradgate has been dismantled of its timber, and its keeping, tho' not stock'd with deer; and the house was long since burnt.—It was, I conclude, and might be restored to, I am certain a noble place; for the grounds are very bold, and diversified, and a trout stream, capable of any formation, twines thro' the valley; but it wou'd require a great sum to render it complete. _{Bradgate Park}

Beneath the ruins, and within old walls, Ld Stamford's fox hounds, a noble and celebrated pack, are kept; these I saw, and *honor'd* with my approbation: Ld S— has a hunting seat, at 2 miles distance.

Mr O— having attended me about the kennell, and the ruins of the old house, we climb'd the scarry hills of this park; whence is much more to be seen than I could see, (tho' with a new pocket telescope) even as far as Coventry, the Vale of Belvoir, &c, &c.

Mr O— now led me to, where he had never surveyed himself, (for what do rich people, but puddle at home for more?). The lonely, sequester'd ruins of Ulverscroft Priory; lying in a vale at the edge of Charnwood Forest; well screen'd by woods, and water'd by a trout stream. _{Ulverscroft}

Here I did in haste what I cou'd with my poor pencil, from my poney's saddle, serving as a desk; and first, in sketching this north view of the remaining southern wall of the church. It has been surrounded by a wide and deep canal, and as usual with ponds, orchards, &c; and as usual now, all is left in desolation. But happy I, that can view what will soon be no more, these remnants of monastic grandeur; and how much shall I be envy'd by my grandchildren antiquaries.—

I think that the ruins of Ulverscroft Priory afforded me as much satisfaction, as I ever receiv'd from any observation; (and these are my first pursuits, as filling my mind with noble ideas of former religion, and architecture, and, as I have often declared, that had I in those days survived the dangers, and pleasures of youth, I had certainly retired into one of these asylums;) for it is seated in a shaded sequester'd vale, surrounded by wild, or wood-ed hills; and the roads are so bad, and it is so much out of any travell, as to add much to its solitude, and duration.— But I must, at every such place, express my sorrow, and astonishment, that the owners will not guard, and preserve such ruins; and not allways give them up to the mischief of changing farmers, who destroy wantonly, and for repairs.

In my way hither Mr O. told me of his having sat, some days before, in a jury to examine Mr Arnold's lunatic patients at Leicester, of which number Mr H[oward] (son of the late famous prison-Howard)[6] was one; whom he described as sullen, and hopeless.—He next told me, our discourse turning upon this hunting country, 'That once having a Cockney friend at his house, who affected a passion for fox-hunting, over night, he, on the morrow, equipp'd him with a good horse; and when the fox was found, saw him near a hedge, restraining his horse, when O— call'd out, 'Let him go, and he will clear it'; 'Let him go,' answer'd *the sportsman*, 'What do I hold him in for, but to prevent it'.

He also mention'd his remembrance of Mrs S[iddons], at Hinckley, playing the Irish-widow[7] in a most capital stile; 'Why Sr I imagin'd, then, her comic powers to be very great'. And so did I allways, Mr O. had she not been curb'd!

After a considerable time well-spent at Ulvescroft, we cross'd the fields to another farm, Mr Robys; where Mr O: consigning me to the guidance of young Mr R. took his leave; after being as civil as man cou'd be: I hope I behaved equally well.—Mr R: pointing out our course, soon left us; and we then cross'd the wildness of the forest;

ULVERSCROFT PRIORY

from a water-colour by the Diarist

[see p. 157

which has pleasant dips, and many romantic scars, and rocks.

After passing the Ashby road, and by that very farm-yard, wherein I was, last year, nearly bogg'd, I came very hot, and very hungry to the village of Belton, where yester- Belton day was held a great horse-fair.—

In this morning's ride I felt unusual pleasure; for the weather was fine, it was the first day of my tour, I felt fresh, so did poney; and I hoped much from Blacky: I had al-ready view'd three curious, wish'd for scenes, viz, Brad-gate Park, of noble ground much extent, and capable of being made one of the first of places;—the gloomy soli-tude, with the venerable remains of Ulvescroft Priory; and the cold scenery of a wild forest, whence are many distant, and charming views.

At Belton, to my sorrow, (for I had been too long on horseback) was a second fair-day of sports; a great number of booths, and much clamour of trumpetting; so here could be no stop. After getting what information of road we cou'd from the drunkards, we found a horse path that brought us in three miles to the village of Diseworth; whence, after two miles of smart riding, to avoid a storm, I came to The Turks Head Public House at Castle Duning- Castle ton; at which house having been so well receiv'd last year, Doning-I was resolv'd to visit again, when possible. Mrs H[earson] ton the landlady, at first was cold and shy; but to his old friend the poney, not so was the hostler; who has the care of Mr H.'s horse, left here, to whom he has given the greatest attention, and brought him into the highest order,—it was now 5 o'clock, so no time to be lost; and finding a cold leg of mutton, I sat down to it with a greediness unknown to the fine world; whilst some eggs were poaching, which the maid ask'd me if I would have hard, or *ripe*: the cheese (goose fair) was excellent, the parlour clean; and my horses now give me no trouble, and Poney goes very well indeed. In short, I felt as much happiness as is to be found alone, without communication, and apart from those we

159

love.—Mr H[earson] the landlord, coming in, made me known, and respected, but his turn of politics was curious; as may be read.

(H) 'Any news Sr?' (B) 'Why I think that we shall not have a Spanish War'.[8] (H) 'I'm sorry for that.' (B) 'Why so, Mr H.?' (H) 'Because of the money likely to be taken, and brought in, which wou'd lighten our taxes'. (B) 'I am afraid that you are mistaken there, Mr H, for the money taken wou'd only benefit individuals, and we must pay more taxes to carry on the war'. Perhaps I did wrong in undeceiving him.

At Leicester begins the now overspread, prosperous cotton trade, which populates, and enriches all the neighbouring counties: thanks to the Reciprocal Treaty. This village increases in buildings, and possesses the comfort of coals, at 6d per hundred.—I stroll'd about till it was dark, around the castle hill; and down the road almost as far as Cavendish-Bridge: the views from this hill are very beautiful, of the Trent vale, Nottingham Castle, &c, &c.— After supper I felt as I shou'd do, contented and sleepy; and at 10 o'clock retired to my stucco'd floor chamber, to make up the arrears of the foregoing night.

Wednesday June 9 At 7 o'clock I walk'd to the barbers shop, to be shaved; then visited the church, which is large, and light, with a spire to be seen for 20 miles around; in the church is a very old tomb, well brass'd, of the Stantons, and two fine recumbent, alabaster, figures of the Haselrigges.—The clerk is a schoolmaster, a *larned* man, not like one I lately heard of, who repeating after the minister, concerning Job, 'That he fear'd God, and eschewed evil', made it, 'That he fry'd God, and stewed the devil'.

Leaving C. D. I walk'd quietly to Dunnington Park, my eyes amply gratified with the finest views of the Trent and Derwent vales; and wonder I did, at the foolish fashionable confinement in London, when compared with the chearful, salutary delights of the country.—This bill, too, is of a different complexion, from one at The Star and Garter!

WILLIAM HEARSON. CASTLE DUNNINGTON

June 8th.	Dinner	-	-	-	-	- 0	10
	Porter	-	-	-	-	- 0	3
	Brandy	-	-	-	-	- 0	8
	Supper	-	-	-	-	- 1	0
	Ale -	-	-	-	-	- 0	6
	Wine -	-	-	-	-	- 1	3
	Brandy	-	-	-	-	- 0	8
	Fire -	-	-	-	-	- 0	4
9th.	Breakfast	-	-	-	-	- 0	8
	Horses hay & corn		-	-	-	3	2
	Wrighting paper					0	1
						9	5

Dunnington Park look'd very green and pleasantly; and its hawthorns were in full bloom. Thro' the new enclosures, I came to the village of Kings-Newton, and soon crossing the Ashby Road, above Swarkston-Bridge, was much delighted with Mr Greaves seat at ———— which has a noble front view, and is well back'd by woods, which with some good pools form, what Mason calls, 'an ample theatre of sylvan grace'.

Keeping the hill top, I was soon directed to the rocks, call'd Anchor-Church; above which, leaving my horses at the wicket gate, I walk'd thro' a small wood, (sadly honeycombed by rabbets,) and by a steep descent of turf steps, to this picturesque scenery of delight; and where, even, sequestration, and anchoritism might appear happiness: of all men I shou'd prove one of the fittest for such a plan; my pleasures are few, they are solitary, and I cou'd catch, and dress my fish.

My survey was as good as cou'd be, without getting into any of the cells; which were lock'd up: and, in some respects, better for being alone.—All these places shou'd be guarded by a house, to prevent intrusion; and to receive

Juſt landed from America,

And to be ſeen for T W O   D A Y S   only, in a Room at Mr. CLARKE's, the *Red-Lion, Corn-Market,* Derby,

A BEAUTIFUL

AMERICAN ELK

BETTER than thirteen Hands and a Half high, juſtly deemed one of the greateſt Curioſities of Animated Nature, and probably the only one of the Species ever ſeen in the Iſland of Great-Britain.

The Public are reſpectfully informed, that this Animal, now offered to their Inſpection, (the Species is rarely to be met with even in America) exceeds, in Size and Beauty, any Animal of his Kind and Age. The Shape of his Body reſembles that of an elegant Horſe, which he excels in Swiftneſs, and in the fine Appearance of his Breaſt and Shoulder. His Neck and Head are ſtately beyond Deſcription; the former meaſures four Feet in Circumference; and he can, with Eaſe, reach nine Feet two Inches and upwards with his Noſe. He has a branching Pair of Antlers, near three Feet in Length, each of which is divided into three diſtinct Parts, being ſeparated near the Head, and growing in different Directions. The lower Branch is remarkably curved, inclining towards the Eye, about a Foot in Length, and not unlike a Cow's Horn. But what renders this remarkable Creature ſtill more curious is, his having two Holes in his Head, one under each Eye, reſembling a Noſtril, through which he breathes and ſnorts occaſionally, tho' not perceptibly, (being curiouſly cloſed up by Lids reſembling Eye-lids) unleſs opened by the Keeper or himſelf.

Since the 31ſt of March, the Elk's Horns have grown about a Yard in Length, about forty-two Inches wide, and twelve Inches round the Bottom of each Horn. There are eight Branches, ſome above eighteen Inches long. His Horns grow ſo faſt, they will not permit him to ſtay here more than two Days.

The different Parts of this Animal's Body have an obvious Reſemblance to four Beaſts of the Field,—the Camel, the Horſe, the Cow, and the Deer.

The Elk is on his Journey to London for his Majeſty.

₊ Admittance, Ladies and Gentlemen, Six-pence;—Children and Servants, Three-pence:—From 9 in the Morning, 'till 7 in the Evening.

§‡§ The Public may be aſſured, that whatever is aſſerted in this Bill, is ſtrictly true.

visitors, and those who had permission to fish. Where is the expence of placing an honest, indigent family upon the spot? who wou'd be highly benefited by strangers; and I shou'd add to their advantage, by writing, and printing the history of the place, and of the anchorite who dwelt therein. Here might the owner, then, store up his fishing tackle, some few books, with a snug corner of good wine; and, in the rock might be scoop'd out every kind of cool, comfortable apartment.

About a mile from this pleasant, happy spot, stands Foremark, a house built, within these 30 years, by Sir Robt. Burdett; which is of vile architecture, and in a bad situation; in front there is a paltry pond, with pitiful plantations: I never wish to enter these Venetian vanities.

Turning to the right, a lane of a mile brought me to the banks of the Trent, which I cross'd at Twiford Ferry; Po: was very quiet in the boat, but Blacky was much alarm'd: another six miles of good road, in the second crossing the Mersey navigation, (having one shower of rain by the way) we enter'd Derby.—Here every house was adorn'd with oaken boughs in honor of the old 29th of May; and the boys preparing and begging for their bonfires. The Derby militia are assembled here; and disturbing (as at Northampton) the sick, and quiet, by their uproar.—I put up at the Bell Inn; unluckily for me the players are just gone. After a good dinner on rst fowl, and asparagus, I meant for a ride; but the evening became so thundery, and gloomy, that I cou'd scarcely see to write; but I went to view this really-curious beast, far exceeding the size of red-deer, and with the orifices, described, near the eyes; but his stay depending upon the growing of his horns, is an happy puff.

Afterwards I toured around the town, and long attended to the building of the new bridge over the Derwent; then return'd to see the roll-calling of the militia (no remark necessary) and hear their noisy, useless music, and drummings.

In my walk I bought a Derby paper, from which I cut the opposite advertisement of Mrs J[ordan]'s playing.*[9]

After tea my landlord recommended a walk to me, which I found answerable to his description; keeping above the river, to Mr Holden's house at Darleigh, and passing thro' a grove of tall trees, now number'd for sale; but if Mr H: suffers them to be fell'd, he must be a *Neger*[10] ! I return'd home by the Matlock-Road, before nine o'clock.

—This inn (as being the *belle* inn) is only serv'd by females, who run about like rabbets; and 5 of whom are not equal to one man-waiter.

The noise and crackery of the boys, on this foolish commemoration, is most intolerable, and not to be endured.

Some slices of cold lamb satisfied me; tho' it might be thought (by punsters) a *lamb-on-table* supper.

*THEATRE, DERBY.

June 1st. 1790

Mr. PERO presents his humble Respects to the Ladies and Gentlemen, and the Public in general of the Town and Neighbourhood of Derby, and begs leave to inform them, that as MANY Persons have express'd a Wish to see

MRS. JORDAN,

he has, at a very considerable Expence, engag'd her to perform SIX of her Principal Characters in Comedy, during the RACE WEEK[11] in August next: she will also add some of her favourite parts in the Farces to each Evening's Entertainment.

Ladies and Gentlemen wanting places for any of the above nights, are requested to send in time to Mr DREWRY'S Printing Office, where the Box Book will be open for that purpose immediately.—'Tis also requested those who may have set their names down, will be pleased to take their tickets at least three days before the first Night's Performance, for such Box, Seat or Places they have bespoke, and the Number of it, with the first Seat, second, &c, mentioned on the Tickets; as thereby much Confusion will be prevented, and the Manager will have the benefit of disposing of such Places as may be given up to Strangers, which ever attend at all Publick Times.

Boxes, 5s.—Upper Boxes 3s. 6d.—Pit, 3s.—Four first Rows of the Gallery will be partition'd off at 1s. 6d.—
The back Seats, 1s.

BELL. DERBY.

Dinner & Supper	-	-	-	-	2	2
Wine	-	-	-	-	-	2	3
Brandy	-	-	-	-	-	1	3
Tea	-	-	-	-	-	0	8
Breakfast	-	-	-	-	-	0	8
					7	0

This may be as good an inn as can be found amongst *Thursday* the bad ones of this town! My landlord, fat, stupid, and *June 10* splay-footed, reminded me of Mr Towouse: at my desire he recollected having seen (when a boy) the rebells march into Derby,[12] whom he described as a wretched, wearied set, many bare-legged, and footed; and that they press'd his fathers waggons, and horses: I hinted my surprise that they shou'd not all ride! 'Why, Sr, there were few amongst them who knew how to sit upon, or manage a horse'. I had reason to think my bill very reasonable; think of a fine roasted fowl, asparagus, and cheese for dinner. From Derby, the road is very pleasant, thro' the villages of Mackworth, Langley and Brailsford, whence the Peak hills appear splendidly: of Brailsford small bridge, at some small distance from the village, I made this hasty sketch.—

As I walk'd down the new-made road from the hill above Ashbourne, I stopp'd for some time in admiration *Ashbourne* of the prospect; (the town, the river, Mr Boothbys seat, the vale, with the Peak hills forming the back-ground, forming, altogether, a most lovely view) and there met a civil gentleman, whom I had seen last year at A[shbourne] and we conversed, to my inn, about Saml Johnson, whom he had often dined with in this town.[13]

The trout now being in high season, I order'd one for dinner, prodigally enough, as the family dinner, (ready) was boil'd fowls, bacon, and tart, and a bullock's heart roasted: the trout, tho' in season, was white as an haddock.

BLACKMOORS HEAD. ASHBOURNE.

Dinner	-	-	-	-	-	1	6
Wine &c.	-	-	-	-	-	1	5
						2	11

The cheese of this country pleases me much; being a medium betwixt the Cheshire, and the Stilton. My evening ride was long, but not tedious; for the weather was fine, and the expanse of the country open'd my lungs, and my ideas.

For 5 minutes I stop'd in Bentley church-yard, taking one of my drawings.

My thoughts were, when in the upland country, that all soils might be planted or fructified; and why immense spaces shou'd be left desolate and depopulate, let savage ignorant landlords endeavour to answer. At 8 o'clock after a 20 miles evening ride, I arrived at Buxton; and at the hotel, Mr Halls, I fix'd my quarters: but not finding my trunk come, and resolving, whilst here, to keep my own hours, I retired within my bed room; and there, in reading this* and one long letter, and writing several, and in eating

Buxton

*A BLIND SURVEYOR.[14]

What the mind can do independantly of the senses, or rather, how far it can invigorate some senses, and enable them to supply the place of another, has been often shewn by instances of the intelligence of blind persons.

Amongst these, by far the most remarkable which has ever come to our knowledge, is that of JOHN METCALFE, who, being born blind, became first a waggoner, and then a guide in some of the intricate parts of Lancashire and Derbyshire. In this employment he tried and perfected his means of ascertaining distances and measuring objects, and acquired at length such dexterity in the use of them, that he was engaged as a surveyor and projector of high roads in difficult and mountainous situations. Most of the roads about the Peak of Derbyshire, particularly those near Buxton, were executed by his directions, and in the year 1782, he was occupied in carrying a road from Wimslow to Congleton, upon a plan of his own suggestion, without passing the mountains.

What tends to make the whole nearly miraculous is, that he usually goes alone upon this business, and uses scarcely any other instrument than a long staff.

166

supper, did all I wanted: the evening felt so cold that I indulg'd by a fire. Here I am, and a valetudinarian, but merely stationary to ride about, and see the country; and only to mix with, and dine in company, when agreeable.

Up early to find my cavalry; who are lodged in a most *Friday* ill-contrived, magnificent mews, where all things are in *June 11* common; and where they and their furniture must be hourly watched: nothing like a quiet stable to be call'd your own!

Buxton is a most uncomfortable, dreary place; and The Grand Crescent might be better named The Devonshire Infirmary; 'The whole a labor'd quarry above ground'.— Snug lodging-houses, with adjoining small stables were more necessary and comfortable, than useless, ill-contrived grandeurs: but the Duke, I suppose, was made prey of by some architect,[15] a contrast of his Grace, as having some genius, and no fortune.

I spy'd about for some time, unknowing, and unknown; till I returned to our coffee room, where I subscribed, and breakfasted. To people obliged to fly hither for relief, Buxton, as furnishing hope or health, may be tolerable; but it will not do for my plan; so that tho' I may make it my headquarters for some time, yet I shall skir the country round: and this I began to do, to-day, at eleven o'clock, and upon Blacky for the 1st time, as Poney is going to be shod.

I mounted the hill to Fairfield village, one mile; where *Fairfield* Buxton, and its crescent are seen to the best advantage: at the turnpike, I was surprised to receive in change the Anglesea, and Macclesfield half-pence; a better coinage, and of more beauty than that of the mint, and not so likely to be counterfeited.[16]—Down the steep hills of this country, one horse goes in the shafts of a cart, and the others hold back behind.—I walk'd around Fairfield church yard, whence is a great gape over this bleak country, which is colder by a coat than London.—I kept a foots pace, the only pace I dared ride, till I came to Wormhill, near the high road; where, leaving my horse in a hovel stable, I accompanied the shoemaker (who rents the land) down the steep leading to the River Wye; where I climb'd about, and survey'd all the picturesque scenery of Chee-Torr: (of Cheetors there is no want at any public place).

This river, its rocks, and steeps, form a diminutive Dovedale; this is better for the ladies inspection; but they all want brighter suns, and summers, than those we have lately had. Choughs, and jackdaws inhabit the rock, but the eagle never comes to stay, tho' he has often skim'd his flight here; grouse are upon the hills, and the grey game, they say, within a few miles: the trout and grayling fishing would be exquisite, if poachers were prevented, who destroy more fish in one night, than an angler could catch in a fortnight.—

Mr Bagshaw, the owner, whose seat is near, should build (as I have often said before) a house on the spot, where company might bring their dinner, and where (genteel) fishers might be accomodated.

I pass'd an hour of inspection here, with the civil shoemaker; to whose house many parties come to tea, and breakfast; but how much better would that be upon the spot.—At my return to my horse I ponder'd whether I shall return to dinner at Buxton; or go further on to Tiddswell; and determin'd upon the latter; as knowing no one at Buxton; and wishing for novelty. My ride was up and down the steepest hills; which I walk'd down and my horse walk'd me up.—At Tiddswell, I stopt at a comfortable public house, The New-George; where being instantly served with cold roast beef, and cold pigeon-pye, I felt very contented.—After dinner, I enter'd the church, which, without, is beautiful; (quite a model); and within, of excellent architecture: it has at one corner, a noble stone pulpit, now disused, and there are two fine old tombs, (one of the Meverils,) and several figures in stone; but the chancel, belonging to the deanery of Litchfield, is

Tideswell

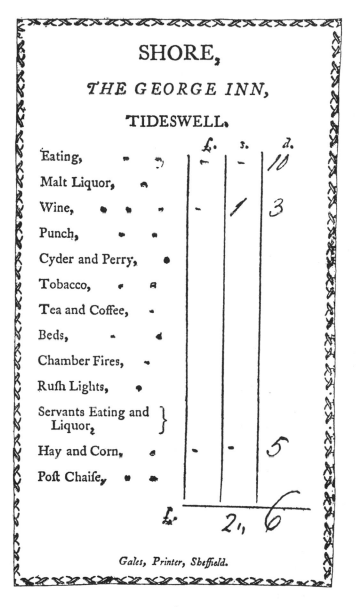

SHORE,

THE GEORGE INN,

TIDESWELL.

	£.	s.	d.
Eating,		-	10
Malt Liquor,			
Wine,	-	1	3
Punch,			
Cyder and Perry,			
Tobacco,			
Tea and Coffee,			
Beds,			
Chamber Fires,			
Rush Lights,			
Servants Eating and Liquor,			
Hay and Corn,	-	-	5
Post Chaise,			
£.		2,	6

Gales, Printer, Sheffield.

in disgraceful waste; and the church wants new benching, most grievously.

They here continue to hang up maiden garlands, which, however laudable, as of tendency to virtue, will soon be laugh'd out of practice; and as I now, visit decay'd monasteries, so will my grandchildren, if of my turn, view the ruins of churches, when they and religion altogether shall be o'erthrown.

The clerks wife said that their music, and singing were good.

This bill will prove how cheaply I was charged for cold rst beef, pigeon-pye, and cheese, with excellent brown bread.—

Buxton

At my return (rather tedious) to Buxton, and its grand stables, and seeing that Poney had been shod, I walk'd into the village, but quickly came back from the threat'ning weather, which soon produced a steady rain.—My trunk not arriving is very vexatious; and now they say it cannot come till Monday.—I pass'd this gloomy evening very gloomily, in my bed room: nor would I sup in company; but had it, as last night, in my bed room.

Saturday June 12

Dr. Warton in his last, posthumous, birthday ode,[17] speaking of health, says

> Haunts she the scene where Nature lowers,
> O'er Buxton's Heath in lingering showers?

It was a lingering shower last night, for it began at eight o'clock, and continued till early this morning.—

As my trunk did not arrive yesterday, which is a matter of astonishment, I will tour about for a day, or two, till it may be supposed to be come.—In general, the company seems to be composed from the adjacent counties; but few people are arrived from London.—Mrs H: my hostess, suffers me to take the sheets, so my nights will be safe; and my days, if fine will pass easily along, from the sight of new objects.—I travell by map, for none can inform you;

the only people who become acquainted with counties, are tourists, or a canvasser at a general election.—

At eleven o'clock I walk'd, with Poney in hand, from Buxton, so call'd I suppose, (for we writers must suppose and assert etimologies) from the number of *Bucks* who frequent it.—A dreary country, with steep hills; and the country *mends in badness*, when the Welch moss begins: here I commented on the wastes and mosses of England, as left at the Deluge, whilst we send colonies abroad to people, and then to rebel! These mosses of a black, pitchy substance,· might, by draining, afford excellent grass, as one sees about the cottages; but how, you will ask, is this to be done? Why, my first fancy, shall be—'Let Government purchase a large moss; (to begin with;) build a sort of prison thereon, properly guarded; and then let the convicts work the country, drain, enclose, dig peat, burn lime, make roads, bore to the centre, plant trees, esculents, &c; and in a few years a smiling garden wou'd succeed to a black wilderness.—The convicts too, instead of being ruin'd for ever, might be draughted to furnish soldiers for the East Indies, and distant colonies; and wou'd prove a resource in time of war, to man our fleets and armies: nay, I doubt not, but this land so improved, might then be resold by order of Parliament, to clear the charge of the establishment'. Upon these hills are grouse; sometimes wantonly destroy'd by firing the heath: in hard weather they descend to feed in the roads, and near the cottages. At Stoney-way Bar I enter'd Cheshire, and the Forest of Macclesfield, an hilly, grassy, steep country, with cottages interspers'd, and some dells, wherein are rapid rivulets; the stream descending from Stoney-way-Bar Hill, affords one pretty cascade.—T. B. now overtook me. Here the flat country opens, of great beauty, and extent; but the day was too hazy to enjoy a prospect: in the vale I cou'd discern some large meres.—I had walk'd on foot half the way; much to the advantage of my health and appetite.

Macclesfield looks well in approach; and one knows a Maccles-field

171

place to be enriching, and increasing when it is surrounded by brick-kilns: the copper works[18] have done this; and disseminate their coin, far and wide, of much better make and value than Government can afford; of these, new ones, I sent for sixpenny worth.—The remains of Macclesfield Castle have been pull'd down, about 20 years; and houses are built upon the ground. I put up at the Old Angel Inn; and was happy to attack a boil'd Buttock of a bull, (such a thing as I have seen in Porridge Island;[19]) but hunger is not refined.

Macclesfield is a large improving town, newly paved; and a new church has been built within these 12 years.—A kind of a stationer that I applied to for old books, answer'd me with contempt, 'That whenever he got such, he tore them up for covers'.

There are silk mills here of good account, but I look not into works to be seen every day; to me castles and monasteries in decay are the daintiest speculation.—I left Macclesfield at 4 o'clock, and with it the hills, and stones; and now enter'd a beautifully-enclosed sandy country, mostly pasture: nothing could exceed the pleasantness of my ride, passing near Alderley and thro' Ollerton; when some
Knutsford clouds arising, hurried me on to Knutsford, a clean, well-built, well-placed town where the cotton trade brings plenty.

Being early, I was obliged to order tea; and then walking thro' the town, enter'd by an avenue, the noble Tatton Park, and therein saunter'd and sat for above an hour.

Of this park more tomorrow; but I got good information (a rare thing) from an honest-looking intelligent fellow.

(B) Who is owner here?

(C) Squire Egerton,[20] who has a vast estate; and this vast park, 10 miles round; and deserves it all; for he is a noble, well-spoken of gentleman.

(B) Did he build the new house?

(C) Yes, he did; where the old one stood: but the offices are not yet finish'd.

S. GOODWIN,

OLD ANGEL,

MACCLESFIELD

Neat POST CHAISES.

	L.	s.	d.
Eating, - - - - - - -			
Wine & Negus, - - -		1	
Rum & Brandy, - - -			
Punch, - - - - - -			
Cyder & Perry, - - -			
Porter & Ale, - - - -			3
Coffee & Tea, - - -			
Tobacco, - - - - -			
Chamber Fire, - - - -			
Writing Paper, - - - -			
Servants Eating & Ale, - -			
Horſes Hay & Corn, - -		1	
Chaiſe, - - - - - -			
		3	6

*T. *and *E. *Bayley, *Macclesfield.

(B) Has he any children?

(C) Aye plenty; and by three wives; and the last he has *in hand* now; and if all the children take after their father, why the more he has the better.

(B) Did he make that lake?

(C) No; it has been there sin Noahs Flood. Good night t'ye master.

(B) Farewell, friend.

How charmingly does this honest voice of praise, and truth, sound.

The next communication was not so handy: for I ask'd a country man, 'If there were any wild cattle in the park?' and he said 'What kind of cattle?' I answer'd 'Of the kind before you'. 'What those?' he replied; 'why those in this country we call bulls'.

I return'd home by the race course, a little common at the towns end, not large enough for a goose to run round; but there is a variety of stands, and at the races of company, I suppose. All the cottages look comfortably; and in most of them I saw geraniums in pots.

This inn is a very good one; the stabling likewise is good, and a wax candle was put into my bed room.—I shall be very sorry not to see some players, as I hear of them around, as at Leek, and at Manchester; and that they will soon be at Buxton.

When in the hill country, I am much offended at the folly, and cruelty of distressing horses, by fast'ning one or more of them behind each cart, to stop it down hill; instead of chaining the wheels: it shou'd seem an ignorant, long adopted, provincial barbaris'm; as bad as the former mode, in Ireland, of drawing by the horses tails.

I had a diversity of viands for supper, as spitchcock'd eel, cold fowl, cold lamb, tarts, and custards; when, from lack of communication I sought an early retirement: cou'd touring in company be well understood, what satisfaction it wou'd afford! But people will pull different ways, and disdain a director; so schis'ms and wrangles quickly arise

174

to disever acquaintance, and friendships, that might, otherwise, last long.—I like to rise early, to bed early, and (from
want of time, perhaps) to fag about much; whilst others
think that the toilette shou'd be a long, and indispensible
duty! Rise as early as possible, and you will, even then,
pass more hours in bed than you ever do in London,
where you must be kept up.—In this inn are built assembly, and tea rooms of spacious grandeur, where are held
monthly assemblies; at which the maid brag'd that none
but gentility were admitted: but *on no account*, any tradesman.—I cou'd not hold up longer than eleven o'clock,
even by the help of tour writing.—So to bed.

I slept in a good bed, till the sun awoke me at $\frac{1}{2}$ past six *Sunday*
o'clock, when I wander'd about the town for an hour, and *June 13*
in the church yard, where all the grave stones are laid
horizontally, and devoid of poetry. The church is of red
brick, and has been built about 50 years, in the Venetian,
ball room stile.—At my breakfast I had a regale of London
newspapers, of so late a date as Friday; for the mail coach
passes thro' the town.—As this was a new, dry church (for
any place of damp gives me cold,) I was tempted to stay
divine service; not that I cou'd be mistaken for an Archer,
or an Aimwell, coming to pick up an heiress: so, having
sent for the barber, and receiv'd a close shaving, a strong
powdering, and a clean shirting, I attended the widow
Hand-biddy, her daughter, Miss Polly Hand do. and
young Mr Hand do., (for they have many names in this
county with the taw[21] termination) in proper form to church
which is a neat, well-pew'd building; and was well fill'd
with well-dress'd company, many of whom came in their
coaches; and there was one sedan chair.—The service
open'd with a psalm, accompany'd by an organ, and the
Te Deum, and—were chaunted; so these with two other
psalms, gave me singing enough: as for the sermon, it had
the merit of being short. The bells are very tuneable; and
they practise ringing.—I had, at my return, to defray this

175

RICH.d HANCOCK   REG.r KNUTSFORD

CHESHIRE

	L.	s.	d.
Eating		1	1
Tea			
Coffee			
Wine		1	
Punch		1	
Negus			
Cyder			
Porter			
Ale & Beer			3
Serv.t Eating & Ale			
Horses Hay & Corn		3	0
£	0	0	3

176

most extravagant bill, wherein my supper, (before mention'd) is thus charg'd 12 *pence.* This is an excellent inn,
with nothing amiss in it, but what seems common in
Cheshire, viz, the badness of the cheese; as if all the good
cheese were sent to London, for the residue here reminds
one of what is to be seen in Newgate Street, with a scure
thro' the paper, importing, 'All this fine old cheese at 2½d
pr pound'.

Good-bye, Miss Hand—
Your Servant, Mrs. Hand—

I now rode slowly thro' Tatton Park, which is a grand
domain of great verdure, and with a noble lake; these are
the charms:—the per contra, no inequality of ground;
(Bradgate for that;) the timber of neither stature, nor
girth; and a house, a patchwork thing, standing ill, with no
plantation on the lawn.—I saw several red deer; but I
shou'd enjoy, in such a territory, to have likewise, many
curious herds of cattle; and horses bred thereon, of the
best race, who shou'd never be handled till they were four
years of age.—Quitting the park, I enter'd a rich country,
which, as to timber, is hourly laying waste, by the destruction of the hedges.—Close to the park, I cou'd not help
trying my pencil at a picturesque spot around *Belton-
Bridge*; where a traveller of my disposition, wou'd enjoy,
after the trials of his fishing rod, to empty his wallet upon
the bank, and revel himself in luxurious tranquillity.—At
a foots pace, I pass'd by Ashley-Hall, seemingly a good old
house, modernly laid open; behind which is a pretty,
(Clapham kind-of) garden: leaving Bowden church, to my
left, soon enter'd Altrincham, a long, straggling market Altrin-
town. cham

At the Unicorn Inn, I was receiv'd, and treated, much
to my travelling wishes, in a clean, white-wash'd room,
with a stone floor (for the day was hot;) where a sirloin of
rst beef, potatoes, cold pigeon-pye, and cheesecakes, were
spread forth, before me, upon a clean, coarse cloth, cover-

ing a large, old, oaken table; and I must needs order in addition a gooseberry pye.—Most unluckily, Dunham-Massey, a seat of Ld Stamfords, (and lately belonging to the Booths, Earls of Warrington) was not to be seen upon a Sunday.

This place, if visible, I had not gone from; or from my inn so soon, (a good summer's day stop,) had not a Jewish kind of a trader been turn'd in upon me; and that destroys all reveries, or touring accounts.

Dinner	-	-	-	o	I	3
Wine	-	-	-	o	I	o
Beer	-	-	-	o	o	3
Horses	-	-	-	o	o	10
				o	3	4

T. B[ush] who has no more religion than my horse, observ'd, with some asperity, that they are all *Methodisshes* here.

Stockport When I was at Knutsford, I remark'd the purity of the country, at seeing young women riding alone: why, within 50 miles of the devilish metropolis, they wou'd have been all robb'd, and r——. The country around this place, and of my road of this evening, is flat, wooded, sandy and populous; and so very pleasant to ride.—Cheadle is a pretty, little town; 2 miles further, and to Stockport, where I made my night halt, at but a sad-looking inn.—I have met some of the newly-adopted Sunday-schools[22] today, and seen others in their schools; I am point blank against these institutions; the poor shou'd not read, and of writing I never heard, for them, the use. There is an essay written on this subject, by Mr R[epto]n, in a publication call'd Variety,[23] (lately put forth) that meets my opinions exactly.—Entering a town on a Sunday evening with all the damsels frisking around is very tremendous to a modest man; and dashes one exceedingly: nor did I ever see smarter lasses, than I met in my strole after tea; with their petticoats so short, as to oblige them to turn out their toes, and exert their best paces.—I walk'd the hill above the town, upon the Manchester road; whence are noble prospects over the rich vale of the Mersey, as well as of the hilly country.— Astonishing is the increase of buildings about this town, and they go on most rapidly; (Stockport contain'd about 10 years since, about 700 houses, now they exceed 2,000, which are insufficient to hold the inhabitants;) even so low as Leicester, the warmth of the cotton trade is felt; and there they told me that they cou'd make a good pair of cotton stockings for a shilling, and gain great profit!

What may not be expected if a treaty and not war, can be made with Spain; and then we shall clothe all South America! Where the old castle stood, are cotton works built in a castellated stile, with battlements, &c, looking like one of the grandest prisons in the world. The church and market-place stand very high; the former is built of mould'ring sand stone. All the houses of this town were formerly built of oaken timber; this, now, in general, has given way to brick, tho, this inn is striped and barr'd with as much black timber, as would build a man of war; the waiter likewise is black, a very Othello, a quick intelligent fellow, who comes to swarth our breed.—The roads are crouded with candidates, and voters, hurrying to the elections.

The port wine here (*Stock-port*) is preferable to any I have drank since I quitted London.

A week is already gone, but no one can say unemploy'd, or that I have been idle.—My bed room of last night was one of the oldest I have ever slept in, all pannell'd with black oak: the finest and oldest I ever slept in was at Broadway in Worcestershire; and at one of the best of inns.—I took a wand'ring walk this morning up and down these steep streets: and threw away six pence in seeing the church, which is as gloomy within, as without, ill-pew'd, and containing nothing curious. *Monday June 14*

The country news-papers are fill'd with announcements

179

of petty oratories, and musicks, after the manner of the abbey.—

This bill is the cheapest I have yet paid, (as you will perceive); breakfast at 7d, and a good supper for 10d, is as reasonable as can be.

I walk'd over the stones of Stockport, which increases hourly; and in every field adjoining, is land to be let for building.—At Bullock-Smithys, a flourishing village, resides

Samuel Bennet
Water Caster;
Instructed by old
Dr Clayton,

a country Myersbach;[24] which inspection, however right, is now entirely left off by physicians.

Taking the Macclesfield road, I soon came, by Norbury Chapel to the confines of Poynton-Park; by which I continued to the lodges. The water is higher than the level of the house, which appears to be a bad one.—Sr G. W[arren][25] with no taste, has open'd all the country around; whereas, to shew a park to advantage, that shou'd be of a different complexion. What is call'd the Towers, near the house, are a sad attempt at something Gothic; and contain a dairy, &c; all the trees in the park are of a paltry growth, and to mend them, they have been as well shroven as if my uncle, Mr M—[26] had owned them.

When I had ascended the hill above the house, I found the park gate lock'd; (a lodge should allways be built at a park gate); so was obliged to make a long detour by the coal-pit engine. A rising road of much command of beautiful, and extensive view soon brought me into the grounds, and park of Mr Leigh of Lime; whose house is in the horrid taste, and manner of Chatsworth, all windows; with surrounding parterres, and a drizzling cascade: some red deer were the greatest ornament about it.—Most of the park is a dreary waste, abandon'd to rabbits: which might be made, by draining, and cultivation, fertile, and beautiful: from the hill tower, is a most surprising prospect.

WHITE-LION INN,

S T O C K P O R T.

B A R B O R.

	£.	s.	d.
Eating	—	—	10
Wine	—	1	
Negus			
Coffee			
Tea	—	1	7
Chocolate			
Rum			
Brandy	—	1	2
Hollands			
Cyder			
Perry			
Beer			
Porter			
Servants Eating, and Ale	—		
Hay and Corn	—	2	3
Tobacco			
Paper			

6 " 10

And now I was soon delighted at finding myself at the snug, little, comfortable inn of Dishley, where the high road is re-enter'd; a neater and more chearfully situated inn I never saw; (for who should, but from force, stop in a black town;) I do not in my praise even except the inn at Broadway: the room I chose, looking upon a small garden, and up to the pretty church, is like one of a good rectory. The stables are excellent; the brown bread, and cheese, so good; the water so cold; the decanters so clean; and the bed rooms so nice; that I wish'd to make a return, and pass more time here.—After dinner, and some enquiries of what was to be seen, to which the answer was, 'Only the views of the valley, and the sight of Lime Park', I walk'd up to the church-yard, and here was not only to be found the sweet view; (mention'd) but these three inscriptions.—

PETER GASKELL

In new ground I have
Chosen this place for my
Grave that for myself
I may it have that my
Bones may here at rest
Remaine and do not
Dig them up again.
Remember man
That thou must dye
And turn to dust
As well as I.

(Well divided!)

JOHN RICHARDSON

Go spotless innocence, and blooming youth,
Go spotless honour, and unsully'd truth,
Go male sweetness joined with manly sence
Go winning wit that never gave offence
Go heaven born infant to thy place above
Go thou who possess'd God's tender love
Go dear John on angels wings arise
Go go to everlasting paradise.

(What a sublime go-cart for dear John!)

WILLM HIBBERT

Cease now my friends, and do not
Mourn, since Christ with me I hope
Will dwell: my days are past, my purposes
Are broken off, even the thoughts of my heart.

(? If meant for prose or rhyme?)

Entering the church, I was delighted at its fitting up; with 3 large windows glaz'd with old armorial bearings, as well as two smaller ones of modern stained glass, all guarded by wiring.—King David is painted under the singing gallery, playing upon his harp.

The outside has been lately wash'd over with a nasty yellow colour—; and the new vane is sadly gewgaw'd with irons, and placed upon a large golden ball.

I now resolv'd, being so pleas'd with the house, views, and all the &c, that I wou'd stay the night, for it may be long'e'r I see such another inn: so I tea'd and cream'd myself well; and then with too much impatience, (my old way) began my evening walk, at an hour when fine London gentlemen are taking their morning rides: and it was too hot, and the hills too steep! After keeping a rough lane for a mile, commanding exquisite views, I turn'd down to the river; where my reveries and quiet, were interrupted by a country man, who enquired vehemently, (good naturedly I believe) about my business; and I did not feel happy in his company.—Afterwards meand'ring alone by the stream, under a wood, I next encounter'd an angler, (this was pleasant); part of whose sport, trout, more than I wish'd for at supper, I exchanged from his pouch into my pocket, for a sixpence: then I stood, for some time, looking at his skill; and art much too hurrying for my eyes, and desires.—I came home nearly exhausted; but, having re-cruited strength, and cooled myself, made another sortie: for thro' life I must be employ'd. Having sent to Buxton for letters, I endeavoured to set up, till the return of the post-boy.

My eyes drew straws[27] to such a degree last night, as to drive me into bed at ½ past ten o'clock, where I took a *short* nap till 8 this morning; when my letters being arrived, employ'd me an hour in answering. But no trunk is come to Buxton; strange that! And that I, (who am *so anxious about dress*) shou'd often meet with such *great misfortunes*.

After breakfast I reason'd with myself about my hour of going; and from dislike to Buxton, resolved to dine here, and return thither in the course of the evening.—

I walk'd Po: on the Buxton road, up the hill; then turning to the right, and passing some small farms, enter'd Lime Park; which I noticed now more than yesterday: the house and park are a tasteless wasteful grandeur, as dreary and as ill-kept as possible;—if the rabbets were destroyed, the bogs drain'd, all the hills planted, and a large embankment made, near the blacksmiths shop, to float the valley with water, it might then be a grand place; but at present it is an horrid wild, with the old wood and hollies all dead, or dying: I saw some red deer, and many starving sheep; all the inhabitants, except the innumerable rabbets.—Returning, I rode my other horse; this employ'd me, with new dressing, (for the *other* shirt goes on to day) till I sat down with good relish, to a good dinner, of mutton chops, cold veal, and gooseberry pye.—In such an house there is a wonderful larder—viz, salmon, pigeons, mutton, veal, cold ham, &c.—Dinner ended, and a resolution taken of going in the evening, (which T. B. wonder'd at). The time hung heavily, having nothing more to see here, and a return to Buxton loathsome.

At five o'clock, (to enjoy the evening) I left Dishley; and found the road good, and very picturesque for the first 4 miles, especially about Whalley village and bridge; but afterwards, the country becomes horridly coarse, and so continues to Buxton, the vilest of all spots.

No trunk arrived!! So I believe I shall shun all company. I supp'd as usual in my bed room; and had, for my amusement, the reading of some newspapers: till, just as stepping

This is more grandly and judiciously emblematised, than any bill I have
ever seen: bottle, punch bowl, glasses, all brought into use!
  Take it for all, in all, I ne'r may look into such inn again.

into bed, I receiv'd so long and so—a letter from Mrs B[yng], as to keep me up till 12 o'clock.

*Wednesday
June 16*   I took a survey of the hotel, and saw the great, and fine assembly room, card rooms, and dining room; all which I shall, probably, never more enter, as I am resolv'd to quit Buxton tomorrow: and now that my trunk is come, I have only to take out of it my sheets, a waistcoat, 2 shirts, a pr of shoes, and a pr of stockings; then all my baggage will travell behind T. B. without further fear of absence.

This might have been managed so at first; had I not thought of an abide here: but all armies take the field in this pompous manner, and are quickly convinced that they cannot do business so encumber'd; so away go the encumbrances, and they become active, and usefull: just so with tourists.—

The sick and lame, who come to bathing places shou'd live in lower floors, in private lodgings; and shou'd not be hoisted up in great noisy hotels.—The D. of D[evonshire] being seiz'd upon by some builder,[28] has here lavished his money upon an huge mausoleum! And this, like his copper-mine may, one day, be exhausted; for these waters depend upon fashion, and the whim of the physicians.— The piazzas are too narrow to defend from either sun, or rain; and the shops exhibit no temptation, like those of Tunbridge.

I ought to have been recommended to some quiet second-rate inn, as the George or the Angel.—The hill before the house might be planted, and deck'd out to much advantage.—My baggage being arranged, and orders given for tomorrow's march, I walk'd, (attended by T. B.) to Pooles Hole, ½ a mile distant, a cavern under the lime stone hill: but whoever has seen the grandeurs of the Castleton cave, will soon hurry back out of this dirty hole; fit only to spoil cloaths, and to sprain limbs. I went on as far as the largest cavern; and then enquiring if

186

there was any thing better, and being answered no, I re-turn'd. It is guarded, and shewn by a colony of 'Weird Women', who are in eternal squabble with each other. Near it is a small house, a very dirty one, scoop'd out of the hill: this cost me sixpence, and the witches had two shillings.

That I might escape the public dinner; (tho' this place is miserably thin, owing perhaps to the elections,) I walk'd up the hill, to Fairfield; (the day very hot;) and there amused myself, with my pencil, in the church yard at taking a sketch of the church, and of the rocky mount at the west end, upon which is the stand of a sun dial: there is also this inscription!

> Stay reader spend
> A tear upon the dust
> that sleepeth here
> and when thou readst
> the state of mee think
> on the glass that
> Runs for thee.

At 4 o'clock I dined, like a traveller abroad, in my bed room; not that I cou'd eat their soup (I am not for the drainings of every scrap) but beg'd for a joint of cold meat, and so dined tolerably; and had good cheese, and bread which wou'd be better if not baked in pans.

In the evening I stroll'd a walk, not deficient in wild beauty, above the stream, where is a shew of rocks, and a profundity, sufficient to astonish a Londoner.

I often sat down to view them, but in pensiveness; and so I started up for exercise, and new objects.

No fat man can walk in this country, as the upright stone stiles are so narrow, as only to admit the passage of a well sized leg.

Letters coming late, left me time sufficient to read and answer them before bed time.

I forgot to mention that in yesterdays morning walk I *Thursday*
June 17

instinctively enter'd the play-house (wherein on the 15th
was this first performance for the season exhibited) which

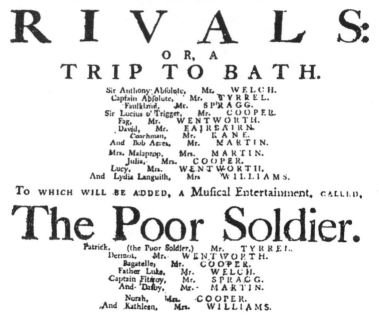

ʏʏ ᴅᴇꜱɪʀᴇ, ᴏꜰ
THE RIGHT HONORABLE
Lord and Lady MACARTNEY.

THEATRE, BUXTON.
On TUESDAY Evening JUNE the 15th, 1790. will be presented.
SHERIDEN's CELEBRATED COMEDY called THE

R I V A L S:
OR, A
TRIP TO BATH.

Sir Anthony Absolute,	Mr.	WELCH.
Captain Absolute,	Mr.	TYRREL.
Faulkland,	Mr.	SPRAGG.
Sir Lucius o'Trigger,	Mr.	COOPER.
Fag,	Mr.	WENTWORTH.
David,	Mr.	FAIRBAIRN.
Coachman,	Mr.	KANE.
And Bob Acres,	Mr.	MARTIN.
Mrs. Malaprop,	Mrs.	MARTIN.
Julia,	Mrs.	COOPER.
Lucy,	Mrs.	WENTWORTH.
And Lydia Languith,	Mrs	WILLIAMS.

To WHICH WILL BE ADDED, A Musical Entertainment, CALLED,

The Poor Soldier.

Patrick, (the Poor Soldier,)	Mr.	TYRREL.
Dermot,	Mr.	WENTWORTH.
Bagatelle,	Mr.	COOPER.
Father Luke,	Mr.	WELCH.
Captain Fitzroy,	Mr.	SPRAGG.
And Darby,	Mr.	MARTIN.
Norah,	Mrs.	COOPER.
And Kathlean,	Mrs.	WILLIAMS.

BOXES, 3s.——**PIT, 2s.**——**GALLERY, 1s.**
TICKETS to be had of the Waiters at each INN, at the THEATRE, and of Mr. WILLIAMS.
Places to be taken for the BOXES, at the THEATRE every Day from Ten to one o'Clock.
To begin exactly a Quarter before 6 o' Clock, and finish at Nine

is a mean, dirty, boarded, thatched house; and can hold
but few people.

188

Last night was the first dress'd ball; (much good may it do them) But, from the generally crippled appearance of the company, little dancing can be expected.

I was in hopes to have got away unknown, and unheeded; but last night T. B. informed me that Lady W.[29] (a infamous character) was there; at which I drew up, and said 'What is that to me?' 'Only, Sr that you might like to meet her, I thought'.—Now, today, this lady proved to be Lady E. W. an elderly lady, who wish'd to see me; and, accordingly, had a conference.—I was also discover'd by

---

BUXTON, June the 16th

The **MASTER OF THE ROOMS**, begs moſt reſpectfully to inform the

NOBILITY and GENTRY,

that there will be a

B A L L

THIS EVENING; and continue every MONDAY, WEDNESDAY and FRIDAY, during the Seaſon, preciſely on the ſame Terms as laſt Year.

Subſcriptions are received at Mr. BRANDERETH'ſ in the CRESCENT.

Mr L., a well behaved young man, (mention'd in my tour of last year) who attended me to my horse, and then, on foot, for a mile of my road.[30]

So farewell to Buxton; where I was obliged to pay for my board, and lodging, of every day that I have been absent; besides all the &c's: they are resolved to make a quick harvest, from the many people that must come, and from the many that chuse to come.

Now my health not obliging me to stay, a longer abode

wou'd be folly; and the expence of this one week has been alarming.——

I pursued my road to Tiddswell; and was soon overtaken by T. B. whose horse coughs sadly, not I hope from the distemper, which is prevalent at Buxton.——At Tiddswell I turn'd to the right, and came to the village of Litton; and thence by a narrow stoney road; to above Monsal Dale, into which we descended.

Monsal Dale

The scenery of this spot is exceedingly beautiful, but not of the boldness or magnitude, described in this exaggerated view; for the hills are not so steep, or the river so broad; and now, from the weirs being broken down, or from the management of the mill, there is little depth, or fall of water:——the millers house lays in ruins; as if a judgment upon it. I here dismounted, and gazed about for some time; but was more pleased, when having pass'd thro' the dale, and mounted the steep hill, I cou'd command the double sweep of the valley, which is a rich, and truly-romantic view; we finish'd by the Hoff, an opposite farm. On this hill top I came into the high road, and in a mile to Ashford, a large and flourishing village, where are two bridges over the Wye; two miles more, and to

Bakewell

Bakewell, a small market town, whose curious church, and monuments, I surveyed last year. A loyn of mutton was nearly dress'd; so upon that, a cold veal pye, and a gooseberry tart, I fared very well; and tho' the inn, the town, and the day were gloomy, yet I joy'd to have escaped from Buxton.——I am now only skimming about, to await the arrival of Col B[ertie], who will get from town as soon as possible; then we shall proceed away together: by that time I may be tired of my own company.——My pleasure in touring is not confined to time; (tho' that I enjoy as much as any man) but the completion of my journal furnishes me employ for the following winter, as I then dilate my former notes; besides the expectant pleasure of an old age perusal.

In the evening I took a walk to Mr Arkwrights great cotton mill, at a small distance from the town; and wou'd have enter'd it, but entrance was denied, for this (no doubt right) reason, however, odd, 'That I shou'd disturb the girls'!—It is work'd from a noble pool of water; Mr A.'s house adjoins it, placed under a steep hill, with a pleasant view.—This hill I climb'd about, and around the outside of a very old house of Mr Winchesters, which having been lately repair'd, and sash'd, wou'd afford no charms for my inspection; and perhaps I might have *disturbed some young ladies* there, too.

I then skirted the town; and above the bridge, seeing some high artificial ground; I said to a countryman, as I often do upon trial, 'Is that the castle hill?' 'Yes, Sir'. (Thus I often find out where many an old castle stood.) Within the top of the keep, where is a hollow, there lay a very proper piece of castle furniture, viz, a large iron cannon; this, at my return the landlord told me, was fired at the Kings restoration of health last year; and this was all he seem'd to know of the town, or neighbourhood, for he answer'd to all my questions, 'I don't know', 'I never heard of it'; indeed he seem'd to have drank up all his beer.—Haddon Hall Park is the great feature of this neighbourhood, and stands well in the vale.—

Cold ham, and cold veal pye for supper. I had no one to speak to, my writing was quickly exhausted, and so I strove to think; but I (*now*) hate thinking;—I left London to avoid thinking; in youth, people won't think, and when they grow into years it is of no use!— — But I will think that I never was in a nastier house, or a more gloomy place; everything dirty, and offensive to the smell; but such places compose the light and shades of touring: and these petty miseries exalt something better into superlatives.

In the night I often arose from my very bad bed to look *Friday* at the weather; which was very rainy, and continued so till *June 18* near morning: this is not a place to stay at; I had done better at Edensor Inn, only 3 miles distant.

When I got up it was a gloomy black morning, all the hills cover'd by thick mists; but I was eager to get away: as for master, or mistress, they were not to be seen, having, probably, been drunk overnight.

E'r my departure I took a walk over the bridge, and this hasty sketch. Of my bill, tho' the chear was bad, the charge was cheap.

During a short stay in an hot summers day of last summer this inn appear'd more agreeable to me; than now, in a gloomy long stay, with little new for observation.

In three miles, leaving the village of Yolgrave, I descended into Alport; where, by the mill is a pretty cascade: the mists now dispersing, it turn'd out a fine day.

Alport

No one here understood my enquiries, or could direct me to the rocks and curiosities that I wanted to inspect: one rock, indeed, of curious formation I saw upon an opposite hill.—And now fortune threw into my hands the very guide I wanted;—('en Attulit ultro'); so Mr Attulit a countryman walking his way, said he knew all my wants, and that he wou'd guide me.— — — First he took me up to the high rocks in sight, Robin-Hoods strides, a cluster of rocks on a barren-spot, very difficult to clamber about (at least I found it so). Now, said he, we will next go to Cratcliff, ½ a mile, a craggy wooded hill, where we dismounted, and climb'd to the Hermits cave, a relict of religious retirement, that neither time or barbarity have yet destroy'd; and most authentic it is by this lasting memorial carv'd upon the wall.

It is a beautiful scenery of steep rocks, happily piled, with a wood beneath them. To the cottager, who dwelt near them, I gave my advice that he wou'd fence in the cave as formerly it was, and clean it out, because it wou'd instantly repay his trouble.

My guide said that the eagle was sometimes seen here, but not being suffer'd to build, took her flight.—How does it happen that those who form parks, and establish residencies, shou'd never chuse to select wonderful, and romantic spots, already furnish'd with wood, water, rocks on cataracts; but that, in general, parks and gardens are deficient of bold features, or natural cascades!

A pleasant walk over some enclosures brought us to Rowtorr Cliff, below which has been a gentleman's seat, who then kept these rocks in good order, and amongst them cut out caverns stone-seats, &c; and on the top whence is a fine prospect, form'd a little bowling green, surrounded by high rocks, one of which of about 50 tons weight, I cou'd move. But it is all, now, going to ruin, and has just receiv'd the last destruction that man can give; for all the oaks, hollies, and mountain ashes, (which, growing for ages, had sprung up in the most romantic way,) are now felling, and are stripp'd of their bark! Poor advantage, and a demolition that another 200 years of care wou'd restore.

I spent much time upon this curious spot.—Below it stands the old mansion, now a farm; and a small disused chapel.

The village of Lower-Birchover is adjoining; and upon the hill Upper-Birchover, with a view of Elton village to the right, and in front, the town of Winstre, to which I bent my course, now taking leave of my useful, and intelligent guide. All the country is scoop'd by lead mines, and their levells; betwixt Winstre and Elton are the great lead mines of Port-Way.

Winster   I stop'd in Winstre church-yard to search for inscriptions, but the nettles were too high; I sketched the west end of the church.

Winstre stands upon a hill, a much better, and gayer place than Bakewell: at a miles distance, upon the hill side, is the village of Wensley; whence is to be seen the beautiful church, and vale of Darley, which I enter'd, after crossing the bridge, over the Derwent at Bridge-Town; and was then upon old ground, which I trotted over, and soon came up to Matlock village, and all the sweet scenery of Matlock vale beneath the high torr.

Cromford   By two o'clock I was at the Black Dog at Cromford; around which is much levelling of ground, and increase of buildings for their new market, (for this place is now so populous as not to do without) which has already been once held, and will be again tomorrow.—This house, and

194

village appear so clean, and so gay, as quite to revive me, after the dirt and dullness of Bakewell.— —

I dare not, perhaps I shou'd not, repine at the increase of our trade, and (partial) population; yet speaking as a tourist, these vales have lost all their beauties; the rural cot has given place to the lofty red mill, and the grand houses of overseers; the stream perverted from its course by sluices, and aqueducts, will no longer ripple and cascade.— Every rural sound is sunk in the clamours of cotton works; and the simple peasant (for to be simple we must be seques-ter'd) is changed into the impudent mechanic:—the woods find their way into the canals; and the rocks are disfigured for lime stone.

So that the intention of retirement is much lost here; and the citizen or the tourist, may soon seek in vain for quiet, and wild scenery:—for it will quickly become as noisy as Cashalton, or Merton in Surrey.

I well know that a peasantry maintain'd by their own ground, or by the cultivation of others ground, must abide; but a fear strikes me that this (our over stretch'd) com-merce may meet a shock; and then what becomes of your rabble of artisans!!—The bold rock opposite this house is now disfigur'd by a row of new houses built under it; and the vales are every way block'd up by mills.

I saw the workers issue forth at 7 o'clock, a wonderful croud of young people, made as familiar as eternal inter-course can make them; a new set then goes in for the night, for the mills never leave off working.—Rocks, mills and water 'in confusion hurled'.

The stabling here is good; but poor Blacky, my new horse, has a bad cough, and begins to day upon green meat, which we hope will cool his lungs.—My walks of to night were not extensive, for much is to be seen at hand: I soon return'd to tea; and, again early to supper.

The landlord has under his care a grand assortment of prizes, from Sr R. Arkwright,[31] to be given, at the years end, to such bakers, butchers, &c, as shall have best furnish'd the market: how this will be peaceably settled I cannot tell!! They consist of beds, presses, clocks, chairs, &c, and bespeak Sr Rd's prudence and cunning; for without ready provisions, his colony cou'd not prosper: so the clocks will go very well.

What the neighbouring market town of Wirksworth says to this, I have not heard.—It might be hinted to Sr Rd, that religion is as necessary as food; and that a chapel might have been built; but trade thought not of this.— One of the worst things in small inns is the being obliged to hear the odious merriment and sad singings in the kitchen. These cotton mills, seven stories high, and fill'd with inhabitants, remind me of a first rate man of war; and when they are lighted up, on a dark night, look most luminously beautiful.—At ten o'clock, it set in for a wet night; as for T. B. he will not repine at confinement here, for I saw him to night, supping with the landlord and landlady, who have lately hired the inn.—

Saturday
June 19

Last night, as the preceeding one, was of continued rain; which began just as I was going to bed, and ended at 7 o'clock, when I arose: this is lucky for the tourist.— After a grand dressing, (for now to my comfort, all my apparatus travells with me,) and a long breakfast, I took a short walk to look at the weather, and at Sr Rd A[rkwright]'s new house,[32] (of which I spoke last year). The inside is now finishing; and it is really, within, and without, an effort of inconvenient ill taste; built so high as to overlook every beauty, and to catch every wind; the approach is dangerous; the ceilings are of gew-gaw fret work; the small circullar stair-case, like some in the new built houses of Marybone, is so dark and narrow, that people cannot pass each other; I ask'd a workman if there was a library? —Yes, answer'd he, at the foot of the stairs. Its dimensions are 15 feet square; (a small counting house;) and having the perpendicular lime stone rock within 4 yards, it is too dark to read or write in without a candle! There is likewise

196

a music room; this is upstairs, is 18 feet square, and will have a large organ in it: what a scheme! What confinement! At Clapham they can produce nothing equal to this, where ground is sold by the yard.——

As the weather was very low'ring, and the clouds hung upon the hills, I loung'd about in uncertainty; looking to the putting up of the stalls for their new market till it became necessary to speak about dinner.——

Upon the inn door, a paper, inscribed with these following verses, was pasted at the last market day: they were written by an old woman.

1

Come let us all here join in one,
And thank him for all favours done;
Let's thank him for all favours still
Which he hath done besides the mill.

2

Modistly drink liquor about,
And see whose health you can find out;
This will I chuse before the rest
Sr Richard Arkwright is the best.

3

A few more words I have to say
Success to Cromford's market day.

It blew a storm the whole day; but never was the tranquility of Cromford vales disturb'd before this hour with the sound of a drum; for here were two recruiting parties striving to inveigle the happy industrious into idle miseries.

As Sr Rd A—— pays so much money, here, every week, of course he wishes it to be spent upon the spot; but then he shou'd procure a charter[33] for the market.

The sight of the booths, of the country people, and of the recruiters, was very diverting; sometimes I walk'd out amidst the stalls, and I expended 6 pence in oranges; two of whom I gave to a little white-headed thing like Frek.——
My dinner consisted of a good batter pudding, a leg of

mutton, and a gooseberry pye. Then cou'd I no longer stay within; a wetting abroad were preferable to the drunken noise at home.— —

Crossing Cromford Bridge, I kept a gloomy, pleasant road thro' woods, and by the river side, till the country rising from Mr Nightingales[34] cotton mill brought me to Crich Chase, whence is a very noble prospect of a wooded, and well cultivated country. Crich is a large village, whose church, with a high steeple, must be a great land mark.— In less than 2 miles further I had a sight of the magnificent ruins I was seeking of Wingfield Manor; missing the right road, I got entangled amongst fields; and when I had ascended the hill, and enter'd the first court of this desolate grandeur, not a creature was to be found. Nothing cou'd be more gloomy; alone, and prowling around the miseries of this ruin! There was a kind of house, but no inhabitants; a sort of stable, but no cattle!!

Wingfield Manor

So I forced my way out; and, near to a new-built house in the valley, encounter'd (with just my luck of yesterday) the very guide I cou'd have wish'd for, a civil communicative man, who saw my humour of antiquity, and indulg'd it; (and where cou'd it be more amply indulg'd than in this old, deserted castle?) He deplored the late desertion and destruction of this place: within these ten years it was (in part) genteely inhabited, and since that by a gardener, till within this twelvemonth; but the present owner, Mr Halton, has demolish'd this grandeur to help build his little meanness, having lately torn up the flooring of the fine old vaulted cellars, and strip'd off the lead that roof'd the hall.—This hall (of which I have a print) is yet glazed, and in it are coats of arms, stags horns, and some stain'd glass (*out of reach*); and in another room a ruined spinnet, from which (as a *true* antiquary) I *brought-away* some of the jacks: amongst many apartments, long fallen in, is sprung up good timber.

My guide (the best that cou'd be) made the most pertinent remarks; led me into every corner; and then around

198

the grand outside. Spake of the siege it sustain'd in the civil wars; shew'd every rent in the walls as if made by cannon balls; and was puzzled, as all countrymen are, about the two Cromwells; the destroyer of monasteries, and the destroyer of castles.—In its present state, from shade, situation, and remains, it is one of the most curious, and well-worth seeing bits of antiquity in the kingdom: (you may take my word, now, after a critical observation of some years). One side of the chapel has been lately pull'd down, as also (wantonly) a high round tower.

Poney was tied up, during my survey (which was amply done) in a kind of a porters lodge. My guide did accept, with civil reluctance, a shilling to drink my health, (unknown); after indulging, and entering into all my opinions.

— — Being highly satisfied with this place, and ungratified with the owner, I return'd, in quiet study of the past, to Crich; where I now had my horse held at the church Crich gate, whilst I hunted for inscriptions (with some success) in the church yard.

> O welcome death, for why thou set me free
> From sin, and sorrow, and all kind of misery;
> Reliev'd from trouble, grief and woe,
> So mourn no more for your Abednego,
> Son of John Hay, and Alice his wife,
> Who in his fourth year resign'd his life.
> Jany. 13th. 1748.

In this epitaph is every thing stated that need to be; with the name (as Dr Johnson observes)[35] properly introduced; as well as the age of Mr Abednego, who might be supposed 60 years of age.

ELLEN CLAYTON.   Aged 20 Years.

> Farewell vain man thou
>   Proved my overthrow
> Thy false deluding has
>   Proved all my woe.
> Now pale death has
>   Ended all my care
> And I a crown of glory
>   Hope to wear.

(The old story I suppose! But I cou'd not learn it.)

199

Cromford   My return was very slow; fearful of encount'ring the
noise of the market folks of the inn; and I was pleasantly
delay'd by accompanying two fishers to the river with their
casting netts, (true poaching dogs,) of whom I hoped to
have procured some trout for supper.——

I came back too soon; for our house was in rustic
revelry, with such a quantity of singing! Solos, and in
parts, and all kinds of chauntings, increasing with the
beer, to an excess of bawling: but some of the voices I was
obliged to hear, seem'd to possess much power. —— —— ——

Sunday   I rose very unwell this morning with a head ach, and a
June 20   lassitude that I wish'd to attribute to having caught cold:
but I strove to rouse myself, and try what the fresh air
would do for me.

Excepting the noise of last night, this inn has done very
well; for they have been very civil, the stabling is good, and
this bill very cheap; besides it is a pleasant, and good station.

		s.	d.
June 19th. Eating	- - - -	1	10
Tea - -	- - - -	0	8
Wine -	- - - -	1	3
Ale -	- - - -	0	3
Brandy -	- - - -	1	0
20th. Tea -	- - - -	1	4
Eating -	- - - -	1	10
Wine -	- - - -	1	3
Ale -	- - - -	0	6
Brandy -	- - - -	1	0
21st. Breakfast	- - - -	0	8
Horses Hay -	- - - -	1	4
Corn -	- - - -	3	0

£0   15   11

After many enquiries, I found that my road wou'd be
shortest, and best, thro' Buxton; and besides, I was tempted
that way by the hopes of finding letters there.

As our way was long, the black horse ill, and well laden,
I went off alone; creeping up a long hill to Bonsall, a long

straggling village; and then two miles more of bad stoney road, till I reach'd the open, and good riding country, where the air was so fresh, as to revive me much. At the public house, call'd Newhaven, I came into the London road; upon which in great leisure, I return'd to Buxton.

By T. B.'s advice I put up at the White Hart, one of the Buxton lodging-house inns, (any thing but a return to the hotel); and was there as much slighted as cou'd be; which I bore with philosophy, knowing that I meant to go on, and that passion wou'd not defriend me: I could scarcely get a room, and I could scarcely eat of the dinner put before me.

At last T. B. arrived; when I sent him to enquire for letters, but none were here; only one had been sent forwards.—From the specimen I have seen of the wine, bread, and victuals of Buxton, I shou'd declare them execrable: the only compensation I receiv'd after my wretched meal, was a cheap charge; only 10d for dinner, and 10d for my horses!—We all seem'd happy to get away; for neither I, or the beasts, cou'd eat the provender.

In the finest, and freshest evening, I continued my ride over the hills; (which afford, as soon as Cheshire begins, gay and populous views;) and found myself quite at home at Dishley; where I made the brown bread and butter pay Disley for the want of dinner.—I saw much company about the inn, and with fear, when I heard of a wedding party, that I might lose my bed; but it would appear to be *quite the genteel thing* for couples to come here from Manchester, and to return back in the evening, after having made the postboys, and ostlers, drunk.

My horses revell upon green meat, which I am sure must do them good, as I ride very gently. If I meant to stay muzzing in a room, I might as well have abode in Duke Street; so I issued forth, and had a lovely walk by the great fish pond in the valley, at the back of the inn; thro' the woods; and home by the church-yard; around whose borders I continued till nine o'clock, catching every breeze in this delicious evening.—

I had a cold supper; and retired early to bed.

A fortnight elapsed; apparently a long one, as being alone, and from so often having changed quarters.—The house was in great laziness, this morning; for none of them appear'd till I had risen an hour.

Having shaved myself, (with Ld Mansfield's razor,[36] as the landlord calls it) and eaten a good breakfast, I took my departure; my host lending me £2 2s (as he cou'd not change a bill) which I am to repay at Manchester; this is a stretch of civility! and of ignorance! for those who know me, are not so civil.

Bramhall
Leaving the high road in less than two miles, and passing by Norbury Chapel, I came in 2 more miles to Bramhall-Hall, which being described to me as a curious old mansion, tempted my curiosity more than all the modern-built houses in the kingdom.—As we approach'd we saw the owner, Mr Davenport,[37] whose family have been long seated here; and are of great antiquity in this county.

My reception was very civil into this oldest of all the old striped houses; black and white, flourish'd into as many devices as a boy wou'd draw upon his kite. The situation is good, so are the views, and there runs a stream on one side; but taste has been little consulted; and the servant maid, whom I beg'd to shew me every antiquity, said that her master loved antiquity, but her mistress the modern taste; so the fine old drawing room, up stairs, and the other inhabited rooms have been lately modernly sash'd! (Cou'd no one have convinced Mr D., (or Mrs D.,) that an old house might be newly sash'd, without quitting the antique taste, and be made as elegant, and commodious, as possible.) The hall is very good, and the drawing room above it is a noble apartment.—The servant then took me at my desire, to the long gallery up stairs, wherein is some old armour, saddles, and curiously-wrought massive stirrups, that shou'd be repair'd, and hung up in the hall; (or given to me;) and therein is, likewise, a chest of old books, rotting,

or used for waste, that contains what I and other antiquaries pant for; (some old plays I saw): if gentlemen have

no taste themselves, why not consult, or bestow upon,
others?

The rooms for use are trick'd up a la mode; and from one, Mrs D. came forth, with very civil deportment.—All the out offices are good; and in one of them (call'd a kitchen) had T. B. according to ancient custom, station'd himself; an intrusion I discourage, or to have my name and history set forth.

The old chapel is undergoing (a good phrase) a repair; let me see it then, e'r the repair be accomplish'd. It is very low, and ancient; they are smearing the wood work with a composition. The books are all fasten'd by chains.—In it is much stain'd glass; as there also was in many of the house windows, much of which is removed into Mr D.'s dressing room.

Mr D. has had bad advice; or lacks taste; or is under management!!! (Ld S[alisbury] has newly sash'd his grand old mansion at Hatfield without offence to the taste of the old building). I cou'd have wish'd to have had a stirrup presented to me: now they, with the old bridles, armour and books, will be consigned to the dunghill.

Cheadle

A bye road (which in winter wou'd be very bad) amidst enclosures, brought me to Cheadle; thro' which I pass'd yesterday sen'night: I here dismounted to peep thro' the church windows, and to read inscriptions in the church yard; at one corner of the former is a groupe of recumbent figures in alabaster, but in the latter I found nothing to amuse, except that Mr Downes lately died a lieut. in the East Indies Companys service, aged 4 years.—The day being very warm, tempted me to an unusual action, viz, to drink ale, and eat bread and cheese, (at the Jolly Farmer upon Galley-Green); not that I believe it lower'd my prow-

Altrin-
cham

ess at dinner, at the Unicorn at Altrincham, upon rst veal, cold ham, &c; where the heat detain'd me till ½ past 4 o'clock.

Eating	-	-	-	-	-	-	0	1	6
Wine	-	-	-	-	-	-	0	1	0
Horses	-	-	-	-	-	-	0	1	0
							0	3	6

Dunham-Massey, the seat of the Earl of Stamford, is distant 2 miles, in a sandy flat country.

There are good woods, around it, and in what is call'd the old park.—The newer park is wall'd, and wooded to the extent of my wishes, in grand shade: but, now from the roguery of servants, and the indolence of masters, there is a sufferance of lopping, shroving, and cutting down trees, nor is any notice taken of the charcoal fires at the park gate! The park is very verdant; and every kind of tree grows to a wonderful stature.—

But judge of my astonishment, when fancying and hoping that I was to see an old magnificent mansion (long the residence of the ancient family of Booth, advanced to the title of Earl of Warrington) I approach'd a modern, red brick, tasteless house, which I had not a wish to enter.

Skirting the sunk fence of the garden, which I cou'd sufficiently see; and then keeping a walk by the made piece of water, little better than a pond, I rode thro' groves of tall timber, to where, in a most sequester'd spot, on the loftiest branches of the oldest, and most magnificent oaks, the hearns build, and take their stations:—here then did I seat myself on a circular bench, viewing their flight, and list'ning to their cries.—Nothing cou'd be more transcendently gloomy, or gratifying (notwithstanding the suns heat) than my station; where, 'Beneath the shade of melancholy boughs' I enjoy'd the cooler air for $\frac{1}{2}$ an hour; viewing, like another Adam, the frolicks of the sylvan natives.

Thro' a long ride in the woods of the park, and again by Altrincham, I kept my way (most slowly, as the evening was very hot,) thro' the populous villages of Chaverton, Trafford, &c, till I arrived at Manchester, or, rather first, at Salford its suburb; where the noise, and drunkenness of the artisans quite overcame me, added to a long crawl over the stones.—At last I came to the great noisy hotel, The Bridgewater Arms, whose clamour, bell-ringing, and want of attendance wou'd drive a man wild.—My letters (of which I receiv'd here a very large pacquet,) were of such a *disquieting* nature, as to make me instantly determine to give up my northern project, and my intentions of a long tour; and, as Mrs B[yng] is unwell, I will set off for London in the next mail-coach; sending my horses across the country, to nearer London, where, perhaps, I may rejoin them, and take a confined ride, e'r I shall be obliged to attend my duty.

What from the worry of these letters, and the excessive heat of the weather, I cou'd not sleep in the night; and arose on

Tuesday June 22

To arrange my plans of departure.—Col. B[ertie] writes, that he will soon meet me at Lancaster, but I shall answer him in town; as well as Mr S— my solicitor, whose brother being dead, most anxiously wishes to see me.—

So there ends my loitering about in touring; and I must encounter the rattle, and fatigue of a mail coach for 200 miles.

After breakfast, I wander'd about this great, nasty, manufactoring town; looking exactly like Spital-fields, and those environs: their exchange is an handsome building, but crouded up in a low situation.

Their market seems a bad one; peas just coming in at 2s. the peck.

I try'd various booksellers shops and one brokering shop, for old books, but all in vain; then to the collegiate church, just at prayer-time; where the singing was too bad to tempt my continuance: the old massive stalls are very venerable, but there are no monuments, or stain'd glass about the church.

From the church yard most of the old town is to be seen.

Adjoining is the college, a foundation of the nature of the Charter-house; and where, unask'd, and uncontroul'd, I enter'd the old hall, walk'd the cloisters, and then ascended into the library (a public one)[38] where the librarian was adjusting the books.

I saw many soldiers about the town, and some officers in our coffee room, who from their *dress*, and *address*, I

BRIDGEWATER ARMS
INN & TAVERN
MANCHESTER.

Consists of a News & Coffee Room, Eleven handsome Parlours, airy bed Chambers, with Dressing
Rooms to accommodate about 120 persons, also a
large elegant Dining Room called yͤ Free Masons
Hall, Coach houses and Stabling in proportion.
Kept by I Hartley who is determined
to pay every attention to Travellers & the Public in
general and hopes for their patronage & Support.

NB. Neat Post Chaise and carefull drivers.

thought might belong to the militia; and I cou'd scarcely credit the assertion of their being a regiment of dragoon-guards.

I cou'd not but recollect, (when in this town,) the year 1745; when several deluded people followed the fortunes of the Pretender, and sustain'd the damage; of whose forfeiture none has been the more ably, and piteously described than the fate of Jemmy Dawson.[39]—

My wander was short'ned by a tremendous storm of thunder, lightning and rain; which drove me back in haste. My second round (after the storm ceased,) was of the new town; hourly increasing in buildings, and of the better sort: opposite to Lever Row is the grand new infirmary; and in Moseley Street[40] now finishing, are chapels for prayer, and assembly rooms for dancing, well built, and bespeaking opulence and an increasing trade.—

And here let me (ignorantly perhaps) impetuously state my wishes, 'That trade was unknown'; (or that I had lived when it was but little known).—Here arises an outcry against me, What no trade! No prosperity to this country! This country so flourishing by commerce!!—Hold you an instant; what does trade introduce? What carries it out? Why, the very vitals of the country are drain'd to import these *most valuable* commodities, rum and sugar from the West Indies, china and nankeens from the East, hemp from Sweden, deals from Norway, oil from the Northern and Southern Poles, furs from Nth America, tobacco from Virginia, and turtles from Bahama-Islands: now cou'd we not go on very happily without these ridiculous luxuries; or raise the useful ones at home?

But trade, Sir!

Aye, trade, Sir, leads to commerce; commerce leads to war; war brings on taxes; and so the whole country, with the king, and minister, fearful of offending a petty merchant; (as in the present instance of Nootka Sound) who chuses to traffic, and encroach where he ought not, are led into a fresh warfare with all Europe; and this island of interior happiness, must be stripp'd to the heart, whilst its true concern, the landed property, is sacrificed to roguery, false pride, and the tricks of merchandise!—'But see you not the great increase of Manchester?'—Yes; I see the hearty husbandman suck'd into the gulph of sickly traffic; and whilst some towns swell into unatural numbers, lost is the sturdy yeoman, and honest cottager!

The business of harvest, formerly the work of 3 fine weeks, cannot now be finish'd in six weeks.—

Go on my poor deluded country; and strain away in trade; enclose; depopulate; build towns; pull down villages; and deal away so largely and wildly, that ye all become swindlers, or bankrupts! Study to impose taxes; and employ 10 people to collect them from ten others; let informers loose; so no man will distinguish a friend from an enemy. Transport felons by thousands: fill the globe with your convicts. Hang by hundreds: and when reason is almost lost, and laws multiplied beyond comprehension, may some surviving few of the nation who do not thrive by politics, and stratagem, endeavour at a reform.

Who but a merchant cou'd live in such a hole; where the slave working and drinking a short life out, is eternally realing before you from fatigue, or drunkenness.—Being in a great *Hot-Hell*, I was obliged (for the 1st time in this tour) to order dinner; which I was drawn from, to wait upon Mr B[ridgema]n[41] returning from his easy election to his own seat, and to discourse about elections.—No person on a touring intention, shou'd ever station in a town, where you are as much lock'd up as in Lad Lane in London; only list'ning to bells, and clamour; or to wander about, as I did this evening, in hopeless distress! Think of their being no play-house, or shew!—In this country, the people are hatefully slow of answer, for if you ask any one of them their next door neighbours name, they are stagger'd for words, and recollection; and, at last, turning about as if to catch the right wind, their answer is, 'Why—I cannot tell'.—I won't say that I have done wrong in beginning this tour; but I feel myself perfectly right in thus hurrying back to town.—

Storm and tempest—Heat—Darkness—Got to inn. Got into a wrong coach. Look'd up T. B.—What misery in an inn yard.—Leave orders, depart alone,—uneasiness of road, rattle—All afloat—Dirty German—Nonsense and trade—Rattled into Stockport—thence to beyond Smythies—Drunken hostler—Vast speed—Morning breaks—Charming country to Macclesfield, remains of fair and booths—Got rid of German—Change horses—Enter 3 gentlemen, one well bred, one elderly, young man, Cheshire—never from home, had been at fair—Description and jokes—Road up hill and down. Forest and hills to the left—Staffordshire fine country to the right—To Leek, a pretty town—Nice road for riding—Wished myself on horseback—Fresh horses—Quick motion—Do.—Stop at alehouse and talk—Views of the Dove and to Mr Okeovers—descend

into Ashburn—I get out and walk up the Hill—Leggs cramped—Charming road—Reach Derby—Very hungry—Good breakfast—hot rolls—To Cavendish Bridge—Loughb'ro—at length to Leicester—Election confusion—Windows broken—Good dinner at 3 Cranes—Hurry'd this return! Quite a break up of touring hopes—to Harbrothage[42]—to Northampton. Our society very good, and good-humour'd; a good tea Drinking—Militia—Dusk coming on—my small bottle of brandy—quite dark—To Newport—Change horses beyond at— Call for a glass of water and take my drops therein—Put on my nt cap and compose to sleep—Sleep to Dunstable—and again to St Albans—Steep Hill and the horse tired—Fine morning—begin to talk—Revive at Barnet. Cheshire lad we devert abt London and horses—Look out at Highgate—Part friends at Islington—Long walk along the new road; here at six—

Short stay in town—Amendment of Mrs B.'s health—Fine weather—
Wish of return—Hide from office—Take a choice of return—must do it—
Not terrified by my former voyage—Mail coach the only coach—Early
walk Saracen Head—Walk on to Islington—The Cram—5 insides—High
heavy coach—Company a shrewd Scot—Contrast a silly Englishman—
who had been in the East Indies—talked of types and the antropophagi—
who each other eat (Othello)—A poor sickly woman—and a quiet man—I
sometimes endeavour'd to humble the Scot—and help the Englishman
right—But these are impossibilities—Dine at Baldock.—Bill.

I am now writing again, as if no intervention had taken Wansford
place, (just of a week,) having left Manchester on Tuesday Bridge
Tuesday
night last, or rather early on Wednesday morning.—My June 29
horses have come hither thro' Buxton, Derby, Leicester,
and Uppingham; and, T. B[ush] says, in much foul
weather: the horses look well, Po fat as an hog, and Har-
binger in better health, and looking sprucer from the loss
of 4 inches of tail.

I arrived here last night, to a good supper, and a good
night's rest, in the best of inns, pleasantly situated; the
bridge, the river, the church beyond, and the all-about,
constitute the right inn scenery: and I have brought with
me a fishing rod, and tackle, to destroy the fish withal.

This morning, crossing the bridge of length, and
beauty, (tho' narrow,) I enter'd the pretty little church-
yard, and therein try'd my pencil in drawing *the church*;
and in transcribing this epitaph; of most *happy* punctua-
tion.—

FRANCIS COOKE

All you that doth, behold this stone
And think how quickly I was gone
I went to bed very well at night
But was found dead by morning light
So death do not. Always warning give
So pray be careful how you live.

A good breakfast, with excellent tea; I selldom remark
upon tea, but here every thing seems to be good. Next, I

JOSEPH BARKER,
At the ROSE-and-CROWN,
B A L D O C K.

Neat Poft-Chaife, and Stage Coaches,
to all Parts of the Kingdom.

	£.	s.	d.
Breakfaft,	0	2	6
Dinner,			
Tea and Coffee,			
Supper,			
Beer,	0	1	0
Wine,	0	2	6
Negus,			
Punch,			
Brandy,			
Rum,			
Holland's Geneva,			
Cyder,			
Tobacco,			
Fire,			
Servants,			
Coachman,			
Horfes Hay and Corn,			
Oftler, &c.			
£.	0	11	0

WANSFORD CHURCH [*see p.* 212

TOWER AT THORPE
from sketches by the Diarist [*see p.* 218

took a ride upon Harbenger; whom I have never cross'd but once; anxious to ascertain my hopes, or fix my fears.— My ride was very pleasant; first, to Stebbington village, where I gave my nag a trial of being tied to a church-yard gate, wherein I took down one epitaph.

NATHANIEL PHILLIPS

A sudden change, I in a moment fell
I had not time to bid my friends farewell,
I left a wife, two children small,
Which caus'd the tears to shed and fall.

Thence to Water Newton; I did not return till two o'clock: my horse is very ungain, but his severe cough is nearly gone.—

Nothing could equal my good dinner, but my good disposition towards it. This is a nice inn; every thing clean, and in order; a napkin with a wash-hand glass at meals; the beds and stabling excellent!

After dinner, at 5 o'clock, I realised my hopes about fishing; by catching some very fine chubs and bream, several that made my small rod to crack: my situation was opposite to some upland closes, under mowing, and well shaded with trees; to my right, at a distance, a mill; to my left, Wansford Bridge, and village; and behind me, the London road descends a gradual hill, where I can see every passing carriage.

Surely to a man much confined in town, and whose days are sunk in disturbance, these scenes afford true pleasure. Being satisfied with fishing, I borrow'd a stick, and walk'd the high road, northerly, for 2 miles; then return'd to a quiet supper, my writing, and to an early bed,—I should mention that T. B. having in my absence, dock'd off several inches of the black horses tail, I order'd, this evening, to complete his Adonisation, and make him look sharp, that his mane shou'd be hogg'd: (Reminding myself of a Cambridge story, where a scholar turning out his horse in the college meadow, was threaten'd by the master that he wou'd cut off his nag's tail; Let him do it at his peril, answer'd the scholar, for if he shou'd cut off my horses tail, I vow I will cut off *his* ears.)

The old folks of this inn are a fine graceful couple; and their eldest son is one of the tallest, and handsomest men I ever saw.—

Wednesday June 30

Here I loiter; but who can help it at such an inn?— This morning, as soon as the post had brought me my letters (7 o'clock) I sally'd forth to fishing, 'The creatures at his dirty work again' but only caught one perch; however the refreshing air sent me home with a fine appetite for breakfast, and the newspapers. I read that my cousin, G. B[yng][43] is elected Knt of the Shire for the County of Middlesex:—(Much good may it do him! Many men, many minds;) He may think fishing, touring, and my ridings, tedious and fatiguing;—and I (weak, and unambitious) cou'd not endure to be pester'd with every voter of Middlesex, and to have my park overun by every butcher of Clare market.—

Then letter writing, then lunging my new horse; for, as Sr Harry Wildair[44] says 'Lifes but a span, I'll every inch enjoy'.—A short ride employ'd me an hour about the villages of Yarrol, and Nassington; in the church-yard of the former I prowled about; (in vain I shou'd not say, as I read of the deaths of but very few aged persons.)—At my return, another lunging of my horse, and another angling of two hours, without sport, brought on 3 o'clock; and then reminded me of a clean shirt, and of dinner.

After dinner, I resolv'd to be gay; and tho' in London I wou'd not (now) go two yards to see a play; yet for exercise, *Stamford* and variety, I rode 6 miles to Stamford, on that account; after putting up my horse, I perambulated the town, and at 7 o'clock entering the play-house, was shewn into a side box (being *too genteel* for the front). The next boxes were soon occupy'd by some old acquaintance, their daughters, &c, who reside in this neighbourhood; and I receiv'd many kind invitations to return with them. (But lack-a-day, I shou'd then have given up my supper, and my bed, at the Haycock Inn!!!) Here followeth the bill of fare; too long by half; but every performer must add more, and more, to tempt the half price comers: 3 acts were enough for me, and they lasted till 9 o'clock. To night was jabber'd over a modern unintelligible, walking novel, instead of a good old fashion'd, easy-going comedy, as the Stratagem, Recruiting Officer, &c &c;—but perhaps this may better suit the affected elegance of the country.—

POSITIVELY THE LAST NIGHT BUT FOUR.

BENEFIT OF
Messrs. SIDNEY, ROBERTSON, and JAMES.

BY HIS MAJESTY'S SERVANTS.
THEATRE. STAMFORD.

On Wednesday Evening, June 30. 1790,
will be presented, a favourite COMEDY, call'd

WHICH IS THE MAN?
Or, THE SOLDIER FOR THE LADIES.

Lord Sparkle,	Mr. PAULET.
Fitzherbert,	Mr. PERO.
Pendragon,	Mr. O'BRIEN.
Belville,	Mr. KING.
Gentleman,	Mr. JAMES
Belville's Servant,	Mr. MASON.
Lord Sparkle's Servant,	Mr. PETERS.
Clarinda's Servant,	Mr. SPENCER.
Beauchamp,	Mr. CAMPBELL.
Julia,	Mrs. KING.
Sophy Pendragon,	Mrs. O'BRIEN.
Clarinda,	Mrs. PAULET.
Mrs. Johnson,	Mrs. PERO.
Kitty.	Mrs. SISSON.
Tiffany,	Mrs. SPENCER.
Lady Bell Bloomer,	Mrs. MASON.

In the course of the Evening, the following Entertainments, for this Night only:

END OF ACT THIRD,

Mr. Robertson will sing a Queer Halting Hobbling SONG, call'd,

COMMEMORATION, CONSOLATION, DISSIPATION.
IMMODERATION, CALCULATION, AGGRAVATION,
EDUCATION, IMITATION, SEPARATION, and
ADMIRATION, ALTERATION, BODDERATION.

END OF THE PLAY.

Mr. Robertson will recite a humorous TALE, call'd,

THE CHRISTMAS PYE:

Or, The Whimsical Freak of the Exton Farmer at WANSFORD FEAST,
After which, A PANTOMIMICAL INTERLUDE, call'd,

HARLEQUIN RAMBLER;
Or A PEEP INTO STAMFORD.

Harlequin, Mr. James.
Pantaloon, Mr. Spencer.
French Lover, Mr. Peters.
Cuddy Soft-head (the Clown) Mr. Sidney.
Columbine, Mrs. Sisson.

In the Course of the Pantomime,

HARLEQUIN will take a LEAP over the TOWN BRIDGE,

To conclude with a COUNTRY DANCE by the Characters.
To which will be added, A FAVORITE FARCE, call'd,

THE ANATOMIST;
Or, SHAM DOCTOR.

Monsieur Le Medicin (the French Physician) Mr. James.
Old Gerald, Mr. Pero.
Young Gerald, Mr. King.
Martin, Mr. Peters.
Simon Burleigh (the Infant) Mr. Sidney.
Crispin, Mr. Paulet.
Angelica. Mrs. Sisson.
Doctor's Wife. Mrs. Pero.
Waiting Woman, Mrs. Spencer.
Beatrice, Mrs. O'Brien.

To begin at Seven O'clock.
Places for the Boxes to be taken at Mr. Newcomb's.

Tickets to be had at the Printing-Offices; of Mr. Sidney, at Mr. Red-mile's, of Mr. James, at Mr. Thompson's, both in St. Mary's Street; of Mr. Robertson, at Mr. Blake's, near the Theatre; and at the principal Inns.

(Newcomb and Peat, Printers, Stamford.)[45]

My time is fully employ'd here; and so, indeed, wou'd it be anywhere, for I shou'd turn botanist fossillist, any thing rather than do nothing:—who is alone, that is employ'd?—I remember, that in one winter in Germany,[46] (long ago,) I sequester'd myself, in a fit of sulkiness, from the regimental mess, for 3 weeks; and, even then, found employ with my books, and my horses.—

Now to bed, says sleepy head.

The month opens finely. At seven o'clock to my fishing, *Thursday* but return'd soon; a letter from Mrs B[yng] wishing to *July 1* come down, but how can that be?

After breakfast, to my usual sports, lunging my horse, and to fishing; where, ignorant of the right haunts, and tackling, I caught but 7 fish, one a bream of a pound, which was order'd for dinner.—Lady E. W.[47] stopt here in her way to London; odd our second meeting so soon, and with a younger lady very suspicious!—I have written many letters to day, relative to my intention of returning here, after a short absence; and where better than to this house, with its surrounding pleasures, and interior comforts, as put most private houses at defiance? I have now stay'd so long here, as to dread departure; but I must be gone to *see the world*, and enjoy touring.—This is the view from my parlour window; taken as well as my (improving I hope) pencil could take it.

At ½ past 4 o'clock, I left Wansford; and here again I made a reduction of baggage, (before I cross'd Hudsons river)[48] leaving it to the care of Mr Norton; who to my questions 'If he knew the country well'? answer'd 'Yes, sir.' 'Why then how far is Thorney from Peterborough'? 'I can't say'. 'How far is Thorney from Crowland'? 'I never went that road'.—I kept my easy pace, hardly above a walk, to the village of Caister; there dismounting to *Castor* admire the handsome old church with its beautiful steeple, and spire.—Over the porch is this carving in stone; and there is an inscription over the chancel door, that I could

217

not decipher.—I read many inscriptions upon tomb stones, of which I thought this the best.

JOHN WHEELWRIGHT. Aged 35.

A fatal blow came on me unawares
So pray be careful how you spend your years
Unthought for accident you see
My gracious God allotted me.

Passing Ld F[itzwilliam's]⁴⁹ park at Milton, a dead flat, I next came to Thorp village, where stands this very old turreted building; about which I enquired in vain; getting for answer 'It is a tower'. 'But what was it?' 'What was it! Why it was a tower'.

Peterborough is a mean-built poor town; the people were all hurrying to a show of horsemanship:

The road from Peterborough is very rough, and laying very low must be impassable in winter; the village of Ayeberry⁵⁰ is well built; and soon after, from Mr Browns neat farm, a fine gravelly causeway begins, and continues to Thorney; a little, melancholy out-of-the-way place, with one mean inn; where, after taking a short walk, I supp'd upon some tough mutton chops.—The weather is warm; so what signifies the inn to the tourist: and my having a servant, and my own sheets give me content and consequence.—T. B. has brought from Leicester a currish kind of dog, whose only exertion has been to dash thro' a stable window at Wansford, and demolish several panes of glass; that's all he seems to be good for!—We are here the day after the fair; that's generally term'd unlucky, but in travelling quite the contrary. There was no sitting up long in my dreary room upon a brick floor, which I did not immediately discover to be very damp from a mornings wash; and that I had better have been sitting in a field: so with much prudence I swallow'd a glass of brandy ere I retired to bed.

Thorney

Friday
July 2

Waking at six o'clock, I arose instantly, (for it was a fine morning, and I had bed enough) and now took my

218

walk of survey to the abbey of Thorney.—This curious old clump of Gothic solemnity, must, surely be only a small part of what was. It is amazingly strong; and wou'd serve as a good model for a small new church.—The figures over the west-window are much to be admired. Within, to my astonishment, there was nothing antient; not one tomb!— The roof has been much lower'd; and the inside is now pew'd, painted, and gallery'd like a London chapel.— Having attentively view'd the outside; the all worth seeing; I walk'd forward from Thorney.

DUKES HEAD. THORNEY.

Supper -	-	-	-	1	0
Wine -	-	-	-	1	2
Brandy (dear) -	-	-	1	6
				3	8

(And here let me retaste my recollection of the highest enjoyment in touring, and of a pleasure that the idle, and fashionable can never know; viz, the passage thro' a new country, upon a safe horse, in a charming summer morning; when nature in all her charms, and fullest fragrance (for now the hay is cutting) courts us to be happy: Oh! how I despise the sluggards of fashion, and the folly of late hours, when such a morning ride comes like a renewal of youth, inspiring every hope, and fraught with every wish.)

Nothing can form an happier contrast with my late, hilly, stoney Derbyshire ride, than this flat of fine roads; for there is not a stone to counteract fancy, or overturn a castle in the air.

I had to observe the richness of the soil, and its happy produce, till I view'd the grand remains of Croyland Crowland Abbey; when I soon enter'd the little town, quite Dutch-looking (tho' not as to neatness) with a canal thro' it, and many crossing foot bridges.—I was so eager for breakfast, as to fancy it good; when the tea was, I believe, made of ash leaves, and the butter, and bread intolerable.—At leaving London, I ask'd a friend about the inn here, and at Thorney; and he described Thorney as the best, which I thought impossible till I saw this; impossible of a nightly reception.—The hostler, a civil fellow, wou'd attend me, and first over the bridge; this might have been the extent of the abbey ground. The hostler luckily came with me, for the sexton was old, foolish, and blind; so no history, or anecdote was to be learnt from him. In the church yard is this epitaph,

JANE SCOTT.

Life is a journey of a winter's day,
Where many breakfast, and then pass away,
Some few stay dinner, and depart full fed
Fewer that *sups*, and then retire to bed.

Nothing can be more noble, more Gothic, or more elegantly carved than the front (now tottering) of Croyland Abbey; a beauty of the richest workmanship; my eyes gloried in beholding, whilst my heart sick'ned at the destruction: this my guide said, was owing to O. Cromwell.—There are 5 bells in the steeple, which is built for long endurance; but the present church, an aile of the old one, has been pillaged, like Thorney, to the very bone; not the smallest remain of stain'd glass, monuments; or any thing antient, except a grand holy water recess. After a looking at this nothing of inside, we went into the outer open space—formerly the body of the church, (wherein the dead are now buried, and the ground cover'd by grave stones). Of the great 8 southern windows, 4 have been lately taken down, for fear that they shou'd fall down; 'Why let them fall, and it saves trouble, and the over-care of blockheads': so only 4 remain! The front is so seam'd by rents, that down it must soon come; the finest monument in the kingdom: and wou'd I were near it then (not too near) to save, and carry off some of the carved figures. The old clerk was so stupid, and so ignorant, as not to

220

deserve my shilling; but that was bestow'd on age, and dimness of sight.

I now made the outer survey; and express'd my astonishment at all bonfires on rejoicing days being made under the eastern-window; as if to try if fire wou'd weaken what time had spared.

So MUCH for CROYLAND.—I am glad to have seen thee in thy last decline; it is like the comfort of having taken leave of a friend upon his death bed.—The fertility of this country is amazing, and might produce infinitely more burden, and variety than at present, were the land lesser leased and subdivided; with a swarm of inhabitants like Holland: for the clearing of the ditches afford fuel, and manure.—My charge here was cheap, and so it ought for vile tea, rank butter, and bad bread.—The roads are excellent, of a light gravell; whilst I expected stoney causeways.—

From Croyland, a high causeway continued, with much flaggy ground to my left, undrain'd thro' idleness; the pewits, who are the inhabiters, almost buffeted my head.— I had heard of St Guthlacs Cross, (but where uncertain), and therefore enquired after it at the toll bar, when the woman said 'Why there it stands, close to our house': so I dismounted, and faithfully copied it.

My road soon brought me to the village of Cowbett; whose miserable little thatched church I walk'd around.— Soon after, being overtaken by a storm of rain, I hurried into a shed which I occupied for $\frac{1}{2}$ an hour, unoticed.—

Another mile, and to Spalding, a large, clean, well-built, Spalding Dutch like, canall'd town; and to a good inn; whence I first took my bookseller, vainless, walk, and then to a more curious speculation:—for as I enter'd the town, I had observ'd a very antient house of bay windows, surrounded by yew hedge gardens; I now desired an admission, and was receiv'd by the master, Col^l J[ohnson],[51] a very old, worn-out man, who led me into his parlour, and began with saying, 'That he had served in the 1st Regt of foot

221

Guards,[52] and had a company therein'; 'And I had also one therein'; but this, even, did not rouse him, being apparently in pain, and having lost his memory: griev'd was I to see him, and vex'd not to have a servant to attend me.——

This good old parlour was cover'd with portraits, some seemingly very good; but it was heated by a fire, as was also his bed-room, in which were several excellent cabinet pictures, that I had not time to admire; for I expected the old gentleman to drop down dead, from his horrible grunts, and groans. I mention'd my fathers name to him; but all was forgotten! He spake of his family to me, and that one of his sons was the minister of this town; and he carried me into a room, where his daughters had been drying roses.——

The very old hall was properly furnish'd with armoury, buff-coats, and many curiosities of ancient warfare; but I had not permission for quiet observation, as I cou'd have wish'd.

There are many good pictures of esteem'd masters; but all in disorder and decay; like the owner.——At my return to the inn, my landlord wish'd to persuade me to order dinner, and not to wait for the house preparation; but I wou'd not, and so fared the better, and the cheaper, for I had boil'd beef, a pudding, a roasted rabbet, peas, &c; for the charge you see.

WHITE HART. SPALDING.

Dinner	-	-	-	-	1	0
Wine	-	-	-	-	2	3
					3	3

But I forgot to look into the play-house at the back of the inn.

In this town they fatten ruffs, and rees;[53] whose numbers, voluptuousness, or agriculture has thinn'd; they are 5 shillings the couple, male and female.

To inspect thoroughly, to ride slowly, to sketch, and to

write, this mornings distance were sufficient; more were too much: but having, in my mind, fix'd my return to Wansford, I was resolv'd to push on as far as possible.— Leaving Spalding before 4 o clock, I had not ridden a mile, e'er an horrid storm approach'd, which urged me to gallop Po furiously to the village of Pinchbeck (for the 1st Pinchbeck time T. B. said that he had ever seen me gallop Po) and to the Bell alehouse, which I had scarcely enter'd, when the clouds brake, and there fell one of the heaviest storms of rain, with repeated thunder, and lightning, that I ever remember: T. B. remain'd with the horses, whilst I sat with the landlady in a parlour; tho' she press'd me to go into the kitchen, to keep company with their clergyman,[54] whom she said was 'A fine *larned* man', but so addicted to drink as to have wasted all his money, after having sold the next presentation, and now cou'd not live out of an ale-house, where he wou'd accept of a glass of gin from any-one, 'to keep himself drunk'.—I did go in, and saw him sitting before the fire, smoking his pipe.—After an hours continuance of the pelting, pitiless storm, the weather rather bright'ned; and I pursued my way.

The road was excellent, and the country pleasant, affording a pretty village every 2 miles; but the evening was too threat'ning for a stop, else I shou'd have look'd into Gosberton Church: here I contrived to lose my way, by keeping straight forward, instead of turning to the right, wander'd two miles out of my road; which was what I cou'd not afford; so that I made my evening ride 20 miles, (too far by half) and did not reach the town of Boston till Boston near 9 o'clock.—I then was refused, after a long crawl over the stones, a room to myself at the Peacock Inn; but, (here) I exerted myself, and bluster'd, and threat'ned to go to another inn with MY SERVANT, AND MY HORSES;—and suc-ceeded!—

I supp'd upon boil'd soles.—Fish has been most abun-dant during this summer;—turbot 3d. pr lb, good soles 3d. the pair, mackarel 1d. the couple!

223

This inn is of the Gravesend cut; but I had a goodish bed-room.

A fresh, fair morning, wherein I took a pleasant hours walk before breakfast; admiring with all my eyes, and a strained neck, the beauty, grandeur, and loftiness of the tower of Boston Church, a building of most wonderful workmanship.—Within, tho' large, I recollected nothing (peeping thro' the windows) that mett my love of antiquity.

I next rambled by the rivers side, where the tide seems to rise very high; but how high, nobody (wou'd you believe it) cou'd tell me, tho' I ask'd several old sailors, and fishermen! My breakfast of to day, explain'd to me the badness of that of yesterday; for the sugar was fine enough for Col¹ B[ertie] who had perhaps been better employ'd in riding about this country with me, than by staying in London.

The cross, of which nothing now remains, stood, (I believe) in the market-place, and was (I suppose) removed at the time of the new paving of the town.—Before eleven o'clock, hearing the bell ring for prayers, I took that opportunity (to save my sixpence) of entering the church; which is very handsome, light, and lofty; the chancel is neatly kept, and there are stalls in it.—I made my round of observation within it, and found but one or two tombs; there have been many brasses upon the floor, all *carefully* removed, and what little continues, *was too firmly fixed*.— The market was plentiful, and the country lasses who came with poultry, eggs and their other little commodities, were neatly dress'd; but in the country they understand not the arts of decking out shops, for the geese here were not dress'd out like a finely-powder'd coxcomb goose in London: there was also a recruiting party, and the dirtiest I ever saw; of this I shou'd know something, having enacted Capt. Plume myself.

Hope not to learn any thing by asking questions of the natives, for they are all in vain! 'Whose house is that?'

'I don't know'. 'What street is that?' 'I can't tell'. I enquired, to-day, at a vessel, where she traded to? 'Sometimes to one place; sometimes to another'. What do you
freight with? 'Sometimes with one thing; sometimes with
another; just what we can get'.—The smell of shipping
and of coals, is particularly grateful to my constitution. As
I walk'd along the town, I saw an old monastic building,
now by a strange reverse turn'd into wine vaults; and
opposite to it is the old town hall,[55] which must have been a
part of the former: these, an old woman said, had been
mass houses, That Mr F[ydell][56] the great wine merchant,
shou'd chuse to represent the town he lives in, is most
wonderful to me! Nor wou'd I ever vote for a man who
sells such bad wine, as I have often drank of his merchandise.—At the towns end I beheld a very antient brick
ruin (untold to me) which a woman said 'Was a castle
built in the wars'. It must have been part of a grand mansion; many walls are about it; and near to it a very old
school house. I had now seen enough of Boston; having
paraded up, and down, the market-place 50 times; and
was not sorry when my dinner appear'd at one o'clock.
There were unluckily, but some small soles, and some
shrimps in the market; except one or two large turbots,
and one might as well eat of a shark, as of those.—The
removal from every house, the fear of change, the uneasiness of statement, make allways a dismal time that all
are happy to get over.

PEACOCK INN. BOSTON.

Gentl^m Supper	-	-	-	-		1	9
Wine	-	-	-	-	-	1	0
Brandy	-	-	-	-	-	1	6
Breakft	-	-	-	-	-		9
Dinner	-	-	-	-	-	1	9
Wine	-	-	-	-	-	2	0
Paper & Rushlight	-	-	-				1½
Hay & Corn	-	-	-	-		3	2
					£0	12	0½

Hence I was glad, then, to remove, to be free'd from a gloomy inn, and again to get off the stones, and into the country.—(perhaps I had done right in remaining here 2 more days, and to have excursed; this I thought of; but then there is no stop, and my object was only a survey of the fens: these are now so drain'd and cultivated, as to deceive my expectation, which fancied an infinity of canals, causeways, reeds and rushes; instead of which I travell'd on fine gravelly roads, and the country was till'd for grain). My road of return was by that of yesterday to Kirton, (which I then hurry'd by) but now having time, I made an inspection of the church; and was attended— thro' civility, by a gentleman I shou'd deem the apothecary from his knowledge of the deaths of those at rest in the church-yard!

Kirton

'Let him thank me that holp to send him thither'.

It is a magnificent, well-kept country church, and contains an old font, with an inscription in Latin; which I had neither time nor curiosity to make out.

Here I turn'd to the left; and in a charming evening, and in a pleasant road, (for in this country the horses might go without shoes) came in 5 miles to the bank of the washes, where is a public house—call'd Fosdike—of the bathing sort; where is a large room for company, some good bed chambers, and a bathing house: and if a person would study to find out a quiet place with a fine sand in front, and good roads with a pleasant country behind, and with cheap living, this is the spot.—Quiet enough it was, of all conscience, at present (for this was not the flow fort-night, when some people may come) for I had the house to myself; and drank tea most comfortably in the great room; with a view over the sands, (beautiful when the tide is in,) and to the opposite country, and the churches of Fleet, Holbeach, &c.— — It is stated as necessary, that a guide shou'd be hired here, who, for 3 pence a horse, escorts you to the opposite land; inventing, or magnifying the danger you might have sustain'd with his pilotage: sometimes, for

226

their advantage, a drunken man is drown'd in the passage.
—I shou'd not forget to state, that (as an addition to our
company, and trouble,) a young pointer follow'd us out of
Boston, attaching himself to T. B.'s cur, Jock; and did
hunt about, violently, for my amusement: so he came
along with us, and may be mention'd hereafter; I call'd
him Sancho.— — From the last guide house it is 4 miles
to Holbeach, a pretty clean, little town, with a snug civil Holbeach
inn (of my sort) fronting their noble church, whose porch
is flanked by round towers.—Around the churchyard I
walked a dozen times: but the poetry was *too good* for me:
there was one tolerable inscription upon 3 children—
Greenwoods.

> The Great Jehovah full of love,
>   An angel bright did send,
> To fetch away three spotless doves,
>   To joys that ne'er does end.

I stroll'd about the town, and environs till nine o'clock,
my supping hour, and the hour of the chimes, which were
very musical.—In this church yard are many walnut trees,
of more use, now, both as to fruit, and wood than the
quondam-deadly yew.—Fancying I had read of an old
cross here, and had seen a print, I was half angry at the
denial of any such building; so all memory of this cross (so
well described by Dr Stukeley) is now lost. Where it stood,
there is a mean brick building, a kind of a small market
house.

Of a market, this place might have boasted formerly;
but markets and market-days were, some years ago,
different exhibitions from those at present; and were
chartered[57] to encourage open and fair dealings, and to
suppress combinations.—It was, then a day of joy, and
hope in the town whose bells rang merrily; at a fixed hour
the corn was pitch'd, according to rule, in the market
place; where the jolly farmers assembled, and afterwards
dined together at the several inns.—The careful matrons,
and the ruddy country wenches attended, beneath the

market house, with their cheap poultry, ducks, eggs, pigs, &c, &c. (the produce of their own care, and the support of their little families): whilst the sage housekeeper, and the widow ladies came forth for their purchases. Here was every right intention of fair sale, and honest dealing.— — Now let us view the present state, and the disuse of the markets. *Some* farmers *may* ride there in the morning, for a cabal of an hour, to raise, or keep up, the price of corn; which great farms, with such management, can easily accomplish: and has, *entirely* demolish'd the right intention of *free* markets! As for the sake of smaller commodities, that is ended; for the cottages are pull'd down, and the smaller farms are swallow'd up by the greater: and what poultry may be rear'd, is hourly pick'd up by forestalling higlers, for the supply of London, or of great manufactoring towns!!—Thus is lost all hope of, and encouragement for, the poor; an end of cheap residence in the country; and a general increase of expence over the whole kingdom; besides the advantage formerly accruing to the market-town, which on that day display'd all its wares, that were carry'd off in the returning carts, and waggons; as well as (what so much diverted me in my 'sallad' days) the harmless asseverations of a pompous mountebank, with the feats of his Merry-Andrew; or the wit of Mister Punch, and his most facetious family.

After supper, I call'd in my landlord, for some information about the country, but he knew full as little as others, only the common high road; boots knew full as much, with a beard of an inch long; for he allways shaves 'like a gentleman, once't a week'. The waiter said, that their church musick, and singing were good; but did not advise me to stay the service of tomorrow, as their poor curate who has so many children, had but a bad delivery: (his wife beats him in that:) as for the rector of this rich living,[58] he never was here but when presented to it. Think of that ye bishops: and yet this living was given to him by the Bishop of Lincoln!—I have written enough for to-day; so D.—I.—O.— —

The storm of Friday fell here with great violence; but I *Sunday* did not hear of any damage sustain'd. My first business of *July 4* this day was to see the inside of the church, which is a noble pile, but like most others in this neighbourhood contains little of the antique; in this, indeed, there is a knight carv'd in stone, but whose name is (here) unknown. In the bellfry is a ring of eight bells. The chancell is neat, but much darken'd by the blocking up of windows.

Before breakfast my hair was comb'd, and powdered in a barbers shop; but I could not get any account, there, of the place, or of the country. My bill was remarkably cheap, for I had a fine roasted fowl for supper, &c, &c. Luckily there was no other traveller in this house; for I doubt if it afforded more than one good parlour, and one good bed room.

My horses (for the 1st time) were charged only at 8d. for hay!

CHEQUERS. HOLBEACH.

Supper	-	-	-	-	-	1	3
Brandy	-	-	-	-	-	1	3
Wine	-	-	-	-	-	1	
Tea	-	-	-	-	-		8
Horses hay & corn	-	-	-	-	2	7
						6	9
Rushlight	-	-	-	-	-		1

It proved a pleasant morning of the September cast: the country is flat, fertile, and famous for breeding horses and cattle, witness the great ox now to be seen in London, who was bred, and fed in the village of Fleet; part of which I pass'd thro', leaving the church, at some distance, to my right; so to Gedney; and thence to Long-Sutton, a large, straggling, well-built village.——Beyond this the open country has been lately enclosed, and so continues to near Tid-Goat (Tide-Gate I suppose it shou'd be) where crossing a bridge, I enter'd Cambridgeshire; and in a few miles came to Wisbich, an ugly, dull town, with a large canal *Wisbech* thro' it, in the Dutch taste, over which has been lately built an handsome stone bridge of one arch.

When I enter'd the inn (the Rose and Crown) I was instantly prejudiced against it by the sight of a fine, conceited, dress'd-out landlady; and from the ostler having two (deserved) black eyes: neither would she let me eat of the family dinner, but I *must* order something.—There was I suppose a castle at Wisbich; but when pull'd down?

I walk'd to the church, just as the good folk were issuing out of it; and there I saw Mr L[indsay], the rector,[59] from whom (introducing myself) I receiv'd many kind invitations, and pressures to stay; which were by me, all evaded and refused.

My dinner was bad; my charge was dear: my horses could not eat the hay, and I could not drink the wine.— The wine of last night at Holbeach was tolerably good.— This is certainly not the Isle of Dogs from the termination of these neighbouring towns, Hol-bitch, Wis-bitch.

The canal from Wisbich is wide and strait. By its side I was overtaken by a sort of rider, who wish'd me to accompany him; but I advised him not to ride my slow pace: so finding me glum, he push'd forward. (Why shou'd one throw away time and thoughts upon strangers: I come abroad for quiet, country air, fresh scenery, and to go my own way and my own pace; to escape from London blockheads, and the many who will, without caring for you, ask how you do? It concerns very few how I do; and why then be pester'd with the question? This fellow had no thoughts of his own, and wanted to make prey of some of mine; but this is a species of highway robbery I can defend myself against: so I made the fellow sheer off.)

As for any gentlemen to be met travelling, or touring on horseback that the refinement of the age forbids;—a true fine gentleman takes most of his riding upon the stones of London.—And when he travells—it is asleep at the corner of a post chaise: now I maintain that would you enjoy impartial air, wholesome exercise, or intend to see *your own country*, it must be on *the outside* of a horse: nor since I left

Peterborough have I seen one improved place of residence; fenns are not the seats of taste, and pleasure.—

I came in a gloomy evening (which glooms the mind) in eleven miles to March, a scrambling kind of a market town, where I proposed making my night stop; but the largest inn look'd so shabbily, and the casements so broken, that I walk'd forward; when another public house presented itself, whose landlord (with good premonition) said 'Your servant master', to me, and to Mr T. B. 'Goodnight to you, *young man*'; upon which Mr T. B. trotting up, remark'd, 'That house wou'd seemingly do for us'; but I overruled his motion.—At the end of this town, has stood a grand cross, as one might judge from the remains of steps, arms &c.—I allow'd that we had come far enough, quite far enough; but a bed inn must be look'd to. So we travell'd another 4 miles, to Duddington; and, here, the sky long overcast, turn'd to rain; a quick movement was therefore necessary over the remaining, dreary 4 miles which led to Chatteris; where my fears return'd if we had Chatteris forwarded for the better: but the town looking much better than March, and the clean, comfortable inn, The George, put me quite at my ease.—To our new dog Sancho, I am much obliged for his activity, and hunting, which have beguil'd my time, tho at the end he rather tired, for I have ridden 34 miles! After the horses were settled, and I had order'd supper and procured my rooms (for *the rider* stop'd here) I prowled the church-yard.

> JOSEPH BROWN, Aged 3 Years.
> Our dear loved child has lost his life
> His life was but a span
> His blessed Lord call'd him away
> What is the life of man.
> Much did he love his loving friends
> Yet loved the blessed Jesus more
> He beat the waves to seek his Lord
> And found him on the heavenly shore.

A man, that was near me, said that the child was drown'd in a pond; which may account for the two last lines: the others are very elaborate, and curious!

Then found my way to the old nunnery, which stands within the old boundary; and the house built upon the scite (for of the original I think there can be none) is in tolerable preservation.

A twining walk of reverend walnut trees lead to it; an elderly gentlewoman of the house, invited me in, and shew'd the old hall, two parlours, (with some old books) stair-case, &c.—All in the ancient, thick wall'd stile; a comfortable, warm, sequester'd building it is: to a little child with her, I gave sixpence, and advised her to physic him for the worms, for which she was very grateful, and took me for one of the faculty.—I had a cold supper, and much writing to make up; so that I did not get to bed till eleven o'clock.

Monday
July 5

Yesterday I rode too far; but then I came to a good inn, and find I shall gain a day by it: the road of yesterday was barren of observation; but the difference betwixt this county, and Derbyshire, has been truly striking, therefore they have well follow'd the other; here we have had smooth riding, there, all hills, and stones; here, no view, there, a diversity of beautiful prospects;—of fens, and flats, one quickly tires.

Whenever any person in travelling changes a note, a guinea, or a shilling, he is sure to have, in change, bad money tender'd to him, as if it was part of the profit of inns, and turnpikes.—This I found a good inn, and most certainly a cheap charge.

GEORGE INN. CHATTERIS. 4. July.

							s.	d.
Supper -	-	-	-	-	-		1	0
Wine -	-	-	-	-	-		1	2
Brandy -	-	-	-	-	-		1	0
5. Breakfast	-	-	-	-	-		0	9
							3	11

WITCHFORD CHURCH: NORTH SIDE

[*see p.* 233

*This little dirty Chapel, by the North Road Side, We may Suppose
as being dedicated to S[t] Andrew, to have been a Place, where Votaries
from the North head offered up their Prayers for future Fortune.*

CHAPEL AT ALCONBURY
from water-colours by the Diarist

[*see p.* 241

The country from Chatteris continues very dreary flat common; and I was hurry'd over the last part of it by a severe storm that drove us into a farm-yard under a hovel for shelter, at the village of Maypole; over whose stocks are Maypole inscribed

'Those that are wise
These will despise'.

Written, I presume, in gravity, and good intention.

From Maypole there rises a small hill into an open corn country, which gave me pleasure; for I sicken'd of the flat fen.—I left Sutton on my right, with a good-looking church, and soon came to Whichford, where I idled some time under a walnut tree, in the church-yard; sketching this miserable, little church. (Such attempts will I hope mend my pencil; at lease, they gratify my intention.)

Hence I was soon at Ely, pelted in by the rain; and Ely there receiv'd such a pacquet of letters from Mrs B[yng], as, with the cold rst beef served me an hour, and a half; when I recollected that I must view the cathedral.—Now, perhaps, I was not in a humour to be pleased; for, except the centre dome, what is there?—I think it a shabby, ill-kept, edifice, I mean the inside, for the outside is very lofty, and fine, only sadly disfigur'd by the northern side of the west front being down; the chapels are dawb'd over by a whiting; and the stalls, and the altar are in very paltry taste: I enquired for a chapter house, but the woman said there was none; however I found it out, when she shew'd me the adjoining parish church, for which the old chapter house is used; and is the only one I ever saw of the long square form, and much inferior to the circular ones with the pillar: adjoining to the church have been cloisters.

At a small distance is the castle hill, now call'd Cherry Hill; and the old porters lodge, which I shou'd rather think belong'd to the castle, than to the close.—Perhaps, I was neither fit for a Lt. Col¹. or a Bishop; for I am for high dress, subordination, forms, and discipline: as a church-

233

man, I had endeavour'd to imitate that great and good prelate, Archbishop Laud; for without pomp, order, and method, neither the priesthood, or parade will flourish; and was I in my stall, or my pulpit, I wou'd call to an offender, as I wou'd to an offender on a field day: dirty surplices, and slurring over the divine service, are surely, more reprehensible than dirty gaiters, and slovenly motions?

The appearance of truth that I saw, last year, at Southwell, runs in my head: here, I am sure, it exists not. There is much old building to admire, about the close; and the bishops palace I wish'd to enter, but was refused: the gallery, particularly, I shou'd like to have seen.

The town is mean, to an extreme; for if any man chuses to observe, he will find that castles, and religious houses were the safeguards, and comforts of the country; those withdrawn, their dependencies must decay: what must the decrease of genteel residence occasion in the country? Why, starvation and any wish of change; from sceneries of woe, and oppression, to a hope never realized; from a wretched village to Botany Bay!

LAMB INN ELY.

Dinner & Ale -	-	-	-	-	I	0
Wine -	-	-	-	-	I	2
					S2	2

I was away in good time from Ely; but then I fear'd that the heavy storms, around, might impede me; and so Streatham they did, for as I reach'd Streatham village (4 miles) the rain fell most heavily.

My horses being lodg'd in the stables of a public house, I took my station (for some time) under the gateway of the church yard entrance; there sketching the cross, which, from its slope, and decay, must soon fall to the ground.

Such erections as these which survived, were obliged to

234

assume the uses of dials.—After a long, fretting delay here, with the horses, and dogs, shiv'ring in a cold stable, I remounted; tho' but for 2 minutes, when I was driven into a wheelwrights yard, and there we skulk'd for another half hour. These rains, and glooms, quite despond the tourist; who then wishes himself in London, in a drawing-room, or a coffee-house. After these delays, and the evening being so sour, I only thought of making my way; nor did I wish to view the ground where Denny Abbey stood, upon which there is now a good farm-house, but not a remaining porch of antiquity.

Notwithstanding my haste, I was overtaken beyond Milton village, by another storm, which I endured into Cambridge town; where I crawled over the stones, to the Cambridge Black Bull Inn; and there, with difficulty, procured a parlour, and a bed room. (For I shou'd not have come hither had I known of the morrows commencement.)

I never was in a worse or a dirtier inn; for ALL Cambridge is in comparison of Oxford, (what France is to England) about 100 years behind hand: the best Cambridge inn wou'd form but a bad Oxford alehouse!—Dirty glasses; bad wine; vile cookery; but I answer to any question of hope, 'Oh, it is excellent'; and why should I not? Now Col¹ B[ertie] takes another plan; and roundly reproves them: but I, resolv'd never to come again, don't like to vex myself; and so I say 'It is all very good'. Tho here it went much against the grain.—The evening soon settled in for a desperate rain; which I had the pleasure of hearing, when in a miserable tent bed, in a dark room, opening from an old gallery. This wretched inn, with most of this wretched town, ought to be burnt down!

It was with difficulty a bed cou'd be procured: had I *Tuesday July 6* known of this commencement I had gone 20 miles another way.—The rain continued thro' the night with unabating violence, to the mischief of the corn, and to the destruction of the young partridges.—The town is newly paved (*after*

235

a fashion) which unluckily gives the walker an opportunity of viewing the houses.—Some antiquities here I wish'd to see; and for information of their situation to whom must I apply? Why to inkeepers, or to the booksellers; and of these Mr Lunn and Mr Morrell, knew very little: the latter did hint some kind of direction to find out Phythagoras's School (formerly, I believe, a preaching house of the monks of Crowland); but my search was in vain.

I next walk'd within the castle limits, and to the top of the castle mount, whence is the best observation of this filthy town, and the vile surrounding country.

Of the old castle nothing remains but the entrance; which, with additions, now serves for the county prison.—

My walk was much lengthen'd, by my meandring thro' several of the shady walks at the back of the greater colleges; which, with Kings College Chapel (into which, from the clerks absence I could not enter) constitute the only beauties of Cambridge.—

I saw all the gownsmen (the Mr Williams's of Pompey the Little,)[60] handing ladies; and much crop-ear'd country company, hustling to The Senate-House. . . . I know *nothingsh* of *commencements*!

If gentlemen, and artists put forth topographical prints, why will they not state their situation, and vicinity? else it is often impossible to find them! (Mr G.'s[61] and all other publications are guilty of this omission!)—How difficult it is to find people out in a street in London, if they will not plate their door; think then, how the tourist must wander over a wild country, in doubt, and despair: venting himself upon the print sellers who have encourag'd his travell!! Of my intended way in this town whom shou'd I ask? Why I will say of whom I asked; the landlord, the hostler, and then the two greatest booksellers.

Of the hostler, enquiring the road to Grandchester, only 3 miles distant, he answer'd, (after a long stammer) 'Were you ever there, sir?' 'No, or I wou'd not have ask'd you the way'.—At last I got an information to go by

Trumpington, to Grantchester; and this was all the information I got in this seat of learning; in this dirty, cheating inn; for my charge was excessive; the brandy was charged at the rate of 7s. the quart! and no redress; you may fly; but you cannot fight!

It was a very blust'rous day; after the heavy rain. Trumpington is two miles from Cambridge; where turning to the right, thro' some lanes, and crossing the stream, I soon came to Grandchester; long the intention of my visitation, to find out a family monument.

Grant-
chester

A civil old clerk shew'd me the church, (the sacred storehouse of many of my family, a branch from the trunk of Wrotham, in Kent,) where, I found the monument.—It has been the ornament of the chancell; and SHALL BE AGAIN; for I will repair it.—The writing is much obliterated. (The arms are, quarterly 1st and 4th sable; 3 lions heads erased sable and argent; a cheveron or, between 3 lions heads erased argent.)

From the old walling, the mote, &c, there must have been a large mansion here. (Thomas Byng of Grantchester[62] (from the Wrotham stock) was, I believe, the first of the family settled here: he was L.D., Master of Clare-Hall 1571, and Regius Professor.) And this is surely a more honourable mention than one I heard of at Cambridge, viz,

> 'Of whom there is no other memorial
> But that he was a fellow of Oriel',

as if they were to state of me hereafter,

> 'His early days were spent in camps
> His latter days were pass'd at stamps.'

After quitting G, we came into open-field riding, that might have been tolerable in a dry summer, but was now as deep, and as slippery as in winter. After many a slip, and many a slide, I came into the village of Haslingfield, willing to observe an old house I had heard of there: but this old house when I found it, was of no curiosity, or worthy

237

of observation; and the farmer, half sulky, kept me at a distance.——

[And here I cannot help deploring, in my old stile, the desertion of the country, by the gentlemen, and good yeomanry. An hundred years ago, every village afforded 2 good gentlemens houses; and within these 60 years, the hall, or the court still remain'd. These were the supporters of the poor, and of their rights; and their wives were the Lady Bountifuls of the parish: there was then a good country neighbourhood, whose families intermarried with each other. But since the increase of luxury, and turnpike roads, and that all gentlemen have the gout, and all ladies the bile, it has been found necessary to fly to the bath, and to sea-bathing for relief: there the gaiety, and neat houses make them resolve upon fixing on these spots; whilst the old mansion being deserted, and no longer the seat of hospitality, and the resort of sportsmen, is left to tumble down: and, with it, the strength, and glory, and, I may add, the religion of the country.——For whilst decent, and pious families therein resided, the minister attended to his double Sunday duties, and to the weekly prayers on Wednesdays, and Fridays, besides the keeping of holidays; to which the aged, and virtuous poor were urged to attend, by good example.——But the families being gone, no longer are these duties continued; and the divine, himself, from lack of company, pays a pitiful stipend to a hackney curate (who rides over half the country on a Sunday) and retires to London, or to Bath.

The poor cottagers, who are soon reduced to half their former number, are consigned over to the few farmers; and nothing remains of the old hall, but some tottering walls, and uncultivated kitchen gardens. So endeth the prosperity, the beauty, the support, the religion of the land!]

When I arriv'd, in what they call another mile, at Halton-village, I stopp'd at an alehouse for some bread, and cheese, and ale, (remarkably bad.) Upon the opposite hill is a prospect pole; whence I saw, below me, the woods,

and park of Wimple;[63] and was happy to get into shade, Wimpole
and upon a good road. Some enclosed, wooded grounds
brought me to the house, where, I sought, in vain, for
admission; and after a waiting of 20 minutes, (a sufficient
time for a view) was refused by the servants; tho I knew
that Ld and Lady Hardwick were at the Cambridge
commencement.—I did, to be sure, feel a *little* vex'd:—
but what can be seen in such an ugly, modern, house?
Around which appears not a glimmering of taste; nor are
the stables, and offices, planted off from sight!—Riding
thro' the park, (like that of Wrest, in flatness, and views)
with only one hill to my right, on which is this ugly
summer-house building; I came into the old North Road at
the little village of Arrington.   Arrington

It was now 3 o'clock, (time for dinner,) and therefore
after reconnoitring the Talbot public house, I put up;
and had a good room, dinner of plenty, and pass'd one
hour, and an half, in contentment. The landlord is an old
stupid German; formerly, I suppose a servant in the York
family: but the house is a good horse halt, and pleasantly
placed for walking and riding in the park.—

Dinner -	-	-	-	-	-	1	0
Wine -	-	-	-	-	-	1	2
Beer -	-	-	-	-	-	0	3
Hay & Corn -	-	-	-	-	-	0	10
						3	3

I am now on the old North Road,[64] almost abandon'd
for the new one, upon which are better inns; and leads better
into the west end of the town.—There was no reason for
my being deny'd at W: House; as I mett, two hours after,
(when I had left Arrington,) Lady Hardwick on her
return.—To the right of the road is a view of foolish,
fantastic, mock ruins, unlike every thing they wou'd wish
to represent.

The road is, generally, enclosed, and with some woods,
till I came to Caxton, a poor mean place, probably ruin'd

239

from the loss of the passage; whence a wild, open road, good to ride however, brought me to Godmanchester, at $\frac{1}{2}$ past seven o'clock: having pass'd by Beggars Bush, (now an elm tree planted there and call'd Kings-Bush).

Hunting-
don I dismounted before I descended the hill, and had a walk of two miles, (sending the horses forward,) thro' Godmanchester, over the bridge, and to Huntingdon; where at the head quarters of the Blues, I hoped to have found my old comrade Major S[taveley];[65] but he was not with the regiment, so I left a letter for him.—I had sent my horses (luckily) to The George, an old and unfashionable inn, but I knew there was good stabling, and I was civilly receiv'd, and well-treated at supper; after I had walk'd about for near an hour.—My writing, after supper, commonly employs me till eleven o'clock, my hour of retiring.—

Wednesday
July 7 I put in practise, this morning, the right intention of touring; viz, to rise early, and ride away to the first stop to breakfast. By these means, you get forward on the day, enjoy the morning air, and go to your breakfast with true relish.—I did not wait T. B.'s call; but was down stairs by $\frac{1}{2}$ past six o'clock; and as soon as I cou'd was walking forward.—(Having had a fine rst fowl, peas, &c, for supper, this is certainly a cheap charge.)

GEORGE INN. HUNTINGDON.

						s.	d.
Supper	-	-	-	-	-	2	0
Wine	-	-	-	-	-	1	3
Brandy	-	-	-	-	-	1	
Paper	-	-	-	-	-		2
						4	5
Horses hay & corn	-	-	-	-	3	2
					£0	7	7

The road from Huntingdon is pleasant, (at least the morning sun made it appear so,) passing thro' the two

Stukeleys (that is stiff-clays): and before the night lodgers had got away from the Wheat-sheaf on Alconbury Hill, I was sat down, there, at my breakfast.

Huntingdon, since the new pavement, is a much improved-looking town; and from situation, soil, roads, river, &c, may be thought a pleasant place. In my walk of last night, I went round the old circuit of the priory of Black Canons to the honor of St Mary.[66]

Upon a door, at the end of Huntingdon, I read this (well formed) direction—

> Tho⁸ White chimney-sweeper lives here
> Sweeps clean with great care
> All that please on me to call
> Masters and mistresses I serve you all
> Town and country fire defender
> Chimney sweeper and smoke jack mender.

Alconbury Hill inn, The Wheatsheaf, as standing single, high, and free from noise, is most agreeable; but as to furniture, waiting, &c, it is little better than an alehouse; and in winter must be a cold abode.—My stay here was very pleasant; the garden was fill'd with flowers; and the morning was gay; these are the delights of touring.—I hence took a walk, endeavouring to make my dogs hunt, for above a mile, to the bottom of the hill below Monkswood; below which, to my right, stood Saltry-Abbey, where are now some cottages, and many foundations of old buildings.—Of this place mine host of the Wheat-sheaf told me a *wonderful* story 'That some few years ago he found there, amidst an heap of stones, a gold ring with a Latin motto, which he gave to the woman of the house, who suff'ring the children to play with it, it was soon lost'.

— — The day was unusually pleasant; and I trotted along, anxious to reach my late home at W[ansford]-Bridge; and to receive letters from my true home.—

My only stop was to take a sketch of this poor church.

Except another small stop, at the village of Allwalton, near the road, to observe the staring built house of Mr

Belford; where I walk'd around the church-yard, made my usual peep into the church windows, and look'd about for inscriptions: the best I cou'd find (especially for rhyme) was this upon

SUSANNAH WYMAN.

Here lies a rose bud just cropt'd by death
Which now lies sleeping in this bed of earth.

Upon the church wall is a dial, under which is written '*Watch and Pray*'.

Wansford Bridge

I hail'd my return to W. Bridgé with pleasure, as a place of comfort, and content; after being worried about at nasty inns, in a bad country. Here I had a regale of letters; but not half finish'd when my dinner was announced; and now I had to return to my domestic fishery; in the which I proved unsuccessfully, for an hour, on the opposite bank of the river, amidst the uncarry'd hay.—Being as yet unacquainted with my dog Sancho, I next try'd to coax him to walk with me; and we went together to the wood above the hill, and there stroll'd about, with many hares, and rabbets in sight, which my dog was too steady to run at, as I wish'd, but pointed at them most steadily. However I had a pleasant walk; and at my return, to my great surprise, found Col¹ B[ertie]'s⁶⁷ chaise in the yard: 'What is Col. B. here?' 'Yes, Sr and his two nephews'. (Now this I might have expected had I properly receiv'd Mrs B[yng]'s letters.)—After mutual salutations, enquiries, and seeing our several stables, we had only to order supper; he comes, last, from Peterborough, and is in his way into the north. —An early supper; the boys eat as boys, and retired soon as boys shou'd do; when we stay'd up till ½ past eleven o'clock.—

I endeavour'd to persuade the Col¹ (from my own feelings) against any long flights; and how much better it were, *now*, to hover about home; within reach of friends, and physicians; for I, really, begin to feel that enough is to be seen near home, without wandering like the Guardian frigate, into unknown seas, against rocks of ice:—but the Col¹ contrives to encumber himself with loads; and one shou'd think loves inconveniences arising from a false love of grandeur and relationship. —

I early try'd my fishing rod but without success; and was glad when the breakfast hour arriv'd; but not till my black horse had undergone a good lunging.—Sancho, the pointer, now takes to me, from my often feeding him, and was happy to accompany us in our ride after breakfast.—I undertook to shew to the Colonel, the country, and succeeded—*a marveille*; for knowing no further than Elton, I soon became bewilder'd, when we plung'd thro' the water at the mill; then passing along a causeway by the river, at last came to a strong stile that was to be leapt: 'Come Poney try away'.—But so unluckily he managed, that he knock'd his hinder leg upon the bar; and seem'd much hurt. We had, after this, some deep dangerous passes to lead our horses thro' or over; and I was heartily vext to find myself upon a limping horse.—My intentions were to lead Col¹ B[ertie] to Fotheringay, where we soon arrived; and there observed the old keep of the castle, the old inn, &c; and then got the key of the church, which whilst Col¹ B: was observing, I employ'd myself in sketching the old font.—

In the church yard is an inscription to the memory of

Thursday July 8

Fotheringay

> WILLm. FALL, aged, 22 years
>
> The stars we know do us incline,
> But hard was this sad fate of mine;
> The powers above decreed that I
> Was born, and in deep water die:
> Reader, be carefull how you spend each day,
> Least you like he be snatch'd away.—

This place, I had, before, fully seen; and the Col¹ was, now, much pleas'd with the church.—The village is dirty, and contemptible; but famous for its horse fair.

From Fotheringay I again proved an excellent guide, for I again lost the way, and went a mile roundabout to the village of Nassington, which is only two miles distant from our inn.—We dined well; but the Col[1] does so control the boys, that they know not what, or how much they shou'd eat; and sit in dread of his commands.—After dinner Col. B. wish'd to ride to see Ld W[estmoreland]'s[68] seat at Apthorp, 5 miles distant; but my horses stiffness prevented me.—In his absence I try'd, in vain, to fish; and then took a walk to meet their return;—a comfortable supper, and sitting.—

Wansford
Bridge

Friday
July 9

A newspaper, and my daily letter from home; with one, the earliest effusion, of the dear Frederick. The party now were moving forward on their northern circuit.—Col. B. by delaying here a day on his road, shews much civility; but resting here as I was, and not wishing for interruption, he never cou'd come at a worse time: to share your intentions were friendly, but thus entering like a visitor deranges me; besides the Col[1] has allways, and allways will have his incumbrances!—He now brings two nephews with him, (nepotism like a Pope) whom he chides, and directs everlastingly: the Col[1] loves not snugness, and quiet, as I do; for he must be in company, or whisking along; and cannot endure a day in a place: he is now hurrying into Lancashire, that he may hurry in Lincolnshire, and hurry thence back to London!! When the weather clear'd up, about 12 o'clock; (for it rain'd all night, and this morning) Col[1] B. proposed to be going: but I shou'd not have been sorry to have kept myself and my limping horse at home.—The day proved very windy, and very clear; and I continued with the northern party till the hill above Stamford, where we shook hands, and parted.—I, now, turn'd over the race course, by the stand, which is a very handsome one, and the spot very chearful, to the village of Easton, where is an house to be lett.

TO BE SOLD,

A Very handsome large HOUSE, at EASTON, (near Stamford), in Northamptonshire, with good Garden, cold Bath, Out-offices, and every Conveniency, for a Gentleman's Family; in a most delightful healthy high Situation; fine Air; excellent Roads, in a fine Sporting Country; with great Plenty of all Sorts of Game; and a very good Neighbourhood, within little more than a Mile of Stamford, a very genteel Town, and an excellent Market for Fish, Flesh, and every other Conveniency; and about the same Distance from the great North Road from London to Edinboro'.

It is a grandish stone-house, fit for a retiring tradesman, with a pleasant look to Worthorp-Grove. The church, at the end of this village, commands a fine view over the vale, and town of Stamford; and is a beautiful building. In the church-yard is this epitaph of good division of rhyme, and of good spelling to the memory of

JOHN BLACK.

> Farewell to you my lovely
> Spouse: Your years for mee
> Refrain. We'f only parted
> for a while in hopes to meet
> A gain.—

Opposite to this village is Worthorp-Grove, which I rode by, in my return; and which brought me to (what no one will tell you of) the lofty ruins of Worthorp House;[69] where Lord Burleigh retired to, 'To be out of the dust whilst Burleigh House was building'.

The roof is off, the stair cases almost rotted, but it is yet of loftiness, and magnificence; why Ld C.,[70] living so near, and finding this within his own farm should neither restore this building as a mansion, nor embellish it as a ruin; and that Ld E., (as man of supposed taste) should let it abide within a farm-yard, exposed to wretchedness, apart from use or ornament, I do not conceive!—Enclose, and leave it, and the natural growth of trees and ivy, wou'd soon form a beauty around it.—(But I am tired of offering reforms, so let my lord of E. indulge his taste his own way).

The gates of these grounds being lock'd, I was oblig'd

to return under the wall, which road brought me back to the race-course stand, which is an handsome building, wherein tea drinkings used to be held.—I now made a detour, to the right, to the village of Wittering, and then back into the high road, where I met the Duke of A[ncaster],[71] in his way, to Grimsthorpe; and held a long discourse with him about his cousin.—The day proved very pleasant; and Sancho hunted about much to my amusement. I was most eager, at my return, for dinner, being 4 o'clock; and was instantly well serv'd—a roasted chicken, and a hot ham, &c, and I found that a pint of port wine (never even the half of an inn bottle) would scarcely serve my dinner time, so was obliged to call for another, and thus lose my measure.—My dog and I had a long walk in the evening; then a cold supper; but not till I had attended the horses, who look very well.

Saturday
July 10   Time runs away; my holidays will soon expire; and I must begin to think of the stamp revenue; and of trudging every morning, to Somerset Place.[72]—Most pleasures have attendant pains; since I came last here, I have a crickish pain in the back of my neck, and, to-day, a rheumatis'm in my shoulders, and chest; all got by going from a warm bed to stand, in a cold wind, upon a rivers brink: very idle that! and yet one cannot foresee what shou'd happen, and might be prevented; or we should live too long, and happily: so now when I fish, it must be in a warm evening, after a pint of port, and when the air has been soften'd by the sun.—I rode Blacky to day; tho now determin'd that he will never be a horse I can approve of.

In passing thro' our village, I espied the lid of an old stone coffin by the Gully Way; and applying to Mr Medmar (the Duke of B[edford]'s agent) who lives at the end of the bridge, I had it removed into my landlord's garden; the old woman, before whose door it lay, said she had remember'd it there, for 50 years. At the little village of Stebington, a mile from this place, to which I rode,

WANSFORD BRIDGE: TURNPIKE HOUSE

WOTHORP HOUSE
from water-colours by the Diarist [*see p.* 245

there is an ancient stone mansion, inhabited by a farmer; this I ask'd leave to enter: in it is a good old fashion'd parlour, and a picture of one monkey shaving another. Over the porch of entrance is written

Deo: Trin: Uni:
Sit. Gloria
1625.

If a man were rightly to indulge a pursuit of antiquity he shou'd go from village to village; from church to church; then wou'd he frequently discover some curious monuments, some very antient houses, some castellated ground: the worse the roads, the more, probably, of unexplored curiosity; for good roads have removed ever stone, and stick, as navigations have spoil'd the beauty of rivers.

Near to the village of Water-Newton, a pretty village, 2 miles distant, there has been a Roman station[73], in the fields (still call'd Castle Fields;) where coins are frequently found.—I rode there this evening, and applying to an old woman, she said that her children had lately brought her two; which she call'd mites: they are, I believe, of the Emperor Claudius, are very perfect, and I cou'd easily discern *Imperator*. My angling rod next took its turn, (for the moments of life shou'd not be lost,) and I caught one good perch; besides having caught on the bank, in the course of the day, a cold, if I may judge by my evening feels.—The minister of Water-Newton, being visiting at this house, and hearing that there was *a learned* antiquary within, (for this coffin lid will set my name up) was usher'd in to me; and then talk'd so learnedly about Roman emperors, and Roman coins, as thoroughly to confound one, who cou'd only how, and pretend not to be ignorant. (Besides my researches are only after English antiquities, and lead not to the Romans; *whom* I gave up, when I quitted the Guards.)[74]

Owing to a change of weather, and my fishings late, and early, I found myself so unwell this evening, that it became necessary to take care of myself; so I retired to bed at

10 o'clock (ordering that I shou'd not be call'd) and having taken many analeptic pills,[75] suderificised most plentifully till nine o'clock.

Sunday   And when I did rise, and had mounted an hot, dry
July 11   shirt, I was not very handy after a night so bewilder'd.— Breakfasted I lung'd Blacky, and then rode him; and a rough bad road I took, leading thro' woods, and everlasting gates, the only road too that leads to Lord Westmor-
Apethorp   lands seat at Apthorp.[76]—No way made; no direction posts; no lodges! After that, you know what you are to expect; a deserted seat, all weeds, no attempt at cleanliness, or improvement! Open corn fields opposite without a tree planted; a river running thro' a rushy morass, and a ruinous mill in front.—

It is a very old mansion; where King James 1st often abode for the pleasure of hunting: whose statue, of stone, stands under the front arcades; and this I had to observe for a long time, till they would listen in the house to the bell I rang. This was, certainly, the garden front. The housekeeper now attended me, and to my desire of viewing the oldest parts of the house, she shew'd me what were the old hall, and buttery-hatch, now left to ruin!

The house is built around a collegiate quadrangle; the old dining-room has been modernised, tho yet retaining a fine antique ceiling. King James's bed, and the tapestry hanging of the chamber, are in the same stile he left them. But the beauty of this house is the gallery, a very noble one, 120 feet long, and not narrow, wainscotted with oak, and fill'd with full length family pictures, neglected to decay.

There are many noblemen I would not know or visit; amongst them, those that have no road of safety, or finding, to their house; and those who neglect all the pictures, and portraits of their ancestors; (which give to me, I say, with the stain'd glass they suffer to be destroy'd, and the books they permit to be torn up,) for such men must be cruelly ignorant of taste, civilities, or comfort; and therefore I will not know them: and of what must I talk, and what reception meet; in a house thus neglected? Here are many fine old portraits; some in the housekeepers room; and an excellent picture of a painter and his wife, stuck up in a small bed-chamber: many others are tumbled about the house; which is most vilely disfigured by a tea room of Lady W.'s! Why shou'd a lady shew her little modern taste at the expence of grandeur, and the stile of an old mansion. At my desire, I was shewn the library, a good room; but like the dining room, looks gloomily into the court: these two rooms are (savagely) glazed with great, heavy, square panes. During my view there fell a heavy storm of rain. The housekeeper, and servants were very civil.

(Keep it in thy memory, reader, that I introduce the most trivial occurrences, to refresh my mind on a distant perusal.)

I shou'd suppose, (from this banishment,) that the viceroyship of Ireland, tho in danger of sword, and bottle, afforded more satisfaction to some lords, than the quiet enjoyment of an English estate!

(The older, and more severe my remarks, the nearer may they be presumed to have advanced to the truth.) Some curious stain'd glass was given from the windows here, to the Earl of Exeter at Burleigh, to put up in his (more modern) house! He should have had from me, my eye teeth, first.—By a master of any taste, or intention, there might be form'd in the front, a piece of running water of any extent; and then planting the opposite hill, it wou'd look nobly: Newton Church is not brought into sight sufficiently; and the ministers house is, without any reason, quite block'd out.

After this visit, of a kind to afford more pain than pleasure, (for you cannot carry off any thing, improve any thing, or save any thing from destruction,) I meant to have dined at Kings-Cliff, a small town, at little more than one mile distant; but when I saw the best public house, which appear'd very bad, and recollected The Hay-cock Inn to be only 6 miles distant, I made my way back, (a very rough, and bad one, thro' woods,) by ½ past 3 o'clock ; and there was regaled with good cheer, in a good parlour.

Wansford
Bridge

—The ride was, at times, warm, and the flies, in the wood, troublesome. Sancho made an excellent point at some par- tridges; it seems quite cruel in me to endeavour to ruin his qualifications!—The bells of this church compose a miser- able jingle, which I remark'd to a gentleman who lives opposite the inn, 'Aye Sr,' said he, 'it is odd that it shou'd happen in every place belonging to the Duke of Bedford!' 'Not at all', I answer'd, 'for His Grace is not famous for his attachment to *the belles*'.[77]

I rode, this evening, upon my grey jennet; but joyless, from the weight of a cold, that I am most eager to get rid of: so I supp'd very early, and after liberal libations of warm wine, and water, was in bed by 10 o'clock.

Monday
July 12

If bed can remove a cold, I ought to be better, for I was eleven hours in mine; but it, still, continues very heavy, and will not quit me so soon as I hoped for.—Breakfast, and horse lunging finish'd, I rode the black horse for 3 hours; and now having try'd him several times, I find it impossible to keep him, as his paces are dangerous; so when I return to town I must put up with a loss, without getting any wisdom into the bargain!—This horse was, unluckily, puff'd down my throat, at a time too when I was peevish, and when it was necessary to have a horse, or stop my tour; so my hope now is that his loss may not much exceed the hire of a horse; that will appear a sort of consolation.—My ride was (first) to Elton, where Ld Carysfort has a tolerable seat, on a chearful spot (this, the church, &c, I have before mention'd); then to Chesterton, where Mr Wallers old mansion seems to be kept in dis- graceful sort: all old houses were built in villages and sur- rounded by groves; modern taste orders that all should be laid open; to do this a village must be destroy'd, and this

250

seems to have been done at Chesterton.—Here I came
into the high road at Cates-Cabbin; where the new landlord has put up his own head for a sign, tho not quite after
the manner of Abel Drugger,[78] else he had chosen a *crow*. I
return'd, by Water-Newton, at two o'clock, just as a venison pastie was ready; of which I eat, tho' it is a nasty
greasy business.—This morning, uncheck'd barbarity was
destroying the swallows nests around this house.

The race of birds will be quickly extinct, even the
breed of game is with difficulty preserv'd; for as ignorance
is the offspring of barbarity, the farmer and gardener are
taught to believe that all birds rob and plunder them, and
that they should be destroy'd by every engine, and scared
away by every invention. By these means the country is
stript of a chief beauty; and the contemplative man misses
a prime satisfaction.—On the few remaining tall trees the
rook is forbid to build! The blackbird and bullfinch are
shot in the kitchen garden! The sparrow is limed in the
farm yard! And the swallow is driven from 'the coigne of
vantage'!

Now wou'd these blockheads but consider the works of
Providence who sends all things for our uses, or comforts,
they might observe (what even the gentleman, who forwards destruction by his sons, and servants, will not) that
these birds independent of the pleasure from their song,
their flight, and their company, are of several most material
uses.—The rook (in my opinion) does one shillingsworth
of advantage, by destruction of the slug, for a pennyworth
of damage sustain'd by the corn. The blackbird, and bullfinch destroy the worms and insects inimical to greens, and
fruits; and richly deserve their small rewards of peas, and
cherries.—The sparrow hardly earns his poor pickings
from the stack, by his destruction of the caterpillar.

I once ask'd a lady, if she loved to be stung by gnats?
She answer'd with horror No; 'Why then, madam, do you
order the swallows nests to be pull'd down from the window,
who wou'd keep them away from your chamber ?—Exclu-

sive of the melody and notes of birds, which every one must admire, surely their various flights, the operations of their lives, their nest-making, and the rearing of their young, with the variety of their calls, chearing us thro' day, and night, ought to inspire us with consideration for ourselves and them.—Yet there is not one gentleman who will, or dare, defend them: afraid of their servants, or of their children, they wink at barbarity, give up sense, and forego satisfaction.—The Duke of Marlborough[79] suffers not the birds nests to be taken in the shrubbery of Blenheim; but the gardener is permitted to shoot them when they hop over the kitchen garden wall!! Hedges being nearly destroy'd throughout the kingdom, a nest can no where be built in secresy, and security. I now look at a bullfinch, or a nightingale, as a great curiosity: nor can the former domestic character any longer avail the swallow, or the robin.—Children are taught to harrass; men delight in murder; else wou'd the birds hop before us in security, and sing on every spray around us.—Cruelties early indulged, open the navigation to Botany Bay.

After swallowing a cascade of tea, in the evening, I took a long walk with Sancho, who is too valuable, and useless for me; for I find him to be very stanch:[80] now the dog for me, is a chacer; whereas, Sancho tonight, pointed steadily at two hares and wou'd not pursue them; and from the rabbets he turn'd in contempt.—At 8 o'clock, the chilliness of the evening drove me in, and now for a trite, and true remark, viz—that summers have left us with all their pleasures, and all their pains; times were, I remember, when the sun arose, and retired in splendour, when the middle of the day was too hot for exercise, and people talk'd of grottos, arbours, and cool retreats; when you could keep abroad till ten o'clock at night, list'ning to the beetles hum, the partridges call, and those sounds of evening coming from afar; and saw the bats wheel, and the white owls flight: now we all creep home at 8 o'clock, wishing for fires. Wasps are unknown; the frog croaks

not; nor does the great moth extinguish our candle.—We
had 2 hot days in this summer; and then a storm restored
the cool weather.

Having no letter this morning, from Mrs B[yng] *Tuesday*
assures me of her company in the evening. I shou'd not *July 13*
appear ill before her who wants spirits, strength, and
comfort.

T. B. is rode to Apthorp, to endeavour to get a basket of
fruit from the gardener; and to enquire if the gamekeeper
will come over to shoot rabbits with Mr C[olman], who
intends, most kindly, to escort Mrs B[yng] from London.

I am vex'd to find that both the Stamford and Peterboro' companies of comedians have quitted those towns, as
it might have afforded a pleasant evening.—If Poney is
ridden 30 miles a day, so much the better, else he is as
frisky as possible; as I found him to-day, when riding
thro' the wood to where stood Suley-Lodge, the stables *Sulehay*
whereof, of great antiquity, now form a miserable farm-
house: but it is seated in a most sequester'd spot, with a
pool below it; and upon the lawn adjoining, I saw a herd
of the Kings deer.

Tho the road to Ld W[estmoreland]'s is almost impassable, instead of being render'd of great beauty, and
with Gothic lodges at the gates, yet have they stuck up
amidst the woods the mean modern Lombardy poplar.—
There lays a tree by our warf side which measures 5 feet in
diameter; and they say that some are brought of 6 feet in
diameter.—T. B. came in soon after me, with a basket of
fruit from Apthorp; but could not see the gamekeeper.—
My next employ was arranging the bed rooms, changing
mine, and setting up a bed therein for Mister Frek: then I
unwisely went to my old dangerous haunt upon the rivers
bank, for an hour before dinner.—In the evening there fell
a violent shower of rain; otherwise, it is impossible to go
abroad, when in expectation of arrival; and the time moves
slowly indeed, when fear of some accident obtrudes as the

cause of delay.—At every glympse of weather I walk'd before the door; they came upon me unexpectedly; and then were disembark'd, Mrs B[yng], Miss C[ecilia] F[orrest][81] and my little Frek,[82] under the guardianship of Capt. C[olman].[83]

Of an evening of meeting there is no description; but that we talk'd little, and eat less: C., and F., wander'd with me into the stable; and over the bridge.

There was an early call for bed.

Being now in company, touring account ceases: of our society there is little to relate.—Mr. C[olman] early try'd at fishing.—In the garden I cramm'd Frek with currants. —My tour writing comes up to Cowley's description;

> 'Nothing there is to come, and nothing past,
> But an eternal *now* does allways last.'

Mr C[olman] and T. B. went to Ld W.'s gamekeeper, to settle abt rabbet shooting: whilst C[ecilia] and I walk'd to the pretty church of Thornhaugh, and the retired house of Dr P[roby] Dean of Litchfield.[84]—Mrs B. does not mend in health, and spirits; like her sex she dares not to be well: the weather is bad, and we are all gloomy; so I forced C[olman] to go to the play at Peterborough.—

More walking on my part—more attempts at angling, brought on the evening; when my grand and unexpected pleasure was the hearing my dear Frek repeat his prayers audibly, and with feeling: this happens, to the dear childs eternal wellfare, from the having about him servants of some religion; (of what kind that is, signifies nothing,) who teach him to reverence the Divine Being, and bow at the name of Jesus.—

After the ladies indulgence of tea, and their retiring, I took to prosing, and a pint of port.—

C[olman] was not up when I arose; for he had stay'd throughout the play, and to supper at Peterborough, even

till one o'clock; so he did not come down till a late breakfast: when he retail'd to us a description of his evening,
but forgot to bring home a play bill!

We then, for a small proof of skill, try'd to take a sketch
of *The Turnpike House*, seen from our windows; mine—
here inserted—bore I believe the bell.—He, and I, employ'd, or rather lost two hours upon the rivers bank, endeavouring to catch fish; but the wind was too high and
cold: Oh, that the soft south wou'd come.

T. B. was sent to Apthorp to procure fruit.

I wish I cou'd say that Mrs B.'s health mends by
country air; but she is yet not strong enough to walk, or
attempt riding: so we live a confined inn life.

Dinner finish'd, Mr. C., (attended by T. B. his master
of the horse now, tho' but just return'd from Apthorp with
fruit) went off on his rabbet shooting intention; when I
rode to Mr C[utteridge] the minister of Water-Newton,
to thank him for his civility about the antiquary paper:[85] but
he not being at home, I return'd by ½ past 5 o'clock to tea.
Part of my evening was past at fishing, with very little success; during much time, I lost my line and top of the rod.
C— return'd satisfied with his sport, and with full hands,
for he had killed 6 rabbets.—At evening close, just as the
cloth was spreading for supper, C[ec]y and I walk'd, out,
and further than we intended, for we got to Stevington
village; and did not return till near 10 o'clock.—The
weather is cold, and windy. Poor Frek had a sad fall,
to-day, over a stile, and bruis'd his face exceedingly.

Mrs B. appears so much better this morning, as to re- *Friday*
solve upon a drive, and to Burleigh, which place C[ecy] *July 16*
and Mr C[olman] have never seen; and shou'd not quit
the country without seeing.—Mr C. was most extravagantly idle this morning, nor wou'd he wake tho several
chambermaids shook, and call'd him.

There was such a run of post-horses at our inn, that
when we required them, they were not to be had.—At

noon, I rode forward, with Frek carried before T. B.; nor did the chaise come up to us till two o'clock, having waited an hour at the park gate; when we descended to the house.—(Of this place I have often spake before). The kitchen is grand and shews nobility; as for the rest of this superb-looking, useless mansion Italianised from comfort —it affords neither rooms of intention, or living; not a trait of Gothic grandeur; all gilding, and foreign indelicacies; a drawing room chapel; a pitiful music room, tho too good for the fiddling company that come here.

The hall might be made noble, but will not be by this Earl of E.[86] From the park which is green, and shady, tho' without features Uffington House and church are seen to advantage; in driving about, our ladies were nearly overturn'd by the sleepy postboy.—

A dinner well serv'd; with much civility; and our waiter is very quiet.—My philosophy suits fishing—as its disappointments I can endure; but not so, affection and fine feelings of which I had a surfeit this evening: coldblooded negative virtue, (which men should not coincide with) declaring the impossibility of eating an animal it had seen slaughter'd! Pretty conceits, which would soon die away, were they not supported by civil male acquiescence, which hardens these delicate mongers!!!

Saturday July 17   High time to be employ'd in some active pursuit, or to return; an inn is not the place for idleness or sickness.— Mr C., the minister of Water-Newton, call'd upon me; and forced upon Frek a quantity of Roman coins found in the Roman camp near to his village.

At our dinner time, Mr O[sborne][87] stept in for a minute; he was in his way to Ld W.'s to see a great cricket-match.

C. went to his rabbet-shooting, but with no great success; neither had I any luck at my last fishery: shou'd I ever return to this place to make a stay, I must find out some intelligent fisher to guide, and instruct me. The evening was very gloomy, and sultry; with sun it had been

intolerable.—In the Stamford newspaper, was an advertisement of the dog (Sancho) who follow'd us from Boston;
so I wrote in answer, desiring that he might be sent for:
heartily repenting my ever suffering him to come after us,
as he has been an incessant plague.—Just below this inn is
a paper mill, of some benefit to the poor; but I wonder,
not to find the cotton mill erected in this country, whose
advantages are now so manifest.

Frek and I took an early and long walk; for the rest they *Sunday*
are sad sluggards: Mrs B. most idly breakfasts in bed; *July 18*
C[ec]y is tediocity; and Mr C[olman] never appears till
eleven o'clock. Tho' we breakfasted late, we determined
to have an early dinner, (an excellent one it was) that we
might take an evening drive. This, was under my escort to
Apthorp, around which place is plenty of game, and our
dogs had one very good course of a hare.—The civil housekeeper attended us into every corner. The gallery was
admired; but as much money has been thrown away upon
foolish dressing rooms, French chairs, and useless tables,
and in forming a silly menagerie, as wou'd have made a
fine piece of water in the front of the house; where is now
a vile rushy meadow.

The kitchen garden is very mean; and cou'd only furnish our baskets with some of the small common fruits.

We had an excellent supper.—After which, and the
ladies retired, we had our bills to settle.—And now, behold, my long-expected visitor, Major S[tavele]y;[88] the
ladies descend; and we sit up another hour.—The Major
seems so attach'd to his old (and now tiresome) mischief,
the regiment, that they cannot part, tho' a separate main-
tenance were now proper for them both.

It was necessary for, and agreeable to me, to be going *Monday*
early; and my old, restless, friend (after his *long* and *com-* *July 19*
fortable visit) wou'd be going at the same hour, to breakfast with a brother Blue, who lives 4 miles off, at Allwalton:

so leaving the care, and trouble of payments to Mr C. and
T. B. being order'd to follow me, the Major and I were off
by 8 o'clock, (the Major mounted on a broken-winded
poney of our inn!) in a very fine, summer-like morning;
and crept along at a foots pace (a quick motion had been
impossible for his nag) till we parted at Kates-Cabbin.—
The Major (my oldest military chum) will not let me have
him in peace, and comfort, for he hurries about like a boy,
and cannot determine to part from his regiment, to settle
and be quiet.—Feeling hot, and hungry I was not sorry to
find myself at Alconbury Hill (the Wheatsheaf), where I
had breakfasted, and Poney finish'd his feed, before T. B.
arriv'd: I then wou'd not allow him any time, (he having
used so much at parting), so instantly walk'd forward, and
was overtaken by the cavalry, in two miles, near Alconbury
church.

Buckden   I had often try'd, in vain, to see the inside of the Bishop
of Lincoln's palace at Buckden; and, now, unexpectedly
succeeded: its appearance is castellated, and within the
walls, certain strong turrets with apertures.—This ancient
appearance diminishes hourly, as much of the mote has
been lately fill'd up, and many walls pull'd down.—The
interior is grave, strong, and useful; something to vener-
ate: a good dining parlour, a neat chapel, tower stair-cases,
and some stain'd glass in the windows: all places of this
low, shaded situation, I prefer to the modern hill-top
stareabouts.

Having now time sufficient, for the chaise company were
not to leave Wansford till noon, I resolv'd to meander from
the road, right and left, to peep at churches, and church-
yard poetry: which pursuit now becomes fresh.—So I
walk'd from the road, over the fields, to Dodington church,
dirty and gloomy, and built of brick (for all the churches
here are mean in comparison of those of Lincolnshire). Mr
Thornhill, whose house is near, has entirely planted it up.
—Next I turn'd to the right to Southhoe, a mean dwind-
ling village, where many farms, and cottages have been

taken down (for the fewer farms, the fewer cottages, of course!!)

Here I rejoin'd the high road, but soon to leave it again, to pass thro' Little-Paxton; around whose church, and church yard I made my circuit. I should fancy that some painted glass was in Doddington church; but no houses being near, I would not, with trouble, seek the key.

From Paxton, I chose the lower road over the Ouse, to the town of St Neots, which has a good market-place, and St. Neots a lofty steeple to a well-built church: in the church-yard I read this inscription.

SARAH PAINE.

In faith she dy'd, in dust she lies
But faith foresees that dust shall rise
When Jesus call while hope a rumes
And boosts her joy among the tombs.

(A very good steady incomprehensible epitaph! Faith forseeing that dust shall rise!

A rumes puzzles me.—)

The day was so warm, as to make me glad to arrive at our dinner-quarters at the Cock at Eaton; where the chaise Eaton soon arrived. Nothing, luckily, had been left behind but Socon Frek's hat.—Our dinner and wine were bad; but the landlady, Mrs W., and her son were very civil.—In this church-yard I find the two following epitaphs,

MRS E. ROGERS.

Grief and pain daily did me oppress
A great sufferer was I here
My husband gone, relations was severe.

THOMAS GIMBER.

I need not to confess my life
For surely thou canst tell
What I have been, and what I am
Thou knowest very well.

At Buckden I could find no barber but one in the tap room of the George Inn; and tho here are two barbers, one

259

was gone to *size*[89] at Huntingdon; and the other, as not employ'd by the house refused to come! (Liberty, and property, and no excise.)—However at last I did get a razor and a brush—and made out a tolerable toilette.

At Eaton was quarter'd a quartermaster of the Blues—a quondam trooper (when I serv'd in *the wars* with my *Lord*

Biggles-
wade

Marlbro')[90] who seem'd heartily glad to see me.—At Biggleswade we arrived at seven o'clock—supper to order—and to try to equip Frek with a new hat.—Supper was good; but all in haste for bed, as Mr C[olman] was obliged to be in town by the morrows noon, so necessary to be off by 4 o'clock. Hard work this! and little sleep to be expected!!

*Tuesday
July 20*

Circle and intention of this tour now finish'd; and with some shame, and no over-satisfaction.—Buxton and its waters, soon vanish'd; my grand ride with Col. B[ertie] was prevented by Mrs B[yng]'s illness; and my latter tour of the fenns has been very gloomy; my stay at Wandesford, at last, tiresome: so that upon casting up the balance of expence and pleasure, I find myself out of pocket.— The purchase of Blacky was an hasty job; and he must be sold instantly to prevent broken knees, the certainty of his paces. This is a sad vexation; and from which, too, I shall not learn wisdom!

We were up at 3 o'clock; ladies shivering, I creeping about in my nt cap; but they were soon gone, and I quickly return'd to bed: a rainy morning—which clear'd up at noon, when I rode with Mr K[night] (on a well intention'd errand) to find a good field in his farm, where Poney may be left; whence I may allways (coming down in a stage coach) take him up in a hours time: he will here refresh myself, for he has been up and down many a hill lately) and I leave a box with my nt cap, shirts, fishing-tackle, ready for any trip; to which I may add wine, &c, and then it becomes my country seat.

This appears a good plan, and Mr Finch the barber, (who speaks of himself as an expert angler) will be allways ready to attend me upon the rivers bank.—Having settled about Poney, I made my old strole by Southill, to Chicksands; where I meant to have paid my respects to Sr G. and Lady H. O[sborne],[91] but they being gone out to dinner, I wrote a letter to him in his stewards room.—At Shefford I allways stop to shake hands with a respectable couple, who seem ever delighted to see me; he served my father when I was born, and they both lived with my mother, at the time of her death.[92]

I return'd by 3 o'clock, very hungry; so lost not an instant with the cold round of beef.—In the evening I took my master of the horse (now about to resign his office) to view the two closes appropriated for Poney's grasing; and he did me the honor to approve.—Till 9 o'clock I continued my saunter about the good roads near this town; but the evening was very cold, as threat'ning wet weather.

My supper was short; and I hasten'd to bed, as I must be up early for the coach tomorrow.

EDITOR'S NOTES

(1) A poor impression of probably the second state. (British Museum—Parthey No. 1226.)

(2) Bagnigge Wells Gardens lay on the west side of King's Cross Road (once Bagnigge Wells Road). It was a fashionable pleasure resort from 1759, when it was opened, but declined from about 1780 and was closed in 1841. There is an interesting account in Wroth's *London Pleasure Gardens of the Eighteenth Century* (1896), pp. 56-57.

(3) The reference is no doubt to Kitts' End, a halt on the Islington-Chester road between Barnet Pillar and South Mimms Church. See Cary's *New Itinerary for Coach Times*, 1817, p. 279. (Information received from the Editor, *London Topographical Record.*)

(4) George III's birthday was June 4th.

(5) This local official managed the issue and sale of Government stamps and saw to all matters requiring stamp duties and also many of the taxes. These officials continued as late as 1885, but soon after most of their business was transferred to the post offices, and the word 'revenue' was added to 'postage' on the stamps. The author of these diaries, being himself in the Stamp Office in London, would no doubt have special facilities for collecting fees and money for the expenses of his journeys.

(6) Probably the child born to John Howard on March 27th, 1765, whose mother died four days later. This younger John died, 24th April, 1799, hopelessly insane.

(7) This was a play of Garrick's published in 1772.

(8) In 1788 the Spaniards seized some fishing ships at Nootka Sound and the country expected war, which, however, was avoided by the Nootka Convention, 1790. This incident is referred to later on in these Tours and also in the other Tour of 1790. The Reciprocal Treaty, referred to in the next paragraph, is no doubt the Anglo-French Commercial Treaty of 1786.

(9) Mrs. Jordan, the famous actress, who was born in 1762 and died in 1816, appeared on the stage first in Ireland. She ran away to Leeds in 1782 and played in that circuit until 1785, when she made her debut at Drury Lane as Peggy in *The Country Girl*, remaining in London until 1815. For a long time she was mistress of the Duke of Clarence, afterwards William IV. Derby had a theatre from 1773, and Mr. Manley with a very

good company of performers, who were frequently aided by the most popular actors and actresses of the London stage, attended here at regular seasons.

(10) Probably a slang expression derived from niggardly.

(11) The Derby Races were held on August 17th and 18th, 1780. In the *Derby Mercury* of August 19th, 1790, we have the following:

MRS. JORDAN'S fourth Night.

Theatre. DERBY.

On Thursday Evening, August 19, will be presented
A Comedy, called

THE BELLES STRATAGEM.

The part of Laetitia Hardy by Mrs. JORDAN.
To which will be added the Musical Farce of

THE VIRGIN UNMASKED.

The part of Miss Lucy by Mrs. JORDAN.

And on Friday and Saturday will be presented a PLAY and FARCE in which Mrs. JORDAN will perform principal Parts.

(12) During the invasion of England by the Young Pretender, Prince Charlie, he and his men reached Derby on December 4th, 1745, and started their retreat the next day.

(13) See notes 45 and 86 of Tour of 1789. According to Boswell (Ashbourne Journal, 1777; *Isham Collection*, XIII, p. 24), the following formed Dr. Taylor's society at Ashbourne: Mr. Alsop, 'a roundheaded squire . . . when he is asked "Jack, what time do you go to bed?" he answers, "I don't know, about the time one gets drunk, I think"'; Mr. Longdon, 'a civil rather spruce squire, intelligent enough'; Mr. Davenport, formerly landlord of the Blackamore's Head, and Counsellor Leigh, 'more squire than counsellor.'

(14) John Metcalf of Knaresborough, the famous roadmaker and bridge-builder, was one of the most wonderful of blind men and very well known at this period when England had very few good roads. His first work was on the main road between Harrogate and Boroughbridge, and later between Harrogate and Harewood Bridge. Soon work poured in upon him, and he had as many as 400 men working for him at the same time on a single road, but he did all his own surveying and made all his own plans. His fame as an engineer and builder spread far and wide, and he carried his operations all over Yorkshire, into Lancashire, Cheshire and the Peak of Derbyshire. In all he made 180 miles of main roads, including their bridges, water courses, walls, etc. He died in 1810 at the age of ninety-three.

(15) The Duke's architect was John Carr (1723-1807), v. *D.N.B.*

(16) Very little copper coinage was issued in the reign of George III; until the year 1797 halfpence and farthings had only been coined between 1770 and 1775. To meet the deficiency in small change large issues of

copper tokens were made by trading firms and by town corporations; as many as 250 tons of pennies and 50 tons of halfpennies were struck by the Anglesea Mines Company alone, and halfpence were also issued by a Macclesfield trading company called Roe & Co. The tokens usually bear on one side the name of the place or firm which issued them and on the edge the places in which they were redeemable, and this class of token is very common. The shortage of coin of the realm also provoked the issue of masses of pieces, sometimes more or less resembling the regular coinage but with altered or bungled legends, which can only be regarded as forgeries. All these issues attracted the attention of collectors and sets with portraits of popular heroes, buildings, etc., never intended for circulation, were struck to meet the demand.

(17) This ode, composed for George III's birthday (4th June), commences:
'Within what fountain's craggy cell,
Delights the Goddess Health to dwell.'

(18) The copper from the mines at Alderley Edge, a few miles away, was taken to Macclesfield and manufactured there. The mines, and presumably the works also, were worked for a long time by Charles Roe of Macclesfield, but in 1790 the owner appears to have been Mr Patten of Warrington. There is an account of the Alderley Edge mines and the connection with Macclesfield in *Lanc. & Ches. Antiquarian Society Transactions*, xix, 108.

(19) Porridge is used in the sense of pottage. Captain Francis Grose in his classical *Dictionary of the Vulgar Tongue*, edited by Eric Partridge (Scholartis Press, 1931, p. 267), has the following reference: 'Porridge Island is an alley leading from St. Martin's Church Yard, to Round Court, chiefly inhabited by cooks, who cut off ready-dressed meat of all sorts and also sell soup'.

(20) Samuel Egerton of Tatton, the last of the male line of the family, who died in 1780, was succeeded by his sister, Mrs. Tatton of Wythenshawe, who took the name of Egerton and died in 1780. She was succeeded by her son, William Tatton, who also took the name of Egerton. He was born in 1749 and died in 1806. His eldest son, whose name was Tatton, died in 1796, in his father's lifetime. The next son, born in 1781, was Wilbraham Egerton of Tatton, ancestor of the Lords Egerton of Tatton, and the next son resumed the Tatton surname and was the ancestor of the Tattons until recently of Wythenshawe.

(21) Biddy—a chicken or fowl.

(22) In Stockport, Sunday schools were adopted on an all-denominational basis, and the Stockport Sunday school still flourishes. The school dates from 1784 and the present building from 1805. There is a full account of it in Henry Heginbotham's *Stockport—Ancient & Modern*, i, 349, ii, 385-398.

(23) A collection of essays written in the year 1787-1788. Mr. R—n was Humphry Repton, to whom it is usually attributed, but it is also ascribed to Anna Seward. The essay referred to contains most entertaining arguments against educating the lower classes.

(24) An eighteenth-century quack of German origin who began to flourish about 1774. He was exposed by J. C. Lettsom. See *Lettsom*, by Abraham (1933), pp. 169 *et seq.*

(25) Sir George Warren of Poynton and Stockport, M.P., Knight of the Bath, who died 31st August, 1801, aged 67. He was the last male of the ancient family of Warren which had owned Poynton and Stockport from the fourteenth century.

(26) Possibly Montague, the 2nd Viscount Torrington's wife's brother.

(27) A well-known expression at the time implying sleepiness.

(28) This is probably a disparaging reference to Carr, the architect. William Newton, the Peak Minstrel (see *Dictionary of National Biography*), was a carpenter on the job, but the Duke of Devonshire probably did not let out the work to a contractor as is usually done to-day.

(29) This is perhaps Maria, widow of James, 2nd Earl Waldegrave, although she had since remarried clandestinely in 1766 the Duke of Gloucester. Her second marriage was published and declared valid in 1772, although the only witness, the officiating clergyman, was dead. She was separated from her second husband in 1787. Her name appears under Gloucester in *The G.E.C. Peerage* and there is a reference in *Notes & Queries*, 10th series, iv, p. 242, to the Duke of Gloucester and Lady Waldegrave figuring in the Têtes-à-Têtes Histories as Dorimont and Maria in *The Town and Country Magazine*, 1769, p. 13.

(30) See p. 136, note 3 f.

(31) Arkwright tried to establish a market in his factory colony by giving prizes at the end of the year to those bakers, butchers, etc. who had been most regular in attending and selling at the market which he had started for his employees at Cromford.

(32) Willersley Castle, near Cromford. The house was roofed in 1788, but had not been occupied when a fire occurred there on 8th August, 1791, which did much damage and delayed occupation until after Sir Richard's death.

(33) Sir Richard bought the Manor of Cromford in 1789, and shortly afterwards created a market—he does not appear to have obtained a charter.

(34) Mr. Nightingale was no doubt the Peter Nightingale from whom Arkwright had purchased the Manor of Cromford. Nightingale was a country gentleman and had been High Sheriff of the County of Derby. He left his property to his great-nephew, William Edward Shore, who later changed his name to Nightingale—he was the father of Florence Nightingale.

(35) Johnson in his essay on Epitaphs writes, 'It may seem very superfluous to lay it down as the first rule of writing epitaphs that the name of the deceased is not to be omitted; nor should I have thought such a precept necessary had not the practice of great writers shewn, that it has not been sufficiently regarded'.

(36) In the great actions as to the validity of the patents of Arkwright, the quietus was given to the application on his behalf by the great Lord Mansfield. The Lancashire spinners were the great enemies of Arkwright, and he set up a rivalry to Lancashire by forming a partnership with a Lanark mill, in allusion to which, as a taunt to his enemies, he said that 'he would find a razor in Scotland to shave Manchester'. This must be the reference to Mansfield's razor.

(37) The Davenports had been at Bramhall in Stockport parish from the fourteenth century. William Davenport (1745-1829) was the squire in 1790, and was High Sheriff of the County of Cheshire in 1781. He was the last of the family, the estates going to his illegitimate daughter, whose husband took the name of Davenport.

(38) The only public library at Manchester was Chetham's Library, which was founded in the seventeenth century by Humphrey Chetham, and which still exists. There is a short life of Chetham in the *Dictionary of National Biography*.

(39) This is a reference to the poem by Shenstone.

(40) The reference is to a scheme in preparation—The Assembly Rooms, Mosley Street, were opened in 1792, and were taken down in 1850.

(41) Henry Simpson Bridgeman (Tory) elected 21st August, 1780, for the Borough of Wigan. There is a full account of the Bridgeman family in *The Historical Catalogue of Staffordshire* (Archaeological Society, vol. 20, 1899).

(42) Merely a pencil note. Probably Market Harborough.

(43) George Byng, great-grandson of Admiral Lord Byng, first Viscount Torrington; brother to Lord Stratford. Born 1764; married Harriet, daughter of Sir William Montgomery, Bart., who died in 1845. He was of Whig principles and opposed to short Parliaments. He sat for Middlesex ever since 1790, and would probably have sat ever since 1780 but for the fact that he did not sit in the Parliament of 1784-90. He was apparently first returned in 1780 at the age of 16.

(44) This refers to Farquhar's comedy.

(45) Both these plays are mentioned in Allardyce Nicoll's *History of Late Eighteenth Century Drama*, 1927. On the outside of the building which used to be the Stamford Theatre is a plate with the following : 'This building was erected in 1768 as the Stamford Theatre and was in use for more than 100 years. Macready, Kemble, Edmund Keen, Sheridan, Knowles, Mr. and Mrs. Charles Keen and other notables performed here.'

(46) The writer's military career was as follows.—(See Introduction.)
Cornet, Royal Horse Guards, 11/1/60.
Capt. 58th Foot, 29/3/62.
Lieut. 1st Foot Guards; Capt. in the Army, 11/8/62.
Capt. 1st Foot Guards; Lt.-Col. in the Army, 19/2/76.
Retired, 18/5/1780.

(47) See note 29.

(48) One of the oldest inhabitants states that it was customary temporarily to name a part of the river after the owner or occupier of land adjoining such part of the river. A farmer named Hudson may have farmed near one of these backwaters and so have given his name for the time being to the water.

(49) The Fitzwilliams were the great leaders of the Whig Party in Northamptonshire as the Cecils of Burghley were of the Tories. The kennels at Lord Fitzwilliam's seat are built in that quaint style of pseudo-Gothic which often marks the third quarter of the eighteenth century.

(50) For notes on this village see *Victoria History of Northamptonshire*, p. 491.

(51) Lieut.-Col. Maurice Johnson, of Ayscoughfee Hall, Spalding, died 3rd December, 1796, aged 79. He was present at Dettingen (1743) and Culloden (1745). (See also p. 361.) [In the *Gentleman's Magazine*, vol. xliv, 1774, pp. 206-209, there is an interesting tour of this district by Thomas de Quincey, father of the opium-eater.]

(52) The author's third and last regiment.

(53) A ruff is a bird of the sandpiper type, and a ree is the female of the species.

(54) There were three Vicars of Pinchbeck in the eighteenth century who bore the same name:

1726. Thomas Townsend.
1752. Charles Townsend.
1780. Charles Townsend, junr.

(55) Formerly the Hall of the Guild of St. Mary, and by Mary I granted to the Corporation.

(56) Mr. Thomas Fydell, M.P. for Boston, who died on 6th April, 1812, aged 72.

(57) Sir Richard Arkwright bought the manor of Cromford in 1798, and shortly afterwards obtained a charter from the Crown entitling him to establish a market at Cromford.

(58) The Vicar of Holbeach in 1791 was Jacob Mountain, who had been collated to the vicarage, 1st December, 1789, descended from Mons. de Montagne, one of the French Protestants driven out in 1685. In 1788 he was made Prebendary of Caistor in Lincoln Cathedral, and the following year came to Holbeach. In early life he was intimate with the statesman,

Mr. Pitt, and being both learned and pious he had the best prospect of advancement in England, but the call came to lay the foundations of the Church in Canada. On 7th July, 1793, he was consecrated at Lambeth as first Anglican Bishop of Quebec, and there he laboured with great honour till his death on 16th June, 1825, at the age of 75. Eleven years later his son, G. J. Mountain, became third Bishop of Quebec.

(59) There has not been a Rector of Wisbech since 1252. The vicar in 1790 was the Hon. Charles Lindsay, son of Lord Crawford and Balcarres. He was vicar from 1787 to 1795, and was educated at the Grammar School in the town.

(60) 'There was in the same college, a young Master of Arts, *Williams*, by Name; who had been elected into the Society in Preference to one of greater Genius and Learning, because he used to make a lower Bow to the Fellows, whenever he passed by them.' etc. See Coventry, *History of Pompey the Little*, 1751, p. 234 *et seq.*

(61) The well-known maps of Gross.

(62) Thomas Byng was Public Orator at the University 1565-70; Master of Clare Hall 1571-99; Vice-Chancellor 1572-3; Regius Professor of Civil Law 1574-99, etc. and died 1599.

(63) At the village of Wimpole the houses are all modern, and no church is to be seen amongst them. A church there is belonging to them, but it stands a mile to the west, where the village also stood till towards the close of the eighteenth century. At that time the mansion and parts of Wimpole Hall were being enlarged to their present magnificence by Philip, the 1st Earl of Hardwicke (the builder of Lord's Bridge). Plebeian cottages were not to be tolerated 'betwixt the wind and his nobility', so he pulled down the entire village and planted it, where it now is, along the Akeman Street. The church, which could not well be moved, he faced with red brick to match his new-built stables, close to which it is situated. (Rev. Edward Conybeare, *Highways and Byways in Cambridge and Ely*, Macmillan, 1910.)

(64) The history of the Great North Road is well described in Charles G. Harper's two volumes on the subject, published in 1901.

(65) Major S— or S—y, of the Blues, is undoubtedly Miles Staveley, who began his military career as a cornet in the Royal Horse Guards on 9th January, 1759, and served in the regiment in various ranks until 4th September, 1799, when he was appointed Colonel of the 28th Light Dragoons. This regiment was disbanded on 25th June, 1802. On the 12th March, 1803, he was appointed Colonel of the 4th Dragoon Guards, which post he held until his death in September 1814, by which time he was a full General. He served during the Seven Years' War in Germany and in Flanders under the Duke of York.

(66) *The Victoria County History of Huntingdon* gives full particulars of the Austin Friars Priory—Huntingdon Priory.

(67) Colonel Bertie, afterwards 9th Earl of Lindsey (see note 1, p. 239, vol I.).

(68) See Bridges' *History and Antiquities of Northamptonshire*, 1791, vol. 2, p. 423.

(69) For an account of Wothorp, see Stamford Baron in Bridges' *History and Antiquities of Northamptonshire*, 1791, vol. 2, p. 578.

(70) Possibly Lord Cecil of Burghley.

(71) Brownlow Bertie, 5th Duke of Ancaster and Kesteven, and cousin of Col. Bertie.

(72) Now Somerset House, and still the headquarters of the Inland Revenue.

(73) *The Victoria County History* (*Northamptonshire*) has a map showing the Roman remains near Water Newton (vol. i, p. 168).

(74) Referring to his military service abroad.

(75) *I.e.* Dr James's famous pills.

(76) See Bridge's *History and Antiquities of Northamptonshire*, 1791, vol. 2, p. 484.

(77) *Cf.* the *tête-à-tête* portrait in *Town and Country Magazine*, vol xvi, p. 9 (1784), where he appears as 'the Bloomsbury Youth' coupled with a Miss St—ns—n.

(78) Abel Drugger, the famous tobacconist in Ben Johnson's *Alchemist*, which was a favourite character in the eighteenth century, Garrick's performance being very famous; and another actor who distinguished himself in the part being the now almost forgotten Weston.

(79) The husband of Caroline, only daughter of the 4th Duke of Bedford (1739-1817), and therefore a connection by marriage with the author, through the marriage of the 4th Viscount Torrington's daughter to the 6th Duke of Bedford.

(80) A colloquial use of the verb, *to retard*.

(81) Miss Cecilia Forrest, Mrs Byng's sister, m. 1797 Rt. Hon. William Windham.

(82) Frederick Gerald, 5th son of the author, who entered the Foreign Office and became Gentleman-usher of the Privy Chamber. He died 5th June, 1871.

(83) George Colman, the younger (1762-1836), dramatist and from 1824, Examiner of Plays (see *D.N.B*). His friendship with the Byngs is recorded in Peake's *Memoirs of the Colman Family*.

(84) The Dr. P—, Dean of Lichfield in 1790, was Dr. Baptist Proby, who was Dean from 25th March, 1776, until his death on 16th January, 1807.

He also held—after the fashion of that time—two rectories—Doddington in the Isle of Ely and Thornhaugh in Northamptonshire (apparently the 'retired house' mentioned). There is an obituary notice of him in *The Gentleman's Magazine* for 1807, vol. i, p. 275 (the March section), the phraseology of which certainly suggests the pen of Miss Anna Seward (who died in 1809).

(85) *The Victoria County History* (*Northampton*), vol. i, p. 170, gives full details regarding the discovery of an old cylindrical stone now in the Library of Trinity College, Cambridge.

(86) See Bridge's *History of Burleigh, History & Antiquities of Northamptonshire*, 1791, vol. 2, p. 586.

(87) Possibly the 'sincere friend and affectionate relation, John Osborn', to whom the Tour into South Wales is dedicated (1787), and who was the author's cousin. Cf. Vol. I, Tour in South Wales, 1787.

(88) See note 65 above.

(89) The assizes.

(90) When the War of the Spanish Succession broke out Hanover and Celle placed under Marlborough's command more than 10,000 troops which fought with distinction at Blenheim and elsewhere, and in 1707 he was appointed to the command of the Army of the Rhine.

(91) Sir George Osborn (the author's cousin) of Chicksands Priory, Beds, married first in 1771 Elizabeth, eldest daughter and co-heir of John Bannister, Esq., by whom he had an only son, John, and secondly in 1788 Heneage, daughter of Daniel, 7th Earl of Winchilsea, which lady died in 1820. Sir George was a general officer in the army, and Groom of the Bedchamber to George III. He died 29th June, 1818, and was succeeded by his son.

(92) George, 3rd Viscount Torrington and Elizabeth Daniel, granddaughter of Sir Peter Daniel, Knt.

A TOUR IN BEDFORDSHIRE

1790

Day	Weather	To What Place	County	Inn	Miles
Saturday Aug. 21	Hot.	To Biggleswade, in a post-chaise	Beds.	Sun.	45
Sunday 22	A charming day.	Morning lounge. Evening ride.	—	—	12
23	Morning showers. Fine eve.	To Eaton; and back.	—	Cock. T.	22
24	A pleasant day.	To Potton; and to Barford.	—	Alehouse.	20
25	Fine morn. Rainy eve.	To Silsoe.	—	George. B.	20
26	A dark wet day.	Fishing in the evening.	—	—	—
27	A gloomy wetting day.	Evening ride.	—	—	12
28	A charming day.	Morning ride.	—	—	10
Sunday 29	Do.	Morning ride.	—	—	6
30	Do.	To Bedford and back.	—	Swan. B.	22
31	Do.	Rides.	—	—	16
Septr. 1	Do.	Rides.	—	—	18
2	Do. but windy.	To Sandy, Hasell-Hall, Potton, &c. and evening ride.	—	—	17
3	Wind & rain.	To Potton, and back; evening ride.	—	—	13
4	A fine day.	To Arlesey—Clifton, &c.	—	—	13
Sunday 5	Do. but showery.	To Stevenage, Barnet and to London	Herts.	Stevenage Swan. B. Barnet. Red Lion. B.	45

(miles. 253.)

A Tour in Bedfordshire

1790

E VERY return to the haunts of youth renders age
pleasanter to itself

> When years no more of active life remain
> 'Tis some delight to trace them o'er again.

In such recollection, vigour, and animation return:—if
so I am right in thus marking down my tours; to feel in
them, hereafter, a renewal of capacity, and a re-entrance
into the haunts of youth; else they would soon be

> Gone like traces on the deep,
> Like a sceptre, grasp'd in sleep,
> Dews, exhal'd from morning glades,
> Melting snows, and gliding shades.
>
> *Cooke.*

I am rather afraid that universal trade, and universal
foreign travel, have not only rendered my countrymen free
thinkers as well as citizens of every clime, but have destroy'd the soft links of love, and relationship, and have
banished all affection for our early home, and abodes!

I never knew, amongst the herd of my relations, and
acquaintance, but that those who long lived in Italy, became at their return, worse English people, having imbibed some unatural tastes, and humours; and when they
felt the cold of England, exclaimed about Italian sunshine,
forgetting that one is a bracer, easy to be endured, and that
the other was a calamitous enervator: so likewise, when
raving of Italian pictures, are they uninformed of superb
collections in every adjacent street in London.

Being thus quench'd of hope, not longing, mine Italian brain
Gan in your duller Britain operate most vilely.
W. S.

An English settler in Italy becomes, in my mind, an undone, abandoned wretch; seeking food from macaroni, conversation from fiddlers, and etc, etc, etc.

I return, now, frequently, into my first vortex; where every lane, and every field furnish traces of youthful days,

And as a hare whom hounds and horns pursue,
Pants to the place from whence at first she flew,
I still had hopes, my long vexations past,
Here to return—and die at home at last.
Goldsmith.

With the hope of composing my mind; to adapt it to the last grand retirement without gloom in the present, or regretting the past; for

Who, again . . . would fardels bear,
And grunt, and sweat under a weary life.
W. S.

To indulge, likewise, my new passion for drawing, this tour will be cramm'd by numbers of such attempts as my pencil may produce; for myself; this happy memorial 'Hoc est Vivere bis.'

Here, as with doubtful, pensive steps I range,
Trace every scene, and wonder at the change,
Remembrance wakes with all her busy train,
Swells at my breast, and turns the past to pain.
Goldsmith.

Upon Saturday morning August 21st 1790 I resumed my old walk to Barnet; choaked, not tired, by the heat and dust, where I am to be overtaken by Mr. C[olman] with Mrs B[yng] and Frek[1] in a post-chaise. John[1] was my companion; but he disdaining my slow pace, push'd forward to the Lower Red Lion, a very bad inn, with a dirty, puzzle-headed Irish waiter; these when sober, are stupid and when drunken, insolent. My agreement with Mr C. was to pay

274

the first stage—to the rest: Mrs. B. with her sons, returned to town; we continued our route; changing horses at Hatfield, and at Stevenage. Mr. C. was completely armed with pistols; which after some debate were at my desire (tho' by him unwillingly) concealed. 'Why oppose yourself, my dr Sir on a levell, to a poor but civil maroder? Surely hazards, and blood-shed, are cheaply avoided by a payment of five guineas?' To this argument Mr C. urged the feelings of youth and resentment; and inwardly grieved at my obstinate cowardice, in thus forcing him to hide his implements of valour, and revenge.

The roads are now crowded as London empties in August, and fills in February; everything thrown back with the hours; for such old-fashioned fellows as myself there will nothing left but the sun to keep us in countenance; but things will go round, and we shall be all right in time.—My nerves are either so weak or my fears so overpowering, that I never (but from necessity) ride in an hackney post-chaise; jolted, winded; harness that don't fit, horses that won't draw;—and left at the mercy of an ignorant, drunken post-boy, who cannot drive, and is everlastingly brutal to the poor beasts under his lash.—Young gentlemen are ever in violent haste to hurry to nothing; and laugh when I desire a post-boy not to gallop; not to hurry down hill; or to abstain from cutting at the horses eyes!—Glorious weather; and abundance, God has sent us; but man has rooted out man; and the wide-stretching farmer has de-populated the land; poors rates were high, so the poor were abolish'd!—And now that they be wanted, in vain may they be sought.

The children, with the aged few, struggle to collect for the rich, the blessings of heaven.

A month might formerly serve for harvest: now half the seed returns to earth e're it can be gathered; or the wet retards it, till it is half rotted—this is the miserable, destructive economy of the day!!—One man dying under fatigue, reaping away in a field of 20 acres.—

Several farmers trust wholly to the arrival of Irish itin-
erants (Mr W[indsor][2] of Gastlings Farm allways) and
should these ever find empty at home: let them reflect
upon what they are to do and upon what they have done—
the legislature might deign to look to this calamity—and
know that neither the dropsy of London nor the wens of
manufactories constitute the sound, honest, laborious,
flesh of the nation.

My friend (Mr C[olman]—a native of the north)[2a] allways seeking if possible, for disparagement of one country
and exaltation of another seem'd to glory at the want of
hands here compared with the numbers he had seen collected together in his ane country. 'That, my friend, said I,
arises from the small spaces of cultivated land there;
whereon the labourers must consequently make a greater
show than twenty times their number dispersed over a land

Biggles-
wade of all cultivation.' Arrive at Biggleswade. Here Mr T. a
cunning trickster, has been in an underhand manner set-
ting up a new inn against the very people who hired the
remaining lease of his inn at a highly advanced rent.
Surely the justices will in such case refuse a license? *

After dinner in our walk we espy'd a fine trick'd out
London damsel, lolling at the window, 2 pr of stairs of the
adjacent Waggon Inn!—'It is the East and Juliet is the
Sun'.

* FOUNTAIN INN

BIGGLESWADE, BEDFORDSHIRE

The Nobility, Gentry, and Public in general having lately experienced
much inconvenience for want of another inn at the above place to accommodate them in the posting line,

J. SCARBOROUGH

Butler to the late Duke of Chandos, Begs leave to inform them, that he has
opened a new House, delightfully situated at the south end of the Town
where he has laid in a stock of the very best Wines and Liquors and respectfully solicits their patronage; He has provided new and commodious Post-
Chaises with good and able Horses and Careful Drivers.

N.B. The greatest attention will be paid to Gentlemen Travellers.

TURNPIKE HOUSE: BIGGLESWADE BRIDGE

[see p. 277

TURNPIKE: UPPER HILL LANE: BIGGLESWADE

from water-colours by the Diarist *[see p. 277*

Mr. C. is a novice at an inn; one of my colts; I am a touring rough-rider—

Poney being sent for, arrived soon at his grass-field, and cow company; looking well, tho his feet are much shatter'd: attended his shoeing; and made them leave his stable-door ajar during the nights which are now very warm.

My fishing tackle examined; great cry and little wool; in how long a time would my caught fish pay for the purchased apparatus?—

An early supper; C. lives upon eels, I play away upon apricot tarts and custards.—

A fine fresh morning—I took a long walk before break- *Sunday* fast and was for some time, busily employed in sketch- *August 22* ing some drawings————(finished in the following summer).

Mr C. thinks to increase strength, or to gain pleasure, from sleep, an idle notion indeed. Enough for refreshment is all that is needed. More is loss of time. Life is too short to cut from it some hours of every day? No man in his space, has lived longer than myself, from never having been a dormouse; or wasted hours in tedious dressing.

The barber (and fisherman) has been with me in deep debate, against the scaly tribe; and we have fix'd upon our Tuesdays intentions—the when—the where—the how?

I could not pass the morning without a ride, and Poney went delightfully, only too frisky, for he is not to be rode carelessly,

Before dinner—at one o'clock the now risen C. walked with me for an inspection of the river, to find out good fishing holes, and safe bathing for himself after our dinner of eels and roasted rabbets—the painted lady (ugly enough) attended by a suivante passed the window, with a hope, we supposed of being noticed, 'I am out of the case, but to you young man, this is a challenge, dishonourable to refuse'—so C. was obliged to go forth, and to coquet—his account, at return was, that the lady was very conceited, and very secret. 'She had chosen to sequester herself from the gay world; that she boarded at the inn with her faithful servant; and that she objected not to walking with him but was *too discreet* to suffer any visits'—

I led C. (mounted upon a high-bred hack of Mr K[night]'s)[3] one of my old rounds, passing at the back of Hill Grounds stands this ancient oak pollard near a gate reminding me of many old hunts;—the poem entitled The Loves of The Plants,[4] may explain the *sexes* of trees; of which science I am ignorant. Half a mile from this tree is the turnpike house in Upper Hill Lane.

Over Southill grounds; called upon Mr W.; and returned over Southill fields. The evening was dull; so was my conversation with a new friend: for one cannot prate of old times to young ears.

In our way home, stopped at K[night]'s farm at Lower Caldecote; and saw Poneys pastures, after a walk about— and a bow to *Juliet*, we had our eelish supper and retired to an early bed.

Monday August 23   Some intentions on my part, with much conversation about Powel's walking journey, urged C. to ride as far as Huntingdon (20 miles) to see him there, in his way; and so eager was he, that I scarcely restrain'd him till 9 o'clock —when he went off in a gallop. At eleven o'clock I followed by the way of Biggleswade common to Sandy; in passing thro' Chesterton (Castra) Fields,[5] I conversed much with a man about the Roman coins so frequently found therein; and stopped to sketch a drawing which means to exhibit Julius-Caesar's camp.

Eaton Socon   At two o'clock—by my slowest pace I arrived at Eaton; where I strolled about for 2 hours.

Awaiting the arrival of C. who at 4 o'clock came in full tilt and breathless.

When recovered he told me that Powell[6] arrived at Huntingdon at 12 o'clock; that he (C.) walked forward with him about 5 miles to observe his pace and manner.

Mr C. would be a famous walker with some little practice. But he does everything by starts; either very tediously, or with violent rapidity.

Our return home was very slow (lucky for Mr K[night]'s Biggles-horse) and most charming by moonlight; but Mr C. and I wade had not been long enough acquainted to enter much into conversation.

> # L O S T,
>
> By a GENTLEMAN, in paffing from DEADMAN'S CROSS TOLL-GATE, through SOUTHILL, BROOM and BIGGLESWADE to POTTON,
>
> ## A L O C K E T,
>
> *The Picture of a Young Lady, Set in Pearl;*
>
> A G U I N E A Reward, for any Perfon who carries it to Mr. Beaumont, Coach-maker, at *Bigglefwade,* or to Mr. Smith, Printer, *Bedford.*
>
> Auguft 10th. 1790.

I never heard to whom this locket belonged, or if it was recovered.

After supper, indeed when our bottle was ended—I could not refrain from joking him about his *unecessary* armament of pistols, and not bringing with him a gun so *highly* necessary for his intention of partridge shooting. However if he has no gun he has brought with him a load of shot, flasks, screws nets etc. etc. purchased at no small cost!!

War Office August 21 1790

26th Reg. of Foot, Edmund S. J.
Byng, Gent. is appointed Ensign,[7]
without purchase Vice Samuel
Crooke promoted.

One of our bumpers was to ye future fortune of the young ensign: of which receiving no announcement from Mrs B. I shall take the liberty of informing her. C.'s eyes became soon closed; I could not sit up alone.

Tuesday
August 24

St Bartholomew, with his cold dew. But then formerly it was eleven-days in advance: so our old proverbs are all kindly.

Horseback at 10 o'clock. Took the Potton road:—passed *this well known turnpike* and in another half-mile crossed the rivulet near the *foot bridge* described in the next page. Then to Potton, there called upon Mr H.[8] my brother's agent (and the gamekeeper of this excellent manor) and went around the church which stands over the brook above the town on the eastern side.

Sandy

Over Sandy Warren to Sandy village—around which, in the adjacent fields, culture is brought to great perfection, and cucumbers cover the ground; this I made Mr C. to observe; and to pick up what he liked for our dinner—

The new enclosures beyond rather puzzled me—but I broke down some rails most courageously.

Then crossed Blunham common and these two bridges; and in two more miles to Gt Barford; where we put up at Mrs Bakers, The White Hart Alehouse. Here Mr F[inch][9] our conductor was not arrived—dinner being ordered we walked over the bridge—and about the churchyard when our puffing barber came in and speedily our ale house fare was a bottle of fine choice wine belonging to a club here, whose book and rules we read; scarcely to be outdone by those in Bunbury's print.

At 3 o'clock we issued forth to our fishing; catch a few perch at the stanch below the bridge.

Then foolishly and with much loss of time change our situation and go to another spot, lower down the river 2 miles to be unecessarily tired: here tho' the evening was fine we caught but few fish, and had then a long walk back to our alehouse there to settle our account and order our horses.

Eating - - - - - -	2	0
Wine - - - - - -	1	3
Old Beer & Mild Ale - - -	0	8
Brandy - - - - - -	1	0
Corn & Hay - - - - -	1	4
Mr. Finch, Eating and Liker - -	1	5
	7	8

At seven o'clock we put forth, in a cool evening, with a moon to light us home, to a good supper; then C. is in haste for bed: he will not sit up with me, tho' he rises four hours later. . . . *Biggleswade*

As usual I rise at seven o'clock; but no C. stirring! Well let him lay if he likes it. *Wednesday August 25*

My waking hours were well employ'd in an early walk with my rod and line by the river-side—(upon which stands Biggleswade Mill—and here is the road into the meadow) where some casting-netters caught the only fish that were caught.—After breakfast Mr H. my brother's agent from Potton, called upon me, to settle about Mr. C.'s shooting with him on the 1st September. Papers and letters from town to read, and to answer.

Mrs Byng hopes E[dmund] is an ensign (laughable enough this after the insertion in the Gazette) writing to her, to E[lizabeth] L[ucy][10] and then transcribing from our door post, this long, ill-done advertisement was a business of some time.—

Wanted a few, active well-made Lads, to Compleat the gallant Corps the 19th Regiment of Light Horse, now Cantoned at Chevilimodoo, in the East Indies.—The Regiment is Quartered in a most plentiful country abounding in all kinds of game; and the Men at full Liberty to Hunt, Shoot, and Fish as they please! They are mounted on the finest Horses in the World, from Arabia, Persia and Bengal: and each light Horseman is allowed two Black Servants to take of his Horse so that He has nothing to do but to Ride Him.—The Pay in India is nearly double; and the necessaries of Life not half the Price they are in England. On the Passage out to India, The Recruits are Supplyd with every Article of Comfort, and Convenience; Bedding, and Provisions, Gratis; and will receive every Shilling of their Pay, which runs on during the voyage when they arrive at Madras; from thence to the Cantonment is but 48 miles.—Young Men not above F5 18 high nor under F5 15 who are willing to enter for this most Honorable and profitable Service by applying to Cornet Neville at the George Inn, in Potton, shall Receive One Guinea Bounty, and a crown to drink his Majesty's Health.

God Save the King.

N.B. As the Ships do not sail for India before February, the Lads will have near 7 months to amuse themselves in England; and the whole time in full pay the same as if on actual Service.

Now for our ride—thro Southill village—by Southill House; and then over Romney Warren thence into Wrest Park; where I intended to have ridden about, and have shewn to C. the Prospect House, gardens, etc. etc. but the rain falling fast, hurried us along under an avenue of trees, to the George Inn, Silsoe; where we housed ourselves and stabled our horses.—C. thought of a good dinner, but I confined his wants to the situation, and to an half eaten, half-hot leg of mutton; to which were added eggs and bacon: C. praised the ale and I quaffed brandy and water.

Silsoe

Such a deluge of rain fell as to drive even the drovers into shelter; once I ventured out into the garden and from a seat well sheltered in a yew bush, took this drawing.

GEORGE, SILSOE.						s.	d.
Dinner -	-	-	-	-	-	I	6
Beer -	-	-	-	-	-	o	3
Brandy -	-	-	-	-	-	I	o
Tea -	-	-	-	-	-	I	4
Horses Corn & Hay	-	-	-			I	4
						5	5

BIGGLESWADE MILL

[see p. 281

GARDEN FRONT, THE GEORGE INN: SILSOE
from water-colours by the Diarist [see p. 282

The misery of the inn, and the misery of the day could not but gloom us; C. had no great-coat and mine could make only a short defence against the weather. We were obliged to drink tea; and to stay as long as possible.—

At ½ past six o'clock we braved the weather; the roads so lately dusty now streamed with currents—C. was quickly soaked to the skin, but I held out better from my gt-coat.

At Shefford I advised a stop at my old friend's M[artin]'s[11]—where we used many glasses of brandy—within and without our bodies; with many thanks to brother Martin.

In our way of return we met Sr G[eorge] O[sborn][12]— who gallop'd by us; I know all my acquaintance that I meet; and so perhaps does he— Into Biggleswade we came Biggles-
wade like two drowned rats; and were instantly in our bed rooms —washing—shirting, etc,

At supper I sat in Knights[13] coat; all I wanted of change; and C. in his shooting jacket: we feasted again upon eels; and drinking freely of the port made us defy the danger of our souxing.

I slept better last night, than I have yet done here.— *Thursday* Poney went rather heavily yesterday, and coughed fre- *August 26* quently;—so this morning he lost a quart of blood, which was deem'd by the hostler (as usual) to be of a very bad quality! A damp, rainy morning. Writing long letters to town; whence I received a newspaper, and many letters.

In the morning we were confined by the weather; but were urged to an evening fishery by the fisherman who hires the water, and would go away tomorrow—— So we dined at one o'clock; and at ½ past 2 entered our boat with the fishermen, and the barber's Finch's son;[14]—after being punted down the stream for 2 miles, we began our operations—by laying down flew-nets[15] and driving the fish with poles; in 2 hours time we caught a great quantity of roach, and other small fish.

Being tired of the pastime, tho more with the weather,

283

(for it began to rain hard) I walked home across the meadows; and returned well wetted; C. did not come in till after dark. C. return, history—if—his redressing—Oh! Oh!

> Let me have men about me that are fat,
> Sleek headed Men.

Friday
August 27
A gloomy morning.—Vex'd at the thoughts of the last nights folly; but recovered by letters of announcement of Freks fortune, in succeeding his brother Edmund as page to R.H. the P[rince of] W[ales].[16]

Writing letters till noon: then rouse C. and the weather clearing up we took a pleasant walk to survey Knights farm—and by the hamlet of Upper Caldcote; where being caught in a shower of rain, and sheltering under a hedge I had no other employ than to sketch the only cottages in sight.

After dinner, I open'd the first bottle of my own wine; which we soon finish'd to the healths of the ensign, and of the page. Their success—with my hopes, gave my spirits a fillip, otherwise I feel myself very low, and enfeebled, relaxed by day, and spasm'd by night as we supposed that Powell, the famous walker, might arrive here this evening in his return from his York expedition to be perform'd, now in 5 days and 18 hours;

We mounted our horses and walked them to Girford Bridge, where Mr C. gallop'd forward 5 miles to reconnoitre; but return'd to me without tidings. It was a pleasant autumnal evening.

Much company, and more noise in our inn than usual; (for in general it is very quiet) probably from shooters on their road. The evenings now begin to grow cold: but I oppose a fire, which as once begun cannot be discontinued. We stay'd up till eleven o'clock: but no news of Powell!—

Saturday
August 28
At one o'clock this morning I was awaken'd with an account of Powell's arrival; but being very sleepy, I would not arise; only ordered him to be supplyed, to his wishes,

with supper and wine—A return of summer; Mr C. has resolved upon seeing Wooburn, but no horse being unlet, he
walked by my side to Ickwell Green, a rural pleasant spot.

By Ld O[ngley]'s[17] dogkennel: ignorance of youth! To
Ld T[orrington]'s gate of approach: a Gothic lodge I
think it is called! for Lord T. disfigured the country by
building some of the strangest ill-fashioned buildings that
ever were conceiv'd; and tho in the constant waste of
money, and pursuit of taste.—Never produced anything of
beauty or utility!—did; and undid; built up and pull'd
down; and never was wrong!!! A Gothic lodge!!!

Then to Mr Gastling's farm, where we saw Mr
W[oodman]'s horses, and were treated with bread and
cheese, and wine under his porch.

Thence, to where the priory of Warden till very lately, Old
remained in good preservation; but now nothing but a Warden
back part of the offices remain preserv'd as the whole would
have been, by the late purchase, Mr Whitbread[18] had he
come in time: (being an improver and preserver:) the
chimery and the stone work above the door are much to be
admired— — This, as a farm house, an excellent one
might been form'd—or as a shooting box— — Thro fields
to Warden Church, whence is a most pleasant and varied
view.— —

Returned home hungry to a quickly prepared dinner—;
to which we sat down without form: how unlike a private
invitation? From most of which—deliver me!—Our
bottle soon empty'd and longing to enjoy more of this fine
day I walk'd up alone to the new fitting inn: where I heard
and saw Mr T.'s plans and cunning: It will be a clean
comfortable inn.—As for the captain, he took a flirt with
our incognita neighbour—seemingly a lady of the Wardour Street life, for whom a country retirement may be
necessary.

She would not own any thing to the captain, who described her as all conceit, and affectation.

Our suppers are slight: and we retire early, not being of

the same age to form a long conversation; old men will not explain and should not narrate.

Sunday
August 29
This has been a very quiet week: however, unluckily chosen, as my own house at present is empty'd—The weather is now very pleasant, but cool, and will suit the partridge shooters.—I give up fishing, for this season; and here it is a joke, where every man throws a casting net; and where the fisherman use flew nets.—The post came in late; and C. rose much later. With much pleasure did I peruse this announcement:

G A M E.

WHEREAS the GAME on the CROWN MANORS, of BIGGLESWADE, STRATTON & HOLME, in the County of Bedford, has been for many Seasons very much disturbed and destroyed by unqualified Persons and Others, — NOTICE is hereby given, that whoever in future shall be found trespassing on the said Crown Manors, will be rigorously prosecuted, by Order of LORD CARTERET.

H A Y N E S H O U S E,
August 28th. 1790.

How rediculous to suppose that these paper pellets will deter the poacher; or preserve the game!

Put your gamekeepers, my lord, to bed at 8 o'clock in the morning; and let them rise at 8 o'clock at night.

Having enquired, for Mr C.'s diversion, about the Duke of B[edford]'s hounds, I received from Mr W[indsor] this notification:

> I, Windsor, Duly to Mr. Byng, the Duke of Bedford's Hounds will be at Chicksands Wood tomorrow Morning at 5 Clock.
> Gastlings.
> Augt. 29.

286

WARDEN PRIORY [*see p.* 285

'Upon this spot, in a blacksmith's shop, was Tompion brought up; who, from making plough chains, took in clocks to repair: and so followed the watchmaking line, till he attained the highest excellence'

from water-colours by the Diarist

Mr H. (my brother's agent at Potton) came to dine with us—This is very fatiguing! For these gentry are half familiar, half formal, half truth, half brag, half honest, half ——: tired out; but I did it for C.'s future sport.— He rode a mare of good make and description—that he would * have tempted me to buy: I try'd her but was not in a purchasing humour, tho I wanted a taller horse than Poney; besides a latent wish for hunting, a passion not quite extinguished in my heart.

On the south side of Biggleswade Bridge (my evening sketch) is written:—

'The River Iyvell was made navigable in the year of Our Lord 1758.'

I heard that Mr C. had set off at 5 o'clock (not at 4 *Monday* o'clock as he threaten'd) to meet the hounds: as I ride very *August 30* slow and take my grand pleasure in passing through the air, and over a country at my ease, I was soon after breakfast, at 9 o'clock, on horseback, to enjoy, completely, this fine weather; for I see no reason in idle delay, and then to gallop away to make up lost time.—Thro Northill, to Cople Cardington and to the Swan Inn, Bedford; it was a *Bedford* fine drying day and the harvest advancing merrily—Bedford is a dingy mean town; my first visit, after ordering dinner, was to Reeds,[19] the odd, printing man, but unluckily for me, he was from home, else I had invited him to dinner: but his wife shew'd me all his curiosities—Returning to my inn, I walk'd to the northern end of the town to the Moravian College; where civilly attended by their priest and matron I was shewn their chapel, dormitries etc etc etc.

From the inn window I took this upper view. The bridge till lately was blocked up by gateways, serving for the county gaol.—

At two o'clock Mr C. arrived with a long account of his hunt, in and out of Chicksand Wood; into corn fields, and

* I have since repented of my haste and want of judgment.

287

being pelted by the labourers.—When we were setting off C. wished likewise, to see the Moravian College;[20] so I rode slowly on, and he did not overtake me until I was past Cardington: when our return was very slow and pleasant, but hurried at the last by the rain.

SWAN, BEDFORD.

Ducks Veal Cutlet -	-	-	-	-		4	o
Beer -	-	-	-	-	-		3
Wine -	-	-	-	-	-	1	3
Brandy -	-	-	-	-	-	1	3
						6	9

Tuesday
August 31

I had premised that this tour was to be only a vehicle of my drawings,—at this time, just attempted, and which then sketch'd were finished in the year 1792 when this tour was written out; fairly.

As C. was not stirring early this morning.—I went away at ½ past nine (after the post came in) to Gastlings farm; here C. overtook me; and then Mr Walker with us to my favourite spot, Rowney; where we examined in vain about fishing the moats—now very shallow and fishless.

Clifton

Thence took our way by Southill Avenue towards Clifton, *whose church* is view'd to advantage from the Stanford road—Clifton Bridge, nearly at hand is of rural and picturesque scenery. The church of Clifton is of sufficient size and building for the village.

Adjoining to the pale of these grounds, stands the turnpike house—upon the road leading from Baldock to Bedford.

Returned home thro Langford, with an eager appetite, having been long on horseback; after dinner C. went out to try a gun, and I went to try a walk;—both returned at 8 o'clock, he having had a flirtation with the conceited incognita. Supped at nine o'clock upon cold beef; and at eleven retired.

Poor partridges! and poor hares! For all the world issue *Wednesday*
out to destroy calling it sporting; and game being thus *Sept. 1*
sought and pursued, makes every one adopt the vile
principle of commiting what destruction he can, for he
judges that what escapes will never again be seen by him.
C: at six o'clock went to this sport at Potton to meet Mr
H. I took a cool refreshing walk before breakfast—after
reading newspapers (for I cannot move till I have read
about the Spanish War)[21] my ride was first to Sutton; at the
end of which village stands this old stone foot-bridge over
a stream that flows thro Sutton Park, most of which is to
be view'd from this bridge.

In this, poor, village the houses are numbered, but why
I know not.

Thence I proceeded over an open ugly country, (where I
saw no shooters!) and by Potton wood, to the village of
Cockayne-Hatley[22] a miserable mean one, in grazing
grounds, and to view what might remain of the old family
seat of the Custs.—It is moated round, and now in a
delapidated state; therein is an hall with a wooden roof and
a bad gallery:—I picked up a little bit of a panel picture
but there are no books, except some fusty law and divinity.
A new mean addition of rooms has been made at one end,
never to be inhabited; for the place and soil are truly
wretched, and not to be improved!—I crossed over pastures, an intricate way into Gamlingay Field, and so to G:
village to view the famous weeping ash tree; but of whose
history, and planting I could learn no account!—

Passing the demolished Gamlingay-Park and Everton
village, I came to The Hasells a pleasant, dry, shaded seat
of Mr Pym;[23] which is soon to be put under taste by Mr
R[epton],[24] and where Mr P. has *employed* (already) a large
sum of money in building a new house. Over Sandy
Warren to Sandy village, and by the lane to Girford Bridge.

And in another mile to a alehouse, The Cross, upon the
road at the end of the hamlet of Beaston; where, in a
shabby room, I eat of boiled beef, and bread and cheese,

whilst F[inch], the fishing barber, (who came here to meet me) drank his ale in the kitchin: my horse got some oats in an outhouse.—At 3 o'clock, we repaired to the not distant, rivers bank; and angled there for several hours, catching many small fish; when I returned to the alehouse to pay the bill—thus charged

			s.	d.
Mr. F's Eating and drinking	-	-		3
My Brandy	- - -	-	I	
For my Dinner what I pleased				
So I generously gave	-	-	-	6
			s.I	9

Soon after my return home, C. came back tired, bringing only 3 birds. Our supper conversation turned, principally, upon his day: his having first dined in the field: and afterwards with Mr H. at Potton, where he was much charmed with his pudding.—

Thursday Sept. 2   I read in the newspapers of P.'s arrival in London; and most certainly a surprising performance! From a lack of roguery has this poor devil gained nothing by his powerful labours; whilst a cunning cheat would have brought his abilities to a most profitable market.—May some subscription be set on foot to reward him.

POWELL

This celebrated Pedestrian has won his wager—he arrived in York on Wednesday, between one and two o'clock—and on Saturday at St Paul's London; at twelve minutes after *four*—being an hour and forty-eight minutes within the time wagered for:

He was met, at Highgate and Islington, by about 200 horsemen; and when he reached London, the crowd was immense. As soon as he had touched St Paul's Church-door, the mob gave him three huzzas. He then got into a hackney coach, and was drove to the *Pheasant* public-house, at the back of *Astleys* Amphitheatre, where he went to bed. *Powell* said he would undertake to walk *one hundred miles* this day, if any person would make it worth his trouble by a wager.

BIGGLESWADE BRIDGE

[*see p.* 287

GIRFORD BRIDGE
from water-colours by the Diarist [*see p.* 289

He declares he never tires; and this journey was performed with a very uneasy *Corn* in the sole of one of his feet. When he was opposite Islington Church, an old man was thrown down by the mob pressing forward in order to see *this* Walker pass: and as the crowd was very great, the poor fellow, in all probability would have been trampled to death, if it had not been for *Powells* humanity. As soon as he came up to him, he made a full stop—nor would he move further, till the old man was set upon his legs, and taken care of.

C. was early out to his shootings. I had done well to have gone with Mr B[arnett]'s hounds—which passed our house to wash in some not distant large covers.—

It was a charming day. After breakfast I took my gentle ride by the end of Beaston hamlet—, there amusing myself by taking these two sketches of the same cottage.

Over Girford-bridge, to Sandy—where I cheapen'd a quantity of Roman coins—; then wander'd up many of the vales of Sandy Warren—at the end of won of them stands this cottage; the drawing of which, *I presume* is *very like.* There are many of these pleasant vallies, and some steepish hills: the hills are stocked with rabbets, and the vallies are till'd as garden grounds.—These urns etc. were dug up in the great sand pit of the south east end of the village.

Thence to the Hazells Mr P[ym]'s—: there is a cottage at the foot of the Warren in a lane, at the edge of his grounds, whose situation is truly picturesqe, and retired; my wonder allways was that such a place was not taken within his pale and improved into something more:— every such place of mine should hold a happy dependant to rear my poultry etc; etc;—

Old Mr P. has as little taste about these things as his friend Ld T: and yet for ever they discourse about these things! And, of course, highly flattered each other.

If a man wants to erect a Gothic building—or any thing in the way of ruins, let him not blunder on in his oun conceit but refer to Hearnes, Middimans, and Groses[25] prints and he may be furnished with an intention in an instant.—

Young Mr B. enticed by some builder, has just finished an, Apollo-garden-like, house, all window'd:—[26]

From his grounds I came upon Potton Heath, to look out for the shooters but in vain; call'd at H.'s house at Potton; and then took my way of return by the foot of Sandy Hills, over Girford Bridge, and thro the hamlet of Lower Caldecote, to Biggleswade.

Not a moment of waiting for dinner; (this is the joy of an inn) a boil'd fowl, and pickled pork being ready soon satisfy'd my cravings: C. came in quickly after, with *3 more* birds.

At 6 o'clock, I rode and C. walk'd to see Mr T.'s new house, at Holme, who has here built a nice retirement:

H. understands odd contrivances, lean-tos etc—into all which, we were obliged by him to enter; nor did we get home till ½ past 8 o'clock; in good time however, for C— to play the window scene with Juliet.—We had a cold supper, and were early to bed:—most people lay more in bed in the country, than in London, where they never can retire in good time.

I had an early and most pleasant walk, by the rivers bank to Frog-Hall, and returned by the new-fitting-up inn; which tho established in an unmanly way, will be a snug shop, with better rooms, stabling, and garden, than this old house can boast. Papers and letters read—(and the latter answered.) We trotted away to Mr H.'s at Potton; when tho it rain'd, the sportsmen would sally forth.

My intention, here was to try H.'s mare; but she having been ill-rode did not please me; then not finding the shooters, I returned quickly to Biggleswade, to avoid coming storms.—C. returned birdless.

D[uke] of P[ortland] and Ld F[rederick] both changed horses, at our inn; and to both I *introduced* my civilities[27]—
—!—!—!

C. devoured 12 mutton chops at dinner! No man possesses an happier appetite; but we never exceed our bottle. Our evening exit was, I riding, he walking, to K[night]'s farm—a retired gloomy spot with plenty of apples in the garden; and returned over Brome Field and by Holme-Mill, into B[iggleswade] just as a violent shower began which we sheltered from in the Swan Inn gateway.—Tea and toast, and a wish for a fire; which I opposed: our latter evening was passed in drawing.—

Saturday
Sept. 4

Theatrical Crowning of Mr Powell

The Celebrated Pedestrian.

— — —

Royal Grove

Astley's Westminster Bridge.

This present *THURSDAY* 2d Tomorrow Friday 3d and Saturday 4th September 1790.

This famous Englishman will be crowned with laurels upon the Theatre which is purposely prepared for the occasion, as is the Scenery, Machinery, Dances, Songs, Chorus, etc. and the ceremony of Theatrical Crowning will take place in the same manner as was represented at the Couronement of Mons. *Voltaire* at the Comedie Francaise at Paris some few years past.[28]

Mr Powell will appear in the dress he wore on the road on his last journey to York, and give spectators a specimen of the pace he commonly keeps on the road which is superior to that of any Horse for a continuance of time.

Mr Astley, in exhibiting this famous Pedestrian to the Public has had an eye to the ceremony of the Roman Victors (who were peculiarly distinguished by that brave and Warlike people) under an idea that it would be equally pleasing to Englishmen whose superiority in Athletic Exercises and bravery stand unrivalled through the world.

C. off early to his sports. I after a morning walk, newspapers, and breakfast, rode thro Langford, a place of misery, of ruined cottages, (and where the house of God is as wretched as the house of man) to Arlesey,[29] to the old mansion there, where in my sallad days I visited and sported: now all ruin and desolation!

·And the long grass oertops the mouldering wall.'

A large old hall back'd by a large parlour wainscotted with oak; some good carving therein and a tolerable old portrait of Ld Chief Justice Lee: all the elms and avenues are cut down; and the house must soon fall for the stairs are dangerous to ascend. Returned to, and entered the church; wherein are some monuments of the Brown and the Edwards families, with a curious old font, well worthy of removal by some antiquary. Some brasses strongly fix'd! Returned by Clifton, and thro the hamlet of Stanford by 3 o'clock. C. came in from his last days sport, with another leash of birds making in all 4 brace and ½:—all shot by H. for C.

C. has never touched a feather! Nor could I now conceal a sarcastic laughter after all the expence that C. put himself to for shooting apparatus;—for everything, but the most necessary, and first to be thought of article, a gun; and to my calculation of his costs, he pleaded guilty.— Exactly one guinea a brace!

	£	s.
Game Certificate - - - -	2	3
Patent Shot - - - - -		8
Powder - - - - -		4
Flask - - - - -		8
Gaiters - - - - -		5
Shot Bag - - - - -		3
Flints - - - - - -		1
Horse Hire to Potton - - -		12
To Mr H. - - - - -		10
	£4 14	0

Dinner and tea; then a walk over pleasant grounds to Stratton and back. At our return to settle a long tho reasonable bill, and all the trouble of feeing the servants.—

Sunday Sept. 5

Rose at 5 o'clock; eager to go but sorry to depart. A family at home!!! C. soon stirring; and early abroad on foot to attend me: near Baldock I stop'd to take a sketch of this poor mill once celebrated for the beauty it contained. At a bad inn The Swan, at Stevenage we badly breakfasted. Attracting much notice by our method of march; and had not C: been overruled by me in preventing his walking in a jacket, we had been followed by a crowd: as

BALDOCK MILL

[*see p.* 294

WELWYN CHURCH
from water-colours by the Diarist [*see p.* 295

it was, people were abroad, and inquisitive of me; thinking it a walking wager.

From Welwyn Hill C. mended his pace, and from a fear of being follow'd passed thro Hatfield, and for some miles, with much celerity; at the rate of 5 miles in the hour.—An approaching storm hurried me forward for shelter which having procured in the stable of an unlicensed alehouse at the 13 mile stone C. overtook me; within sight at a small distance is a cottage by the road side near the 13 mile stone beyond Barnet; this was one of the keeper's lodges of Enfield Chace.[30]

The rain continued fiercely; but hoping to find Mrs B[yng] at Barnet I hurried forward; luckily she came not, for it was their fair: all noise and uproar.[31]—C. soon came in, well wetted, to a bad scrambling dinner: then in a cold, damp evening, we pushed our way to Duke St M[anchester] Square,[32] where we arrived before 8 o'clock; C: coming in quite fresh, and proving himself to be equal, nay superior, to the most braggart walkers.—

EDITOR'S NOTES

(1) John, third, and Frederick Gerard, fifth son of the diarist.

(2) Jack Windsor at Gastlings.

(2a) This was doubtless Colman the younger, referred to as the gentleman from the North, since he was educated at King's College, Aberdeen, from 1781 to 1784-5. (See *Memoirs of the Colman Family*.)

(3) Mr Knight of the farm at Lower Caldecote.

(4) Refers no doubt to the edition of 1789. The well-known illustrated edition with the Bartolozzi frontispiece, and Blake's engraving of The Fertilization of Egypt, did not appear till 1791.

(5) A considerable quantity of sepulchral remains, pottery and coins have been found from time to time in a field called 'Chesterfield', lying to the east of the village, between two small hills, on which are the remains of earth-works, popularly known as 'Caesar's Camp' and 'Galley Hill'. Judging from the size of the cemetery there appears to have been a considerable settlement hereabouts. The old Roman coins are known locally as 'chesterpieces'. There is a description of this field and the remains found there, on p. 60 of *The Gentleman's Magazine* for 1764.

(6) Powell was sufficiently well-known for his portrait to have been made, a print of which is inserted in the Diary.

(7) The author's second son.

(8) Mr Hinson. Potton Manor (or Potton Regis) was owned by the diarist's brother, George, 4th Viscount Torrington, who sold it in 1795 to Samuel Whitbread.

(9) Mr Finch, the barber and angler at Biggleswade.

(10) E. L., Elizabeth Lucy, his eldest daughter.

(11) Martin, the host of the inn at Shefford.

(12) Sir George Osborn. (See p. 270, note 91.)

(13) Borrowed from Mr Knight of Caldecote.

(14) Young Finch, the son of Finch the barber fisherman.

(15) Flewing was the process of fishing with a net behind a chair, both being dragged slowly along. (Wright's *Eng. Dial. Dict.* vol. ii.) Flewers sometimes used nets with unlawful meshes to destroy fish under size, or out of season. (Gardner, *Hist. Dunwich*, 1754.)

(16) The author's fifth son succeeds the second.

(17) The Right Hon. Robert Henley Ongley, Baron Ongley of Old Warden, was created a peer, 22nd July, 1776. In 1792 Southill Manor was in the possession of Robert, 2nd Lord Ongley, who still held it in 1797, and whose family had acquired considerable property in Southill at different times. The greater part of his land in this parish he exchanged with Samuel Whitbread early in the nineteenth century for an estate at Old Warden. Lord Ongley, however, retained the manorial rights in Southill, and they passed at his death to his son Robert, 3rd Lord Ongley, who conveyed them to Joseph Shuttleworth.

(18) Mr. Samuel Whitbread, the elder, who died in 1796, came of a Nonconformist family in Bedfordshire, from which he inherited a small property. As a young man he entered a London brewery and in course of time rose to possession of the business. After realising a large fortune, he purchased in 1773 the manor of Old Warden from Charles, son of Sir William Palmer, and in 1795 the Gastlings Manor of Southill from George Byng, 4th Viscount Torrington, the brother of the author.

(19) There was a John Reed, a painter, in Bedford at this time, to which this probably refers.

(20) In 1744 a Moravian congregation was founded at Bedford, but the autocratic behaviour of the 'chief labourer' and the squabbles that arose on the building of the chapel were the chief causes of Wesley's final break with that body. It nevertheless flourished; the brothers and sisters lived in separate houses, but had a common chapel for worship. The women later founded a very successful school for young ladies which still exists.

(21) In 1790 the Spaniards seized the fishing ships at Nootka Sound, and the country expected war, but on 24th July a convention was signed for the ships' release, and on 25th November, 1790, the King's Speech at the opening of the session announced peace.

(22) Cockayne Hatley had passed, owing to the failure of the male line, from the Cockaynes to the Custs in 1745, and was at this date owned by Francis Cust, who died in 1791.

(23) Mr. Francis Pym was High Sheriff of Bedford in 1791. His house, the Hazells, a mansion in the Italian style, was built in 1660 and enlarged 1720-1740. This manor at Sandy, known after the dissolution as 'Hasells Manor', belonged originally to the priory of Chicksands, but upon the dissolution of the priory by Henry VIII in 1542, passed to Francis Pygott, who alienated it to Robert Burgoyne, whose grandson, John Burgoyne, in 1635 transferred it to William Britain. His grandson in 1712 sold the manor to Heylock Kingsley, whose daughter and heiress married William Pym in 1748. The son of this marriage is the Francis Pym here mentioned.

(24) Humphry Repton (1752-1818), landscape-gardener (v. *D.N.B.*).

(25) The prints of Hearne, Middiman, and Gross were amongst the best known of the period.

(26) This was no doubt Charles Barnett of Stratton Park, Bedfordshire, who was born in 1758, entered the Foot Guards at the age of 17 years and rose to be a major-general, dying in 1804 at Gilbraltar. The property he owned was purchased by the executors of his grandfather in 1764 from the heirs of Sir John Cotton, Bart. His son, another Charles Barnett, took over the Biggleswade Harriers about 1825.

(27) William Henry Cavendish Bentinck, 3rd Duke of Portland (1738-1809), and his son Lord Frederick Cavendish Bentinck (the 4th), born 1781.

(28) Descriptions of the amazing ovations to Voltaire, as an old man, are to be found in Mrs. Toynbee's edition of *The Letters of Mme. Du Deffand*.

(29) Arlesey was owned by William Bedford, who took the name of Edwards.

(30) Enfield Chace, of which only a portion known as Hadley Woods and Hadley Common and the Rough Lot in Trent Park now remain, was a royal hunting-ground and originally formed a portion of the great forest of Middlesex. It was disforested in the eighteenth century.

(31) Fairs were held at Barnet on 8th, 9th, and 10th April, for linen drapery, toys, etc. On 4th and 5th September the Harvest or Welsh Fair was held for Welsh cattle and horses, and on 6th September for mercery, etc., and sometimes for a few horses, pigs, etc.

(32) Boyle's *Court and County Guide* for 1796 gives the Hon. John Byng as residing at 29 Duke Street. The house (a corner one) was in existence until a bomb of World War II practically completed its destruction.

A TOUR INTO LINCOLNSHIRE: 1791

Day	Weather	To What Place	Inns	County	Miles
June 13 Monday	Cool & windy.	Coach—To Biggleswade.	Sun. G.	Beds.	45
June 14	Gay but cool.	To Cana Manor Farm; &c.	—	—	20
15	Cold.	To Chicksands Priory; and back.	—	—	14
16	Dripping morn: dull eve.	To Southill; and back.	—	—	7
17	A calm day.	To Chicksands Priory; and return.	—	—	14
18	Dripping morn: pleasant eve.	To Bedford; and return.	—	—	24
Sunday 19	A cool day.	To Eaton; to Alconbury Hill.	Cock. G. Wheatsheaf. G.	Beds.	23
20	do.	To Ramsey; to Huntingdon and return.	George. B. George. T.	Hunts.	26
21	Pleasant morn: cold eve.	To Wansford Bridge.	Haycock. G.	—	20
22	Pleasant day.	An evening ride.	—	—	5
23	Fine day.	To Market-Deeping.	Bull. B.	Lincoln.	13
24	Fine day.	To Bourn. To Folkingham.	Bull. B. Greyhound. G.	—	20
25	A warm day.	A morning and evening ride.	Greyhound. G.	Lincoln.	18
Sunday 26	do.	Church. To Sleaford.	Angel. T.	—	9
27	do.	A morning and evening ride.	—	—	23
28	do.	To Lincoln.	Rein Deer. G.	—	18
29	Hot day.	Cathedral. To Lincoln.	—	—	—
30	A pleasant day.	To Bardney. To Thumby.	Angel alehouse. Swan. T.	—	24
July 1	A cool day.	An evening ride and back.	—	—	12
2	Pleasant but rainy.	To Tattersal. To Sleaford.	Angel. B. Angel. T.	—	20
Sunday 3	Fine morn: rainy eve.	To Dunnington. To Spalding.	Red Cow. T. White Hart. T.	—	28
4	Windy & showery.	In Spalding.	—	—	—
July 5	Charming day.	To Holbeach, &c. To Boston.	Chequers. T. Peacock. T.	—	32
6	Pleasant day.	To Spilsby.	White Hart. T.	—	17
7	A fine day. An evening storm.	To Skegness &c and back.	Bathing Inn. B.	Lincolnshire.	28
8	Charming day.	To Horncastle.	Bull. T.	—	16
9	Fine day.	To Louth.	Blue-Stone. B.	—	14
Sunday 10	Fine morn: missling eve.	An evening ride.	—	—	6

Days	Weather	To What Place	Inns	County	Miles
July 11	A stormy eve.	To Saltfleet.	Old Inn. B.	—	33
		To Cleathorps Inn.	T.		
12	A pleasant day.	To Great-Limber.	Ale Ho:	—	30
		To Barton-upon-Humber.	George. B.		
13	do.	To Glanford Bridge.	Angel. T.	—	24
		To Spital.	Inn. T.		
14	A warm day.	To Gainsborough.	Blacka-Moors Hd. B.	—	33
		To Lincoln.	Reindeer. G.		
15	Hot.	To Nocton-House and back.	—	—	14
16	Hot.	To Ancaster.	Red Lion. B.	—	28
		To Grantham.	Angel. T.		
Sunday 17	Hot.	To Greetham.	Royal Oak. T.	Rutland.	23
		To Stamford.	George. B.	Lincoln.	
18	Hot & stormy.	To Wansford.	Haycock. G.	Hunts.	23
		To Alconbury Hill.	Wheatsheaf. T.		
19	Charming day.	To Buckden.	George. G.	Hunts.	23
		To Biggleswade.	Sun. G.	Beds.	
20	—	Evening ride.	—	—	7
21	—	Morning and evening ride.	—	—	16
22	—	Evening ride.	—	—	8
23	—	To Southill, &c.	—	—	10
Sunday 24	Rainy morn. Fine eve.	To Wellwyn.	White Hart. T.	Herts.	20
25	Heavy showers & stormy.	To Barnet.	Mitre. B.	—	25
		To London.			

FINIS CORONAT OPUS.

43	Good.	Total	41	5	806

(I have examined the above; and found it to be true. J.B.)

A Tour into Lincolnshire
1791

'THERE is nothing, Sir, too little for so little a creature as man.—It is by studying little things that we attain the great art of having as little misery, and as much happiness as possible.'

So says the great Johnson; much to my approbation, who study only little things, and therefore ought, according to him, to be a happy man:—and now I fly in quest of comfort, and peace, leaving out of sight the fineries and follies of London, and out of hearing the eternal raps at my door, with the never-ceasing admission of milliners, (who must be follow'd up by bills,) and the endless discourse about wavering fashions, and balls commencing at midnight.—

These I shall now, for a short time, be delivered from; but yet to recollect the two last dinners I was drag'd to in London; (surely people will tire of my manners, yawning over unatural hours, as much as I do, & over the forms, and miseries of most invitations.)

To the first dinner I was forced, upon a promise of a *very* early hour; (even at 5 o'clock).—The day was unusually cold, with a strong nth east wind;—I left my house at ½ past 4 o'clock; being hungry, warm, and in tolerable spirits; and when arrived, I found no readiness of dinner, the grates were burnish'd up, the tongs and poker laid up for the summer, and the windows open!—Nor did the company drop in till past six o'clock;—then wond'ring at their early coming.—— — My limbs ached with cold, my appetite retired, my intention of conversation subsided;—and when, at last, dinner was announced, (in a grotto room,) the wine was so execrable, that from it, neither warmth, nor comfort, were to be receiv'd.

The conversation was like the wine, poor, and sour; (men, and women equally want restoration from dinner;) with an universal complaint 'That never was felt so cold a 25th of May'! I look'd towards the grate;—'Would you chuse a fire, Mr B?' I bowed:—a servant was order'd to spoil the brilliancy of the grate (the lady of the house pouting) and return'd with a parcell of chips, which being soon burnt out, left us in more misery!

It was a cruel attempt upon my feelings.—Men do not assemble well without a fire, nor care to talk without wine. —We broke up dissatisfied;—the ladies prepared for Ranelagh; I crawled, sulkily, home.— — —

The following day, upon a similar invitation, I went, invitus;—dined much later; a small quantity of peas at a very high price;—fish spoiled by the delay;—but where's the wine? Bad, thick port, and new madeira!—Now with such a dinner, might one not have expected some tolerable madeira, and some goodish claret? (Cut off your side-dishes, I did think, and wish'd to have said; and if you do not pretend to know wines ask a friend of judgment, and of foreign correspondence, to assist you.)—Here were no fires; but an elegant assortment of geraniums, and of myrtles, forced you to endeavour to hope that summer was coming.—

What am I? Am I too old? Too eccentric? Or too observant?—I hope neither;—but I require warmth, genuine wine, and regular hours;—I deny over-flattery, and despise fashions:—but drag me not from my desk, and my fire side, to polite conversation, and cold rooms.—

Besides these, there are two topics I abhor; viz, politics, and children; of the one, few will talk calmly; and of the other, none can know, nor feel, but those who have *long endured*; and shrink from a recollection; neither choosing to expose their miseries, or to suffer the assertions, or contradictions of ignorant batchelors.

(I am not averse from, nor, perhaps, capable of other than matter of fact conversation, which is generally held, I think, in too much contempt; for the reporter is, at least, an honest man, one who cannot, or will not run away from the truth.—Matter of fact related simply, and unadorn'd, makes the surest way to the passions; whereas flourishes are commonly so unadvisedly, so idly added, as to take off from every belief and attention.—Catching every good circumstance, and enjoying every passing occurrence, form the foundation of happiness, and the delight of conversation;—being therefore a matter of fact man, I will dilate into two more (seemingly fond of guttling) narrations, in the description of two gentlemen I frequently visit.

Commentator, of spruce, formal manners, of critical taste, and of classical acquirements—passes his mornings in a well-stored study;—he keeps late hours; and is never punctual at any place of appointment:—his conversation is extremely refined; with an eternal praise of the fair sex; with whom he maintains no improper connection, or, indeed, much intercourse, nor has he been able to procure a wife from these highly-flatter'd females.

To this gentleman, a week since, did I make my first visit of the day;—and after some (*very decent*) conversation, happening to mention potatoes, he ask'd me if I knew how, and when they were first introduced into this country?—This question stagger'd me;—and I mumbled something about Columbus, and America; Aye but, says he, nobody should answer with uncertainty; we should allways apply to books, and be ready on every occasion; let us search the dictionaries.—And so we did.—

Now supposing I had dined with this gentleman, (which formerly I have done) tho' he might read in books of The Culture of the Vine, and of the Origin of Potatoes; yet at his board, I should find wretched wine, and miserable esculents.—

I next visited my friend, Regulus, rough, hearty,

303

vulgar, free, ignorant of grammar, swears without knowing it, and never saw a dictionary;—but he understands
the comforts of life, and where *they* are to be found:—
'Dammee, you shall dine with me, to-day, I'll give you a
bit of fish from Phillips's, a nice ham from Burgess's, and
I know my wine will please you; my Lafite claret is excellent,—and I think (by G—d) my old port is the best in
England'.— —

Now I take the body, you the mind;—who has the
better bargain? Are you for refined conversation, and thick
wine;—or for honest vulgarity (and a bit of B.) with
delicious wines?—Why who would hesitate an instant?—
The good things that enter the stomach, make you relish
what enters the ear;—without them I sit peevish, and
miserable, and laugh at the acquirements of *larning*, when
a man cannot acquire useful knowledge from it: it then
becomes all moonshine;—and whilst the jolly *ignorant*
dog is tasting life in reality, the scholar is looking for it in
a dictionary!—

Monday
June 13

Upon Whit Monday, June 13th. 1791.—I begin a
new tour; and later than last year; (that's all the better;)
after having been delay'd for two days, by the coaches
being full:—whose goings out I have, in vain, attended,
till this morning;—when I was receiv'd, the sixth passen-
ger, into the Paul Jones York Coach.—My servant Garwood, now appointed my master of the horse, went forward to Biggleswade two days ago:—and where is
T. B[ush]*—that G— should gain this appointment?

*T. B[ush] came to live with me, in the year 1765, as groom, two years
before I married; and continued in my service for more than two years
afterwards:—Since which time he resided in my neighbourhood, in various
capacities; a dependant upon my house; and my assistant about horses,
ridings &c.—From long observance of my manners, he knew me so well, as
to render orders unnecessary; and to leave me at ease about his care and

Why, gone to

> 'The undiscover'd country, from whose bourn
> No traveller returns'.

This hints, with other *gentle* touches of the mind, and body, that my touring thro' this world may quickly subside;—therefore, as a pleasant, harmless pursuit, not to be delay'd.

The weather is now cold and uncomfortable; succeeding a very hot, and forward spring. Of my coach company there is nothing pleasant to remember; all conceited ignorance; I could not refrain from snapping them up sometimes: at Baldock, where I walk'd forward, leaving them at dinner, I allways find my journey nearly at an end, attention.—Soon after my getting into the Stamp-Office, I was lucky enough to be able to find a situation for him there; that reliev'd his family from a wretchedness I could scarcely conceive:—Perhaps my satisfaction was almost equal to theirs.

From that time his life and history have form'd a part of my Tours.— Such a loss is an amputation of contentment. His illness, of a weeks duration, in May last, was caught from his attention to a friend who died but some days before. To the honor of Mrs B[yng]'s humanity, and fortitude, be it told that she went and sat beside him, when he had just heard his death warrant pass'd.—He said, 'That his greatest wish, here, was to see me, hoping that I should arrive in town, before he died, to receive his thanks; that his mistress's presence, and conversation, had afforded him infinite consolation, and that he doubted not but his master, who had ever watch'd his fortunes, and had redeemed him, (unsought) from misery, would prove a protector to his two children'.

Such meeting bestow'd comfort upon either party. He was quiet, resign'd, hopeful of mercy; and with a strength of mind that can only be bestow'd upon us by the divine goodness in the minutes of poignant affliction! His latter hours were pass'd in devout attention; till the last delirium came on, when he listen'd for my coming, hoping I should soon arrive.— Thus died T. B.—

Let us draw the veil over human failings; attributing to great temptation, or bad company any wanderings from the rule of right; and throw into the other scale, sobriety, civility, and decent deportment.

> 'The evil that men do, lives after them;
> The good is oft interred with their bones'.

W. S.

Biggles-
wade

and myself quickly at Biggleswade, unpacking my trunks, resident there.—'*I am too much i' the Sun*'. W. S.

My dog Pero is lost; and with him some hope of entertainment. This is the Fair day here; but I am not young enough to walk up to it; and feel happier over a good fire, waiting the arrival of Poney, from a grass field at Mr K[night]'s farm;[1] where he has been passing a pleasant month with 2 cows: but it would be dangerous to have him shod, on the evening of a Fair day. I had my tea, my walk, and my solitude: any thing preferable to London noise, and London hours.—There is a company of comedians here; think of that! Where they cannot find salt for their porridge: there will shortly be as many companies as there are market towns.—These idle indigents traffic their follies for the pence of the poor; and when they have exhausted a neighbourhood, and are deeply in debt, they either run away, or are suffer'd to escape. The tour I now meditate is to be undertaken with Col. B[ertie] who fixes upon the county, to gratify family curiosity: any unseen county is the same to me; may he come soon ere I tire. A walk over the bridge; and then a slight supper.

*Tuesday
June 14*

Arose early to a cold morning. The mornings are now frosty; and they say that much snow is fallen in the north! My first employ, of much import, was the having Po: well shod; upon the which depend the movements of my march. G: my new follower, is to be taught, and told all my methods: he appears very quiet, and attentive, and I think will serve me well.

Breakfast over, and to my ride; G[arwood] attending me upon a hack. To Gastlings Farm; there settled with Mr W[indsor] my winter horse-keeping account. Thence to Chicksands Priory; met Sr G[eorge], and waited upon Lady H[eneage];[2] then to Cana Manor Farm, there saw the mares, and with difficulty caught mine.—Paid Mr C., the stupid, grunting farmer; and partook of some bread and cheese, and brandy and water. This is a bleak spot; but the view is fine. My mare, who is very young and awkward, was led away by G—; she is a present to me from Col. B[ertie], was bred by Mr Hall, and is a daughter of the Useful Cub.—I rode home by Southill; saw Ld E[xeter][3] walking before the house, then call'd upon Mr Dilly, a yeoman, and farmer of great account, with whom I made a dinner engagement.[4] (Popularity is a great punishment; but it is encouraged, often, from envy—or from hatred of others, for the pleasure is none, and the mind is trick'd into it).

Of the players company here, I meant to invite the manager, Mr Brook; but he, poor man, is confined by a rheumatick gout; tho' out must he come tomorrow evening to play the 'so young and light of foot' Romeo.— Finch, my fishing barber, is the companys dresser, and was to have been the inviter; then sould I have *shone away* with my *grand* knowledge of poets, and players. I took a long evening walk; but it was cold and chearless. A full inn to-night.

Lady B— call'd upon me in her way home: I am strangely popular; and must stand (I believe) for the county at the next election.

Passed a better night than my first; for any one used to a bedfellow is unhappy to find himself alone. Up early; this I must stick to for pleasure, health, and right intention. Lunging, and riding my young mare, who goes awkwardly; but I hope that a quiet journey, with gentle treatment, will settle her paces.— — Reading and writing letters: one from Col. B—,[5] saying that Pero had been found, and lost again.— — After breakfast, at eleven o'clock, I rode out, followed by G[arwood] upon the mare, under my equipments and instruction; she went quietly, and will move well.

At Shefford I sent him back; there call'd upon Mr M[artin], who was in town; then to Chicksands Priory, now in great beauty by the haymaking around; but the air is cold, *Wednesday June 15*

Chicksands Priory

307

and gloomy, and when Nature desponds, man will likewise despond; for we all depend, more or less, upon the wind and weather, and rise up, and fall down, with the barometer and thermometer.

Sr George drag'd me a long walk about his (well known) place. Mr and Miss W— dined with us; cold extreme, and no fire! I came warm, and in spirits—I sat in cold and formality;—here is the difference betwixt private houses and inns: all dinners are hurried over, as if a necessitous misery, to be got rid off as soon as possible.—

Let us hear what the great Dr Johnson thinks of inns.[6]

When at Chapel-House Inn, Oxfordshire.
'There is no Private House in which People can Enjoy themselves so well as at a Capital Tavern. Let there be ever so great Plenty of good things, ever so much Grandeur, ever so much Elegance, ever so much desire that every body should be so easy; in the nature of things it cannot be: there must allways be some degree of Care, and Anxiety.—The Master of the House is Anxious to Entertain his Guests; The Guests are anxious to be agreeable to him; and No Man, but a very impudent Dog indeed, can as freely Command what is in another Mans House, as if it were his Own.—Whereas, at a Tavern, there is a general freedom from Anxiety.—You are sure you are Welcome, and the more Noise you make, the more trouble you Give, the more good things you Call for, the Welcomer you are.—No Servants will attend you with the Alacrity which Waiters do who are incited by a prospect of an immediate Reward, in proportion as they please. No Sir: There is nothing which has yet been contrived by Man, by which so much Happiness is produced as by a good Tavern or Inn'.

I think Mr B. has often spoken the same language.

We walk'd, after dinner, for some minutes into the hay field; but the men were all shivering, and the women wrap'd up; no loose stays, with a fine, easy, sweaty dishevelment. After tea, at seven o'clock, I set off home, in a dull dripping evening, and was return'd, going my best speed, in 50 minutes. I then bethought me of the playhouse; and to it I went; more barnish misery exists not; the company seem starving: one fiddle—and 13 candles composed our music and lights. I could not laugh; I could not cry; or stay more than two acts. Except the pronunciation the acting was of the nature of the lordly theatres.

THEATRE, BIGGLESWADE

On **WEDNESDAY** Evening the 15th. of **JUNE**, 1791,
Will be prefented, the Celebrated *TRAGEDY*, of

ROMEO and JULIET

Romeo,   Mr. B R O O K E,
Friar Lawrence,   Mr. P R I C E,
Capulet,   Mr. C R I S P,
Benvolio, Mr. F R I M B L E Y,
Paris,   Mr. S M I T H,
Tibalt,   Mr. H O B S O N,
Peter,   Mafter C R I S P,
And Mercutio,   Mr. B L A N D F O R D,

Nurfe,   Mrs. M O N K,
Lady Capulet, Mrs. B A K E W E L L,
And Juliet,   Mrs. C R I S P,

End of Act the 4th. — A folemn DIRGE, with the Funeral Proceffion of JULIET
to the Monument of the fAPU LETS, — The Vocal Parts by Mr. BROOKE,
Mr, HOBSON, Mafter *Crisp*, Mifs BROOKE and Mrs. WILKINSON.

Comic SONGS, by Mr. HOBSON & Mafter CRISP

To which will be added, a Favorite Mufical ENTERTAINMENT, called

THE W A T E R M A N;[7]
Or, Firft of AUGUST.

Tom Tug,   Mr. S M I T H,
Bundle,   Mr. F R I M B L E Y,
And Robin,   Mr. B L A N D F O R D,

Wilhelmina,   Mrs. W I L K I N S O N,
And Mrs. Bundle, Mrs. C R I S P,

TICKETS to be had of Mrs. Brooke, *at the THEATRE.*

Doors to be Open'd at Half-paft Five — and to begin at Seven o'Clock.
PIT **2s.** —— GALLERY 1s.
DAYS of PLAYING, — MONDAYS, WEDNESDAYS, AND FRIDAYS.

*** No Admittance behind the Scenes.

309

Three acts, only, were finish'd at 9 o'clock. It was an evening for a fire; and over one I muzz'd till 11 o'clock.

Thursday June 16 Last night was of the blust'rous November kind.— Some rain fell, which must do much good; and bring warm weather, I hope. Having now no employ in the country but visiting, I am slow in rising, and getting forth.

I quitted town to avoid company; and now I go to dine in company every day in the country! How often does thus acting opposite to intention, and assertion, happen? I do it here from delay; and having no objects of observation. An Hibernian Capt remark'd when his regiment was order'd from the sun of the West Indies to the frosts of Canada, 'Why this is going out of the frying pan into the fire'!

Fashion now permits people to leave London; so the roads are crouded: in this, as in every other thing, sense, health, pleasure, or convenience are not to be consulted, but only fashion ('that deformed thief!!'). Fashion orders long-neck'd spurs to be worn; so all the post horses are restive at going off from this inn, from being violently spurr'd on the first motion.—At one o'clock ride slowly

Southill to Southill; call upon the Smiths; then to Squire Dilly's* to dinner: where I was well receiv'd, hospitably treated, and drank of good wine. Mr P—[8] and Miss D.[9] made the four.   I was in good spirits; talk'd away upon some few topics that I may understand, and upon many that I did not understand.

*Mr Boswell—in his Life of Dr Johnson, just published, (which is greedily read, and so universally admired) mentions that 'On Saturday June 2nd, 1781, I set out for Scotland, and had engaged, as I sometimes did, to pay a visit, in my way, at Southill in Bedfordshire, at the hospitable mansion of Squire Dilly, the elder brother of my worthy friends the booksellers in the Poultry.—Dr Johnson agreed to be of the party this year, with Mr Charles Dilly, and me, and to go and see Ld Bates Seat at Luton-Hoe.—

'He (Dr J—) found himself very happy at Mr Dillys, where there is always abundance of excellent fare, and hearty welcome.—

'On Sunday, 3d June, we all went to Southill Church, which is very near to Mr Dillys house.'

310

D[illy] is so puff'd up by the above insertions that he talk'd of soon giving up farming, and seeking in or near London the conversation of learned men, 'who are not to be met with in the country'. 'When you do that', said I, 'you will give up all your comfort and happiness; and with you, D., it is too late in the day. Remember the dog and the shadow'.—'What happiness', D. remark'd, 'it must be to belong to the Literary Club'. 'If you belong'd to any club', I replied, 'it should be to the *Dille* tanti'.

The evening pass'd off well, over good wine, and a good fire. D— told the history of the neighbourhood; and recollected many meanesses of —

At 8 o'clock I crawled back on foot, gloom'd by the weather: what no warm weather for the comfort of the poor, and us old folk; and is winter to return, before summer is come? cold beef; a good fire.—

Having no canine companion, I have written to Col. B[ertie] to say that Rangers company were welcome; but he is not yet arriv'd. G[arwood] by his strut and manners might pass, I should think, for a lawyers clerk, following his master on the circuit.—Rode the mare for $\frac{1}{2}$ an hour.— A tedious morning; and not in motion till 12 o'clock; when, G— following, I took my ride thro' Langford, Clifton and Shefford to C[hicksands] Priory; where I met Mr, Mrs and Miss S[mith][10] at dinner.—No discourse of pleasantry: but I opposed Sr G[eorge]'s praise of *Gilpins Life of our Saviour*,[11] lately published in common historic writing. 'What divest,' said I, 'the New Testament of the grand scriptural stile, so truly descriptive of our saviours words and deeds? Who but fools would turn Miltons Paradise Lost into a ballad; or sink, almost wickedly, the solemnity of divine writ, by this frittering away the holy Evangelists in modern biography'.

We also discoursed about schools; and in praise of Rugby, as out of the way of vice; and a place more under the management of the masters than any other, and I was

Friday June 17

311

for keeping boys backward, and long at school; and not hurrying them into men, and frisking them away to foreign travells.

Left Chicksands at 8 o'clock, where the inside of the old venerable court is just cover'd over with a smart rough cast, like a new farm house! Adieu to all the gravity, and respectability of such a place;—no longer can I pace about it by moon-light, in religious meditation, fancying all the monastic retirement, of such a happy retreat from the world.—I shall now look at it as the outside of a dairy; and so only wish for cream!—Boswell,[11a] meeting Sr G[eorge] some time ago, said 'I do like that Colonelle B[yng]; for he cuts'—'I thank him for his liking, Sr George, but pray, who does not? His friend Johnson mowed with a scythe; every man uses his weapon; I sometimes cut with a penknife, and others prick with a pin'.—I had a pleasant ride; and at my return found Ranger, the Col.'s dog, was arrived by a coach: he is a trouble I have sought, being a fat, stupid creature. Having been late this morning, in rising, I sat up late; even till ½ past eleven o'clock! Hear this, ye gay world.

Saturday June 18 A cold, drizly morning. I must go to Bedford before I quit the county; for my carriage will not move till I have *greased the wheels.*—Receiv'd a long letter from Mrs B[yng]; but when she writes fully, she is complainant, and refines upon pleasure till it becomes a pain! I being form'd of grosser mould, am perhaps, the happier mortal. The weather clear'd up soon after breakfast; but from a fear of returning wet, I took the shortest road by Northill, and to Cople and Cardington, (G— turning back at the end of 5 miles; for now I must attend to the mare, and his maremanship). Cople Church is a strong-built, little pile; at Cardington are some of the tallest and stoutest Lombardy poplars I ever saw.—At the end of Cardington where several roads join, stand the remains of an old cross. A scud of rain hurried me into Bedford; where calling upon

Cople
Carding-
ton

Bedford

Mr P[almer] a lawyer,[12] I engaged myself to an early dinner.
Mr P— is gouty, puddling, and knock'd up; and looks
only to the main chance: as may be seen in the following
hand-bill.

Bedford, 1789

M I S T A K E S having happened, no **GAME**
CERTIFICATES will be made out, without the Money, —
which may be sent by the same Opportunity that
the *Certificate* is sent for.

He, Mr *Fish* P[almer], order'd a tench out of his stew
pond, and shew'd me his garden, before I walk'd up into
the town to Mr H[ensman],[13] our distributer of stamps;
whom I touch'd for my journey; or all had stopp'd. Surely
a swindling tour might be made upon the distributers of
stamps, by a man resembling any of the Commissioners,
and going to those who did not come often to London.

Upon a board affix'd to St Marys Church in Bedford
is written this threat, of strange implication, and folly,

> Whoever defaces the grave stones,
> Plays at games; or commits any
> Indecent acts in this churchyard
> Will be prosecuted.

I was sorry not to find Mr Read, the painter, at home;
because he is a greater curiosity than any thing in his two-
penny museum; which his son most laughably display'd.
—I have only dined two days at Biggleswade, quietly, and
without form; for my other dinners have been so formal,
and so hurry'd over, (the modern method) that I am half-
starved; and except the wine at Dillys, the rest has been
poison; especially the lawyers, (he would not, surely, give

313

such wine to a client!) But that there was no object for me to ride to, and that I am delaying upon the road, or I should not have been so extremely courteous.——[14]

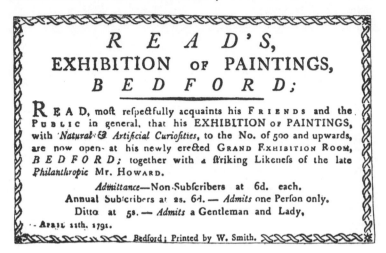

R E A D ' S,
EXHIBITION of **PAINTINGS,**
B E D F O R D;

R E A D, moſt reſpectfully acquaints his F R I E N D s and the Pu b l i c in general, that his EXHIBITION of PAINTINGS, with *Natural* & *Artificial Curioſities,* to the No. of 500 and upwards, are now open- at his newly erected G R A N D E x h i b i t i o n R o o m, *B E D F O R D;* together with a ſtriking Likeneſs of the late *Philanthropic* Mr. H o w a r d.

Admittance—Non-Subſcribers at 6d. each.
Annual Subſcribers at 2s. 6d. — *Admits* one Perſon only.
Ditto at 5s. — *Admits* a Gentleman and Lady.
- Aprir 11th, 1791.

Bedford; Printed by W. Smith.

Mr P[almer]'s clerk, Mr K., dined with us. Our discourse consisted of accounts of court leets, and of the history of neighbouring properties, and purchases: saying, unluckily, that I meant to do a new way home, the clerk was order'd to ride with me; to destroy my own thoughts, and quiet. I wish'd to see if any remains existed of Newenham Priory; but here are only a widely surrounding wall, and many mounds of earth: at the bottom of the grounds, where the river runs, is the Priory-mill.

In a mile and an half, upon the rivers brink is an old castle keep. To this hill-top I climb'd, thro' the bushes, and had, thence, a pleasing view of the river, and the country: my companion soon discovered himself as a sportsman, talk'd eagerly about fox-hunting, and 'that this castle ground was famous for breeding foxes; that the miller, below, was fee'd to preserve them, and could bring in a bill of their damages'. 'Then', said I, 'he never loses a fowl or a duck by illness, who is not thrown into the bill'.

'Look here', added he, 'here is a fox earth—with a litter of cubs within; you may know that from the quantity of feathers at the mouth of the hole!' 'He must know little of artifice', replied I, 'who thus tempted, will not deceive; and strew feathers before every rabbet burrow, to increase charges, and magnify his supposed care'.—In my way from Newenham I pass'd over Goldington Green, whereon are two well-built houses.—Of Bedfordshire there is no county history: none antiquary or draftsman, have ever troubled themselves about the county! But this river seems to have been a strong boundary; and a difficult pass: for another fortification soon presents itself, above the river, of an horseshoe form.

Near to this is Howberry House, an old mansion, (now *Renhold* almost abandon'd) where I remember Mrs Beecher[15] (call'd by the farmer, the present occupier, Lady B.) to have resided; and to have come to Bedford Races in her coach and six, with a good cavalcade.

It is a bad place, in a nasty country, and there being nothing to see in the house of worth, or curiosity, I dismounted not: tho' I rode up to, and around it. My civil guide, Mr. K., here left me; and I soon found my road to Great-Barford, and then being within my Biggleswade *Biggles-* vortex, quietly came my way home by Blunham, and *wade* Girford Bridge, in a fine tho' cool evening: happy to have no more engagements upon my hands.—I indulg'd with a roasted fowl for supper; and soon after ended my pint of port-wine, the best of all the neighbourhood.—Sorry I am to pack up; being here so quiet and so much (*unlike being*) at home: and the servants all know me, and my methods.—

The weather has been too cold for fishing.—

One hint, however, I must give the kind reader, which *Sunday* is, that if he should be able to find no sort of amusement *June 19* in the book, he will be pleased to remember the public utility which will arise from it; "if entertainment, as Mr Richardson observes, be but a secondary consideration in a romance; with which Mr Addison, I think, agrees, affirming the use of the pastry-cook to be the first." (Fieldings Voyage to Lisbon.) [16]

A week gone, without novelty; and little new of inspection: I dread a disappointment, like that of last year; and from being obliged to catch the time, I hope that the Colonel will hurry himself.

Attendance upon my package; and setting Garwood off. A small portmanteau, containing 2 shirts, 1 pr of *articles*, 2 necks, 2 hands, 2 pr of stockings, and one waiscoat, besides his things; together with a portmanteau holding my sheets, go behind him upon the young mare, (not yet named): my night cap, as usual, in my own pocket.

And now that G: can go alone; I shall commonly send him forward: hating to have a servant dodging after me.— Letters receiv'd to answer; bills (cheap) to pay.—The dramatick service here, tho' ill perform'd, 3 times a week, brings tolerable houses;—but the divine service here is so much worse perform'd, that there are seldom more than 30 people at church on a Sunday!!

Going off alone—I am ready to cry. A dreary day, with a nt. east wind, too cold to rain. The view from Beaston-Lane, 2 miles from Biggleswade, towards the church and village of Sandy, with the houses of the Baronet, and clerical Monoux, and the backing hills, is much to be admir'd. In Tempsford village, are the remains of a stone cross, the base and 4 or 5 ft of the shaft.—Tempsford Bridge is now repairing, idly with wood, instead of being well built with stone, which such a road demands, and the Turnpike Trust could well afford; so I was obliged to cross the ford at Wroxton, which had not the water been let down had been impossible for Poney: with much difficulty could I induce Ranger to follow me. I was known, and well receiv'd at the Cock at Eaton, where before me was instantly serv'd a roasted shoulder of veal, and a dish of peas; I love an instant dinner, tho' I cannot say that I now know the feel of hunger! Another reason of my present haste was

Eaton
Socon

a resolution to go to evening service; (to pray for better weather, and a healthy pleasant tour;) so I summon'd in old Mrs W— for a conversation after dinner, and then with her, young Mrs W— and her children, devoutly march'd into the church; which is large, and handsome; and has been adorn'd with much stain'd glass.—The psalm singing, in a singing gallery, was tolerable, accompany'd by a flute and a hautboy: but such a reader, and preacher, as Mr L[ittlehale]s[17] I hope is not often heard; tho' I fear so! Nor can a gleam of instruction dart from such drawling explanations about St Peter, and St John; instead of enforcing practical virtues and wringing sinners hearts, which added to the wind and cold made me almost repent of coming.

> 'By our pastor perplext,
>   How shall we determine?
> Watch and pray, says the text,
>   Go to sleep, says the sermon.'

This business ended I paid my bill;* and then for a ride in an October evening. Nor was I sorry to get to Alcon- Alconbury bury Hill, and clap myself into a parlour, before a great Hill fire. I drank tea for warmth; and then walk'd out for cold.

Ranger renders me peevish, by his immoveable stupidity, for he will not stir five yards from me.—Numbers of the genteels are going to Ld W[inchilsea]'s cricket match, which begins tomorrow at Burleigh-on-the-Hill. I have, likewise, mistaken the season; and fancy'd it to be June! So shall be obliged to return to London, before the summer begins.

I slept well last night, upon an excellent well-mattrass'd *Monday* bed: not the case, I assure you, at my *country seat*, where *June 20* the beds are bad; and every thing belonging to them seems to be stuff'd with lead.—This inn stands so bleakly, as to catch all winds; and must not be endurable in winter.—

*For dinner and wine 2s. 6d.

At rising this morning I enquired of master, brother, and hostler, the way of my intended ride to a *short* distance; but they all directed me different ways! And ended alike with advising me to ask as I went along.

Breakfast at 8 o'clock; off at ½ past 8; took down the first lane, by direction; met a countryman, who said 'I was wrong, but he did not know the way'. Crossing several grass fields, from this lane, I got to a farm-house, and from the farmer good directions; (much wanted in such an untrod country;) but for the dry weather, Poney could not have crawled along, nor could any man in winter, but a fox hunter eager, in the chace, get over, (not thro') this country, of deep clay pastures, encircled by woods.

Here let me introduce a common conversation I have often held when speaking about my favorite pursuit, touring; some ladies, or young London beaux will express their wishes of going in a post-chaise, and the bucks in their curricles, and phaetons: here I smile at the impossibility. 'Why smile in derision?' 'We are capable of going, and are sufficiently good drivers.' 'Yes, I doubt not, on a tour to Hampton-Court, or to Windsor'. After a tedious, and only to be supported in a morning, ride, I came to the mean village of Reveley; (having had a view of the fens, for some time, to my left;) thence to Upwood, where in a miserable situation, in a wretched country, Admiral Sr R. B[ickerton][18] has a house. (But admirals are ignorant of soils, and of every thing, by land).

Ramsey   The road now mended, and in 3 more miles (having perform'd a journey, nominally of 8 miles in two hours and a half) brought me to Ramsey, a place of mean buildings, with a navigable canal, over which are many foot bridges; and put up at the George, a wretched inn, only fit for ½ an hours stop: indeed, the whole place is out of all intercourse, and seems quite at the end of the island. Just below the bridge, I enter'd a glaziers shop, in the hope of finding stain'd glass (a part of my pursuit) and was lucky enough to fill one pocket with fragments from Upwood Church (of which the glazier is *repairer*,) offering for them so high a price, as to confound the shop-boy, viz six pence.

Now to seek the clerk;—and I ask'd the very man for himself: but when arrived at the church yard, seeing the old Abbey House, belonging to Mr F[ellowes][19] and meeting likewise the steward who keeps the keys, I first went with him thither; a civil old man he was, ready of gratification. —In this very old, strong-built, mansion, are several good rooms, and a stair case to the leads of the tower, upon which I went (tho' I allways shudder) to view the wide prospect, to Ely, and Peterboro' Cathedrals, and of much fen, and flat; there are no old pictures, no books, and what is more extraordinary, not one servant therein; tho' Mr F: does sometimes come here for a short autumnal visit. Under the house, around the kitchen, and cellars, are very ancient, curiously carved stone recesses, like those of a chapter house: a row of sycamores leads up to the house.

Within the church is not the grandeur I expected; (but I might have enquired, and known that the Abbey Church was pull'd down:) tho' the pillars and arches are of Saxon architecture: brasses and stain'd glass *are gone*.

The font is as old as need be.—Around the church yard, for stiles, are placed old grave stones, or fragments of stone coffins. Of the many inscriptions, this seem'd to be the best; and *a good one* it is.

MARK TRUE.

WHOSE DEATH WAS OCCASION'D BY A MURD'ROUS STROKE.

Heaven gave the needfull tho neglected call
What day what hour but knocks at human hearts
To wake the soul to sense of future scenes
Deaths stand like Mercuries in ev-ry way
And kindly points us to our journeys end.

What, not mention'd. This is, truly, a grand epitaph! Heaven giving a *needfull* tho' *neglected* call; and deaths standing like Mercuries to point us to our journeys end!! Very sublime!

This is all the remaining of the old abbey gateway. How diminished in 60 years from the print! But yet enough is left, to make us guess what was. What models would these, and other ruins of Gothic architecture afford.

About this ground I was employ'd a full hour: nor did I leave Ramsey till near one o'clock.

After drinking a large tumbler of brandy, and water, eating some bread and butter—packing up carefully the pieces of stain'd glass and defraying this *heavy* charge,* I return'd by the turnpike, and roundabout road; (of cross roads I had sufficient this morning.) In a mile to the village of Bury—whose very old church stands on high ground: as usual I paraded the church yard, and peep'd thro' the windows.—Two more miles brought me to Warboys, once notorious for its witches. It is a tolerable village, with some genteelish houses, and a well-built church: my walk around as usual. Another 2 miles, and to the shabby hamlet of Oldhurst; having left the large wood of Warboys to my left. The road now changed from stone, and clay, into pleasant gravell.—At Herford village, rather a pretty one, there was a feast, (a pretty fair); but the weather chills these festivities. Growing tired, I was glad to get to

Huntingdon Huntingdon; which is eleven miles from Ramsey. At the George, which is an old and shabby inn, tho' well stabbled, I dined comfortably on beef steaks, peas, and gooseberry pye, with a pint of port; then walk'd thro' the town to the bridge, and return'd over the castle hill: Huntingdon is a pleasant-looking town; and the environs chearful. I had to take tea at my return! A quiet ride

Alconbury Hill of five miles brought me back to A[lconbury] Hill, at 8 o'clock: having done enough; and alone, too; that tires.

*Stable	-	-	-	5d.
House	-	-	-	4d.
Servants	-	-	-	3d.

S. 1.

GEORGE INN. HUNTINGDON.

Dinner	-	-	-	-	-	1	6
Wine	-	-	-	-	-	1	2
Fire	-	-	-	-	-		3
Tea	-	-	-	-	-		9

£ 3 8

If my journals should remain legible, or be perused at the end of 200 years, there will, even then, be little curious in them relative to travell, or the people; because our island is now so explored; our roads, in general, are so fine; and our speed has reach'd the summit.

In 1775, Dr Johnson writes——[20]

I am now return'd from the annual ramble into the Middle Counties. Having seen nothing that I had not seen before, I have nothing to relate. Time has left that part of the island few antiquities, and commerce has left the people no singularities.—I was glad to go abroad, and perhaps, glad to come home; which is, in other words, I was, I am afraid, weary of being at home, and weary of being abroad.

Is not this the state of life? But if we confess this weariness, let us not lament it; for all the wise, and all the good say, that we may cure it.

Dr Johnson, however, wanted curiosity, activity and eye sight. But where, tell me, is a journal to be found of travelling in the reigns of James, or Charles 1st? These would afford to me the highest entertainment: I who can trace all the hollow ways, nay, remember some, lately, betwixt Huntingdon and this inn. Could a coach and six have come further than to Huntingdon from London in two days? I should have liked the travell of those times: the reception, and comfort at an inn; and the getting, at every distance of an 100 miles, amongst a new people with a new dialect; and where every thing was cheap too, because it could not be removed. Tho' yet, the posting on horseback might have been very quick; as we know from several accounts; particularly in that entertaining life of Henry Carey Earl of Monmouth.[21]—

'Who to outstrip his fellows, and gain the favor of the new Monarch— set out from Whitehall betwixt 9 and 10 o'clock in the morning of March 24th 1603, and reach'd Doncaster that night'.

The inn appear'd to be very crouded; Ld H[arborough][22] and much other company: but I was secure of the two best rooms. Were I to dwell in any stile, or with mine own equipages, I should certainly send (at least a day) forward, to bespeak the best rooms, the best beds, the best stalls, and the best viands; and not to find them occupied at my coming in late, and tired, by a dirty rider, or a *little Commissioner of Stamps*!

With the company I attended the throwing of the casting-net; and I desired an eel from the trunk for my supper.—

Tuesday June 21   Wishing to get forward to receive letters. Yesterday may be call'd my first day of touring.—The stables of this house, speaking of it as a hunting halt, are very indifferent. —Off at ½ past nine o'clock; thro' Upton village; and in

Hamerton   two more miles to Hamerton; whose handsome steeple appears to great advantage over an ancient grove of trees. Hamerton seems, truly, the deserted village: cottages fallen and falling! These led me (properly,) to the great ruin of a magnificent family hall; (belonging with the village, to Mr B[arr]y[23] of Cheshire;) near to which an Irish surveyor was standing, giving orders for the demolition.—(My intention is to catch a sight of these old mansions, 'ere they all be pull'd down, and removed to London.)

The old lodge is permitted to exist some years longer; as a blacksmith's shop. As for the house, which an easy reparation had render'd an excellent mansion for the rich; or an abode for many poor families; ignorance of real advantage, or of comfort to his tenantry, goaded by ill advice, has demolish'd.—Justice, example, charity, every help and every succour, removed from the country; in whom, soon, this London suction, must be potently, and lamentably felt.—I would that Mr Wilberforce, and Mr Burke were obliged to survey, and report upon Hamerton, to a select committee of the House of Commons; and no

I. HOLMES.
Nephew to the late Mr Warburton

Alconbury Hill

Neat Chaises
Stilton Cheese

Tea		"	6
Chicken & Deser	2	"	
Wine & Brandy	2	3	
Bread			1
Breakfast		"	6
Supper	1	"	6
Wine	2	"	6
Break.t		"	6
Fire & Brush.t	1	"	2
	11	"	6

more to think and prate of East, and West Indian miseries, and depopulations.

Those who travell with fashionable haste, (or slowly for the first time,) will not discover the decrease of halls, farms, and cottages; but I well-acquainted with the county of Bedford can sigh over the decay of its yeomanry and cottages: so may I suppose of this county; and most wretchedly does Hamerton proclaim it.—To be convinced that such houses were, (in opposition to some who fancy otherwise,) let them observe the numbers of small narrow enclosures, formerly, and severally, belonging to the cottages; of these, the hedges are, for the most part, stock'd up, tho' some banks or trees mark the line. Where any apple or walnut or plum trees remain, you may be certain there was an orchard; and a well, cover'd over, or choak'd up, leaves no doubt of a building having been near: of these, and such like remembrances, what numbers I could shew.—How should the poor exist, when the landlord that should protect, and support them, is gone off to reside in Marybone-Parish; whilst of his formerly squire-like place nothing remains but some decay'd garden walls.

How wisely did the fost'ring hand of ancestry provide for the poor, by an allotment of a cottage right of common in the open fields; the village green before their door; the orchard adjoining the house; and the long close behind it! —These two latter being seiz'd by the greedy farmer, and the two former being forced from them by the hand of power (upon some inadequate infamous bargain) has driven away the poor; has levell'd the cottage; has impoverish'd the country; and must, finally, ruin it. When the gentle perspiration, and the smaller ducts of the human body are stopt; with difficulty, and pain, will the larger vessells pant to the heart; and idly may the possessor brag of his bone and his courage.—

I, sometimes, perceive a large farm rebuilt; and a violent addition of barns, adequate to the increase of the farmers land, and rent: but where do you perceive a revival,

324

or renewal of comfortable cottages, and to be kept by a proper portion of land alloted to them? For without that, it becomes a cruel fantasy to decorate without, what you must know to be miserable within; it is like the skinning over a sore, without properly probing the wound.

This, once grand mansion will be levell'd in a month; I mounted up the stair case, and, with danger, into some rooms. At the other end of the village was another seat, now a farm house; and we may suppose that formerly £1000 pr ann: were spent at the great hall, and £300 at the smaller; and that these two houses by their alms, and generosity, protected, and made happy the neighbouring cottagers: to whom now are they to look up? The curate cannot befriend them; the steward will not!—

With these reflections I was glad to leave Homerton; and having good directions, found my way very well thro' many a gate, and over rough fields, to Saltry, a mean village; where Mr Hinde (Sr —— Steward) has added to his house front, one of the long venerable bay windows taken from the old hall.—Hence, I soon join'd the great North Road; and at my easy pace, in a very charming day, arriv'd at that pleasant spot, and excellent inn at Wans- Wansford ford-Bridge: where being receiv'd by Mrs N[orton] with Bridge the civil terms of 'There is your *own* parlour disengaged', I had to condole with her on the death of her husband: the house is now carried on by the handsome gigantic son.— My dinner came quickly, and good.—There was a feast held in this village; country fellows tippling, lasses bawling, and frisking about,

> 'And to crack'd fiddle, and hoarse tabor,
> In merriment did drudge, and labor';

which makes me presume that green gowns are a fashionable wear here!

In the evening I took to the fancy of fishing, when I had 3 instant bites; the last of which, luckily for me, carried away my tackle, else a cold might have forwarded my

325

carrying off: a walk was a sensible plan; and I took that, even till dark, around my well-known haunts, and up the avenue of the wood; but my friend, Ranger is of no pleasure to me, for he is so timid and thoroughly broke, and never chases the game.—At returning, the cook told me that a rsted chicken, and peas were ready; so I supp'd instantly, and bedded early.—

Wednesday June 22 I was awaked in the night by a fallen uvula (nothing else); and rose very early to get a port wine gargle, and then return'd to bed for 2 hours: the N.E. wind of last night brought on this.

Letters from town; and to answer.—The road now is full of carriages: Mr Pelhams[24] coach and six stop'd at this door, whose horses and coachman arrested my attention; for the horses were in such order, and driven by just such a coachman as (had fortune favor'd me) I would have hired: those in a carriage must feel the difference betwixt good, and bad driving; how then can gentlemen sit behind bad coachmen, and hear their horses flogg'd to blindness! And yet I see it every hour in London.

I took a pleasant walk to the retired village of Thornhaugh, whose church shaded by a plantation, and back'd by lofty woods would afford scope for *an able* pencil.—I had, by desire, beans and bacon with &c, for dinner: bad port wine, and a sulky drunken hostler are the only drawbacks here.—

Yesterday forenoon was pleasant, and warm; but in the evening the wind return'd to the N.E; and the night was excessively cold, with a sharpish frost!! What an uncertain climate! From which cause they say that Englishmen can endure the varieties of climate better than any other nation. —This evening I rode my mare to Water-Newton, to call upon Mr C[utteridge] the minister; and afterwards up the avenue of the wood: She is good temper'd; but my fears are that she is too much of the loping hunting breed, and not of the compact make of an hackney; one great

proof of quiet I am sure she gave; for a piece of pack thread
that lengthen'd the headstall of the bridle coming undone,
the bits and headstall fell upon her knees!! She stood still,
and I dismounted, else what had befallen me? Why every
danger from a skittish horse; and here was sufficient to
terrify any horse, or any rider!

The remainder of this evening, which again turn'd
chilly, was pass'd in dawdling about the garden, or upon
the bridge. Some good cold roasted beef closed the day,
and the orifices of my stomach.

The Colonel will not come up with me till Sunday *Thursday*
sen'night; a long time that; and how to be employ'd? But *June 23*
as nothing is to be seen, or thought of, by me, about
Wansford, I will move a march forward this evening,
taking post upon the nth side of the River Weyland, with
my left to the Fenns and securing the town of Market-
Deeping.—This is a hasty sketch of the sign of our inn;
and does, somewhat, resemble the place. After this long
drought, I should fear that when the weather changes
there will be incessant rain; and then we shall be immoveable.—

Mr C[utteridge], the minister of Water-Newton, return'd my visit this morning, and was very prosing.—
Garwood walk'd to Apthorpe, to obtain strawberries, and
did get some miserable things; but, (strange to relate,)
he says that all the fruit, of every sort, is to be preserv'd,
and sent to Ireland! I hope no sarcas'm upon that country;
else they may hoot the Ld Lt[25]; for wrong they will be,
wrong they must be: and how any man is found here who
will accept the Ld Ltcy there, is, to me, most wonderful!!
These thoughts made me wonder at a gentleman, not
young, who dined here to day with two ladies, in im-
moderate haste, ringing away for dinner! Now where is
the use and pleasure of such like gallopings? A gentleman
walks to his pleasure; a blackguard hurrys to his folly.
Nothing can be done well, that is done hastily: let the mind

327

forestall with celerity, and the body act with composure. *This appears to me the truth.*

The opposite sketch is intended to represent the view from the end of the meadows, below the inn, (of that part of the river where I lost my line,) and of the turnpike house upon the Peterborough road.—I left Wansford at 4 o'clock, in a very fine evening, and soon overtook Garwood, whom I again sent forward. On the hill above Stamford I met a hare: is that a good omen? Here I dismounted, and led my horse thro' the town, where I receiv'd civil information; which, as costing nothing, I wonder is not off'ner bestow'd! At the towns end I pass'd by a gateway of the old priory enclosure, and the remains of the church, now a barn.

Newstede Mill is in a pleasant bottom. In another mile Uffington to Uffington village; and there observ'd the mansion house of the Berties; and had to reflect upon the wickedness, and folly of testators, willing away their old paternal properties, as done here, about a family quarrell, but now likely to return again soon (by much mortality) to its right heir, my friend, Coll B[ertie] whom I yet hope to visit in this the residence of his ancestry: seemingly a good house of the King William cut. The church is of an handsome appearance.

On leaving Uffington, there is a fine shew of churches in the flat; which the sun shew'd to great advantage.—To the right the noble woods of Burleigh Park—Stallington, a long village, with some goodish farms; leave Sr Thos Trollops seat to the left; West Deeping to the right; and by a canal side, upon which are two very neat mills, Market arrived at seven o'clock at Market Deeping, a mean long Deeping town.—

Till nine o'clock I wander'd about, by the river side; and into the church-yard, my old strole. The weather, tho' shewy, is not genial and warm. This is a very low, damp situation: and the natives appear Flemish in their looks, and the length of their round hair.[26] The stables are not

328

THE HAYCOCK'S SIGN: WANSFORD

[*see p.* 327

THE NENE AT WANSFORD

from water-colours by the Diarist [*see p.* 328

glazed; and the house rooms are sanded: for such stables, and houses, summers should be hot. As for my landlord, he was civil; but his red *wind*[27] was not drinkable. (Fielding —who excels all other writers in pleasant description, says 'This wind is a liquor of English manufacture, and its flavour is thought very delicious by the generality of the English, who drink it in great quantities: it resembles in colour the red wine which is imported from Portugal, as it doth in its intoxicating quality; hence, and from this agreement in the orthography, the one of often confounded with the other, tho' both are seldom esteem'd by the same person'.)

I supp'd at nine o'clock; and retired early to bed; after having gone over the Stamford news paper.

STAMFORD.

On Monday, Tuesday, and Wednesday last was played at Burley, in Rutland, the seat of the Right Hon. Earl Winchilsea, a grand match at cricket, Hampshire with five gentlemen, against England with five gentlemen, for 1000 guineas, which was won by the latter.

State of the play as under:

ENGLAND

	1st Innings.		2nd Innings.	
T. Walker	13	b. Taylor.	1	c. Taylor.
Fennex	0	c. Purchase.	18	c. Small, sen.
Beldam	7	c. Harris.	63	c. Taylor.
Aylward	13	c. Taylor	1	c. Purchase.
A. Smith, Esq.	1	b. Harris.	0	c. Taylor.
John Wells	23	run out.	3	b. Taylor.
Hon. E. Bligh	28	c. Taylor.	14	b. Harris.
G. Louch, Esq.	9	c. Taylor.	0	b. Harris.
Earl of Darnley	3	b. Harris.	0	c. Small, sen.
C. Anguish	1	not out.	4	not out.
Bulling	3	run out	8	b. Harris.
Byes	2	Byes	2	
	103		114	

329

HANTS.

	1st Innings.		2nd Innings.	
Freemantle - - -	1	c. Walker.	6	not out.
Purchase - - -	5	c. Beldam.	7	b. Fennex.
Small, jun. - - -	10	c. Beldam.	15	run out.
Col. Lenox - - -	7	b. Bulling.	36	c. Wells.
Earl of Winchilsea - -	24	c. Beldam.	2	b. Fennex.
Small, sen. - - -	14	c. Wells.	7	c. Lough.
Hon. H. Fitzroy - -	9	b. Walker.	0	c. Beldam.
Taylor - - - -	0	c. Bulling.	4	c. Beldam.
G. Cumberland, Esq. -	1	b. Fennex.	6	b. Fennex.
G. Talbot, Esq. - -	0	run out.	1	c. Fennex.
Harris - - - -	1	not out.	0	c. Beldam.
Byes - - -	5	Byes -	2	
	77		86	

At the above rural entertainment were present,

The Duke and Duchess of Ancaster—Lady Mary Bertie—The Earl of Exeter—The Earl of Gainsborough—The Earl of Harborough—The Earl of Winchilsea—The Hon. Mrs & Miss Fielding—Lord Darnley—Lord Sherrard—The Lady Noels—Lady Elizabeth Chaplin—Two Miss Chaplins—Lady Charlotte & Col. Lenox—Lady A. and the Hon. Mr Fitzroy—Sir Horace Mann—Sir John Trollope—The Hon. Mr Blythe—The Hon. Mr Harbord—two Mr Delaines—Mr and Mrs Mann—two Miss Manns—two Miss Trollopes—Mr and Mrs A. Smith—Mr. Powis (Member for Northamptonshire)—Mrs and Miss Powis—Colonel and Mrs Pochin—Mr and Mrs Arundel—Mr Louch—Mr Cumberland—Mr Bouham—Mr Maddox—Mr Swan—Mr Sale—Mr Istead—Mr Neville—Mr and Mrs Clementson—Dr and Mrs Willis—Dr John Willis—Capt. Renouard—Mr and Mrs Wingfield—Rev. Mr and Mrs Foster—Mr and Mrs Tryon—Mr and Mrs Barker—Mrs and Miss Wingfield—Miss Lucas—Rev. Mr and Mrs Brereton—Miss Brereton—two Mr Browns &c &c.

On Wednesday night a superb supper and ball were given at Burley, at which most of the above respectable persons were present.

The races at this place begin on Tuesday next, which are expected to be more numerously attended than for several years past.

(These fleeting entertainments are most ungratifying; when compared with regular hospitality, and well bestow'd charity!!)

Peterborough Races ended yesterday: all the quality *Friday* of this place return'd in the evening; much satisfied with *June 24* the last days sport. My bed room was cold and miserable, with an horrid putridity of blankets, over which I prudently pour'd part of my half pint of brandy; as I have often done in Wales. Nor does the cheapness of a bill make any amends for such dangerous wretchedness: here my landlord, upon consideration, has added another 6d. to my supper charge.—This town appears to be large and populous; owing, perhaps, to its low fenny situation affording commonage, and plenty of fuel. The morning open'd gloomily, with much shew for rain: had it caught me at Wansford, or at a tolerable inn, I had said 'Very well'; but to be penn'd up here, would make me wild.

PETERBOROUGH RACES.

Tuesday, June 21, the hunter's plate of 5 gs. each, with 5ol.
given by Earl Fitzwilliam was won by

Mr. Mewburn's ches. mare, Country Girl by Orpheus - -	1	1
Mr. Destow's brown horse, Dutham - - - - -	3	2
Capt. Hart's bay gelding, Convention - - - - -	2	3
Mr. Wing's bay gelding, Amaranthus - - - - -	dr.	
Mr. W. Hopkinson's bay mare, Mayfly, by Shark - - -	dr.	

Mr. H. Cole did not name.

Wednesday, the city plate of 5ol. for 3 yr. old, that never won

Mr. Broadhurst's bay colt, Spider - - - - -	1	3
Mr. Walter Vavasour's bay filly, Hope - - - -	2	3
Mr. Golding's bay filly, by Jupiter - - - -	6	3
Mr Brewster's bay filly - - - - - -	4	4
Sir Chas. Turner's chestnut filly - - - - -	5	5
Earl Fitzwilliam's chestnut filly - - - - -	3	dr.

Thursday, the members' plate of 5ol. weight for age.

Mr. Richardson's bay horse, Wonder 5 years old - -	3	1	1
Mr. Povall's brown gelding, Sweetbriar - - -	1	2	2
Mr. Clarke's bay horse, Merry Andrew, aged - - -	2	3	3
Mr Cox's Yellow Jack, aged - - - - -	4	dr.	
Duke of Bedford's brown colt, 4 years old - - -	df.		

I was up early, glad to quit my nasty bed; and breakfasting (badly) in haste, was urged to ride to Norborough, 2 miles south, by the prating of my host, about an old house there, wherein Oliver Cromwell resided. My mare carried me there, safely and slowly; but I fear she will never have the active, compact pace of an hackney.

BULL INN. DEEPING.

						s	d
Supper	-	-	-	-	-	1	6
Brandy -	-	-	-	-	-	1	0
Wine -	-	-	-	-	-	1	2
Hay & Corn -	-	-	-	-	-	3	2
Wine &c	-	-	-	-	-		2
					£0	7	0

Nor-
borough

At Norborough, there are the remains of the old mansion house of the Claypole family, now inhabited by a farmer, and approach'd to, as formerly, by an old gateway. —The hall, with lofty bay windows, is now subdivided, with a lower'd ceiling; and over the buttery hatches, are curiously carved stone arches.

The farmer, who had civilly shewn me his house, went with me to the church, and held my mare when I enter'd. It is a poor, but oddly-built church, and deserves to have a good drawing taken of it.—The Claypooles were buried in a vault, under a chapel, built by that family, attach'd to the church: therein are only bones; and none of Nolls I dare say: his skull I should like to see, from the quantity of brains it once contained.

I had finish'd this inspection, and return'd to Deeping, before nine o'clock.—Happy in a fine day, I hastened my departure, from a miserable inn; where I was sure I had caught cold: Garwood was to follow me. Two miles to Lovetoft, where has been a grand mansion; of which now, only the garden walls, and orchards remain, with the pillars of entrance. In the church yard (which, as usual, I

332

paced about) is a tombstone—of scupture painted, well bestow'd on this honest shepherd.

RICHARD WRIGHT.

A true and honest Shepherd lieth here
Who watch'd his masters flock for many a year
He's now conducted to a land where he
Can feel no storm, but in a calm shall be
There crown'd with glory he shall sit and sing
Eternal praise to his redeeming king.

Thence, I passed thro' many villages, (which makes riding pleasant,) Baston, Thurlby, and so to Bourn, by 12 o'clock. Bourn

Order'd dinner; then walk'd to the church (with the sexton,) which is large and damp, with an old font, but no monuments. The sexton a communicative old man, walk'd with me over the castle grounds; and to the spring of water that supplies the town: he told me, that they had good psalm-singing here, of 30 *hands*, and several musical instruments.—This inn, another Bull, is not so dirty as the Deeping Bull, but full as ill-managed: at the Deeping Bull I fancy'd myself at an inn (such as I should suppose) in a certain western island, with a waiter (too) of long black hair, and low'ring shaggy eyebrows.

From the altogether of last night I find myself very unwell to-day, and my throat very sore: dinner ended, I go in search of better quarters.—Pass thro' the village of Morton; Bourn Woods to my left; with a view over the Fens to the right; road very stoney, but I was glad to get out of the flat country: at Aslackby, somewhat out of the Aslackby road, stands a turreted building, call'd the Temple, from being I suppose, part of a preceptory belonging to the Knights Templars;[28] and of such places I know several bearing this name.

I was civilly shewn into the lower room, now a dairy, curiously arch'd with stone, and with coats of arms in the centre. Around this house was a great park, well timber'd, and stock'd with deer, which was destroyed about eighty years ago,—

Several misses were here on a visit out of Leicestershire; with whom going to view the church, I made one, and was *witty* with them at the altar, near which lay a speaking-trumpet, which 'I supposed was used to deaf brides'. The church is neat within, all but the chancel.—The prettily-placed town of Folkingham, upon a rising ground, soon appear'd in sight, with its grand new inn at the top of the market-place; an inn worthy of the Bath road, but here sees not 2 post chaises in a day.—

Folking-
ham

The trustees of Sr G. Heathcote[29] having bought this estate are nobly laying out its annual produce upon new buildings in this town; and have already expended £4000 upon this inn, without raising the rent: but then the landlord is to furnish it adequately, and so he seems dispos'd to do; but custom adequate he cannot have. I wish it stood at Biggleswade.—After a long talk with the landlord, (who is of the Spanish kind, proud and lolling in his chair,) and having seen his great kitchen, and superb range, I walk'd around the mounds of the old castle; reflecting upon the alteration of this country;—the defence of castles; the religion of monasteries; the assistance of yeomanry;—all lost! The poor now exist by scanty pillage; dog eat dog; no leisure for honesty!! How grander, easier, and happier did the gentleman live formerly, farming his own grounds: for supposing his land to be well let for £300 pr ann: to a tenant, manage it himself, (aye and ignorantly too) and he may live at the rate of £1000 pr ann: This I have frequently known; and hope it is yet practised.

The church here is of excellent building. In the church-yard was no particular inscription; the opposite was the only one I took down.

HERE
Lies the Body of
George Boheme;
Born at the City of Colberg
in the Dukedome of Pomeron in Germany
who died Septemb ye 9th MDCCXI
aged 83 years.

334

TOWER OF THE MOORS, KIRBY

[see p. 353

ASLACKBY PRECEPTORY

[see p. 333

from water-colours by the Diarist

This, with other walks, and my stable attendance, brought on my supper hour, nine o'clock, when I was comfortably serv'd; and now I drink *Hollands* most plentifully.—The lad waiter says 'That sometimes a chaise, or so, does stop here'. However this inn must soon attract, and benefit the town; and then the expence upon it is properly bestow'd. As this is a country of stone, numberless are the remains of crosses, as the steps, and shafts; and to most of the old houses are porches; a good plan, pleasant and cool in summer, and must keep off the winds of winter.—(*I will build them to all my new farm houses*).—

I gave, this evening, to the boot-boy a glass of gin, which he swallow'd thankfully: for to the lower part of the world, this appears to be clear gains, never to be refused; like offering fruit to children, who cannot refrain, tho' rhubarb must follow.—

I was very unwell all day yesterday, with a sore throat *Saturday* and an aching head; for which I gargled much, and at bed *June 25* time took several analeptic pills, which gave me thro' the night a violent perspiration, during which I toss'd, and tumbled, in a bewilder'd state.—This morning I drank a quart of tea; and having put on hot linnen, walk'd to the glaziers, (a very civil man, in a neat new house) to enquire after stain'd glass; he had some by him, (the best was a St George leaded in the windows of his workshop) of which he gave me many small pieces, brought from Donesby Church.—At eleven o'clock, I rode, upon the mare, to *Threkingham*,[30] 2 miles; and there call'd upon Mr Craggs, a Threking-yeoman farmer of an antiquary taste, who corresponds in ham the Gentlemans Magazine, and has a collection of topographical books: he receiv'd me hospitably, and would have rode with me but for his sheep-shearing;—the poor man look'd miserably, (which my host of Folkingham calls a judgment of God upon him, for having married successively, two sisters (a thing I did not know to be allow'd).

He shew'd me the church, a well-built one, in which are

335

two, curious, large recumbent figures of Lambert de Trekingham, and his wife, temp Rich: 1st. In the church-yard are placed the three stone coffins of the three supposed kings, which coffins have been removed from the church: the alehouse has the sign of the Three Kings.—All this from old record, and memorial. Over the doorway of his granary, Mr C. has placed a fine porch, brought from Sempringham Abbey; whose curious stone work, he said, had repair'd many a rut.

Mr C. is zealous; but he has never travell'd from home, or knows 10 miles from his own threshold! He ask'd me if I belong'd to the A.S.S.,[31] or could draw well? I answer'd as if I was *somebody*; and *hazarded* my drawing book; which he seem'd to approve.—From his house, a lane brought me to a green, call'd Stow-Green, on which were many skeletons of booths, it being a spot whereon large fairs are held.—Here turning to the left, (too much) I came to the village of Horbling, thence, in company of a ploughman on horseback, to Billingborough, a pretty village, and then by his advice, to Poynton village, there to find the clerk who keeps the key of Sempringham-Church, which stands amidst grazing grounds ½ a mile from any house. It may now be fairly call'd (according to the country tongue,) a *dissolute* place.—The church stands upon a small eminence: within, it is truly wretch'd. The steeple is yet beautiful; and upon it is legibly written

IN TE DOMINE SPERAVI

and under it

Singe prayses unto the Lord o ye Sayntes of His.

Tradition reports that Sr Gilbert was buried under the large blue slab at the top of the middle aile; which I should be tempted to remove to discover any stone coffin, or any crozier &c, that might remain.—My mare was tied up in a hovel, where the clergymans horse is placed during service time.

Thence I blunder'd my way, much round about, being

336

obliged to dismount at many gates from the awkwardness of the mare, into the high road; and got back, hot and jaded at ½ past two o'clock;—a solitary, tedious fag! For it is most melancholy, and fatiguing, to inspect, and observe alone; and yet where is the company of the same pursuit to be found?

My dinner consisted of beans and bacon, with good Folking-cold rst beef. In the evening I took a long drawling ride ham (upon the mare again); and once I dismounted to walk around the church-yard of Walcot.

Being not well I eagerly sought my bed.

After breakfast, which rather refresh'd me, for I was ill Sunday and feverish, I took a pleasant walk, and had a long con- June 26 ference with my friend, Mr Watson, the glazier, who found out my antiquary humour, and indulged it; as did, likewise, Mr Cooper, of this town, who shew'd me some petrefactions, an old castle key, and other little findings.

As tedious a morning to me, as to any other, idle, country lad, who wishes for the hour of eating, and then for the hour of sleeping. The London newspapers came in at one o'clock, just before dinner time, when I ate of the family preparation, boil'd fowls, rst beef and young potatoes; which all travellers should certainly do, parti-cularly on a Sunday.—My landlord then came in, 'fearing I was lonesome'; he now gets familiar, and will soon put his paws upon my lap; he prated away 'About the Duke of Orlines's[32] coming in here from hunting; whom he knew to be a foreigner by his earings, that he gave 9 guineas for a chaise to Grantham, 12 miles, and 10s. 6d. to the boys;' that the High Chancellor[33] was also here, last year, and ask'd him 'If they grew good wheat hereabouts.' There would have been no end of my landlords jaw, had not the bells rang for church, to which I repair'd with my landlord, and landlady; (this I may call my religious tour, tho' I sadly fear that curiosity oft'ner than devotion leads me to church); he, fat, large, black, and shock-headed, in new bluff and blue; she, very like Mrs Hall in a brown silk.— Here were a numerous, and decent congregation, with a singing loft crouded; and amongst them one lady in a blue silk bonnet, who sung *notably*; but the bassoons, and hautboys, were too loud and shreiking: as for the clergyman,[34] he went off in a loud, unintelligible key, like a lawyer reading deeds, and was truly intolerable. Had I been in the company of those I knew, I could not have refrain'd from laughter.—Much singing before the service; likewise the Magnificat, and two psalms: during the sermon mine host slept, and I slumber'd.

My landlord said that any gentleman coming to his inn at the season, may shoot with Sr G. H.'s gamekeeper, and that partridges are plenty. At quitting church, my friend the glazier told me that the D:-of-Norfolk, of Q. Eliz. reign, was buried in this chancell; (probably he possess'd the castle.)—A stay even like this, makes one to dislike a change; for the bed begins to fit, and the people to understand you: but these are not notions for a tourist.— G[arwood] went off first; I follow'd in $\frac{1}{2}$ an hour: a very

Osburnby stoney road; at Osburnby Church yard I dismounted, and paced around;—a poor village;—thence to Aserby, another churchyard patrole, where is a seat of Sr T. Whichcote, who seems to have been building kitchen garden walls; but of a place, and park, I never saw worse-kept, nor more ugly; the park is a moorish flat, with the paling visible all around; and of the few trees, Sr T. is felling several! At one corner of the park, by the road-side is a seemingly-tolerable public-house, The Fox with a tally-ho. —A nasty common I cross'd briskly to Willoughby, a mean village, from the name, one knows the low damp situation by willows.

The country now rises; leaving Quarrington village to
Sleaford my left, I soon arrived at Sleaford, where, in the market place, I housed myself at The Angel Inn; then calling for tea, and receiving a cargo of letters, I had little inclination but for reading, and writing.—It was a very warm even-

RICHARDSON

FOLKINGHAM

Neat Post Chaises

	June 24		
Tea			8
Supper		1	0
Hollands		1	0
wine		1	2
25 Breakfast			8
Dinner		1	9
Wine		2	4
Hollands		1	0
wine			4
Supper			9
26 Breakfast			8
wine			4
Dinner		1	3
wine		1	2
Horses Hay & Corn		7	8
		£ 1:1:	3

This bill is as reasonable as can be; and unless the inn should not find better customers than myself, it must be quickly undone.

On a future day, I shall be happy to hear of the success of Mr R. and of The Greyhound Inn at Folkingham, in Lincolnshire.

339

ing; but the country I pass'd thro' I thought gloomy, tho' well villaged.—When I send my letters, people never conceive that I allways direct to myself. Asking the clerks age, at Bourn, he told me; and then guess'd so closely at mine, that I did not like it, for till old age comes decidedly, and with wonder, there is yet a hope of a youthful lock. Speaking to-day of the preacher, or rather being ask'd by the landlord my opinion of him, he said that two gentlemen travellers were so offended by his reading, and preaching, they wrote to him a letter of admonition, desiring the landlord to deliver it, which he properly declined; but that they afterwards put it into the post office of Peterboro' for him; whilst the holy gospel is thus administer'd by curates at low salaries, what else can be expected? The day must come when this country will be convulsed by interior commotions, on the claims and oppressions of the clergy, their non-residence and their neglect of duty.—

Monday
June 27
Pass'd a better night, than I have lately had: tho' I always wake at 4 o'clock.—This is a market day here, and the stalls are spread in front of this inn, with plenty of butchers meat.—In my walk before breakfast, I noted this sign, and inscription, which has great merit!!

WILL POYNTAL

Tinker and
Chimney Sweeper
lives here.

He'll Sweep your Chimneys Clean and not too dear,
And if your Chimneys be on fire
He'll put them out at your desire.

There are few sightly men, or handsome women to be seen in the country; (of the lower class I mean;) for the army gets one, and *Bond Street* the other.—

The church here is a cumb'rous pile, and crouded with

340

niches, wherein but two saints remain; within (I only peep'd thro' the windows,) it is choak'd up with pews, and galleries: town churches seldom afford antiquity; it is only, now and then, in an obscure country church, that brasses, an old font, and stain'd glass windows are to be found.—After breakfast, I mounted the mare (a heavy creature, who never can be a roadster, nor hunter,) and took the high road thro' Lessingham, to the 5 mile stone where Lincoln Heath begins, (or did begin) for now it is all enclosed, (generally with high stone walls), and thence, by an easy road of two miles to Temple-Bruer, (from the French) upon the Heath, which was a preceptory of Knts Templars.[35] Adjoining is a lone farm house, where I was civilly receiv'd; then walk'd around the turret, and by tolerable stairs to the top: which upper part forms a pigeon house; the lower room is exactly like that of Askarby, with niches, as if for a chapter-house. It belongs to Mr Chaplin, who cares not for his possession: a man of taste would plant about, and embellish it, at a small expence. *Temple Bruer*

After my survey I enter'd the farm house, and there eat of bread, and butter, and drank gin and water; for the day was hot.

Some thoughts I once had of going to the Green Man, a public house upon the Heath; but I reflected that it would be better for me, and my mare, to come back, which we did in tolerable haste: in the way, at Lessingham church-yard, I transcribed this epitaph. *Lessingham*

WILLm. WHITTAKER. 1774.

Destructive death, thou hast thy power display'd,
On our dear friend who now in dust is laid;
He that in literature shone most bright,
Alas! No more to us must be a light:
As he was wont to youth for to suggest
Wise precepts of the virtues paths carest;
Now for his merits on expanded wing,
His Makers praise allways is gone to sing.

Dinner was tolerable; wine intolerable. The sight of the market tired me, for there was nothing to enliven; and I did long most heartily for a shew of any kind, a mountebank, or a company of strollers.

Life is a tiresome business; little else but packing, and unpacking, buttoning, and buttoning!—Here is a hatters stall opposite; with what trouble has he unpaper'd and display'd his hats: why now, at 4 o'clock, he is beginning to paper the greater part of them again, and to prepare to depart; life is not long enough, or too long for such nothingness!—I am just in the state of the hatter; for having dined, and being yet alive, I must do something more; and so I will try a ride, (tho' perhaps a ride around the ring of Hyde-Park had been the most prudent, and equally salutary.)

This evening, I found myself upon a fine gravelly road, which brought me to Asgarby village, near the road to Boston; here my map tells me is a seat of Ld Bristol, but nothing of the sort could I find: however, I walk'd about the church-yard, and admired the building of the church.

Within view, at a short distance, are several churches: my wonder was when or how all the churches of this kingdom were built! What all at the same time? and what has preserv'd them? I am of a very superstitious turn; and must think that the same Providence which urged great and pious people formerly, to build these houses of God, still guards and preserves them. Who would, or could build them now? The expence would be enormous. Around, and belonging to the many I see, there are but some vile cottages attach'd; at Asgarby are not a dozen. How beautifully does our land now look, from the spires and steeples; and what useful land and sea marks they are; numbers are gone to ruin, and yearly suffered to fall down: how happens this? Have we no bishops, or do they not visit their dioceses? I also went to Kirby Church, which has either lost, or never had a spire; and is of our blunt Bedford-

Kirby

shire make. In the church yard is this epitaph to the memory of

SUSANNA GOODBARNES. aged 57.

Oh cruel death to separate us here
A tender mother from her children dear
Who was a tender mother all her life
And to her husband a most loving wife
All her days she spent in grief and pain
Everlasting joys in hopes to gain.

This is most happily written; whether as to the cruelty of death separating a mother from her children; and one too who had been a tender mother *all her life*; and had purposely spent her days in misery, in hopes of future joys.—

Not hearing from Col. B: and having time enough upon my hands, I will push forward to the city of Lincoln. My bill was very reasonable; but Sleaford is truly melancholy. Yesterday evening my company was requested by a Dr B— (possessor of Tickhill Castle[36] in Yorkshire, who was on his travell) to know what I heard of the King of France's flight; whose curiosity was roused by my host fancying I had said that the K. of France had quitted Paris,[37] and was now in London: the Dr and I conversed politics for some time; and ended with drinking our Kings health in a bumper.

Tuesday June 28

ANGEL INN. SLEAFORD, 1791.

june							s.	d.
26	Tea	-	-	-	-	-	0	8
	Supper	-	-	-	-	-	1	6
	Wine &c	-	-	-	-	-	2	8
27	Tea	-	-	-	-	-	0	8
	Dinner	-	-	-	-	-	1	6
	Wine	-	-	-	-	-	2	3
	Supper	-	-	-	-	-	1	0
	Brandy	-	-	-	-	-	1	6
	Tea	-	-	-	-	-	0	8
	Horses	-	-	-	-	-	7	4
							19	9

The first 5 miles from Sleaford was of my road of yesterday, (when I thought not of this route); then the Heath beings, where the side roads are good riding: I wish I had, before the enclosure, hunted upon it; my former happiness, and what I, yet, often dream about. Hare-hunting heretofore, with the hounds of those days, must have been exquisite sport; but now unknown, from the folly of speed!—

The day was very fine; but my ideas, like the country, were confined by the stone walls; behind one of which Ranger happening to stray, was by me, with much difficulty pull'd over!—At ten miles end, I stopp'd at the Green Man public house; where, on a bench I sat and refresh'd for some time. In two more miles I came to Dunston Pillar,[38] built by the late Sir F. Dashwood; one of those gentlemen, who fancying themselves architects, erect the horridest piles around them, and for others, who will be misled! Of what use, nature, or taste, is this odious obelisk? It can only incur ridicule! The original fancy was (I have heard) to form a lighthouse for the guide of stray travellers; and to make his Lordships 'Light so shine before men'. This is like all his Ldships other buildings, all a waste of stone! The last grand work he guided was the ugly, narrow, new bridge at Oxford!!—

Lincoln   No one should ride far alone; for the mind seeks succour, and the tongue attention. Lincoln Cathedral looks nobly in approach; from the descent of Cannock Hill, the lower town is enter'd; from this hill, the course of the River Witham is to be traced: Swan Pool, a large over flow of water, in the meadows, seems to be only useful as a comfort to the cattle in summer; and of fine scating in the winter.

Near the entrance of the town are the remains of the palace of John of Gaunt, viz the entrance, and that part of the house to the right; that part to the left has, but lately, fallen down; and the stables are pull'd down; what remains is in horrid decay.—

344

The Rein Deer, a large inn, (at the foot of the hill, and close to the strong-bow gate of entrance to the upper town) receiv'd me, hot and weary: most eagerly did I seek my dinner, and as eagerly drink of the very tolerable port-wine; till a little muddled, and refresh'd by tea, I took my evening walk, (wishing for a companion) of the upper town steep-hill, and to further end, to the Newport Gate, which all our antiquaries deem to be Roman—and that much of the Roman wall is to be seen. The close is well gated; and well housed. The view from the south gate over the lower town, and a wide extent of country (even to Newark) shews at this season in high beauty.

For half an hour did I stand with admiration, gazing at the cathedral, of the noblest architecture I ever saw; and Gothic in the highest preservation, except the loss of some saints, and of more of their heads, which a bishop of any head, would restore. What is the number of the windows? This question none here could answer! This is the finest of our cathedrals I ever saw: and why not, when rebuilding in London, follow such a model? How superior to a lumbering Grecian St Pauls. Upon such an eminence, too, is this placed, as to give it, *above* all others, the *pre*-eminence.—

The clergy seem'd to be placed in comfort; so they should be, if devout, and doing their duty: I would have them reverenc'd, I would have them envied, as Gods servants in this world.—Why is our land to be betray'd to attornies; and to all the unintelligible jargon of the law!!

My walk was long, and fatiguing, (owing to the heat); at my return I was shewn into a good front parlour, and serv'd with the newspapers, and much civility, and excellent cold meat; but I allways like to have for a touring companion, the moon, to light up the evening, and as gayly send me to bed, as the sun calls me from it.—

Which he did this morning, with most garish beams.—*Wednesday* Below hill, here it is very hot; I hope it is cooler above hill: *June 29*

345

the cathedral will be a pleasant place.—Nothing at the booksellers; no information; no *blacks*!

Climb hill to cathedral; was shewn the cloisters, now in great disorder, but going to be repair'd; (I hope, as the French lose their faith we shall receive it, with all its proprieties, all its splendours); and to the library, wherein a great collection of old manuscripts are soon to be arranged: but my guide knew nothing; and I could not find any finely illuminated.

The service was nobly perform'd; Drs Douglas, and Smith, canons residentiary,[39] attended, in all form, and at the communion service; a choir of 10 boys, and 5 men, of whom one boy and two men appear'd to have good voices; the Litany was chanted in the middle isle by two lay-vicars with voices like bulls. When this duty is well done, it becomes the best spiritual concert; better than those at which you are overwhelmed by fiddlers, and Italian singers.

The east window is of new stain'd glass; but how inferior to the old ones, especially those of the north and south ailes.

This well survey'd, I went to view the ruins of the old bishops palace, which I was shewn by a silly gardener; and if a sight of caverns, sutteranes, door ways and ruins, is wish'd for, here is enough to serve an antiquary for a week; a glut likewise for a draughtsman. I left no corner unexplored;—the gardener remark'd 'that these were fine places before they were *inherited*'; any words at random the lower people use. Few families in the country encourage, sufficiently, the breed of pigeons, or will build a pigeon house, which is of everlasting assistance to a table; fewer, enclose any ground with a wall for the keeping of rabbets: — now within these walls, in what he calls the old bishops dining room, has the gardener turn'd in hares, who breed abundantly. Why not encourage a place for them; and keep hares as well as pigs and poultry? Of which, indeed, nobody has a sufficient stock; but from idleness, inattention, and ignorance make every thing a trouble, and a rarity!—Some of the inner grounds the gardener has till'd; the rest is overgrown by weeds, elder-trees, &c; and the walls are cover'd by wild-flow'ring plants.——This place might be adorn'd; and would then be visited, and admired as the *compleatest* parcell of ruins in the kingdom. ——I was tired, and worn-down at my return; when no strawberries could I get to cool my tongue! Who rears any? Or ever could get any, but at a London fruit shop? Where in a plentiful season you may procure enough for your own eating, at ½ a guinea a day.——I had for my dinner two soles, six inches long, and a great, coarse, duckling, the remembrance of which makes me sick.——Great Tom, the famous bell at Lincoln, weighs five tons, and requires 12 men to raise it. 6 o'clock morning prayers, that were used formerly, have been disused about 5 years; (sad proof of idleness, and irreligion;) for nobody came but those who were obliged: I should suppose, that, in old times, decent people attended the morning service, before they began, or could think of beginning, the duties of the day. ——No sooner had I dined, than all evening intention of walking, or riding, was prevented by a gentleman of this county, (whom I knew) stopping here in his way home: to avoid him was impossible; and he, being very loquacious, and tedious, kept me with him till seven o'clock; when he pursued his way, and I mine.

> His ordinary rate of speech
> In loftiness of sound was rich,
> A Babylonish dialect,
> Which learned pedants much affect.
> It was a parti-colour'd dress
> Of patched and pyball'd languages:
> Twas English cut on Greek and Latin
> Like fustian heretofore on sattin.
> It had an odd promiscuous tone,
> As if h' had talk'd three parts in one.
> Which made some think when he did gabble,
> Th' had heard three labourers of Babel;
> Or Cerberus himself pronounce
> A leash of languages at once.
>
> *(Hudibras).*

347

SOME PARTS OF OUR CONVERSATION.—

(D) Ask me any questions about the county, and I will resolve you;—bring the map; let me see; you want to go to Barlings?—Aye—Why—Then you should go by Cherry-Whellingham;—or, rather, I think, by Reepham;—let me see;—there is a wood near there I have often hunted; and then, let me see, you will find the road intricate; but that is your way:—have you any more questions to ask?

(B) You were a great hunter; do you hunt much now?

(D) Oh, no;—quite left it off:—it was the same thing over and over again.

(B) Pray is not this the case with all pleasures?—Less in hunting, perhaps, than in any other; it is in ourselves to form the variety: a horse is a horse; wine is wine, woman is woman; and yet their difference and merits constitute the joys of life: how many changes will 8 bells produce; yet it is still ringing the bells! Surely no one hunt exactly resembled another! Thinking as you do, you had better lay down, and die.

(Here was weak argument on my part, against refined logick, and abstruse speculation. How some people love to deviate from right notions, and, yet, without any settled counter-opinion, contradict others into warmth, and fancy they have won the day, and that they shew a power of criticism, and fortitude, by eternal dissent, and contempt!!!)

The evening was extremely warm; and after my supper time, about ten o'clock; the sky was over-cast, emitting much and continued lightning.

I read in the newspapers, with amazement, the accounts of the flight of the King of France; and of his capture, and being brought back: what a quick and wonderful retribution, for his wanton assistance to our rebellious colonists, whose flame of liberty has now so scorch'd him, and his regal vanities! The pride, and pomp of France consisted in her army, her clergy, and her nobility; now debased, ejected and degraded!!!—My opinion of France allways was, 'That they were 150 years behind this country in comforts, arts and science'; and now they are at our æra of 1640; wanting (only) men of abilities, and a Cromwell: at present it is all fanfaronade. Let them send here for a model of our constitution; and not pretend to cobble one at home.'

Of touring the joy and business is to haste away; and *Thursday* wish for fresh quarters. This, I believe to be a very cheap *June 30* town; at least from this bill, so reasonable, one should be tempted to think so.

REIN DEER. LINCOLN.

						s.	d.
Dinner	-	-		-		1	6
Wine	-	-	-	-	-	2	3
Tea	-	-	-	-	-		9
Supper	-	-	-	-	-	1	
Wine	-	-	-	-	-	1	2
Gin	-	-		-	-	-	1	
Breakfast	-	-	-	-	-		9
Dinner	-	-	-	-	-	1	6
Wine	-	-	-	-	-	2	3
Supper	-	-	-	-	-	1	
Brandy	-	-	-	-	-	1	
Breakfast	-	-	-	-	-		9
						14	11
Horses Hay & Corn		-	-		-	7	10
					£1	2	9

At ten o'clock I left Lincoln: of the first man I met I ask'd the road to Barlings—'You must go by Reepham'; 2nd. man.—'You must not go by Reepham'; 3rd man 'Keep this high road for 5 miles to the village of Langworth; there you will see a direction post to Barlings, an easy way to find'.

This road I accordingly pursued; and in two miles from Langworth, thro' grazing grounds came to Barlings, a Barlings

349

small dismal church, with a farm house near; look'd about for ruins; for of these I got no account at Lincoln from Mr D.

Whilst I stop'd, I sketch'd the miserable church and transcribed this epitaph.

WILL^m BESCOBY. 1768. aged 60 years.

> With streaming ey, and broken heart,
> I from this sinfull world depart
> For you fals man my place you have
> You have sent, me to a lonely grave.

This epitaph was meant, originally I suppose, for some injured woman; but here adopted as grand verses.

I then learnt from a woman in the farm-house, (dressing food for the shearers,) that at Lower Barlings, a mile further on, the ruins of the abbey were: what remains I have here endeavour'd to delineate, which must soon come to the ground; for they are daily carting away the stones and much has fallen, or been pull'd down within these 3 years.

Most religious houses have the same kind of low sequester'd situation; and were well orcharded, and well supplied with ponds. Just below, runs the River Witham, now very shallow; but in winter crossed in ferry boats; it is call'd Short Ford. A sixpence was well bestow'd upon the poor people, who live in an adjacent cottage, and walked with me about the ruin.

All this day the long-wish'd-for rain appear'd to be coming; but it fell not: let me be but housed in a good inn, and then let it fall: the air requires purification.

'I do not wonder that, where the monastick life is permitted, every order finds votaries, and every monastery inhabitants.—Men will submit to any rule by which they may be exempted from the tyranny of caprice, and of chance.—They are glad to supply by external authority their own want of consistency, and resolution; and court the government of others, when long experience has convinced them of their own inability to govern themselves. If I were to visit Italy, my curiosity would be more attracted by convents, than by palaces; though I am afraid that I should find expectaion in both places equally disappointed, and life in both places supported with impatience, and quitted with reluctance. That it must be soon quitted, is a powerful remedy against impatience; but what shall free us from reluctance?

'Those who have endeavour'd to teach us to die well, have taught few to die willingly; yet I cannot but hope that a good life might end at last in a contented death.'

Dr. Johnson.[40]

From Short-ferry I soon came (having from the road a fine view of Lincoln Cathedral) to Stainfield House, an old deserted seat, with a dismantled park, of the Thrywhit family: to the house I rode up and desired an inspection; it has been a grand thing, but most of it, within these 20 years, has been pull'd down. Part of the old hall forms a good kitchen, such a one as is often shewn in a pantomime: there are some tolerable apartments and some bad family pictures.—The farmer spake of the former gallery; and of a fine billiard room: all the timber of the park is gone.

This was a melancholy survey!—At one o'clock, tired and hungry, I stopp'd, in two more miles, before the Angel, a poor ale house, in the mean village of Bradney; Bradney and enquired of the landlord, 'Have you any corn for horses or meat for man?' 'Yes, Sr, I have a bit of mutton in the pot, and oats in the stable'. 'Say you so, then I put up'. —He shew'd me into his best parlour—alias bed room; and wanted the *other gentleman* to come in likewise.

I had for dinner the scragg end of a neck of mutton, with young carrots, with a pint of ale, and $\frac{1}{2}$ a pint of brandy. After dinner I sought epitaphs in the churchyard.

MARY, the Wife of John PARROT. 1790. aged 47 years.

> She was too good upon this earth to stay
> So Heaven in mercy, took my wife away
> It was Thy will O God that this should be
> It is our duty to submit to Thee.

(Mr P— argues this very *submissively* and *patiently*. As for Bradney Abbey, that is all gone;

> 'The solemn temples, the great globe itself
> Yea, all which it inherit, shall dissolve.'

351

When the payment came, I encouraged mine host to charge liberally—and so he did!*

I chose this road, because books and maps have mark'd thereon many old religious houses. At Stainfield was a Benedictine nunnery.—A pleasant ride thro' grass grounds (the gates of this day innumerable) and by woods, to near Tupholm Priory—whereof some small remains are attach'd to a farm house, a large venerable gateway, I went up to examine it; when the civil farmer came out, and observ'd to me that of the religious building the gateway only remain'd. 'Aye', said I, 'your neighbourhood seem'd to be famed formerly for religion; now I suppose a curate can take charge of ye all!' 'And there are no more remains of Kirkstead Abbey?'—'No, Sir; I have lived here 60 years, and only remember this gateway: all this field was cover'd by buildings, and we now dig up great quantities of stone'. We next talk'd about coursing; and then of the coursing, and recoursing of the King of France!—A small shower detain'd me near Kirkstead Church; beyond which a moor has been lately enclosed, whence I could see the church and castle of Tattershall. Passing thro' some ling, and woody grounds, I saw a very high piece of building to my right; 'What is that, G?' 'Why it looks, Sr, like the ruin'd steeple of a church'.—Thro' some fields I rode up to it.—Now for something odd, and droll to the tourist. I enquired of every one, for a morsel of antiquity; I visit a gentleman farmer at Kirkstead village, 4 miles off; and he shews me his ground for the religious foundation: and behold here stood Kirkstead Abbey!—Which I discover'd *promiscuously!*—A miserable common, with some miserable cottages around it, shew this lofty relict to the greatest advantage.—Returning into the road, I accompanied a farmer, who advised me to avoid Tattershall, and to turn to the left, about two miles further, to a snug comfortable inn, much better than any in Tattershall: with him I cross'd a

Kirkstead [margin note]

*For eating, ale, ½ pint brandy, 2 horses hay & 2 feeds of corn - 2s. 6d.

moor, part of Tattersall old parks; which I should think were impassable in winter; and where I saw some of those grey rabbets, which abound in this county, and are so valuable, their skins being a third better; if so, why are they not transported to other counties?

Leaving the farmer, (as slack as others of information, and guidance,) I blunder'd my way to the little inn at Tumby, in the road from Tattersall to Horncastle, where Tumby I was civilly receiv'd, and lodg'd to my liking, in the snug parlour of a thatch'd house; feeling myself in quiet and coolness, after the noise, and heat of the Lincoln Inn. Every wish was for rain; (here I cared not,) and there fell a refreshing shower. My supper (after many short walks) consisted of a fine roasted fowl, cold ham, pickled salmon, artichoke, and tarts; all in comfort: and I sat up till past eleven o'clock, writing, and reading; for here were books!—

A new month; and yet alone! These little inns are *Friday* pleasant pass-the-day spots; but not so well at night, when *July 1* you want mattrasses and comforts: my double bedded room was like that of a farm house, with a deal door, and a latch and joices white wash'd; however, I slept well till seven o'clock this morning.—Coffee for breakfast; a lounge about morning near home; only one walk of the hour betwixt twelve, and one, the family dinner time, when I ate of (an old dish I think) a boil'd rump of beef; this, with some peas, was equal to my wishes.—But not to throw away a day, I took an evening ride, on one mile of our road, then descended to the left to the village of Kirby; and thence over a staring, black moor to the tower of the moor, built of brick, and of excellent workmanship: there is a stair-case to the top, but now very ruinous at the bottom; tho' up which an active man might climb to catch a wild, dreary prospect: it seems to have been built for a review of falconry; and other field sports.

Sr F. D[ashwood]'s pillar, upon Lincoln Heath, will

shew as unintelligibly as this in 200 years.—The air of this evening was quite chilly; and I was sufficiently gloomy, thus hunting out old towers upon a gloomy moor, by myself! Two days ago, at Lincoln, I panted for air; but this cold must introduce rain.—I enquired of a turf-cutter, what he had heard concerning that tower? But all he knew was 'that it was an ancient place'.—

Return'd, I shut myself up for the evening; and having dined early, was eager to sup soon:—sooner *than some folks I know* dine in London! I felt anxious for letters;—those, I look'd for, however, on the morrow.—

Saturday July 2

Up at seven o'clock to a missling morn; and as soon as mine old hostess would descend, call'd for the bill.

The rain being of no terror, I mounted Po: at 8 o'clock; (G. to follow) and was soon at the village of Conisby, whose church is lightsome, and well-built, with a bellfry under which is a thoroughfare.—Crossing the little river, at times very deep, I came in ½ a mile to Tattersall, a small market town, with a mean market-place. When I enter'd the Angel Inn, I felt happy to think I had gone to Tumby-Swan; and did not put up at this bad quarter.—A short ride before breakfast is just what I like, to enjoy the meal, and forward the day.

Tatters-hall

G. soon came in; and when breakfasted I took him with me to view the castle, the most perfect, the grandest piece of brick work in the kingdom. The ditch around is yet fenced by a wall, but all the outer buildings are pull'd down; except a part of a porters lodge and an old stable. A poor family dwell in one angle; up which staircase with an excellent grooved banister, we mounted to the top; and half around the battlements, whence is an unbounded prospect: the walls are 15 feet thick; the cross beams, and the iron work of the windows are left; but what is most to be admired are 3 antique stone chimney-pieces, laden with armorial bearings of the families above mention'd; which should be *taken care of*, and might be remov'd; as most of

THO:S HALL   T: UMBY

FROM LEEDS GATES

	£	s	d
Breakfast		=	8
Dinner		1	6
Supper		2	6
Coffee & Tea		=	8
Wine		3	=
Negus			
Punch &c		1	6
Cyder			
Ale			
Porter			
Servants Eating & Ale			
Hay 2:4 & Corn 3:6		6	10
£		= 16	8

355

the magnificent stain'd glass of the chancell of the church has been by Ld F[ortescue], the owner of this place. This was the only epitaph I transcrib'd from the churchyard.

MARY ATKIN. 1783. aged 26 years.

She that lie hear was a virtious youth
Who new her Saviour and embrace his truth.

The Collegiate Church is, truly, a venerable pile, with beautiful pillars, and one paint'd window; it is now parted from the chancell by a deal door (the altar table standing in the middle aile) to keep out the wind; as every pane of its wonderful stain'd glass has been pillaged—and not re-placed by any other! Of the noble brasses much remain in the *keeping* of the clerk, but, now, should be in the hands of a collector: so had they been in mine, could I (*easily*) have removed them: only one plate of arms (the Cromwells I believe,) *came* into my possession.

When plunder commences, let it be complete: why did not Ld F— (the Gothic owner)[41] take all? Why does not Sr J[oseph] B[ankes][42] (who is an antiquary and comes here sometimes) seize the rest?

One might suppose (without any indelicate reflexion upon *our bishops* and their *well-order'd* dioceses) that visitations were never made; or questions about churches never ask'd! Else might not a bishop ask—'To whom belongeth this chancell? Who removed the windows;—and the flooring, and the monuments of the dead? Why standeth not the altar at the proper place?—Let every thing be replaced, and repair'd with decency; so as to keep out shame, and cold: or I shall try whether the arm of the church have yet sufficient power to punish shameful sacrilege, and to impose reparation.—See that it be instantly begun; and let those who removed the painted windows be thankful that I do not oblige them to replace those, or put in others of equal value'.

A flat country of a mile brought us to the River Witham, (which flows from the Trent to Boston, making an island

THE DASHWOOD PILLAR

[see pp. 344 and 353

RUINS OF BOLINGBROKE CASTLE

from water-colours by the Diarist   [see p. 374

of the northern part of this county): here to my grief, was a nasty ferry, where my horses cross'd with much trouble; (from disuse); but Ranger gave us yet more trouble, from his dulness and delay.—

A long flat succeeded; over a country now drain'd, and enclosed; which has destroy'd the breeding and coming of all the Fen birds; tho' of the greatest advantage to the country and landholder.—

Pass'd near Billinghay Church, which has been newly spired; thence to Nth Kyme; and after some loss of way, to South Kyme; the roads are good now, but in winter must be very bad.

South Kyme

Here is much for observation, tho' little observ'd, I believe, as being much out of the way: this old tower must have been part of some grand building, of which all memory is now lost.

I then walk'd, across the road to the most venerably-looking church; which I was attempting to sketch, when I was driven off, in much nervous disorder, by a drove of bullocks; nor could I collect myself to renew my work.— A gentleman, who had observ'd me from the neighbouring house of Mr Dickinsons, now approach'd me with many offers of civility, and with the keys of the church, and tower: the young farming man, likewise, press'd me to eat, dine, &c &c. The tower is, below, well-vaulted, well-stair'd, and the upper floors well plank'd; from the battlements is an extensive prospect. Then to the church; of such beautiful antiquity, and the porch, with two figures so curious, as merit a good drawing to be taken of it. (But few people will wander out of the road to see, or sketch anything!) Within, the filth and ruin would beggar all description! The roof falling in!—A dirt floor!—An altar table that a pauper would not feed from!!—But there is a curious old monument, 1430, of the Tallbois, of many brasses, with painted labels from their mouths:—I look'd around me; but dared not plunder.

After staying here a long time, and making a most

357

observant, and most gratifying survey, I rode back thro' the village, and, over some fields to a bridge toll; where I was surprised to find myself enquired after, from description by Sr J. G——;—and my poney more particularly described!

After riding for 2 miles by a canal-side, and thro' grazing grounds, I met the same civil intimations of stoppage, left from Sr J. G.[43] and Mr D——; (highly polite this—but of no avail to an obstinate, solitary, traveller,) at the entrance of Sr J.'s grounds;—little, however could I feel a wish of stopping at a place of such vile taste, without design, or intention, in a bad soil, in a bad country, with pollarded trees, and water thrown into an unpleasant ditch!—If any monastical remains had existed lately, no doubt but they are now removed!!

By this place I was glad to trot, unnoticed; when the rain, and my gt coat coming on, I hurried forward, (without any direction posts!) to a large common, whence, (meeting a man and guidance,) I soon found my road to the late inn at Sleaford: where I receiv'd a pacquet of letters from Mrs B[yng]; but not ONE from Col B[ertie]!—After a pint of port wine, I wrote away till seven o'clock; when I stroll'd this dismal town; and at a grave-digging endeavour'd to rehearse Hamlet; and afterwards attended at the procession of 40 women mourners, belonging to a club.

Sleaford

> 'That scull had a tongue in it, and could sing once:
> How the knave jowls it to the ground, as if it were
> Cain's jaw bone that did the first murder!'

Either from damp, uneasy letters, or too much of my own society, I felt gloomy; tho', surely, I have had prosperous weather, and have done tolerably: how I had pined alone, if the weather had proved rainy.

*Sunday
July 3*

Beginning a fresh week; and hoping for company. Up at seven o'clock; hast'ning to go from a known place.

Met, at the inn gate, a civil gentleman (Mr F[arde]ll, Proctor of Lincoln Cathedral)[44] who knew the county well; and did not appear to be of the *logical, puzzling conceited* sort.—I find that gin and water does not agree with me; neither does tea; so I allways breakfast upon coffee; without much delay, that I may go early, and ride gently; not so with servants, who would be an hour at breakfast, and then make up their time by riding hard:—G. do I see loitering every morning, with the maids, or mistress, over a tea-board; sip, sip, sip, by the hour; (which makes me sick;) and complimenting about the lumps of sugar!

Who will say that this is a dear bill? The first 3 miles from Sleaford I knew; then the country rises to Heckington, a well-built village, with an handsome church; in two more miles to an hamlet of pleasant sound, and the very best of hamlets it ought to be, *Garrick*.

ANGEL INN. SLEAFORD.

july							s.	d.
2	Dinner -	-	-	-	-	-	1	0
	Wine -	-	-	-	-	-	2	3
	Supper -	-	-	-	-	-	1	0
	Brandy -	-	-	-	-	-	1	6
	Coffee -	-	-	-	-	-	0	8
	Rushlight & Paper -	-	-	-			0	3
	Letters -	-	-	-	-	-	0	8
							7	4

Great-Hale Fen is now all enclosed, and flourishing with corn; and the roads over it are super-excellent, of a light loomy sand. Arrive at Swineshead, a small market Swineshead town; here I made enquiries after the old abbey of Swineshead, (by all the names of enquiry) of a young man; to whom, at last, I said, 'Are there any ruins?' Who answer'd, 'I know of no brewings'.—An old man did assist me: 'Why it is to the left, not a chain mile out of town'. So I found the scite thereof, and a good farm house upon it:—where long did I call and halloo, as I saw a cap at a window, seemingly of a woman; at last out came an old fat farmer in his nt cap, who was very civil, begg'd me to alight, and drink rum and water, or what I chose; and explain'd to me where he believ'd the old priory stood. He then took me into his garden, and shew'd me where a famous yew tree grew, that was a sea mark; the stem of which was sold to a miller for £20, for a mill post.—Mr G[ough] in his new edition of Camden, says that this tree now stands.—Most authors write from hearsay, and from the books they consult over their fire-side; but never move to an observation: now I examine the place with my own eyes.—He shew'd me, likewise, the stone figure, fixed in the outside of the house wall, of a Knight Templar; of which he accused himself of having (when a boy) often shot at with a pistol, and then glorying at carrying off his nose:—which he now thinks of repairing. 'When I buried my cattle', said he, 'that died of the distemper, I got into the burying ground of the monks, and dug up many of their skeletons'.—The arms of the Lockton family are in two places upon the house.—

This inspection threw me 2 miles about; and I return'd into the road at Bikar; where another 2 miles brought me to Dunnington, a small market-town, where I dined, comfortably, on a shoulder of lamb, peas and tart; in a quiet house, but not a night-stop. When I had dined, and was going forward, it began to rain; so I waited for some time: but resolving to continue my punctuality (and little doubting but that Col: B: would arrive at Spalding to-day, as he was to leave London on Thursday) I put forth; and tho' it rain'd all the way, so as to hurry me, yet it was not a pelter.

Dinner	-	-	-	-	-	1	0
Wine	-	-	-	-	-	1	2
Horses	-	-	-	-	-	0	10
						S3	0

A good dinner. A good parlour. Good attendance. Where do people dine cheaper?

360

I had soon to recollect, and a melancholy feel it was, where, last year, at an alehouse in Pinchbeck-village, I put up (with T. B[ush]) to avoid a storm of thunder, and lightning.—These were my chief thoughts; with an almost certain hope of meeting Coll: B: but at Spalding I Spalding receiv'd a letter from him, saying he would be there tomorrow; also one of an old date from Mrs B. Here, at the White Hart, were my quarters of last year. The evening continued wettish, and gloomy, and I lower'd in a back room not too merry in my own society; so a walk was necessary, and I stroll'd about, for ½ an hour, by the canal side, where are many good houses built: the very old one I visited last year,[45] retains its old master, Col J—, whom I then thought upon the edge of the grave; but grunters (man, and horse,) they say endure the longest, and are the stoutest.

My walk was well taken, if only to hear a conversation at the bridge foot, where the town watch had assembled, taking their nightly orders; and one would imagine only rehearsing the scene in Much-ado-about-Nothing;[46] for these old feeble creatures were arm'd with rusty bills, now a curious and unknown weapon, (these had serv'd for centuries).—Two superior watchmen *commended* the charges to the *dissembly*; one bidding them to avoid drunkenness, and another from the watch-house cried out 'Have a care that your bills be not stolen'. The very words *S.* —used. The whole assemblage, and their management differ'd not a whit from the company and orders of those venerables Messrs Dogberry and Verges.—Mr *W. S.* must have observ'd just such a meeting; (*at Long Crendon in Buckinghamshire perhaps*).

> *Dog:* Well masters, good night; an there be any matter of
> Weight chances, call up me: keep your fellows
> Counsels and your own, and good-night. Come, neighbour.

I remark'd to an old satyrical-looking lady, standing near, my wonder at their *good* guard. 'Aye', says she, 'a'nt we *finely* güarded by such cripples? Sure never town was so guarded! And only in summer time, too! In winter when one may suppose a watch wanted, we have none!!!'—This was, curiously, explain'd to me by my landlord, as derived from old law, and donations, for watchmen to keep off wild beasts, who formerly infested the neighbouring woods, and fens; in winter they were secured by inundations.—

This is a curious relation!

In this county as in many others, the bread is baked in pans (to be distinguish'd I suppose) which renders it heavy and sodden. My pint of wine at supper was the meanest measure I ever saw; now I can carry a good *pint*, at least of port wine. The wind blew very fresh, and it was a very cold evening. Surely our climate is alter'd for I will not attribute my feelings to age.—

Monday July 4

To-day I am to expect Coll B[ertie]. I have, now, been three weeks by myself; and shall feel the pleasure of society: but how soon does solitary life beget shyness and reserve; and I dread the superior conversation of a London-gentleman; having nothing to speak of but my own petty adventures.—Those who do not attend to their own horses, deserve to be ill carried, and to have their horses spoil'd, and starved; to mine I attend assiduously, and particularly at that dangerous hour of shoeing, when a blacksmith would willingly cut to the quick, and drive his nails at a venture. Yesterday the mare lost one of her shoes, and the others were so bad that she was obliged to be shod this morning: poneys may last another week.—This has been quite an April day.—High wind, and violent showers; I made several short walks; one around the churchyard, and there transcribed these two (not bad) epitaphs.

ROBT. RANDALL.

And is he dead? Is he already dead?
Ah too suri*sing news, sudden as sad!*

362

WILLᵐ BOTHAMLEY. Clock Maker.

What human foresight can from danger screen
The various *movements* of the frail *machine*
A slight obstruction in *the curious piece*
Affects each member, laws of motion cease.

There is a glover of this town who fattens those dainty birds, call'd ruffs and rees, for the tables of the great; but the number of these birds is much decreas'd by the drainage of the fens: however, he sells about 1200 dozen during the summer; and to the King regularly, the Duke of Portland, &c &c &c. These birds, being pinion'd, are render'd very tame, very fat, and very dear; a couple of them I sent as a present to London. My dinner was truly bad, from the rankness of the meat, and the buttering of the cookery: I find there is nothing but fowls and fish to be depended upon.

At 4 o'clock Coll B. arrived; a flurry of meeting; he comes in a curricle, his servant on horseback; then his dinner, bad like mine; no wine drinkable, else *we* had *sat* quietly: some discourse arose about touring, the present, the past, and the future.

(C) Touring alone must tire. (B) Aye, so it does; but then you know yourself, and are safe: where is the man to tour with you? You may meet a pleasant tavern man; but none who will go thro' the rubs of touring, and be agreeable. (C) We must quit it soon? (B) So I fear; with many other things; and then to stick close to London, its warmth, its play-houses, in the winter; a summer walk, sometimes, to White Conduit House, and the Apollo Garden, and if desperate, and your will made, then to Richmond, or Maidenhead Bridge.

A town walk was proposed—therein went over the history of the 1st Regt of Guards.—Return'd to tea; then out again; this is life! We, afterwards, saunter'd along the Boston road for a mile, and back again. Obliged to order supper; better manag'd this in France, where 30 or 40 sous may be your price, and you are serv'd accordingly,

363

without the distress of choice.—Our bad service here, parted us too soon.—Inn wine is good, according to the time of credit.

Tuesday
July 5

First day of the combined forces. The Colonel has purchased a pair of small tight-moulded, foreign horses, with a curricle, in which my *heavy* baggage will be placed; and this must be of much use to my mare, who should not trot far, even with such a weight upon her. Settled my own account.

WHITE HART. SPALDING.

Coffee -	-	-	-	-	-	o	9
Supper -	-	-	-	-	-	1	6
Wine -	-	-	-	-	-	1	3
Brandy -	-	-	-	-	-	1	6
Breakft.	-	-	-	-	-	o	9
						5	9

WHITE HART. Spalding.

Breakfts.	-	-	-	-	-	1	6
Dinners -	-	-	-	-	-	3	0
Suppers -	-	-	-	-	-	3	0
Sherry -	-	-	-	-	-	1	9
Port -	-	-	-	-	-	3	9
Ale -	-	-	-	-	-	o	6
Paper -	-	-	-	-	-	o	1
Rushlites	-	-	-	-	-	o	6
					£o	14	1

Market day here, quite an installation: saw the stage coach arrive, and all the women descend with such *terror* and *modesty*! This is allways an event in a country town; and what a *critical* tourist should attend to. I then walk'd to view the remains of Spalding Priory—formerly boasting its tenants, and tenements; but now affording only shelter for some poor inhabitants, and a keeping for the ruffs and rees!

Now to our breakfast; and some discourse of our past touring; but

> 'No more yet of this
> For 'tis a chronicle of day by day,
> Not a relation for a breakfast, not
> Befitting this first meeting.'
>
> *Tempest.*

It was a fine morning, and with eagerness did we begin our first march.

> 'They rode, but authors having not
> Determined whether pace, or trot.'
>
> Hudibras.

Over the flat, and (now) pleasant country, first to Weston village; thence to Waplode, and to Holbeach, 8 miles; servants to follow us; and stay here: we went this way, and on further to Long Sutton, at the Coll's desire, to view the church; and any part that might exist of an old house that did belong to a branch of his family, extinct within these 4 years in Mr B[ertie] of Low-Layton. Pass'd near Fleet, and Gedney Churches (my ride of last year) and to Long Sutton Church; which we were shewn Long by an old, wild, clerk, who said he had been wounded by Sutton his son, now in Bedlam; where the old man might be properly placed.—

It is an excellent church, kept, and furnish'd like a London one, with an organ, and a painted ceiling over the altar, in the Verrio[47] taste.—Near the village, Mr P—, a lawyer (who married one of the Miss B.'s) has fitted up a lawyer-liking house; where we call'd, and the Coll left his name.—Then, to where the old Bertie mansion stood; most of which was burnt down: this might have been an approach, either into the house, or the offices.——The day was highly pleasant; and the Coll seem'd completely happy, discoursing of his family, and of how much belonging to them we had to review: so the miles seem'd as short as the country appear'd fruitful, and populous.

Holbeach   Return to Holbeach; where, in our parlour, hung a picture of the King of Prussia,[48] (father of the last) so like Admiral Byng, with the same round, smooth, unmeaning face, and the same little, mischievous nose.——

Our charge was most extraordinary cheap; for we had for dinner, a neck of mutton boil'd, with caper sauce, and vegetables, a roasted duck, tart, collard eel, and a bottle of port-wine and ale.

CHEQUERS. HOLBEACH.

Dinners	-	-	-	-	-	2	0
Wine	-	-	-	-	-	2	0
Ale	-	-	-	-	-	0	3
						4	3

After dinner, we discoursed about health and longevity: my opinion was 'that health was to be maintain'd, and longevity acquired by, only, two methods; (I mean with a tolerable constitution;) early rising, and exercise; the former to be resolved upon and observed rigorously, and the latter never to be eluded: neither sleep, nor idleness to be yielded to, else their mastership would be quickly establish'd; with years, too, on their side.

'I know several men', I said, 'who indulged in liquor, and yet preserv'd their looks, and health, by resolving upon exercise; not by little, paltry, crawlings about; but by good stout exercise: why, you Colonel have kept yourself alive, and hearty, by a bold, and prudent determination of riding every day in the year.——I often call in the morning upon some of my friends, and find them not risen; and when I meet them in the afternoon they complain of head-achs, indigestion &c, &c:—Why they ought to be whipp'd around, the neighbouring square; or tied upon an horse, and obliged to ride'.

A pleasant twining road, (my same of last year,) led us to the water bank, when the curricle coming up, I mounted therein, with the Coll; (as charioteer, for the first time, I believe, in 16 years;) the horses are clever, but ill rein'd and harness'd, and I dislike the carriage, and the attention required: my old-fashion'd, smooth-going Italian chair was the only equipage for touring, ease, and safety.— Over the sands it is customary, (and thought necessary, I believe,) to have a guide; and so you might hire one from Hyde Park corner to Kensington, and of as much use; for when the tide is up, you cannot pass, and when the tide is out, a dog may walk thro' the water.—

At Fossdyke House, a mean bathing place, where I drank tea last year, we stopp'd for an hour; it is a melancholy place, for we saw only one girl who waited on us, but our intention serv'd well for variety.—The chaise went forward for quarters; our road & ride were very pleasant, and we conversed much, in our way, with a pedestrian— who spake highly of his performances.—At Kirton the high road is enter'd, which brought us in 4 miles to Boston, where we walk'd over the stones to the Peacock Boston Inn, and then, till dark, by the river side; tho' the evening was very cold; so cold as to force us to sit over a fire at coming in, when we might have hoped for some tolerable fish at supper; but the cod fish stunk so as not to be endured! In London, fish gasp upon the fishmongers leads; here, by the sea side, they stink!! So, likewise, in the inn of a famous wine merchant, (Mr F[ydell])[49] the wine was not drinkable! One might have expected something less than poison? Brandy and water, and peevishness, soon hurried us to bed.

A blustering cold morning. I was amongst the market *Wednesday July 6* folks at 7 o'clock. No strawberries! So I must defer that pleasure till next year: cherries there are, but these are kill boys; strawberries are the taste of a gentleman, cherries the fruit of the vulgar. Raspberries I bought, but of no better flavour than blackberries. I breakfasted upon coffee; the Col upon tea; when, we, balancing about touring, thus stated,

(C) Is it worth while thus to wander about?

(B) Most certainly for health of body, and improvement of mind. (C) Those men may be right, who assert that none should depart from London, where every comfort is at hand? (B) I think such to be idle, narrow notions;—let me keep that thought for a bonne bouche, a closing scene of goutification; inability daring not to take a wider flight: let the touring of my country be my first object; and then when I shall have completely visited England, Wales, Scotland, (not Ireland), why I will embark for Italy, Athens, Egypt, and Palmyra: but not before, I promise you.

PEACOCK INN.   BOSTON.

Gentl^ms Sup^rs	-	-	-	-	3	6
Sherry -	-	-	-	-	1	9
Port Wine	-	-	-	-	2	6
Malt liq^r	-	-	-	-		3
Breakfts.	-	-	-	-	1	6
Rushlights	-	-	-	-		2
Paper -	-	-	-	-		½
					*10	8½

*Were we not overcharged one shilling?

At 10 o'clock we left Boston; after a walk around the church yard, and our admiration of the lofty tower of the church.

Sibsey

To the village of Sibsey; where walking about the churchyard, and reading the grave stone epitaphs, made me to remark that poor people died early, for they must work when ill; never understood their own management; advice came slowly, and ineffectually: no, it is the rich man who lives longest, who has every comfort, a nice bed, and physicians at hand: look into the mausoleums of the great, and you'll find that they outlive the parish. (C) Don't you think that the air, and the exercise, ought to strengthen the poor? (B) Yes, if properly taken; but their air, and their exercise are obliged to be taken at bad seasons, and with severity; so they wear out; for there is no repose for age.

To Stickney, a village betwixt two great fens, with decoys at a distance: thence to Stickford, where the country now rising, made us to enjoy the change; thence to Keal-coates; mount a steep hill to West Kaile; then to E. Kaile, and to Spilsby: having been 4 hours on horseback.—It *Spilsby* was a chearful, windy day, and our ride was very satisfactory; during which we discours'd about relationship, and family, and keeping well with them: 'It is', said I, 'what pride and poverty make us submit to; but selldom a society of choice: you visit yours; I visit some of mine; but we are neither of us at home! You owe nothing to your family, either from interest, or legacy. Thinking of that, I revert to your London topick, of Hyde-Park; about which you dare to ride, and with a dog behind you; whereas at G:[50] you dare not take a spaniel out!'—

A long delay to our dinner; when sad cookery spoil'd every thing: the mutton of this country is shockingly large, and coarse: I eat nothing but beans, or young potatoes, which can scarcely be spoil'd; to them I order'd slices of bacon broil'd, which the Coll said was a rash action; rather say, Col, that is was a *rasher* action.

After dinner—we eagerly walk'd to survey what might remain of the old family seat of the Berties, at Eresby,[51] near this town; which seat was burn'd down about 30 years ago.—

But first, to the church;—where was a sufficiency of antiquity for me, and of family curiosity for Coll B: (for whose researches of family ground, and estates, we have wander'd this way). Here are several old recumbent figures, in alabaster, of the Berties, &c &c; and several handsome brasses over their old vault; also, with many others, a grand monument of Rd Bertie, and his wife, the Dss of Suffolk, who died 1580, 1582;—under which, is a vault, and coffins: this I beg'd for a lanthorn to explore. In it I found five coffins, toss'd about; but our drunken landlord had never been down, and now would not! All the inscriptions upon the several monuments, and brasses, were order'd to be copied for Coll B.; whom I honor for this spirit of family antiquity; now derided, and neglected!! —The old avenue at Eresby, still in being, led us to the pillars of approach, and to the spot of the former house, gardens, and canals; but

> Such are thy bowers in shapeless ruin all,
> And the long grass o'ertops the mouldering wall.
> *Goldsmith.*

An odd drunken fellow who was there, told us 'that he play'd the engine at the fire which was *only t'other* day; and when every person was burn'd in the house'.—It broke out in the day time, from the boiling over of a plummer's pot, when the roof was repairing.—Herein, were consumed the library, family pictures, &c &c.—Some old stabling, and a dog-kennell are remaining; as are likewise the garden walls, the fruit from which is preserv'd for their new master, Sr P[eter] B[urrell];[52] who possesses 21 manors around this town.—In the church, this evening, were two women church'd by the clergyman (when we were there) in the space of two minutes: which office I did not know could be thus huddled over, privately, in a church?—I added, to my surprise, a wish that the clergy could live together in their own communities, for I allways objected to their society over the board;—'as should they prove proud, and formal, it was disgusting; and if frisky, it was more disgusting'. We return'd to tea; and then try'd a long strole over the fields. This gloomy town seems to be thinly inhabited.

This morning I was awaken'd by the barkings and fightings of dogs, upon the market place; such nuisance, and noise is intolerable: one dog can disturb a whole town. Oh, for a dog tax: and yet its first unpopularity will prevent, what every one wishes! If the dogs had not awaken'd me, my nightly companion, a rush light, soon would, (according to daily custom,) by his expiring stink! *Thursday July 7*

Our ride of this day was thro' Halton to Bratoft, where is a small brick church; and where has been a wall'd park, and a hall, now dismantled, and destroy'd.—Not only gentillity have fled the country, but the race of yeomanry is extinguish'd.

When tradesmen, farmers, and yeomen brought up their children to business, to attend to agriculture, and to assist in their fathers' fortunes; why then truth, society and honesty, dwelt in the land: for the sons were honest, hearty fellows and the girls unaffected, notable housewifes.—But now, from false pride, and idle hope, parents educate their children in fashionable folly; the misses sent to French boarding schools, or convents, and the boys are to become bishops, or generals. Of such blindness what must be the result? Why, such misery and distress of the old folks, that the farm (for ages in the family) must be sold; the sons turn'd out into the world, (to make their fortunes, as the term is) sink into debouchery, disappointment, and end in a jail; whilst the fine misses, vain, pert and ignorant, quickly degenerate into harlots, take lodgings in Wardour Street and perish;—we hope repentant sinners!!

We next came to Burgh, a small market town, with a church upon an eminence, above the marshes; which must be a sea mark; from situation this place resembles (in miniature) the town of Rye (in Sussex).—The flat is not disagreeable, (at this season,) being fill'd with cattle, and besprinkled with cottages. Many churches in sight; to the left, upon the coast, that of Winthorpe, and to our right, in the marshes, the little low church of Skegness; which the Coll aptly compared to a cradle.—Our ride was now over the sands, (with a distant view of the Norfolk coast,) to Skegness Inn, a vile, shabby, bathing place. Here, when arrived, much was our trouble; and the Coll, with difficulty, prevail'd upon the old hostess (une diablesse) to allow us to enter a mean parlour, below, and to have some food therein. A walk upon the sea-sand, and to sniff up the wholesome breeze, till we thought we might return to our landlady's bar room; where we had some miserable smelts, and some raw, rank cold beef put before us.—This wretch'd house was fill'd with strange company; but society is a pleasure; at least, the ladies, old and young, love company, and absence from home: here, indeed, the misses may ripen, from the squeaking of maids, haul'd about by the postilions. There is no garden, no walk, no billiard room; nor any thing for comfort, or temptation!

If a good house were built here, with a clever landlord, it would draw much company, and answer well. Our starvation was great: close to us sat Mother Notable, in all filth, shelling beans, and making tarts.—If we had intended a night stop here, we had been undone, for every bed was engaged; and no abode nearer than Spillsby: for no ale house at Burgh was fit for a bag-man.—(As posterity may be ignorant what a bag-man is, let them learn that he is a rider, who travells, with saddle bags, to receive of shop keepers a list of what goods are wanting from manufactories, and wholesale dealers; and to collect the debts.)

From all these miseries and a kitchen stinking of strong mutton, and a roasting hog, we hurry'd away.—I stopp'd in the marshes, to take this sketch of the miserable little church of Skegness, and then overtook Coll B. at Burgh.

My mare is so hot, when following, that G— is obliged to go first.—The Coll, anxious to see wherever any of his

372

relations have, or do live, desired that we might turn out of our road of return, to Gunby Hall, an ancient seat of the very old family of the Massingberds, but now rented to Sr P. Burrell for a shooting seat; this house, tho' well placed and with wood in view, (of which much spoil has been made) is a most melancholy place: suicide in every room: and if I did come to sport over my 21 manors, I would add some neat rooms to a farm house of my own; or build a neat cottage on some pleasant spot.

Here we left our names.—Hence Col B. wish'd to go to Willoughby village, the first title of his family; so first to Welton, and then by Willoughby-Wood, (swarming with game,) to Willoughby, a large village, and an excellent living; where the Rector Dr [Bouyer][53] has lately built a good parsonage. In the church, much out of repair, which we enter'd, there is one old carv'd grave stone in the middle aile, (Adam de Bertie perhaps) the sight of which delighted the Coll, more than an advancing storm did me: I advised stopping at the Six Bells Ale House, but was overruled; however in a mile, I said—'I would fly for shelter to a farm house; follow me'; and so they did; it proved my weather wisdom, for the storm fell, just as we reach'd the farmer's stable: the farmer came to us, in very civil fashion.—Herein we stay'd for ¾ of an hour, (discoursing about husbandry, oxen, &c) till the sky clear'd up, when we resumed our road to Claxby; here is a pretty dip, and a pleasant country—with a fine view to the right, to Skentleby, and to Portney, whence a lane return'd us to Spilsby; after a longish crawl, and having been a long time on horseback.—Our supper was hurried, being in arrear to our appetites; soon after which we finish'd our bottle of port, and seem'd most inclinable to a retiring.— The difference of the Coll's method, and mine, is that his wants are numerous; he wants many knives, many glasses, and rings away the bell; I hate the waiter's interruption, and like to wait upon myself; it is easy to fetch the mustard, and peppar from the side-board: 'Pray don't ring the bell,

Wil- loughby

Spilsby

my dear Colonel, but let me help you, if the things are in the room; determine, before dinner, upon the sort of bread, and ale, that you want, but don't keep the waiter in the room, asking him questions about brewing, and baking'. The Coll's servant is so over-knowing, and conceited, as to worry me exceedingly; his master has submitted to him, and so he brags and complains at his pleasure; alters harness, manages his horses as he likes, and is as ignorant, as presumptious.—

Friday
July 8
This was a lovely morning.—I walk'd before breakfast to where the old mansion house stood, and there sketch'd these two pillars of approach.—Coming back, I enquired at an old glazier's shop, for stain'd glass; he said, 'That they made no account of it, for that month since, they took down a painted window from Bolingbroke Church, which was all thrown away, or broken by the Boys'!!—Coll B: after breakfast, again betook himself to his ancestors in the church; from which he has had made copies of the inscriptions.—To settle bills, is my province.

At eleven o'clock we left Spilsby.

Pass'd near Hindley, a new house of Mr Brackenbury's, discoursing with the minister of Spilsby, (of as good information as others); and in 4 miles came to Bolingbroke, once a market town, now a mean village.—The church seems to be a small portion of a once noble pile.

The castle ground is a pleasant spot, and deeply moted around; at one point, a small remnant of a tower overhangs the river's margin, which has been unnoticed by topographical pencils; tho' surely deserving such attention.

I thought this a good, and pleasant observation, of what was, what is; thoughts arising about John of Gaunt, Henry Duke of Hereford, even down to their new descendants; the day and country added chearfulness.

An excellent road brought us here, and continued us to
Reavesby Honby; thence to Reavesby, the seat of Sr Joseph Banks.

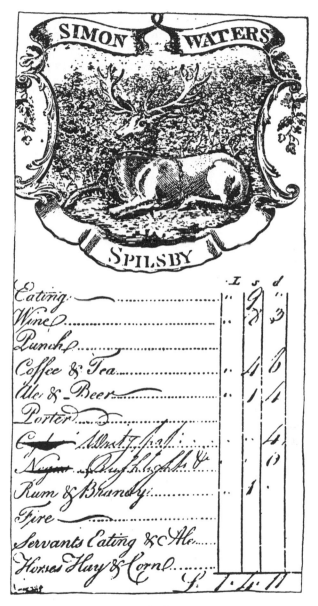

SIMON WATERS

SPILSBY

	£	s	d
Eating		9	
Wine		8	3
Punch			
Coffee & Tea		4	6
Ale & Beer		1	4
Porter			
			4
			0
Rum & Brandy		1	
Fire			
Servants Eating & Ale			
Horses Hay & Corn			
£	1	4	11

375

—The park is flat, dismal, and unimproved; the house mean, and uncomfortable, with an horse pond in front; with no gardens, or comforts; but when a man sets himself up for a wild eccentric character, and (having a great estate, with the comforts of England, at command,) can voyage it to Otaheite,[54] and can reside in a corner house in Soho-Square; of course his country seat will be a filthy neglected spot.—How I do fancy I could make myself adored in my country village; by preventing oppression; by succouring the weak, and needy; by finding them cheap fuel; by giving land sufficient to each cottage; by distributing cloathing to those, only, who frequented divine service; by administering medicines gratis; and by holding out to them support, comfort, and consolation.—I would not live, or dine with people of other description to have a share of their learning.—We left our cards for Sr J. B.— If a man is happy in his pursuits, it becomes real pleasure; let those who fancy it, embark in balloons, or trace the course of a comet; I am a poor sublunary mortal; and will try to imitate Shenstone.

1

At fortune I'll never repine,
Whilst my roses and hyacinths blow;
Few pleasure are equal to mine
If the new-planted trees will but grow.

2

At my porch the swallow may build,
The white-owl, in my barn shall grow fat;
The robin a shelter I'll yield,
And the crumbs he shall pick from the mat.

3

With roses my breast I'll adorn,
Of true love, and of silence the pledge;
Nor think of the lurking sharp thorn,
The defence of my sweet-briar hedge;—

4

An emblem, perchance, that's too true,
Of the giddy enjoyments of life,
In plucking of which we soon rue
The keen thorns of ill humour and strife.

To Moreby, a small village, thro' new enclosures, and Moreby
so to Scrivelsby-Hall, the ancient seat of the Dymockes.
Mr R[epton][55] is here employ'd to improve the grounds;
for him I enquired; as did likewise Coll B— for Mr D—
The stables are very old. I was tempted to enter the house,
in hopes of antiquity; but sadly disappointed, for nothing
in it was there to observe, but 3 champion saddles, and
caparisons. Neither old pictures or portraits here; but most
of the house was burn'd down (which I knew not) about
30 years ago. It is surrounded by a mote. The maid servant,
stupid to an extreme, ill merited our two shillings.

The minister's house lately repair'd upon Mr R.'s plan,
is excellently done, simple and thatch'd, yet pleasant, and
neat. What more is design'd about this place, I knew not;
much new paling is finish'd: but I cannot conceive it can
ever be made a beautiful place. Two miles over a light, open
country; and to Horncastle: here we dined upon a good Horn-
cold dinner, when I ate more than usual, having been half castle
starved at Spilsby; and the wine being found tolerable, we
finish'd our bottle, and resolv'd to stay the night.—Nothing to be seen in this town, (only famous for its horse fair);[56]
so our evening was past, in pleasant walks, before, and
after tea: at our supper the only conversation which
occurr'd, that I remember, was

(B) What a delightful honor is that of being Champion, and to be hereditary?[57] How I should like to purchase
the manor, of a tenure that would introduce me at the
coronation.—(C) This gentleman is not vain of it; and
disdains the name of champion. (B) What a grandeur to
lose your own name in that of the champion!—as—
Where does the champion live? Here comes the cham-

377

pion! This is the champion's seat—and yet—what size is the champion? (C) Of a tolerable size. (B) That's lucky; I wish he was 6 feet, 6 inches high: for tho' the title may tolerably fit a tolerably sized man, yet should it descend to a cripple, then I suppose the next of kin must challenge for him. How strange it seems, that officers requiring superior courage, or politeness, should be hereditary honors; and that a champion might prove a coward, and a master of the ceremonies a driver of stage-coaches.

Saturday July 9

I proposed, this morning, that we should, for variety, take a drive in the curricle. After settling our bill, my enquiry was after any castle here, but all I could hear, or see of antiquity was part of an old wall near the river: in the opposite field they dig up Roman coins; so assuredly it was a Roman station. I walk'd forward; and was overtaken by the Coll in the curricle, whilst I was employ'd in Ashbye church yard, copying this epitaph:

ANN DREWRY. Aged 66.

My dearest friend in this grave is lay'd
Yet I am not the least afraid
But hope that we shall meet again
With Christ in Heaven to remain.

(Commonly the dead speak for themselves; but here the friend speaks.)

I drove onwards a bad, hard, road, tho' a turnpike, very stoney, very chalky, thro' a high and bleak country with very steep hills; which make unpleasant driving, especially in curricles, those most dangerous, tottering carriages, that follow heavily up hill, and press upon the horses down hill; my whole attention was therefore paid to the driving: the Coll walk'd or rode, up the hills; as the horses soon overtook us.—The poor village of Scamblesby lays low, betwixt high hills. In a few miles we saw, to our right, Mr Chaplin's house, and grounds at Tathwell; all the country about, is fit for, and dedicated to coursing. Louth spire like Salisbury, is to be seen from afar; but the steepness of the

378

GOODWIN,
At the BULL Inn,
𝕳𝖔𝖗𝖓𝖈𝖆𝖘𝖙𝖑𝖊.

	£	s	d
Eating, — — —	~	4	6
Wine, — — —	~	4	8
Punch, — — —			
Coffee and Tea, —	~	3	6
Ale and Beer, —	~	~	10
Porter, — — —			
Cyder, — — —			
Negus, — — —			
Rum and Brandy, —			
Fire, *Rush Lights* ~		1	3
Chaise, — — —			
Servants Eating } and Ale, } — —			
Horses Hay and Corn.			

£0 - 15 - 0

Drury, Printer, Lincoln.

Louth road obliging us to go slow, we did not reach Louth till one o'clock. The Blue Stone Inn, so call'd from a great stone at the street corner, gloom'd us exceedingly; before dinner, we walk'd to look at the beautiful steeple of Louth Church; and were, at our return, worn with expectance for our dinner, which, with the wine, proved truly wretched.

In touring the right mode is to chuse a dictator, one who should be obeyed; now the Coll and I go on well together, but neither of us command.—So one orders this— the other waits for that, and a delay'd, and bad dinner ensues: now when I am alone, I run into the kitchen, see what is going on, and likely to be ready; there is a leg of mutton roasting; and a veal pye did you say? Bring them in. So I dine quickly, cheaply, and at the moment of appetite.—

After dinner I drag'd forth the reluctant Colonel; (for we must move about as tourists;) and first to a stationer's, where little intelligence was to be had; then thro' this town, improving in buildings, and business, we waddled in quest of Louth Park-Abbey:—At last we work'd our way to where this abbey stood, of which only the following fragments remain, upon a hill in grazing grounds, with much raised ground and adjoining foundations which have been much scooped for the stone-work; at which they are now at work, and have peck'd up many fragments of pillars, pediments, bases &c; from these ruins, whereon we prowled for some time, we had a good rabbet hunt.

The high road of approach is well mark'd; and on one side runs a stream which fed all the ponds, and the mote of the abbey: at the end of this approach, we met a gentleman, who was very civil and communicative; and explain'd to us the cut, still call'd Monks-Dyke, which supply'd the abbey with water, and, probably, with provisions from Louth.—This gentleman, (whom we soon found to be a surgeon,)[58] accompanied us back to the town; and shew'd us the spring head;—in the way, remarking on the extraordinary breed of grey rabbets, one of which we had just hunted—(Pettener) Sr their skins are worth one shilling each. (B) I wonder then, that the breed is not encouraged in other counties! (P) I wish they were not in this; as the poor people are tempted to kill them; and so get themselves transported. (B) Why, Sir, you might say so of every other temptation; true virtue is an abstinence from our desires; a poacher, and every man, under ready acquirements, is easily tempted: the judges, then, are very proper as to their convictions in the several counties, according to the ease of the theft therein; as sheep stealers in sheep counties, wool in wool counties; therefore I see no reason for destroying rabbets, because they may induce to theft the profligate poor.—

Every town almost produces some crazy poet laureat; who chaunts the praises of the town and hails the return of noted seasons. At Leicester I met the best I ever remember to have seen.

HAPPY
LOUTH.

WRITTEN by RICHARD SALMON.   September 22nd 1786.

> Indulgent Heav'n, on this much favour'd town,
> Has kindly pour'd its richest blessings down;
> Good milk, good bread, and wholesome home-brew'd ale;
> Fine springs of water never known to fail;
> Our markets well supply'd with flesh and fish;
> Here's all that man can want, or heart can wish.
> And for a clear and healthful pleasant air,
> Few situations can with this compare:
> No fenny fogs their baleful influence spread,
> Such noxious vapours here we need not dread.
> These are great blessings, and we yet have more,
> The gospel's freely preach'd unto the poor:
> In such a plain, familiar manner given,
> That all may learn, and find the way to Heaven.
> Such boundless mercies may we duly prize,
> And not the bounties of our God despise.
> May peace and love in ev'ry house abound;
> In every breast may gratitude be found;
> May youth be taught the paths of vice to shun,

And age thro' faith their Christian courses run,
A bright example may this town appear,
It's fame resound thro' ev'ry village near;
May pure religion spread thro' every place,
Sinners repent, and all be sav'd by grace
Thro' faith in the Redeemer's precious blood:
We have no other advocate with God.
 For this my native place, Lord hear my prayer,
And make the people Thy peculiar care;
Bless them with faith and hope, and love and peace,
And let the number of Thy saints increase.
Great Shepherd, Saviour, Thy free grace display,
And guide Thy wand'ring flock in the right way;
The narrow way that leads to joys on high,
That all may be prepared, and fit to die.
Grant this, O Lord, I humbly Thee implore,
Then shall we praise Thy name for evermore.

Mr P[ettener] obliged us to see a fulling mill; he then drank tea with us; and then led us to view the clergyman's (Mr J[ollan]d's)[59] garden; which is almost cover'd with cloisters, seats, &c, all made of roots of trees, and moss, to correspond with an hermitage in the centre, finish'd with curious taste, and trouble: therein are several rooms, recesses, and chapels, all lighted by old stain'd, glass, (once in Tattershall Church;) the ornamental parts are of fir cones; the tables of polish'd horse bones; with many inscriptions around, and upon the ground, from the Scriptures. It is throughout a work of infinite labour, and highly curious; and so must the framer of it be, who was not at home; but his lady was, and she shew'd us her house.

The Coll thought the hermitage too diminutive, and the passages too low; he was right, for Mr J. need not have done so much. My plan was (and to be proposed to Mr J.,) to have his gardener, at grand shewings, properly attired as an hermit, and to be found in some of the recesses, at his studies. Mr P., our guide, said that Mr J. was overun by company 'That', I answer'd, 'might be, in part, prevented or turn'd into a good channel, by fixing up a poors box, and desiring the charity of visitors; then the town would

382

bless and could not deride his work'.—Our latter evening
was pass'd at a stationer's, where the Coll purchased maps;
and at a woolen draper's, Mr *Adam Eve*, where the Coll
bought a piece of the Lincolnshire stuff.[60] We supp'd,
hastily, at ten o'clock, and were in our beds, shabby
things, in shabby rooms, by eleven o'clock, mine, being
under an arch, with festoons curtains, the Coll named the
Tent of Darius. This is a mean, dirty, ill-managed inn; for
the master is dead, and no woman is competent of such a
charge.

A lay-in-bed morning; not up till past 8 o'clock. I had *Sunday*
forgotten to mention our having seen, yesterday evening, *July 10*
their assembly, and card rooms,[61] which are elegant. Our
good ciceroni, the Dr call'd again this morning, with fresh
offers of civility, and of placing us well in the church at
service time; which we meant to attend:—We press'd him
to dine with us, but he would not; *so* I press'd him stronger;
and told him he was the best Xtian we had met in our
pilgrims' progress.—

We were introduced at eleven o'clock, into a grand pew,
in a noble church, with a full, well-behaved, and well-
dress'd congregation; and there is an organ, and a singing
loft. When the minister appear'd, we were not a little surprised at the wildness of his eyes, his sallow skin, and black
flowing locks (altogether Otaheiteish). His reading was
vehement, and turgid, especially in the lessons, but when
he came to his sermon, where I expected declamation, he
sunk into softness, and was inaudible, and unimpressive.
The long service ended, (during which Coll B. sigh'd
piteously) we remark'd the pillars, and arches of the belfry;
and were then introduced to Mr J. the minister; a man
seemingly eaten up by pride, and particularity, with
attempts at every knowledge and art. We now, follow'd by
our two lacqueys, made a thorough survey of his hermitage; of which an accurate description would fill six pages;
wonderful is the art and labor, here bestow'd! Several more

apartments were open'd to us; our discourse upon, and admiration of the whole was abundant.

I advised Mr J[olland] to buy some stone loaves, and cheeses; and to keep a hedgehog therein to destroy vermin: and remarked how well it might shew by moonlight, or properly lighted. With this Mr J. seem'd to agree; and more, when I wonder'd that no country-people would endeavour to make such comfortable chairs, and tables, as he had form'd from sticks and pieces of wood: for every thing is in correspondent taste; even the ink stands are of curious roots.—'Here,' said I, to Mr J., 'an hermitage may be properly constructed; but in open gardens, or walks, they become haunts of impurity'. There are books in several apartments, and on the floors many inscriptions of praise, work'd in wood, pebbles, or horse-bones; but not one cross; probably he might fear to give offence. Most of the doors are composed of fir-cones, or of roots curiously woven together. It would be supposed an almost impossible task, for Mr J. and his assistant, (oddity,) to have put together such a work in a few years! He, Mr. J. appears to be composed of as many curious, and odd materials, as his hermitage. Our lacqueys were wonderfully surprised!

We bowed, and retired.—Our guide then animadverted upon the peculiarity of his minister's mind; saying 'that he had been a most unsettled man, who had try'd all occupations; and now only fix'd by this hermitage-employ; and that madame had much the better, and quieter capacity. At church there was a brief for the re-building of a church in Cheshire: briefs now cannot answer; for from this large congregation I saw no collection come, except from our *elegant* pew!

As we were now fasten'd to politeness and visiting, we could not but accept an invitation to tea, at Mr P.'s. We dined on the house preparation, rst beef, and batter pudding; and then were obliged to ride out with Mr P., against our better intentions: I rode the mare, who went tolerably; and I hope that (as *Mister Beard*, an old stupid groom of Mr Bertie used to say) '*I shall bring her to her proper affections*'.

We took a rough road to a gentleman's seat at 3 miles from this town, guided by Mr P[ettener] and for no other reason that I know but to be introduced to Mr Allington, the present occupier, to perplex him, and flurry some young ladies, who were at the windows. It is a dirty, ill-kept place, and with twining walks in some hedge rows, that made P. to compare it to the Leasowes; and to ask me if I had seen that place.—It is as much like the Leasowes, as the little play-house at Louth resembles the opera-house theatre. Our ride was hurried back by a shew of rain, and it mizzled during the evening; the hours of which we pass'd in a *genteel* tea-drinking at Mr P.'s; or in reading the London newspapers.—No players, unluckily for us, are here; but there are a 3 horse riding man in town, and also a fire worker[62] who will exhibit on Wednesday. This is the worst inn we have enter'd, quite a dirty tap-house; no attendance; all sluggards; and nothing eatable, or drinkable to be had.

The country about Louth is famous, and preserv'd for coursing: Mr Chaplin of Tathwell is the grand leader of this diversion, which brings in winter a society to this place; (lucky it is, that sports can, even yet, draw, or keep people from the metropolis;) and we heard of those, not unfamiliar to us, who were here *in the course* of last winter. —Mr P. spake of his pleasant, and useful sport, by having a greyhound companion with him, on his visits to the sick.

At nine o'clock we left Louth, and the miserable Blue-Stone Inn, the worst we have yet enter'd, with shatter'd casements, and bacon drying upon the stairs.

The steeple is a fine object; but the hermitage is, upon second thoughts, the business of vanity, and folly.

We soon came into the flat country, and for 5 miles upon a well-made turnpike road; after this by marshland

Monday July 11

to Saltfleetby; and there turn'd to the right to see where Theddlethorpe House lately stood, which was pull'd down 3 years ago by the Duke of Ancaster:[63] (for this tour is taken, as I said before, for the observation of Coll B., who must view every relict of family possessions,) some old walls, and yew trees, only remain; and this as a place of long, or winter residence, had been a very bad one, tho' for sea air, sea-sand riding, and sea-fish eating, an excellent station; being but some 100 yards from the sea shore; therefore *some people* might have liked to have kept up a good room or two for a summer's month. Just beyond it, is the house of Mr Marshall, and the church which we enter'd; but no Bertie monuments! Which surprised the Coll who had heard of their existence.—But at going out, the clerk said 'there is another Theddlethorpe; this is E. T.—but in the marsh is W. T.' 'Why then we must ride there, and you, my friend, must go for that key'.— Here the civil farmer came out to us; and put up our horses in his stables, wherein we had a *fine* rat hunt.—We now were right, for in this church is an handsome monument of black marble, with busts of white marble of Charles Bertie (son of an Earl of Lindsey,) and of his wife.

It is a pretty, neat church; with a very old font, worthy of my trouble. We now took to the sea sands, the widest I ever rode upon; and these we continued for 2 miles, with a north wind full against us, impregnating our lungs with the healthful saline air, till we arrived at Saltfleet.—This is a poor place, under the sea bank, with a wretched inn-bathing-house; where we had—Ah! such a dinner! With such cheese!

Two Gentlemens Dinners	-		-	-	0	2	0
Borton Ale	-	-	-	-	-	0	6
Porter	-	-	-	-	-	0	3
Wine	-	-	-	-	-	2	4
					£0	5	1

386

Nothing but the sea view to support us. Only one gentleman there, Dr C—k of Louth; what can a man do here alone,
without a female helpmate?—We, now, enquired our forward road; and got little intelligence except that the distance
was 18 miles: Coll B. would engage the ostler, (a sailor,) as
his guide; and for that purpose, to ride his mare. I push'd
forward for some miles, on a very easy road to find; when
the curricle came up, and I prevail'd upon the Coll to discharge the guide. Then we proceeded together, in the curricle, thro' the villages of Marsh-Chapel, Tetney and Hum-
berstone, for about 10 miles, against a stormy nth wind:

(C) Oh, how this gloom, and cold weather suit me.
(B) Surely it is too cold, and dreary? (C) Better these than
heat, and sunshine: if it had been hot weather I could not
have continued this tour; but should have given up: you
like hot weather! (B) I do like sun, and summer; everything appears gay and happy; nature comes forth with
renovated charms, and *we* grow young again: November
of year, and life, comes too soon, when we languish for
ease, candles, and cards. The sun may relax our frames,
but he exhilerates our hearts.

We, now, came upon the sea coast, opposite the Humber's mouth, and then near, or upon the sands, to Clea- Cleethorps
thorps Inn, a bathing place of a better complexion than
the 2 others we have seen upon this coast; for here are
large dining room, and a card room. But why come we
here? A place to be avoided by tourists, as in no place are
you so much neglected! There to lodge in a cock-loft!
The company shirk you; and conversation were thrown
away. We desired privacy, and procured a dirty little
parlour, with a fire, for it was dismally cold; our room was
fill'd with smoke; at last we did get some tolerable victuals
to eat, and we sat muddling over the fire. I never, by
choice, stop at public places; I may never tour again; and
if I do can I go alone! If in company must I be dictator?
Must I have absolute rule? And have from my comrade an
agreement properly sign'd and stamp'd? At ten o'clock,

my letters (that I sent for) arrived from Grimsby; but they were so numerous, and some so full of worries, that I could only read them over by 12 o'clock. The following—of good presage I hope, chear'd my mind.[64]

My dear father

I hope
I am be-come a
good boy & I hope
Biddy and me will
be come a comfort
to you and my
mother I am
very well Adieu

I remain
your aff.d Son
federick Byng

May peace and glory await his steps;
May health and prosperity crown his hopes;
May he never know want nor feel sorrow:
May his continued duty to his parents, be rewarded by length
Of days, and in the comfort of his own progeny;
And may I with heartfelt reason, wish him to close mine eyes, and to
      receive my latest benediction.

It was a rainy, cold evening, with a cutting nth wind; and I dreaded bad weather here, more than at any place; at a quiet inn, a wet day may be endured; for it freshens our horses; forwards a wash, and gets your coat mended.

These places want a good garden, and a bowling green; here they have no ground of such description!

Such a mixture of odd, unruly company would quite undo my nerves and spirits, where one black sheep perplexes an whole flock.

I was in my truckle bed at 12 o'clock.

I look'd at the weather, at 4, and at 6 o'clock, when it _Tuesday_ was very black, and lowering: however, at 7 o'clock, when _July 12_ I arose, the day mended.

Our breakfast was hast'ned as much as possible, and we felt happy to get away: tho' from the best of the Lincolnshire bathing shops; where the people were civil, and the bill reasonable.

CLEATHORPS. July 12. 1791.

						s.	d.
To Suppers	-	-	-	-	-	3	0
Breakfast	-	-	-	-	-	1	8
Wine	-	-	-	-	-	2	6
Brandy	-	-	-	-	-	1	3
Ale & Beer	-	-	-	-	-	0	6
						8	11
Tea	-	-	-	-	-	1	8
						10	7

Over 3 miles of boggy turf we rode to Grimsby, where _Grimsby_ in religious times stood a priory, and a nunnery, now a wretched borough, existing only by venality; and with such an alehouse as could not have been slept in.—The church and clerk are both very old; the former green with damp and disgraced by dirt; arches, and an arcaded gallery of communication around the body, chancel, and side ailes, mark its antiquity, and former splendour.—The clerk made us observe a very ancient recumbent figure, which he said 'was of one Grime, who *found out* this habitation'.—A rocky road, (here call'd a ramping road,) of a turnpike turn, led to Laceby, a pretty village, then thro' a variety of cross lanes, (leaving Riby village to our left,) wherein much trouble of driving was required, because our cattle are blundering upon bearing reins, (things not to be endured one moment); in a curricle every bump may overset you, it is a carriage of incessant care; whereas in my old Italian chair, the horse chose his way, I loll'd in the corner, observ'd the country, and had my chat; now in the curricle it is an eternal looking to helm, & sail.—At early noon, we came to Gt Limbe, near to which Mr P[elha]m[65] in his grounds is erecting a mausoleum, (a little Ratcliffe library) of which Mr W[yat]t, the famous architect gives the plan, and directs the execution.—Below it, for the sake of contrast, and miserable comparison stands, (for the reception of the living,) an alehouse so bad, as not even to afford cheese!

(When I possess domains, old, foolish, happy thought, those who live under by protection shall taste happiness, ere the dead shall lodge in grand repertories.) We did get a slice of baked beef, not to be eaten, (beer and bread as bad,) and a glass of brandy and water.—We, then, walk'd up to this, not yet finish'd, mausoleum, a fine effort of Mr W.'s genius! And a fine sum it will cost! A lumbring Grecian building, whose lower story is to be the deposit for the dead; and the upper circular hall will be fill'd with monuments.—Ld O[ngle]y's[66] at Warden (before mention'd,) is worth 20 of this, and did not cost a 20th part of the money: this is adorn'd with festoons of flowers, and there are stone baskets at the top: I never saw a heavier clump!—and the expence will be as heavy as the clump. Formerly we buried our dead in a chancel of a church, or in the adjoining chapels; but our new taste is to bring them into our shrubbery walks; which must be very *diverting* and *reviving* to the family, and their visitors! About this grand folly, there are great plantations making without either knowledge, or taste; and with such wide drives as are horridly staring, and disagreeable: these adjoin to Brocklesby-Park; where many more great plans are to be perfected. After a short walk (for the Coll hates walking) we return'd to our inn; and chaise. By a drive of 3 miles to Kernington, Crocton, and leaving Wooton to our right, at last we came to Thornton village; whence in a mile, and a half we arrived at Thornton-College. Thornton College

This is the grand front of approach; exhibiting the finest remains of ancient taste:—nothing here in the Cupolaish, Panthcontic, Wyat-tish[67] manner; but nobly Gothick.—We did not climb to the battlements; but the Coll's servant did, and by a good stair case.—The back front has not the richness of the fore front. At the end of the meadow are the beautiful ruins of a chapel, with some of the nicest arches, carvings, sutterances, and all that observation which delights an antiquary.—Near to this chapel must have stood (I believe) the building of habitation; upon the scite of which is a farm house, with several arched rooms, and gothic windows. All the walls of enclosure are forms of carved stones:—some ash trees have been lately unadvisedly fell'd. This place has been lately sold by Sr Rd Sutton: but neither he did, nor will his successor preserve these glorious relicts.

> Having waste ground enough to build upon;
> Why must we raze the sanctuary walks,
> And plant our mischief there?

At going away we met the farmer, who told us a long story of King Henry the eight having been receiv'd, and grandly treated by the monks here. (I love old tradition) That he remember'd when all the statues remain'd in their niches; of which, now, only the three centre are standing, viz, the Virgin—St John—and . . . . . . That the others were knock'd down, by the boys, by great stones from the top; as was a stone lion over the front gateway.—I never saw any monastic remains, grander than these; and I suppose then to be of the highest rank existing.—The farmer gave us good direction for our route: three miles to the village of Barrow, having a fine view to our right of the River Humber—of the opposite Yorkshire coast, and the town of Hull; a grand, and pleasing prospect; and in two more miles to Barton; where we expected a goodish inn; but the best appear'd dismal, and casemented! However here we must sleep.—Tea drank, and orders given for supper, we walk'd thro' the town, which is mean, and dirty; and to the river side, where the passage-boats lye: here is an inn, wherein, I think, we might have fared better than at our inn, the George at Barton.—After some inspection of the pleasant-looking Yorkshire coast, we return'd, and rather, hastily, as some rain began to fall; so we shut ourselves up, eat our mutton chops and of a great coarse holybut: then quickly to our rooms.—

Barton-on-Humber

Wednesday July 13

The Colonel is not so well form'd for a traveller as I am; he moves in state; trunks laden with dressing apparatus, with snuff, with books, from Shakespeare down to a Court calendar! He is violently offended by all smells; 'Don't you smell the tobacco?'—'Yes, a little'. 'I could not sleep last night from the smell of the feathers! Could you?' 'Yeas, a little'.—During his *hours* of dressing, and of conversation with his valet, they compare notes and join complaints; and then the Col comes down to me (his unpitying friend,) saying, 'Why my servant says he was bit by bugs last night'!—'Was he so? Aye, they will bite in inns'!!

2 Teas -	-	-	-	-	-	0	1	4
2 Suppers	-	-	-	-	-	0	3	0
2 Breakfasts	-	-	-	-	-	0	1	4
Wine -	-	-	-	-	-	0	2	3
Brandy -	-	-	-	-	-	0	1	6
Ale	-	-	-	-	-	0	0	6
					£0	9	11	

Up at 7; Coll at 8. My mare gets thin, cuts behind, and has a warbled back;[68] so she must, now, go on a foot's pace only.

Here are two churches, not 50 yards asunder, both of great antiquity; that to the west is of the handsomest form, and has an elegant border of stone-work, below the battlements: in the eastern church-yard I took down this epitaph.

MARY PICKERING.

Farewell my husband, and children adue
What in my power was I've done for you
Mourn not for me, since it is vain
I hope in Christ, we all shall meet again.

Most glad to part from Barton, which is a nasty, gloomy place, but where we had hoped to have found a tolerable shop.—We rode forward over an hilly, bleak country, good for hare-hunting, tho' lately enclosed: the Col's mare walks so fast that I am obliged to overtake him often by a good trot.—To Elsom village, situated under the hill, pleasantly, and shadily; we descended the hill thro' a grove of firs, leading into an open country, with marshes, to the right, which brought us to Glanford-Bridge, call'd Brigg; a small, neatish, market town, form'd by a conflux Brigg of roads; here is a navigable river—but only a chapel of ease.

During our dinner stay, we discoursed about future tourings, and 'if it were worth while ever to go further than the small round where we are known, and can be civilly treated; as at Biggleswade, Wansford Bridge, Oxford, Woodstock, or Chapel-House'. 'I must finish', said the Coll, 'with Nth Wales'. 'Well', answer'd I, 'when I shall have recover'd this tour; perhaps in 2 or 3 years, I will be your guide; the inns, there, are not so bad as those we have lately inhabited;[69] and then so much to see, cataracts, castles, cascades, and mountains! Trout, and salmon to eat; but should we ever go together again, let us detach

393

our lacqueys, and horses to the verge of observation, there whisk down in the mail-coach; and the tour finish'd, jump into another, and return to London'.

In this town and county a barbarity is practised, disgraceful to Hottentots, for the pointers and other hunting dogs, have, during the summer, a large ring forced thro' one of their fore feet, which obliges the animal to hop about in the greatest misery.—'I remark'd the difference, betwixt good, and bad inns, or well, and ill-managed gentlemen's houses, was, in one instance, the laying the cloth for meals at an early hour, viz the preparing the supper room as soon as can be, after the dinner things are gone; whereas at a common inn, or at a shabby mansion, they never will make a forward arrangement, and so you wait, without end, for the commonest conveniences.'

Our two lacqueys seem to agree wonderfully: the Col's *gentleman* (Mr *Napes*) entirely governs mine, (Mr *Tongs*, from his fine horsemanship) who looks up to him as a complete genius: they walk out together in the evening; and sometimes play quoits: Mr. *N: perfectly* understands the management of horses; throws in a rugg, throws off a rugg; and *Mr T:* imitates him as much as possible.—A goodish dinner (good wine is almost, impossible) in a clean parlour, with civil attendance: after our bad inns, and rooms, and meals, this inn appear'd a charming situation. —Off again; our servants gone forward; puddle along to Hibey-Stow, then to Redburn; where Miss C[arter][70] has shewn much ill taste about her *approach* and *lodges*; her *plantations in front*, are likewise shabby, consisting, chiefly, of Scotch firs; but as these *make a shew*, and *shoot up quickly*, they *may* please the lady. From Redburn, we travell'd upon the old Roman road; nothing to observe, except Mr H[arrison]n's ugly lodges,[71] till we came to the few poor cottages at Spital, and to our inn there, a retired spot, such as we wanted after our shut-ups, at the late several stops: nothing equal to a single house, (if to be found). Tho' the

Spital

394

THOMAS PARKINSON

BRIGG

	£	s	d
Breakfast			
Dinners	3		·
Tea & Coffee			
Suppers			·
Wine	2	4	
Punch — Brandy			3
Negus — Hollts			6
Cyder			
Malt Liquor			4
Servants Eating & Ale			
Horses Hay & Corn			10
Fire in Lodging Room			
Chaises			

0 ... 5 ... 3

greater part of this inn is old, and shatter'd, yet there are some additional parlours, and bed rooms, with tolerable stabling.—Opposite to our inn are two chapel-like old buildings, and some tumble-down alms-houses; whence crawled forth an aged man, who shew'd to me this chapel, wherein service is perform'd once a month.

We enquired at Brigg, (as we do every where) for any place to be seen, and allways get the same answer, 'That they don't know of nothing'.—Now,—close to this inn, there is the seat of Mr. H[arrison]; into his grounds we walk'd, and were most agreeably surprised at viewing an exceedingly pretty place;—nay, more,—one of the finest sheets of water, with surrounding plantations well arranged, tho' composed of mean, and improper trees.—The house commands both near and distant gay views.—So much for praise; but the place is not kept in order; the plantations near the house are of larches, or pitiful trees, shewing an ignorance of planting, for Lombardy poplars are stuck upon hills, and beeches upon bogs.—One of my favorite trees, now much lost, and disused, would highly suit this lime-stone country, viz the sycamore; and where is an handsomer tree to be seen?—We admired Mr H.'s place the more, as being of our own discovery; remarking, 'Why not tell us of it, at the inn?' And say, 'Gentlemen, there is a pleasant walk for you to take, and a very pretty place to see'. The evening became quite cold! So I proposed the introduction of the hot kitchen poker (July 13th) into our laid fire; and with excellent effect!—Supper was good, and well serv'd; the best we have had, as was likewise our Oporto, of which we finish'd the bottle.

Talking over Mr H.'s place; our next intentions; and the past days; soon introduced eleven o'clock:—a late hour for us!

Thursday
July 14

This is the anniversary of the French Revolution.[72] I hope if there are fools in London who think of inflaming their

396

country, that they may be made to repent such folly.——
There is a stage-coach just set up to run from this place to
Retford in Nottinghamshire, 20 miles, joining these 2
great roads; which coach seems not likely to succeed, tho'
upon it is written *I labour for your convenience.* Garwood
goes slowly to Lincoln; whilst the Coll's valet drives the
chaise to Ganesborough: our ride was for 2 miles and an
half upon the high-road to Fillingham Castle, Sr C[eci]l
W[ra]y's,[73] a large wide space of ground, *violently* planted
with Scotch firs, and there is a long fir avenue to the house;
in short the firs have (like their countrymen) overun the
domain, and Sr C. seemingly disdains to try other trees;
altho' the sycamore and the beech would thrive here wonderfully.——The soil, look of the house, must form a
resemblance to a great Scottish seat, with their plantations,
called *Policies.*[74]——

SPITAL.

Tea	-	-	-	-	-	1	6
Suppers	-	-	-	-	-	4	0
Wine	-	-	-	-	-	2	6
Beer	-	-	-	-	-	0	3
Brandy	-	-	-	-	-	1	3
Breakfast	-	-	-	-	-	1	6
Fire	-	-	-	-	-	1	0
Rushlight	-	-	-	-	-	0	4
						12	4

Probably he may have imbibed his fir-taste from some
Scotch friends, and relations.——For when the Col call'd at
the house and left his name (which as a *Lincolnshire man,*
he allways does) we heard that Sr Cecil was in Scotland.——
The house is a poor, inconvenient thing, an attempt at
something castellated, with narrow windows, and corner
towers. The view to the west is not disagreeable, over some
enlarged water in the valley, to the village of Fillingham,
and to the Trent vale.——This place and the upper country

397

must be fine for coursing.—Keeping the hill, we had extensive views, and a good look to Glentworth House and Church; to which place we descended: here is a fine old mansion, now going quickly to decay.—The late Ld S[carborough]⁷⁵ with *special* taste, and folly of expence, added a new, flaring, red brick, back front, which gives the strangest look of age, and youth united!—The old part has been turreted, inner-courted, &c.—and might have been restored to strength, and comforts, for half the expence, laid out upon the unnatural junction. All now, is neglected; the furniture sold; and there is only a steward for its inhabitant! Part of the church seems to be a new building. Returning up the hill, we soon came into the turnpike road from Spital; Harpswell Church lays warm, and surrounded (*a l'Angloise*) with good hedge row elms. When in the bottom, a dull flat country to Gt Corringham, and then by Thonock woods, (Thonock pastures they will be soon, for they are stocking up the woods—viz, killing the goose with the golden eggs; but hearing they had been purchased by a land-surveyor, I wonder'd not at the mischief, as these gentry only look to the immediate produce:) and down a hill into Gainsborough, a busy town of much inland trade.

Gains-
borough

The Blackamoor's Head in the market place is a mean dirty inn; and to the stables there is no way but thro' a stone entry: a better inn, now that the new stone bridge over the Trent is built, must be open'd; formerly, the ferry drove people away.—The landlord was very civil.—No letters for me from London!—Before dinner we took a long hot walk thro' the town; passing some time in and about a very ancient building, (in one corner of which there is a play house with all the necessary green rooms, &c, &c) then to view the new bridge over the Trent,⁷⁶ which must be advantageous to the town. This broiling tedious walk might have been avoided by an enquiry into our evening way.—At our dinner there was no fish. I remark'd to our landlord, 'Why I thought that the salmon leaped out of the Trent into your market place'.——

Din^r	-	-	-	-	-	3 :	
Wine	-	-	-	-	-	2 :	6
Malt Liq^r	-	-	-	-			6
						6 :	

In the evening—very warm—we curricled at a slow pace thro' deep sandy roads to Lea village, and to Knaith, where I stopp'd at Mr D[alton's][77] gate; having promised—after his pressures, not to pass his doors. *Unluckily*, he was from home. I sent for Col B. to come in.

The house is in great *rurality* of taste, with windows to the floors, which are all stucco'd; a small conservatory, forming one side of a study, is enter'd from the dining room: every thing savors of oddity, and meant particularity.

In the front of the house stands the little old church; below which the River Trent flows in beautiful curve, affording a constant scenery of traffic. Take it as a place of soil, and of oddity, it is to be admir'd; tho' I should fear it must be cold in winter, being too much upon the greenhouse cut: however, I think I could live very happily in it. It makes a pleasing variety with our other *videnda*; especially those of this day; and must be a capital spot for fishing.

On the hill near it, very ill-chosen ground—is a nasty place of Mr Hutton's. Two more miles, and to Torksey; where we got out of our chaise to survey the old ruins of Torksey-House, upon the brink of the Trent; and these I think are well described—even at this later day, in the print.——

Happy survey of grand wretchedness, after the smart little green house. The road here gets lighter; and soon brought us upon the side of the canal leading to Lincoln. We stopp'd for 10 minutes at a clean looking public house,

399

call'd Daventers-Nook, where we water'd our cattle, and drank *some liquor*. Before we reach'd the next village of Pwynne the evening became cold, and dusky; so the Coll proposed riding, which we did, for the 4 next miles, into

the city of Lincoln: my second visit. The Rein Deer is a good inn; we had a comfortable supper with tolerable wine; and enjoyed ourselves till midnight!!—

After *mature* consideration, it was determin'd that we should lounge this day here, or hereabout: and to survey a cathedral, and hear the service therein, by me so much commended. A complete dressing; things sent to wash; then good hot rolls at breakfast: at $\frac{1}{2}$ past 9 o'clock, crawl'd up to the cathedral, and walk'd the great aile till the service was beginning, a time well bestow'd; this was a decent, and honourable performance, but, unluckily for us, no anthem, as that is perform'd on Wednesdays, and Fridays, at evening service. How few people attend! Any attendance will soon cease: and I shall live to see when none will be present at a cathedral service, but a reader, a verger, and 2 singing boys; who will gallop it over in a few minutes.

We, next, made the round of the castle hill; and look'd into the (*fine*) new jail; what ornaments to a country!What succession houses to Botany Bay!! What with this trail-about, and walking 20 times up the market and asking the price of salmon, (which is 8d. pr lb,) the dinner soon came on, when we fared upon beans, and bacon, and roasted rabbets.—After dinner, the Coll proposed to visit Norton House, late the seat of Ld Vere Bertie,[78] and since of the Hobarts. I rode the mare; who rather improves in her paces; but she now requires some rest; up Cannock Hill, and thro' new enclosures, to Braunston, thence in 3 miles to Norton, where are a good parsonage house, and an old family seat of the Berties; (Berties enough formerly, and estates in plenty in this county); Ld V. B. was the last Bertie possessor of this estate, now gone with his daughter,[79]

(SO WELL KNOWN) to Mr H[obar]t.—This is a good old (deserted) hall—with its timber fell'd, and its avenues rooted up; there is a large painted stair-case, with several good rooms, and a chapel; also a play house fitted up by Mrs H[obart].—Another generation may settle here, if the house holds out; which none can long do without fires, and inhabitants.—There is a picture of Miss B[ertie] when young, beautiful, well shaped, and, (seemingly) un-affected: how alter'd now!!! We stay'd here too long; but the Coll never tires of family.—They mistook our road of return, and got down to Hanworth village, and so back to Braunston, when we enter'd the church, to view the monu-ment of Ld Vere Bertie, erected by his disconsolate widow. But none will add a line for her!!

The moon shone brightly and lighted us home to a well dress'd supper of tripe, and lamb's fry. This is a good inn, with quick, civil attendance.

My horses being sent forward; we mount the curricle (which I allways drive) and took the heath road; which we were surprised to find so jolting, and disused, tho' good for riding: the village road to the right, had been better, and pleasanter; than

> Where miles immeasurably spread
> —Seem length'ning as we go.

Not one house: not one stop for horses to water at; all *Saturday* newly enclosed heath; villages, in a row, to the right.— *July 16*

Quite tired of driving, for the horses go heavily, and the chaise follows dangerously. See Temple-Bruer to the left, to which I urged the Col to ride, whilst I walk'd forward in the chaise; till at the end of 2 miles, I was overtaken by him, when I was surveying the Roman-road, which runs here, for some distance, in the highest preservation. Arrived, after a drag of 20 miles, at the poor village of Ancaster; (whence the duke's title; and so we came!) and *Ancaster* there expected to have found a tolerable, huntable inn, and an alehouse; where, however, we got some good chops, and were quiet.

REIN DEER. LINCOLN.

Suppers	-	-	-	-	-	3	0
Wine	-	-	-	-	-	2	6
Brandy	-	-	-	-	-	1	0
Malt Liquor	-	-	-	-	-	0	6
Breakfasts	-	-	-	-	-	1	8
Dinners	-	-	-	-	-	3	0
Wine	-	-	-	-	-	2	6
Sherry	-	-	-	-	-	1	9
Malt Liquor	-	-	-	-	-	0	6
Suppers	-	-	-	-	-	3	0
Wine	-	-	-	-	-	2	6
Malt Liquor	-	-	-	-			6
Breakfasts	-	-	-	-		1	8
Soldiers Wine	-	-	-	-		2	6
Eating & Ale	-	-	-	-		2	6

£1 9 1

This is surely, for a pompous inn, in a great town, a very cheap charge.

I walk'd, as usual, about the churchyard, remark'd therein a very lofty old stone; and took down this inscription.

Thomas Abbot. 1781. Aged 14 years.

Here lies a blossom in this clay,
    Who labour'd to surpass
The greatest students of his age,
    Which *soon* he brought to pass:
The sciences most gay, and bright,
    The gospel light also,
Was his delight for to defend
    Against man's greatest foe.

Glad to hasten away (chaise again) from this poor inn, and miserable country: pass by Sr J. T[horold]'s[80] park, whose house is stuck in the clouds—and whose park is scurvily planted.

RED LION INN. ANCASTER.

							s.	d.
Wine	-	-	-	-	-	-	2	4
Negus	-	-	-	-	-	-		
Liquor	-	-	-	-	-	-		
Ale and Porter		-	-	-	-	-	o	6
Eating	-	-	-	-	-	-	2	o
Tea	-	-	-	-	-	-		
Coffee	-	-	-	-	-	-		
Tobacco		-	-	-	-	-		
Servants Eating & Liquor					-	-		
Horses Hay and Corn			-		-	-		

£0 4 10

We now descended, a short, but very steep hill, commanding a fine view of Grantham Vale, to Belton Park,[81] (Ld B[rownlow]'s) cruelly cut in two by the road; a tasteless spot, devoid of grandeur, of quiet, or of comfort!

The Coll heard my *remarks*, but answer'd not, as not liking to give up Lincolnshire to my notions.

The print of the house must prove what that must be! And for the water works (now destroy'd) I repine; as they must have been curiously imagin'd: and I am rather of opinion that fountains and fanciful waterworks are too much discouraged.—

(C) I must turn my head aside, here, fearful that Ld B[rownlow] should see me! (B) And what then? (C) Why, then, he might press me to come in; and being in *the duke's* neighbourhood, and *being a Lincolnshire man*, I should be puzzled to refuse him. (B) Are you not going with me to Grantham? And you know but little of Ld B—!—Now I refused Mr D:[82] who visits at my house; and should have refused him, had we met him at home.—I smile at all these formal, unintended invitations.—(Conversation dropt.)

A stoney, nasty road till out of the park.—Grantham

2C2　　　　　403

spire would appear wonderfully, if we had not lately seen that of Louth, so much more beautiful. The Angel Inn at Grantham Grantham bears a most venerable front, with an angel, cround, in stone, on the top. We occupied a very old room: but there are large ranges of buildings, and of stabling behind.

Our evening strole was around the newly-built cross in the market-place; to survey the George, a great, staring, new inn; and as the emptier, had been the, better for us: and to lounge about Mr M.'s sad house, and grounds. My letters, now, receiv'd in abundance, took up much time in reading, and answering, till our supper came; which, with the wine, were very tolerable: but there was no shews, nor soldiers to beguile the evening (our only lack I remember).

(C) You spake of being here formerly, and at Stamford, with C.[83] and S.; surely you had then an odd set of acquaintances! and I allways wonder'd at your leagueing with them!! (B) Never wonder at such things; wonders will never cease: I may wonder at myself *then*; at myself *now*; —one must live in society, and people are not easily discovered; I *now* get tired of most people: in youth we are easily satisfied. I might remark that I wonder at most of your intimacies; but something suits; flattery, or obligation bind us all. Few exist but knaves or fools! (C) But those were not people of your turn! (B) I had no turn, them; we were thrown together; discrimination, and commentation were not in my mind. (C) You chose better afterwards? (B) Perhaps I did.—As old acquaintance drop off, new ones start up; but no hearty communication:—it is the ease of old fellowship that brings us together now; and makes me not afraid of dashing an opinion; or of divulging a feeling to you; but this is not to be done to old age, or youth: neither do I now dare to comment upon you, but up to a certain mark; you sometimes hear me, and won't alter;—I listen to you, and cannot change.

Suppose at SALTHILL.		s.	d.	Our Bill at ANGEL. GRANTHAM.		s.	d.
Tea - - -		2	o	Tea - - -		1	6
Duck, and dressing -		4	o	Suppers - -	3		
Peas, and Butter -		1	6	Malt Liquor - -			3
Tarts - - -		1	o	Wine—Port - -		2	6
Beer, & Cheese - -		1	o	„ —Shiny - -		1	9
Cold Meat, & Pickles -		2		Brandy - - -		1	
Paper - - -			4	Tea - - -		1	6
Rushlights - -			6	Rushlights - -			4
Wine - - -		5		Wr: Paper - -			2
Brandy - - -		1	6				
Breakfast - -		2		£ 12			
£1		10					

We went, before breakfast, to see old Draper in the *Sunday* stable. Old Draper has been run for 3 years, successively, *July 17* as a post horse; and every year, having been put into training, has won a fifty-pound plate at these races: nor have these performances touch'd his master's heart with compassion; or with curiosity, to try his speed, or further. excellence!—So,—having been a wonder for one day of the year, he sinks into a slave for the remainder;—and blends the high-mettled racer, and the post horse in one animal!!

A very warm morning; as the last two days have been. —A tedious crawl in the curricle, again, upon the hard, chalky, hilly road, tho' pleasant; Ponton steeple is well built, and the vale to Easton, where stands Mr Chumley's house, is agreeably pastoral; heat, and dust obliged us to refresh ourselves, and water our horses at Colsterworth; where a new landlord is soon expected.* The hot weather

*ANGEL INN.

COLSTERWORTH. LINCOLNSHIRE.

Mr. DAVIS, of the Queen's Arms, St. James's Street, *London*, has purchased the above INN, and fully intends entering on the fame, and con-

Greetham made us glad to reach the Royal-Oak Inn, at Greetham; a nice situation, being a single house surrounded by woods. A roasted shoulder of veal was just ready; but when ready, what a monster! 'Prick me down bull calf'. Cold ham as nasty; so in despair eat potatoes; till at last we were recover'd by a tolerable pigeon-pye, which we eat up. We chaised it again in the evening; but soon a storm threaten'd to meet us; (I am very handy, from my feelings, and fears, as to their approach;)—passing thro' Brig-Casterton, a pretty village, and mounting the hill above it, we spread all our canvas, and successfully, as to reach

Stamford Stamford, (just as the storm fell,) and shelter in the gateway of the George Inn; when finding the storm to continue, we order'd beds, and supper, at this nasty, hot, town inn; so unlike the coolness, and cleaniness of Wansford-Bridge, to which we intended: not to the dislike of the Coll, I believe, as being nearer to his point. It was a sowser of rain, with heavy thunder; which added to some tea, wofully shook my nerves.

ROYAL OAK. GREETHAM.

Dinners	-	-	-	-	-	4	0
Malt Liq:	-	-	-	-	-		8
Wine -	-	-	-	-	-	2	6
						£0 7	2

The grand walk of this town, and none more pleasant, is to Burleigh-Park; this we try'd, upon the clearing up of the weather; I, soon return'd from the heat, but the Coll continued to B[urleigh] House to make his enquiries after the

tinuing the Business in that extensive Line for which the Angel Inn has been so many Years distinguished.

Mr. TINKLER, who has declined Business, most respectfully begs Leave to recommend Mr. DAVIS to a continuance of the Patronage and Support of his Friends.

June 1791.

(Newcomb and Peat, Printers, Stamford.)

Earl of E[xeter]—heat excessive!—The players perform to-morrow.—The Coll talking to the people about *the duke*, and of his using their house, is of little avail to us; (on the contrary) as the duke is a miser.

Our supper was of more than ordinary shew, as *we* must make a figure, here.—I felt sleepy; and tired; tho' of *what* can I be? We were put, after some rudeness, into large beds, with festoon'd curtains; which never shut close, being for shew, and not of comfort.—

GEORGE. STAMFORD.

Boiled Tench, &c. -	-	-	-	3	0
Roast Chicken &c. -	-	-	-	2	6
Potatoes &c. -	-	-	-	1	0
Bread -	-	-	-	-	0	2
Cheese -	-	-	-	-	0	2
Brandy -	-	-	-	-	1	0
Port -	-	-	-	-	2	6
Sherry -	-	-	-	-	1	9
Breakfasts -	-	-	-	-	1	6
				13	7
Paper -	-	-	-	-		2
				£ 13	9

In Lincolnshire, a very large county, there is little for curiosity; but few gentlemen's seats, and the sea-coast is flat, and unpleasant. *Monday July 18*

The two grand features of the county, are the cathedral, and Thurnton-College (Crowland I have view'd before). —Being of little travell, the inns are bad. The fens, once a scene of wretchedness, are now the gayest part, and the best inhabited. In general, the county is of a very sombre cast; the pleasantest parts are about Gainsborough, Spilsby, and towards Clacton, and Bulingbroke.

The march of the allies has continued one fortnight; and we have done enough: I have observed upon most of the county; and the Coll has seen all the family ruins,

407

monuments, &c, &c,—we now divided the 3 last shillings of the stock-purse: parting is allways a melancholy time. So much of time, and of money gone! Thus ended the conjunct Lincolnshire tour.

G[arwood] was sent forward upon his reloaded mare; whilst I, '*all by myself alone*', turn'd to the left under B[urleigh] Park wall, and, passing a pleasant common, soon came to Walcot-Grounds, (a pleasant hunting seat); and soon found in these grounds the object of my search— viz, a column of memory; (that *must confer honor* on the *planner*!!) there are those who have erected pillars to the memory of great events, and of great men; but this *honourable* erection is to the praise of that *most valuable animal*, call'd a fox hound! To the memory of *Dolphin*, are written many verses equal to the design: in the second line, *attend ye hoaxers* almost knock'd me up; his nose, and his avoiding to hunt vermin are *finely* described. This column is placed amidst old lime-stone pits; which, if planted, and trick'd up, would be a pretty spot, command-ing a pleasant view of Ufford Church, and House.

This nook of Northamptonshire is gayly wooded, and villaged: this round did not throw me 2 miles out of my way, and the ride was so chearful, (so unlike the many in Lincolnshire) that I came in quite happy to that excellent house, the Haycock, Wansford-Bridge; where I am at home; and Mrs N[orton] met me with 'Pray Sr, walk into your *own* room'. All so neat, and comfortable; with pens, paper, and wafers in my *own* room. The waiter said 'Sr rst beef, potatoes, and fresh tarts will be ready at ½ past one o'clock'.—I shall often return here, I hope, for where can I find a better inn; see a better bridge; or catch more fish?— The mail coach arrives regularly at 7-o'clock every morn-ing; northwards; and at 5 every evening; southwards.— Two theatres within 5 miles: that's extraordinary!—How lucky we have been in the weather! What if I had met bad weather, when alone? And what if we had encounter'd bad weather? March, march, was our word; we talk'd little;

Wansford Bridge

408

and confinement had render'd us peevish.—Yesterday was (*consumedly*) hot, (but *I* can bear heat,); the evening storm did some good, but not enough: this day has been a sweater; tho' gloomy; I foresaw that more storms must arrive. Before my dinner appear'd, a storm was brewing; so I sat quietly, except when I murmur'd, 'Where is your nt cap, Byng? I thought you allways carried that in your pocket"?

The storm was very severe; for $\frac{1}{2}$ an hour it deluged the ground; but this was not enough to cool the air. At 3 o'clock I quitted Wansford-Bridge with regret; and rode in terror of storms, sometimes slow near a stop-house, and then vehemently forward; saunter'd at Kates-Cabin, again at Stilton, when it look'd very black, so I hasten'd on to a new public house, (the Crown, Woolsack) 2 miles further; this house is starting up, as Alconbury Hill, and many others did, and may in time be a good inn! The more inns upon the road the better, for they encourage cheapness, and civility; and this house lays very handily for a fishing scheme upon Whittlesea-Mere: but I was not happy in sitting upon a cold brick floor, after a warm ride, tho' I counteracted with 6 pennyworth of brandy, and water.—Tho' it rains ever so hard, I shall soon be at Alconbury Hill; then, and at the other stops, weather is of no concern.

HAYCOCK INN. WANSFORD.

Dinners	-	-	-	-	-	1	6
Wine	-	-	-	-	-	1	3
						2	9

An intermission of storm push'd me forward; and as it thunder'd all around, I drove poney along, (now here is the plague of ponies, for they cannot move at times of want, and are as long going 2 miles, as a taller horse would go 4); and at six o'clock reach'd Alconbury Hill. G— having _{Alconbury Hill}

409

profited by his tutor's instructions, now minutes my horses, gives them $\frac{1}{4}$ of pails of water &c &c, and, throught, shews infinite knowledge!—The stables here are pitiful; which is surprising upon such a road, and at a hunting rendezvous: Mr H[olmes], the landlord, is now building a new, but bad, stable.

It was a dismal evening: a gentleman, who lodges at Huntingdon, drove here this evening, to enjoy the fine weather; whilst I was wishing for a whist party.—Fowl, and peas, (evermore) for supper; nor did I long after abstain from my bed.—

Tuesday July 19   For the first time upon this tour, I put in practise a plan I so much admire (of such chearfulness, and forwardness,) which is an early ride to breakfast.

I. HOLMES.

ALCONBURY HILL.

Neat Chaises.

Fowl and Pease	-	-	-	-	2	6
Wine & Brandy	-	-	-	-	2	3
*Bread	-	-	-	-		1
					4	10

*An odd Charge!!

The morning was very fine, and fresh, and the roads being smooth, and gravelly the rider glides happily along. What vigour does the morning air give to both body, and mind? All hands are now in the hay-field, which perfumes the country.—When I was sitting at breakfast, after shaving, at the George Inn, Buckden, before nine o'clock, G— pass'd by.—The Bishop of Lincoln,[84] the barber says, resides much here; but why should a bishop have any residence but in his own close, where he can look to his own parade, and his own troops, and review the management of his cathedral? This inn is too much unknown to

410

me, for it appears to be excellent, and with excellent stabling: perhaps I may make some stay here hereafter. There is a pleasant walk behind the house, into the fields. I read, in the newspapers, the accounts of the riots at Birmingham:[85] one party inflames, and then accuse the other of warmth!

I never travelled in a more charming day; no intolerant sun, but a fresh'ning S.W. wind: so my ride appear'd short; and approaching Biggleswade, seems like a return to a quiet home. Biggles-wade

Here again 'Walk into your own room, Sr'. Many letters, which I was hasty to read, and hasty to answer.— Roasted pigeons ready; bring them in, with a bottle of port. So comfortable I felt; and in the hopes of seeing here Mrs B[yng] and my Frek, in a day, or two.—After dinner sent to my *Jonas*, as it appear'd a very *fishable* day, and he appointed me to come to him at 4 o'clock. G— soon arrived, with the mare, who now wants grass, and rest, and she shall have them.—At 4 o'clock I walk'd to the barber's, who weaves lines, and wigs, (a connected trade) and with him walk'd a mile to a pleasant spot; but no fish; the air now turn'd cold, making me repent thus trying the chance of illness. I ask'd him after the players? 'Why they are here still, Sir; and perform to night'. 'Then I suppose they are so hampered by debt, that they cannot move; and must stay till pity and forgiveness permit them to go?' 'Sir, I believe they are very poor; and that my son, who dresses the company, will never see a penny of payment'.—From idleness, or from curiosity, (put charity out of the case) I went again; greater wretchedness is not to be seen! How much they should envy the haymakers.—The play was Inkle and Yarico,[86] with variety of other entertainments: it would be right if they were not tolerated. Tho' they get little, they get all that this town can give; and that is too much by every sixpence: nothing could approach nearer to Hogarth's Barn, for many faces were seen peeping thro' the holes of the barn, which we who had paid, and were in the castle, thought unfair, and repulsed these assailants. I sat next to Mr K[night] and his neice, but left them at 10 o'clock, when the play finish'd, and half the sports were to come; so this threw me into fashionable hours and I did not retire till 12 o'clock.

Wednesday
July 20 Time draws close; and I must return! A morning of refitting myself, and my cattle. My coat, (new when I came out, now nearly worn out) wants brushing; and my horses want shoeing: strange to say but poney brings back the shoes he took hence. This, and arranging my touring books, dawdled away a very fine morning; but I have jumbled about sufficiently, and a little of the sedentary is not amiss. I caught cold last night (as I deserv'd) but I hope it will not increase at these my hours of hope. Mr G——[87] the apothecary, has offer'd (very civilly) to let my mare run in his meadows, which will be very commodious, as there she will refresh her young limbs, wearied by work. —Ranger is come here with me, and is to stay here till his master comes this way; poor thing, he is very orderly, and harmless, but there is no animation, or diversion about him.—It became proper, not necessary, to think of dinner; and I ate, at two o'clock, of the family rst beef; a pleasing change after the brood of chickens I have lately devour'd.

In the evening I rode the mare to Potton, to Mr H.'s,[88] to enquire after his bruises, occasion'd by an overturn in the stage coach; whom I found limping about, and far from a recovery.—Tea at six o'clock: then walk'd to see Mr. G.'s meadow, in which my mare will run; and a clever field it appears to be.

I kept out late to enjoy quiet, and the country, as much as possible.

Thursday
July 21 To prepare for my expected company, and to arrange our bed rooms: they will not arrive till supper time.— Rode the mare to Windsor's, Walker's, then to Southill.— Saw Mr S[mith] call at Dilly's; sat some time with Mrs S.

told her of Mrs B.'s coming; return'd home at 4 o'clock.—
This is the last night of the play: shall I announce it? If I
do not, rebukes will follow; and if I do—what woman will
abstain from going? At seven o'clock, I rode forth, (tho'
with a cold, and swell'd face,) about 5 miles; return'd at
nine: my company, (Mrs B., Mr Frek, Mr and Mrs
C[olman])[89] immediately came in, all eager in an instant,
upon my foolish announcement, to hurry to the play; tho'
Mr C— is very unwell: so crawl'd over the fields—to a
full house; where from civility we got places.—I smiled at
their not knowing my *great friend*, else how had the poor
players look'd up to him! Our return home, by a candle
and lanthorn, was too late, to a good supper. Frek alone
—dear fellow—in spirits: not in bed till 12 o'clock.

I and Frek arose early; and were quickly busied in the *Friday*
garden at the currants, and gooseberries: there is a plea- *July 22*
sure in wholesomely stuffing these little hogs.—
No one else till very late: Mr C— very ill; and when
risen—began to oblige me with a reading (a great pleasure
it was) of his newly written play, the Surrender of Calais.[90]—
Two acts were pass'd thro' before dinner. The 1st act very
good, the second charming; (I am now not writing
panegyrics or criticism, or to say how much I admire the
writings of Mr C— or how much more I esteem the
writer).
In the evening they in a chaise, I upon the mare, took an
airing to the Roman camp, upon whose brow (which with
difficulty *we* climb'd) there was a long sitting to enjoy the
air, and prospect. At our return Mr C[olman] read his 3rd
act, which, tho' excellent, seem'd more the work of hurry
than the 2 former: with him I had a late and pleasant sit up
—even till 12 o'clock.

We had engaged ourselves to breakfast at Mr S.'s, at *Saturday*
Southill; but Mr C—'s ill health kept him, and the ladies *July 23*
at home, whilst I rode to Mr S.'s in good time, with

apologies, &c. After breakfast I walk'd with Mr S. about Southill house and gardens—; which caused many inward sighs—from recollection of the past, and thought of the present. Return'd by one o'clock—when the company were risen. After dinner we all went to Mr S. to tea; but owing to Mr C.'s illness we were dull. However his good humour and pleasant discourse kept me up very late.

Sunday *July 24*

A dawdling morning; taking 2 short walks with Mr and Mrs C., and making them promise to renew their visit here. Dine early, because of departure; which some slight rain might have deferr'd, had I not been resolute. Much theatrical discourse at dinner; then give orders for my mare to be sent into the meadows; and mount poney, almost for the last time, as he gets very weak, and tottering: poor fellow we have had much pleasure together; and were I owner of a park he should run therein for life! Return gloomy, sad, like a school boy; count the mile stones to Stevenage; here overtaken by the chaise, which reach'd

Welwyn

Wellwyn, long before me: here we supp'd wretchedly, and in melancholy.

Monday *July 27*

Last day of this tour. Up before six o'clock, to a very gloomy morning; ride away in haste, till the desperate rain hovell'd me at Lemford-Mills, for an hour: then dashing forth—in spite of the weather, had a horrid wet ride to Barnet. Here, as the chaise had stopp'd before, I put up, by way of trial, at the Mitre; which is of all inns the nastiest; (so I go back to the lower Red Lion).

Now for hot, dusty, empty London! In my way, planning future tours—and if—and how, to be managed.

EDITOR'S NOTES

(1) Knight of Lower Caldecote. (See p. 296, note 3.)

(2) Sir George Osborn and his wife Lady Heneage, daughter of the 7th Earl of Winchilsea. (See p. 270, note 91.)

(3) Brownlow, Cecil, 9th Earl of Exeter.

(4) John Dilly, called by Boswell, Squire Dilly. His house stood near the Vicarage, Southill, but it has been pulled down. He died at Clophill in 1806. (See Boswell's *Life of Johnson*.)

(5) Colonel Albemarle Bertie, afterwards 9th Earl of Lindsey. (See Vol. I, p. 239, note 1).

(6) Cp. Birkbeck Hill's edition of Boswell's *Johnson*, ii, p. 451.

(7) A ballad opera in two acts by Charles Dibdin, in which occur the well-known songs 'Jolly Young Waterman' and 'Then fare thee well, my trim built wherry'.

(8) Possibly Joseph Ashby Partridge of Shefford Hardwick Manor, Southill. (See Victoria County History—*Bedfordshire*, iii, p. 259.)

(9) Possibly Miss Dilly.

(10) Rev. Laurence Smith, Vicar of Warden and Southill.

(11) 'An Exposition of the New Testament intended as an Introduction to the Study of the Scriptures,' by William Gilpin, M.A., Prebendary of Salisbury and Vicar of Boldre. Printed for R. Blamire in the Strand, 1790. Dedicated to Bishop Barrington of Salisbury. Contains: (1) Preface; (2) Life of Jesus Christ drawn from prophecies of the Old Testament; (3) Commentaries on Books of the New Testament.

(11a) Byng appears to have met Boswell fairly frequently at Malone's. On 7th Aug., 1785, Malone gave a dinner to Boswell, 'a good deal intoxicated,' Lord Sunderlin and Mr and Mrs Byng. Again on 15th, there was a dinner at which Boswell, Byng, Gen. Paoli and Sir Joshua Reynolds were present. In 1788, Boswell records for 19th April: 'I dined at Malone's with Mr. Byng, his lady and two daughters, Miss Cecilia Forrest, the two Palmers, Courtenay and young Jephson. We had a very good dinner, though I recollect no particulars. . . . We staid supper, and the Ladies and Byng and the Palmers did not leave us until I suppose above two.' In 1786, Boswell consulted Byng as to whether he should send his son to Charterhouse or Westminster. (*Isham Collection*.)

415

(12) Jeremy Fish-Palmer, Attorney-at-law, Clerk of the Peace at Bedford, 1776-98.

(13) Mr. Thomas Hensman.

(14) John Howard of Cardington, the prison reformer. Died at Cherson, South Russia, 1790.

(15) Possibly the widow of John Beecher (d. 1784) of Howbury Hall, Renhold. (See Victoria County History—*Bedfordshire*, ii, p. 215.)

(16) This reference is to the author's Preface to Fielding's *Voyage to Lisbon* (New York ed. of 1902, p. 185). 'If entertainment, as Mr. Richardson observes, be but a secondary consideration in a romance, with which Mr. Addison I think agrees, affirming the use of the pastrycook to be the first. If this I say be true of a mere work of invention, surely it may well be so considered in a work founded like this, on truth; and where the political reflections form so distinguished a part.'

(17) Revd. Richard Littlehales.

(18) Possibly R.-Ad. Sir Richard Bickerton (1727-1792).

(19) William Fellowes of Ramsay Abbey (d. 1804). (See Victoria County History—*Huntingdonshire*, ii, p. 194.)

(20) See Birkbeck Hill's edition of Boswell's *Johnson*, ii, p. 381.

(21) This is a mistake in the Christian name. It is Robert Carey, 1st Earl of Monmouth (1560-1639), who recounts the journey in his *Memoirs*.

(22) Probably Robert Sherard, 4th Earl of Harborough, who was at Lord Winchilsea's cricket match at Stamford.

(23) This was most probably Mr Barry, as according to Lewis's *Topographical Dictionary* the gift of the living of Hamerton was in this family's hands.

(24) Probably Thomas Pelham, M.P., later 2nd Earl of Chichester.

(25) The Marquis of Buckingham. (See p. 145, note 96.)

(26) A reference to the fenmen.

(27) In old registers the word 'wine' is frequently written 'wind'.

(28) Aslackby was the preceptory of the Knights Templars about the time of Henry II to 1324.

(29) Sir Gilbert Heathcote, 4th Baronet, was M.P. for Lincolnshire and Rutland. He died 26th March, 1851, aged 78.

(30) There is an article on Threckingham in the contemporary *Gentleman's Magazine*, pt. ii, pp. 793, 906. The family of Craggs still reside at Threckingham.

(31) Fellow of the Antiquaries Society of Scotland.

(32) The Duke of Orleans was present at the 'Greyhound,' Folkingham, on the 24th November, 1789, at a hunt. He was guillotined 6th November, 1793.

(33) The Lord High Chancellor in 1790 was Lord Thurlow. He held the office from 1783 until 1792, when it was temporarily put into commission.

(34) John Moore Brooke, rector 1787 to 1799.

(35) Temple Bruer was a preceptory of the Knights Templars (*c.* 1185-1324). (See above.)

(36) Tickhill Castle, which had been in possession of the Crown for many centuries, was dismantled by order of Parliament in 1644.

(37) On 21st June, 1791, Louis XVI and Marie Antoinette fled from Paris, but were recaptured at Varennes.

(38) Dunston Pillar was erected by Sir F. Dashwood, Bart., afterwards Lord le Despencer, as a lighthouse on Lincoln heath in 1751. In 1809 the lantern was replaced by a statue of George III to commemorate his jubilee.

(39) Dr. Douglas and the Rev. John Smith, D.D.

(40) Cp. Birkbeck Hill's edition of Boswell's *Johnson*, i, p. 365.

(41) Hugh Fortescue, 3rd Baron and 1st Earl, who died in 1841.

(42) Sir Joseph Banks, Bart., Antiquary and President of the Royal Society, lived at Revesby Abbey. He died 19th June, 1820, aged 77.

(43) Possibly one of the Grevilles of Thorpe Latimer.

(44) James Fardell, who died 16th February, 1805.

(45) Probably Ayscoughfee Hall. (See p. 267, note 51.)

(46) This refers to the well-known scene of the foolish constables in Shakespeare's 'Much Ado about Nothing.'

(47) Verrio, the well-known seventeenth-century painter, was always noted for his tasteless confusion and exuberance.

(48) Frederick William I of Prussia.

(49) Mr. Thomas Fydell, M.P. for Boston, who died 6th April, 1812, aged 72.

(50) Possibly Gunby.

(51) Descendants of Richard Bertie (died 1592), who married Katharine, Baroness Willoughby de Eresby.

(52) Sir Peter Burrell, Bart., was on the 16th June, 1796, created Baron Gwydyr and died on the 29th June, 1820 He had married the eldest daughter of the 4th Duke of Ancaster and Kesteven, who became Baroness Willoughby de Eresby in her own right on 18th March, 1780.

(53) The rector of Willoughby-in-the-Marsh from 1771 to 1811 was Reynold Gideon Bouyer, LL.B.

(54) Tahiti, an 'outlandish' island in Polynesia.

(55) Humphry Repton. (See p. 297, note 24.)

(56) This fair was held about Whitsuntide.

(57) The office of King's Champion at coronations had been held by the Dymoke family for a very long period. The duties, however, have not been performed since the coronation of George IV.

(58) Dr. Samuel Carter Pettener was born on the 15th of June, 1748, and died on the 18th of January, 1831.

(59) Rev. Wolley Jolland, who died 16th August, 1831, aged 86.

(60) Possibly Thomas Peel's. The stuff was used at the Lincoln Stuff Balls to encourage local industry.

(61) Louth Old Town Hall had a card-room annexed.

(62) A man who shows fireworks.

(63) Brownlow Bertie, the 5th and last Duke of Ancaster and Kesteven, who died 8th February, 1809.

(64) His fifth son, Frederick Gerald ('Poodle') Byng.

(65) Charles Anderson Pelham, created Baron Yarborough, 13th August, 1794, died 23rd September, 1823, aged 75.

(66) Lord Ongley. (See p. 297, note 17.)

(67) James Wyatt, who died 4th September, 1813, aged 67, erected the mausoleum, in 1794, of the Pelham family. He also rebuilt the Pantheon in Oxford St.

(68) A swelling produced by the larva of the gadfly.

(69) Refers to the Tour of 1784. (See Vol. I.)

(70) Probably Charlotte, daughter and heiress of the Rev. Robert Carter, owner of Redbourne, who married Lord William Beauclerk, afterwards 8th Duke of St. Albans.

(71) Norton Place, the seat of John Harrison, M.P. for Grimsby, who died 7th February, 1811.

(72) Anniversary of the fall of the Bastile.

(73) Sir Cecil Wray was 13th Baronet of Glentworth and died 10th January, 1805, aged 70. Fillingham, sometimes called 'Summer,' Castle was built by him in 1760. Compare Byng's account with those of Arthur Young (*Lincolnshire*, 1799, p. 27 and *Tour through the East of England*, 1781, I, p. 457).

(74) The grounds round the house.

(75) The Saundersons—Earls of Scarborough—owned Glentworth House. The 4th Earl died on the 12th May, 1782, and the 5th on the 5th September, 1807.

(76) This bridge was opened on the 26th October, 1790, and was the only bridge, after the Newark one, over the Trent at that time.

(77) Henry Dalton, Esq., of Knaith Hall; said to be an eccentric character and died unmarried on the 3rd of February, 1821, aged 75. He was buried at Leatherhead, Surrey, and a tablet to him is in the church. He was the last of the family.

(78) Eldest son of the 1st Duke of Ancaster and Kesteven (who died 13th September, 1768) by his second wife Albinia, daughter of Maj.-Gen. William Farringdon.

(79) Albinia married, 16th May, 1775, the Hon. George Hobart, of Nocton, afterwards 3rd Earl of Buckingham.

(80) Sir John Thorold, the 9th Baronet, of Syston Park.

(81) Belton Park, near Grantham, was the property of Sir Brownlow Cust, Bart., afterwards 1st Baron Brownlow, who died on the 25th December, 1807.

(82) It was probably Mr. Dalton, who is referred to. (See note 77 above.)

(83) Probably Cust.

(84) Sir George Pretyman Tomline, Bishop of Lincoln (1787-1820) and Bishop of Winchester (1820-1827). Died 14th November, 1827, aged 77, and was buried at Buckden, Hunts. He was tutor to the Rt. Hon. William Pitt, Prime Minister.

(85) There is a full and interesting account of these riots on 14th-17th July, 1791, in *A History of Birmingham*, by W. Hutton, F.A.S.S., 1795, pp. 389-392 and 471.

(86) A play by George Colman, jun., with six male and four female characters. (See Allardyce Nicoll, p. 247 of *The History of Late Eighteenth Century Drama*. 1927.)

(87) Lawrence Gall.

(88) Hinson. (See p. 296, note 8.)

(89) George Colman, jun., married secretly on 3rd October, 1784, Clara Morris, an actress of small parts at the Haymarket. After they had revealed the marriage, they were re-married at Chelsea on 10th November, 1788.

(90) Mr C— is George Colman the younger, whose play 'The Surrender of Calais' was performed at the Haymarket Theatre on Saturday, 30th June, 1791, and subsequently at Drury Lane, of which production the Victoria and Albert Museum possesses the prompt copy. In an early edition of this play Mrs. Inchbald has some introductory remarks in which she says that it is considered by every critic as the very best of all the author's

numerous and successful productions. 'In this drama,' she writes, 'are comprised Tragedy, Comedy, Opera and some degree of farce, yet so happily is the variety blended that one scene never diminishes the interest of another, but they all combine to produce a most valuable composition.' Modern opinion would probably endorse the eighteenth-century opinion of Lord Torrington in the Diary—the first act goes with a swing, the second act is delightful, but the third act seems weak and inadequate. A printed edition came out in Dublin in 1792, but the first authorised issue of the play did not appear till 1808.